THE HISTORICAL ARCHAEOLOGY OF THE PACIFIC NORTHWEST

The American Experience in Archaeological Perspective

UNIVERSITY PRESS OF FLORIDA

Florida A&M University, Tallahassee
Florida Atlantic University, Boca Raton
Florida Gulf Coast University, Ft. Myers
Florida International University, Miami
Florida State University, Tallahassee
New College of Florida, Sarasota
University of Central Florida, Orlando
University of Florida, Gainesville
University of North Florida, Jacksonville
University of South Florida, Tampa
University of West Florida, Pensacola

THE HISTORICAL ARCHAEOLOGY OF THE PACIFIC NORTHWEST

Douglas C. Wilson

Foreword by Michael S. Nassaney and Krysta Ryzewski

UNIVERSITY PRESS OF FLORIDA
Gainesville/Tallahassee/Tampa/Boca Raton
Pensacola/Orlando/Miami/Jacksonville/Ft. Myers/Sarasota

Cover art courtesy of Marceline A. Wilson.

This book will be open access within three years of publication thanks to Path to Open, a program developed in partnership between JSTOR, the American Council of Learned Societies (ACLS), University of Michigan Press, and The University of North Carolina Press to bring about equitable access and impact for the entire scholarly community, including authors, researchers, libraries, and university presses around the world. Learn more at https://about.jstor.org/path-to-open

Copyright 2024 by Douglas C. Wilson
All rights reserved
Published in the United States of America

29 28 27 26 25 24   6 5 4 3 2 1

Library of Congress Cataloging-in-Publication Data
Names: Wilson, Douglas Calvin, author. | Nassaney, Michael S., author of foreword. | Ryzewski, Krysta, author of foreword.
Title: The historical archaeology of the Pacific Northwest / Douglas C. Wilson ; foreword by Michael S. Nassaney and Krysta Ryzewski.
Description: 1. | Gainesville : University Press of Florida, 2024. | Includes bibliographical references and index.
Identifiers: LCCN 2024017901 (print) | LCCN 2024017902 (ebook) | ISBN 9780813079172 (hardback) | ISBN 9780813073460 (ebook) | ISBN 9780813070858 (pdf)
Subjects: LCSH: Archaeology and history—Northwest, Pacific. | Archaeology—Northwest, Pacific. | Indians of North America—Northwest, Pacific. | Northwest, Pacific—Antiquities. | Northwest, Pacific—History. | BISAC: SOCIAL SCIENCE / Archaeology | HISTORY / United States / State & Local / Pacific Northwest (OR, WA)
Classification: LCC CC77.H5 W55 2024 (print) | LCC CC77.H5 (ebook) | DDC 979.5—dc23/eng/20240724
LC record available at https://lccn.loc.gov/2024017901
LC ebook record available at https://lccn.loc.gov/2024017902

The University Press of Florida is the scholarly publishing agency for the State University System of Florida, comprising Florida A&M University, Florida Atlantic University, Florida Gulf Coast University, Florida International University, Florida State University, New College of Florida, University of Central Florida, University of Florida, University of North Florida, University of South Florida, and University of West Florida.

University Press of Florida
2046 NE Waldo Road
Suite 2100
Gainesville, FL 32609
http://upress.ufl.edu

To Tracy, Marceline, and Douglas Jr.

CONTENTS

List of Figures   ix

Foreword   xi

Acknowledgments   xvii

   1. Introduction to Historical Archaeology in the Pacific Northwest   1

   2. Origins of Historical Archaeology in the Pacific Northwest   15

   3. Contextualizing Pacific Northwest Colonialism   33

   4. The New York of the West   59

   5. American Conquest   84

   6. Death, Burial, and Commemoration in the Pacific Northwest   108

   7. Slugs of Gold: The Historical Archaeology of Pacific Northwest Industries   131

   8. Transportation and Urbanism at the Onset of Modernity   158

   9. The Past in the Present in the Pacific Northwest   182

Works Cited   199

Index   263

FIGURES

1.1. Map of the Pacific Northwest   2

1.2. Spirit pole at the Visitor Center of Fort Vancouver   4

2.1. Examination of beaver trap fragments during the 1947 excavations at Fort Vancouver   18

2.2. Excavation of an officer's quarters at Fort Yamhill   26

2.3. Japanese Sometsuke Senbori Gohan Jawan (rice/soup bowl with hand-painted cobalt and carved lines) collected from Minidoka National Historic Site, Idaho   31

3.1. Map of exploration and early fur trade sites   36

3.2. Blue on white Chinese export porcelain sherd remanufactured into a projectile point   38

3.3. Plans of selected early fur trade forts   44

3.4. Hand-painted English creamware tea caddy recovered from Middle Village (*qíqayaqilxam*)   57

4.1. Map of later fur trade and mission sites   60

4.2. Plan of Fort Vancouver ca. 1829 and 1845   70

4.3. Silver spoon (15 cm long) recovered from the Mission House at Waiilatpu   75

4.4. Church of St. Paul, in St. Paul, Oregon   77

5.1. Map of the Oregon and Applegate trails, showing early settlements, Army forts, and battlefields   86

5.2. A remnant swale from the Barlow Road   87

5.3. Excavations at the Newell House at Champoeg   91

5.4. Excavation of the enlisted men's barrack at Fort Lane   98

5.5. View of the Blockhouse, Parade Ground, and Garden at English Camp on San Juan Island   100

6.1. Headstones of Forbes and Maria Barclay at Mountain View Cemetery   109

6.2. Phoenix buttons recovered from the Fort Vancouver village   112

6.3. Unknown Pioneer Woman's Grave on Mt. Hood   116

6.4. Typical Chinese ceramics found at sites in the Pacific Northwest   125

7.1. Map of sites associated with Northwest industries   134

7.2. North wall profile of two units excavated into a Chinese dwelling site in Jacksonville, Oregon   142

7.3. Steam donkey on display at Camp 18 Restaurant, Elsie, Oregon   149

7.4. Map of the Weyerhaeuser Camp 2   153

8.1. Map of railroad networks and archaeological sites   159

8.2. Eric Gleason exhibiting one of the test units behind the Wing Hong Hai Company building in The Dalles, Oregon   171

8.3. Kaiser shipyard welding "practice" artifacts   177

9.1. Kids Dig! at Fort Vancouver   189

FOREWORD

For many of us who hail from outside the region, thoughts about the Pacific Northwest conjure images of magnificent landscapes shaped by their bountiful natural beauty. Vast evergreen forests, towering trees, and lush undergrowth extend inland from the ocean's edge into interior elevations, where cascading rivers teem with salmon and carry icy meltwaters seaward from the snow-capped peaks of the Cascade and Rocky Mountains. The Pacific Northwest is often imagined to be a peaceful wilderness, one of the final frontiers in North America to be settled by Europeans, where present-day inhabitants model environmental stewardship for the rest of the continent. We might recall historical details about the Lewis and Clark expedition, or the treacherous conditions of the Oregon Trail journey, especially as they were depicted by the famous 1980s video game. But the physical majesty of the region conceals the fact that the Pacific Northwest was never really a cohesive cultural or environmental area at any point in time. Its sheer sociocultural and ecological diversity tends to be glossed over in historical accounts and media portrayals. It takes an archaeological perspective to reveal the complicated realities of the social lives and human–environmental interactions that shaped this region's cultural history and its contributions to the wider American experience.

In *Historical Archaeology of the Pacific Northwest,* Douglas Wilson demystifies the Pacific Northwest, enlisting archaeological evidence and interpretations to reveal the area's dynamic social history, illuminate the role that human–environmental adaptations played in shaping the landscape over time, and liberate Indigenous histories from prior colonial narratives. Today, this expansive space between the Rocky Mountains and the Pacific Ocean encompasses the modern states of Washington, Oregon, and Idaho, and parts of the Canadian province of British Columbia. Beneath the forest canopies, along the sea coast, and across the valleys between mountain ranges, decades' worth of historical archaeological investigations illustrate how humans have entered into ecological and social relationships across the Pacific Northwest to suit their needs for new settlements, subsistence, cemeteries, mineral wealth, industrial extraction, transportation, and even the preservation of natural and cultural heritage.

Historical archaeological scholarship focused on the Pacific Northwest has contributed to topics essential for understanding the American experience, many of which have been covered in other volumes in the American Experience in Archaeological Perspective Series, such as fortifications, the fur trade, Cold War production facilities, logging camps, residential boarding schools, and mortuary practices. While each of these themes has been explored as the primary focus of individual books in the series, this volume moves in a new direction. It marks an expansion in the series' scope, as the first book to focus on a particular geographic place as a context for examining the intersections of several topics over time—from colonization and immigration to the gold rush, industrial development, and urbanism.

In this synthetic and comprehensive treatise, Wilson marshals data from an enormous body of academic and cultural resource management literature to examine the place of the Pacific Northwest in the larger North American mosaic. Wilson's historical archaeological approach positions the Pacific Northwest as a place of confluence and conflict. From the outset of his exposition, he debunks the stereotypes of the Pacific Northwest as a natural "hinterland" by acknowledging that signs of modernity are everywhere in the region. Whether in urban or rural settings, material vestiges of the modern era—bridges, roads, military installations, shipyards, parks, commercial centers, neighborhoods—embody and conceal deep histories alongside scenic surroundings. It is impossible, Wilson argues, for historical archaeologists to ignore the impacts of humans and the material traces of their exploitation of and interactions with the many cultures and natural resources present in the region between the late seventeenth and twenty-first centuries, the temporal focus of this book. While calling attention to the imprints of Euro-American colonization, Wilson emphasizes that colonialist and capitalist encroachment into the region has not erased Indigenous peoples and their influence on built and intangible heritage. Indeed, he stresses that understandings of Indigenous peoples, their heritage, and their contemporary contributions are of paramount importance to how archaeologists and the public conceive the Pacific Northwest. The inclusion of Indigenous voices, symbolism, and representation in the visual elements of the built environment, in political leadership, and in cultural affairs are central to understanding life in the region, as well as for considering how historic and archaeologically derived information is interpreted and disseminated.

Following an introduction to historical archaeology in the region, Wilson organizes his journey through the Pacific Northwest's archaeological history chronologically. His exegesis begins with the earliest encounters between Natives and newcomers and brings us into the twenty-first century. When Europeans first arrived in the region during the eighteenth century, they encountered dense, established communities that were as culturally complex as any in North America. The scale of their communal plank houses and wooden carvings matched the grandeur of the surrounding natural setting, much as their ancestors' settlements had for millennia prior. Spanish mariners explored the Pacific Northwest at the northern fringes of their more southerly settlements. Russians, French-Canadians, and European Americans from points east were drawn to the region over land and sea in search of both maritime and terrestrial fur-bearing animals. Most early explorations had minimal impact on Indigenous settlements or lifeways until the nineteenth century after the Louisiana Purchase and the exploits of Lewis and Clark "opened" the region for American settlement. Wilson introduces readers to the archaeological record, buried beneath the forest floors and alluvial sediments, of these forebearers who lived and died exacting an existence from the rich bounty of various ecological niches.

Despite the economic and cultural importance of the Pacific Northwest, the conception of the region as a frontier or "hinterland" persists. Nevertheless, the area has attracted its share of archaeological attention as early investigations of colonial forts and explorers' campsites and the study of post-contact Indigenous sites have given way to studies of the people who created settlements, towns and cities, extractive industries, and industrial and domestic developments in a diversity of forms. Wilson provides a thorough and authoritative overview of historical archaeology scholarship in the Pacific Northwest and contextualizes the region within the American experience, using materiality to bridge past and present, nationalistic narratives, and cultural diaspora. Wilson is sensitive to the ways in which archaeology challenges dominant narratives and recognizes some of the ways that language continues to colonize the past. For example, his use of the term "belongings" in place of "artifacts" awakens us to the idea that objects have different meanings to people, and this etymological shift can convey how people in the past understood their people–object relationships, and how people understand them today. Similarly, the binary terms "colonizer/colonized" are shunned because fur traders often became entangled with Indigenous groups, and their children became part of immigrant and Indigenous populations.

Wilson presents the region's scholarship in ways that move beyond historical archaeology's tendency to emphasize sites of Euro-American and Indigenous contact and European settler sites as grist for narratives that foresee Native disappearance, perpetuate settler colonialism, and marginalize Indigenous people. He demonstrates how historical archaeologists of the Pacific Northwest foreground Indigenous people and their deep history prior to European settlement, focusing on the effects of the cultural interactions and exchanges that took place via colonial projects and waves of immigration, especially from the nineteenth century onward. Wilson's theoretical and methodological approaches are consistent with the New Western History and other post-processual, agency-based, materialist, and Indigenous conceptions of archaeology.

In his comprehensive review of the history of historical archaeological scholarship in the region, Wilson not only discusses archaeological research but also provides ample context for the motivations behind investigations, explaining why archaeologists chose certain sites and problems to explore, which objects they analyzed, how they interpreted the data they collected, and how they interfaced with the overall development and interpretation of regional and national histories. For example, Wilson documents how early historical archaeology of fort sites and missions sought to venerate the colonial past by reinforcing a narrative that appropriated the land for settlement. By the 1970s, more scientific approaches began to focus on documenting the material culture of these sites to explore chronology, characterize the commercial products of the fur traders and missionaries, and compare assemblages using their inferred functions. Much of the work at larger Hudson's Bay Company forts was tied to triumphalist reconstructions that often failed to account for the contributions of Indigenous people. More recent work explores in greater depth colonialism's impacts on Indigenous peoples, documenting resistance to colonialism and Indigenous peoples' persistence in the face of the double onslaught of mercantile capitalism and Christianity.

Wilson demonstrates a longstanding commitment among practitioners in the region to collecting and interpreting empirical data that elucidates the American experience and its expressions in the Pacific Northwest, detailing many such examples. For instance, we learn that excavations of early fur trade forts recovered substantial numbers of Indigenous belongings; these fort sites often are located on landscapes integral to Native lives. The presence of Chinese and English ceramics at early fur trade sites suggests the ability of British companies to trade with Americans to avoid the East India Company's monopoly on Asian goods. These sites yielded significant quantities of alcohol bottles, suggesting that fur traders attempted to manipulate Indigenous people with spirits to create favorable exchanges and encourage dependency. Yet many of these bottles were flaked into tools, evidence that Chinook peoples repurposed these new materials into traditional forms.

The influx of Euro-American pioneers, Chinese laborers, and other ethnic groups to the Pacific Northwest led to various economic pursuits, including farming, ranching, fishing, mining, logging, and manufacturing, all of which have been examined archaeologically. Subtle yet detectable physical traces of the Oregon Trail—the route that so many followed—are well documented. The spatial organization of nineteenth-century military forts supported a status hierarchy, and material culture expressed differences between the enlisted men and officers.

Historical archaeological scholarship in the region shows how immigrant communities maintained their identities by actively constructing traditional landscapes and conducting daily practices while resisting racialized oppression. Archaeological interpretations demonstrate how Chinese communities in the Pacific Northwest acquired imported European, Chinese, and local American products to express their transnational identity. Indigenous people were slow to adopt European and Canadian technology into the twentieth century as indicated by trade goods refashioned into technologically and ideologically useful implements and the persistence of traditional plank houses. The gradual adoption of Western-style houses suggests Indigenous agency, accommodation, and negotiation in an entangled colonial situation. Compared to that of their White American counterparts, refuse from the African American 9th Cavalry at Fort Walla Walla in the state of Washington contained lower relative numbers of items associated with uniforms, such as insignia and buttons. Similarly, there were lesser quantities of horse-related items and high-quality porcelain and decorated earthenware vessels, indicating that the 9th Cavalry was provisioned differently from White soldiers.

Bringing archaeology into the present, Wilson reflects upon the long history of public archaeology in the region, and the evolution of community-based archaeology in the twenty-first century. Early efforts to educate the public about archaeology have expanded to include projects that position Indigenous people and other historically marginalized communities in positions of decision making from the outset. These efforts to decolonize archaeological practice and to redistribute authority in the archaeological process include the investigations of residential boarding schools as sites of trauma and violence, as well as projects that prioritize Indigenous knowledge and community histories in the interpretations of belongings. Wilson suggests that the practice of contemporary archaeology has yet to develop as a scholarly focus in the region. But the highly visible connections between millennia-old Indigenous heritage and the modern landscape, as well as the strong collaborative partnerships between Indigenous communities and archaeologists, are fertile ground for the development of a distinctive and novel facet of contemporary archaeology in the region, one that emphasizes continuity of heritage and Indigenous knowledge in understandings of the present.

Like any region of the United States or North American continent, it will come as no surprise to readers that the Pacific Northwest is a distinct microcosm of the American experience, albeit one marked by a different population and historical trajectory than in other places. In his comparative exploration of cultural and historical similarities and differences, Wilson's *Historical Archaeology of the Pacific Northwest* effectively demonstrates how global processes are materially expressed regionally and locally over time in this distinctive and fascinating place.

Michael S. Nassaney, *Founding Series Editor*

Krysta Ryzewski, *Series Coeditor*

ACKNOWLEDGMENTS

Over many years, colleagues, students, volunteers, and employees have contributed significantly to my understanding of the historical archaeology of the Pacific Northwest. I benefited from many discussions in classes I have taught, and with friends and colleagues who would tell me of magnificent historical sites. I have experienced archaeology with many of you. I greatly appreciate the reviewers, including Mark Tveskov, an anonymous reviewer, series editors Michael Nassaney and Krysta Ryzewski, and Associate Acquisitions Editor Mary Puckett. Your suggestions have helped me tremendously. Of course, all omissions and errors are my own responsibility. Particular thanks go to Portland State University's Millar Library, the Washington State WISAARD and Oregon State OARRA systems, and regional archaeology societies and their journals and newsletters. Unfortunately, due to length limitations, I have had to cut much of the book, and I am sorry for that. The maps were made by the author in QGIS using Natural Earth raster + vector map data (www.naturalearthdata.com) including MODIS satellite-derived urban areas (ne_10m_urban_areas, ver. 4.1.0); world data bank 2 coastline, lakes, and rivers-lakes centerlines (ne_10m_coastline, ver. 5.0.0, pre9; ne_10m_ocean, ver. 5.1.1; ne_10m_lakes and ne_10m_rivers_lake_centerlines, both ver. 5.0.0); North American Environmental Atlas (ne_10m_lakes_north_america and ne10m_rivers_north_america, both ver. 5.0.0); and 1–10 m Natural Earth II idealized land cover raster dataset (NE2_HR_LC_SR_W, ver. 2.0.0 for figure 1.1). The project area was extracted from the 1- to 10-meter Admin 1–States, Provinces (ne_10m_admin_1_states_provinces, ver. 5.1.1). The Oregon and California trails (figure 5.1) are from the National Park Service 1:100,000 Designated Route of the Oregon National Historic Trail (20190411) and the 1:100,000 Designated Route of the California National Historic Trail (20170301), the Cariboo Wagon Road (figure 7.1) was digitized from Leonard (2016: figure 1), and the Mullan Road centerline (figure 8.1) is derived from Townsend et al. (2021) kml file. Railroads (figure 8.1) are from Jeremy Atack, Historical Geographic Information Systems (GIS) database of U.S.

Railroads (August 2015) Vanderbilt University, Nashville, Tennessee (United States) and Cartography office, Geography Department, 2020, "Historical Canadian Railroads," https://doi.org/10.5683/SP2/UCCFVQ, Borealis, V2. The projection is the USA contiguous lambert conformal conic projection (ESRI:102004).

1

Introduction to Historical Archaeology in the Pacific Northwest

One day in the archaeology laboratory at Fort Vancouver National Historic Site, I met a volunteer who was descended from a nineteenth-century Indian Agent, Andrew Bolon, whose murder in 1855 shaped the conditions for the Yakima Indian War. We had been analyzing belongings embedded in the clay floor of a Fort Vancouver Village house that Bolon had rented in the winter of 1852–1853. Hearing of the connections between material things and a poignant family history, we suddenly placed her family history, past possessions from the house, and lived spaces together, illuminating their role in settlement, competition among Nations, and entanglement with Indigenous peoples (Wilson et al. 2022: 244).

Historical archaeology studies material things and sites, comparing them with written records and oral histories. Tacking between these sources, historical archaeologists attempt to confirm past narratives, expose historical myths, and address what everyday people did in the face of events and processes that created the modern world. This book lends insights into the history of the Pacific Northwest of North America, a unique and special place. We seek here to understand the present and future from the basis of a dimly known and sometimes unspoken past.

The Region

The northwestern region of North America is an area of diverse natural beauty, with powerful rivers, evergreen forests, imposing mountains, and fertile prairies, teeming with abundant natural resources. The 1.6 million km^2 area includes Oregon, Washington, and Idaho, within the United States, and the Canadian province of British Columbia (figure 1.1). In comparison, this area is larger than the entire eastern seaboard of the United States, from Maine to Florida, yet its population density is significantly less. Most people live around Puget Sound in Washington, the lower Columbia River Basin in Oregon and Washington, and southern British Columbia, with fewer numbers in the far northern reaches of the Canadian province.

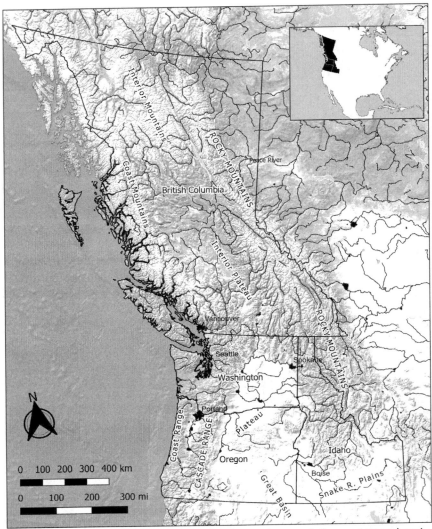

Figure 1.1. Map of the Pacific Northwest showing major population centers and environmental features.

The region is defined by the Rocky Mountains on the east and the Pacific Ocean on the west. In between, rainforest-clad coastal mountains give way to drier interior plains abundant in fertile soil, with the North American Cordillera bisecting the area roughly north–south. Most rivers drain to the Pacific Ocean, except in northeastern British Columbia where the Peace River drains into central Canada. The northern edge of the Great Basin, the Columbia Plateau, and the Interior Plateau comprise drier eastern regions.

Amongst researchers, there is no consensus that this diverse geographic area can be seen as either a distinctive environmental or cultural zone (Dixon 2020: 892; Schwantes 1996: 2). Anthropologists and archaeologists tend to separate the Plateau and Great Basin from the coast, ignoring the international boundary. For example, Ames and Maschner (1999) place the boundaries of their work roughly along the Cascade Range in Oregon and Washington, and the Canadian Cordillera in British Columbia, and include the southernmost "panhandle" of Alaska. Many archaeologists in the region, however, work in multiple environments and easily cross between plateau, coastal, and mountainous areas in the course of their careers. In contrast, many historians link the diverse environmental zones together from the Rocky Mountains to the Pacific Ocean but do not routinely cross the international divide (Jepsen and Norberg 2017). The international divide also hinders much cross-border scholarship. The southern boundary is also problematic with the "State of Jefferson" movement illustrative of the ambiguity of the California–Oregon divide (LaLande 2017). In spite of this, it is the diversity of the natural and cultural environments and the connections between these along rivers that joins the entire region together across time and space. Further, the diversity of people is extraordinary, with people from many regions seeking lives and livelihoods within its borders, and with economic and political factors binding the area together.

Schwantes (1996: 1–14) asserts that the diversity of the natural environment is a critical factor in the human geography, including the connections between regions associated with the great rivers, especially the Columbia, which link people across geographic areas. Likewise, Barman (2007: 5) suggests that the diversity of the environment across British Columbia leads to a less-than-cohesive sense of identity, yet as a Canadian province it has remained cohesive as a political unit. Those involved in the history of the fur trade are the few who extend their work across international boundaries to consider the "Columbia Department" (e.g., Mackie 1997). This may be a key consideration, as it is communication and trade across environmental zones (perpendicular to the coast) that characterized both Indigenous and fur trade patterns (Hobler 2000: 9). Economics continue to drive connections across regions tied to resource extraction, shipping, and trade.

A defining aspect of the Pacific Northwest is the omnipresent art, heritage, and history of its Indigenous peoples. Representations of Indigenous culture are found in public architecture, art, and museums, and modern Tribes are central in political and cultural issues of regional and national importance. The modern Tribes are vibrant, visible, and central to the way in which the Northwest is perceived (figure 1.2).

Figure 1.2. Spirit pole during carving by Yakama Artist Toma Villa at the Visitor Center of Fort Vancouver.

The many waves of immigrants to the Pacific Northwest also have defined the perception of the Northwest. These immigrants include people of European, African, Asian, and Pacific Islander ancestry. From the earliest periods of exploration, and colonialism, these settlers and migrants had a transformative effect on the region. The fur trade and other economic activities of British and American companies fundamentally changed the region's social and ecological dynamics, while the 1804–1806 Lewis and Clark "Corps of Discovery" brought the military agents of Thomas Jefferson, the third U.S. President, to explore lands to absorb into the economic and political sphere of the new and expanding country. American migration over the Oregon Trail redefined the nature of human relations and economic systems in the region, and settler colonists acquired and magnified political and economic power. Pacific Islander, Asian, and other diasporas added cultural distinctiveness to the populations but were largely subordinated to the colonial power structures (e.g., Veracini 2011).

Today, many people in the Pacific Northwest embrace a lifestyle, social and political discourse, and even spirituality that are centered on the natural environment. The area contains a few densely populated cities, notably Seattle and Spokane in Washington; Portland, Oregon; Boise, Idaho; and Vancouver and Victoria, British Columbia, surrounded by areas of great natural beauty, characterized by generally progressive political policies, social activism, and sometimes civil unrest. People in the more sparsely settled areas are more conservative, but also affiliate closely with the land and natural world, often in ways that both complement and contrast with their urban neighbors. The conception of the Northwest as a frontier or "hinterland" persists (Schwantes 1997: 14–16). While the population of approximately 19 million residents is dominated by White people of European ancestry,[1] the history of the Northwest is much more diverse, and there are increasing numbers of people of Latino and Asian descent. Visitors from around the world come to enjoy the cities and natural areas.

Historical archaeology has had a substantial influence on the understanding of the American experience in the Pacific Northwest. Consistent with the books in this series, the geographic region in this case has helped define the United States of America as a distinctive political, social, and cultural entity. In including the Canadian Province of British Columbia, I suggest that the formation of an American Pacific Northwest cannot be separated from its Canadian neighbor, as their histories are closely intertwined, and the similarities in political and social relations with Indigenous, White, and non-White immigrant groups is striking.

Early investigations of colonial forts and explorer's campsites, and the study of post-contact Indigenous sites have given way to studies of the people who created settlements, towns and cities, extractive industries, and industrial and domestic developments in sometimes stunning diversity. Envisioned as one of the "final frontiers" of the American experience, the ways in which Natives and newcomers lived in this region are central to understanding contemporary American life. For example, the Village at Fort Vancouver, the central entrepot of the Hudson's Bay Company in the Pacific Northwest, contained a polyglot community of Native people and new immigrants, some of whom stayed and others who left, but all who left belongings, and remembrances,

---

[1] Following the *Chicago Manual of Style,* Black, Indigenous, Native, and White are capitalized when referring to racial and ethnic identity, but these categories do not necessarily represent positioning equally within political and economic power structures (e.g., Beliso-DeJesús et al. 2023).

that allow archaeologists to explore how they adapted, persevered, and thrived in the colonial period (e.g., Wilson 2014, 2018; Wilson et al. 2022). Likewise, archaeological explorations in Jacksonville, Oregon, have unearthed the remains of Chinese American immigrants who worked, played, ate, and survived under the sometimes extreme burden of racism in one of the first Chinatowns in the Pacific Northwest (e.g., Rose 2020).

This book provides an overview of historical archaeology in the Pacific Northwest from the late seventeenth to twenty-first centuries. It provides an overview of prior scholarship as it seeks to contextualize the American experience in the region, using materiality to bridge past and present, nationalistic narratives, and cultural diaspora. As noted, the region is enormous, and some areas are excluded on its extreme fringes. For example, the Chilkoot Trail in the northwesternmost portion of British Columbia, is not discussed, as the historical archaeology of this area really belongs to Alaska and the Yukon territories. For a number of reasons, including the lower density of academic institutions compared to the East, published works on historical archaeology in the Pacific Northwest are somewhat sparse, although a robust "gray" literature of cultural resources management supplements the published sources (Warner and Schweitzer 2018).

Material Culture, Artifacts, and Belongings

Documents, including diaries, journals, maps, ledgers, and other written records are as important for understanding the American experience in the Pacific Northwest as elsewhere in the world and form a crucial source of information for historical archaeology (Deetz 1988; Little 1992; Orser 2001). The oral traditions of Native people and settlers alike are recognized as critically important to understanding past persons, events, and places in the West (e.g., Gonzalez et al. 2018; Purser 1992; Schaepe et al. 2020; Tveskov 2017). Documents are not perfect reflections, however, as typically they are written by elites and concern the particular interests and cultural biases of the ruling classes. In some cases, like for the Chinese, historical narratives have left out, and even erased, the presence and contributions of large segments of the population (Fang 2021). Oral traditions, while important elements of traditional knowledge, cannot be disconnected from the places and things they relate to, and are affected by the long-term traumas and impacts of colonialism and other aspects of how memory is transmitted across generations, an ongoing debate in anthropology (cf., Lowie 1908; Martindale 2006). With material things, historical archaeologists compare documentary and oral history sources, tacking between them to form a fuller understanding of the past.

Ruins and other human-made remains, including "artifacts," are the primary subject matter of archaeology. "Material culture" is the scientific term used for these remains. It is an antique and ambiguous term that originated out of systematic analyses of object collections in museums to address the patterning of things across space and time, and often within a nationalistic or colonial orientation (Trigger 2006). The subject matter of archaeology is tools and the by-products of making tools, consumable products, such as food and fuel, shelters, conveyances, and all manner of possessions that humans have created, modified, reused, and discarded. Even "artifact" is difficult and ambiguous. Noël Hume (1969: 3–4) briefly explored the term, preferring the *Oxford English Dictionary* definition, "an artificial product," an admittedly simple but elegant designation that captures the usual conception that artifacts are things modified in some way by humans. More recently, archaeologists, anthropologists, and others have witnessed a florescence in material culture studies, much of it tied to understanding how humans are inextricably linked with, and related to, artifacts that explore the social dimensions of material culture (e.g., Cochran and Beaudry 2006; Skibo and Schiffer 2008).

Among archaeologists and museum curators, terms like "artifact" are giving way to expressions that recognize that objects have different meanings to people and that this representation can help scientists and other academics understand how people in the past understood their people–object relationships, and how people understand them today. Schaepe et al. (2017), for example, use the terms "belongings" and "heirlooms" as an alternative to "artifacts" or "objects" to address how some Indigenous peoples of North America relate to ancestral things and places. Simply, the Indigenous Coast Salish worldview places people and belongings in the same space, conveying ancestral knowledge embodied in possessions to people living today. This gives more than a different feeling to the objects but recognizes that there are many different ways to understand the world and how material objects and people interact. Archaeologists explore material things, whether referred to as artifacts, material culture, ancestral belongings, or heirlooms, to address not only what people did in the past, their practices, beliefs, perceptions, identity, and power but also how these objects interact with and affect people living today, be they ancestors, stakeholders, or visitors to heritage sites.

Most artifacts can be seen to have some use. Binford (1962) famously explored the dimensions of artifact function as part of his reaction to the culture history paradigm. For example, Binford's "technomic" function arguably conforms with how many people view a button—a simple device used to fasten clothing together, a "bio-compensatory" tool to assist in clothing one against environmental extremes, like the cold, rainy Pacific Northwest winter. Binford felt that technomic functions of artifacts linked how humans used tools to adapt directly to their environments. He expanded on the means by which people use material things to accomplish tasks in their social settings and to explain and justify the cultural systems in which they live, which he termed respectively socio-technic and ideo-technic function. For example, many recognize the symbolic milieu of buttons, with clothing fashion demarcating meaningful social categories and representations. The higher density and fancier types of buttons within the Hudson's Bay Company Fort Vancouver stockade conforms to orthodox British sartorial standards, suggesting that gentlemen dressed in suits in muted colors, commonly clasped with plainface gilt buttons (Sukau 2022: 163–166). At military sites, coat buttons are designed to reflect rank and duty, but nonregulation buttons at the commanding officer's quarters of an Army fort may reflect their privilege and ability to flaunt military orthodoxy (Eichelberger 2019b: 365). Likewise, buttons at a Chinese store and laundry might reflect business functions in clothing repair and retail but also could represent gambling tokens used to defy laws that racialized Chinese Americans (French 2016: 91–92). Simple, everyday objects like buttons contain many attributes that key into their usefulness but also embody social, ideological, and emotional information. This ties them to many different things, including symbols of colonial dominance and authority, inequality, privilege, and even resistance. This information goes well beyond Binford's original conception tied to evolutionary value and delves deeply into the intertwined relationships between people and their belongings.

What Is Historical Archaeology?

A hallmark of historical archaeology is that it combines the fields of history and anthropology to examine material things. Contrasting material evidence with historical accounts and oral history can support past narratives, or just as likely expose biases and historical silences, often tied to controversial issues or the lives of those who are poorly documented, including disadvantaged or marginalized people. Further, the exploration of the meanings of material culture to contemporary people can examine how some groups persisted through time and the unique role of material things in the preservation and interpretation of past and present identities.

In North America, the exploration of material culture, written records, and oral traditions of people of the historic period (periods and places associated with a documentary record), dates primarily to the European colonial period (Deetz 1996; Paynter 2000a). As a consequence, historical archaeology explores sites that are often more visible, more easily dated using artifacts, and exhibit greater diversity in materials and forms than precolonial Native American sites (Deetz 1996: 5–34). The period is associated with colonization by European nations and the related immigration of other colonial peoples, including those who were enslaved. Two forms of colonial structure emerged from European colonization: colonialism and settler colonialism. Colonialism has been defined as "exogenous domination," relying on colonial agents to increasingly create dependencies on foreign goods, eventually coercing labor and participation of Indigenous people to control resources (Veracini 2011: 1; 2014). The early exploration and fur trade eras in the northwest largely conform to this form (see chapter 3 and chapter 4). Settler colonialism, in contrast, is a political and economic structure that "uses coordinated actions across state-level agencies to conquer, expropriate, and occupy Indigenous lands" (Montgomery 2022: 476). Settler colonialism as a process, uses a "logic of elimination," to remove Indigenous people from their lands, and perpetuates a "native repressed" that sustains the structure (Wolfe 2006: 387, 390). In the Pacific Northwest, the overt extinguishment of Native titles to land, initiated during the Oregon Trail emigration, resulted in momentous changes in social relations between settlers and Indigenous peoples (see chapter 5).

A related nineteenth-century ideology, that of Victorianism, is also important in understanding the colonization of the Pacific Northwest. The Victorian era is defined by the reign of Alexandrina Victoria, heir-presumptive in 1827, and the Queen of the United Kingdom of Great Britain in 1837, until her death in 1901. Some extend the era to the start of World War I. Victoria and her husband, Prince Albert, became symbols of middle-class power and commercialism that stretched into North America via religion and other means (Praetzellis and Praetzellis 1992). Historical archaeologists have explored the role of Victoria and Albert in developing an ideology tied to commercialism, household domesticity, duty, and morality that appealed to the increasingly powerful middle class through the examination of household ceramics, food, architecture, cemetery monuments, and the symbolic use of material culture to both reinforce and manipulate these values (e.g., Francaviglia 1971; Goodwin 2018; Praetzellis and Praetzellis 1992, 2001; Taber 2018). In particular, the cult of domesticity (or true womanhood) placed gender roles on Victorian households, including obligations to perform the British tea ceremony and in the socialization of children. Historical archaeologists often invoke the ideology of Victorianism when examining the Pacific Northwest.

Who exactly was colonized, and the terms used by colonizers, is also problematic. Hajda (2013: 146) submits that people in western Oregon and Washington at European American contact lived in "relatively settled, autonomous, self-governing local groups linked by kin ties and crosscutting social institutions but without any higher-level organization." The concept of "Tribe" was foreign to these people and imposed on them by settlers confounded by the lack of political unity across villages, or small clusters of villages (Whaley 2010: 47–48). The treaty commissioners for the western Oregon Tribes, for example, found that Native people were divided into bands and families with permanent and hereditary "local attachments of the strongest kind," making it "generally impossible to amalgamate portions of even the same people" (Gaines et al. 1851: 469).

The terms "colonizer" and "colonized" are also challenging. As we will see in this book, fur traders became entangled with Indigenous inhabitants, and their children became part of immigrant or Indigenous populations. Likewise, some settlers accommodated their Indigenous neighbors, or had Indigenous wives and partners, and were cognizant of Indigenous cultural traditions, placemaking, and social practices, becoming allies and conspirators in the survival of Indigenous people and their traditions. While this fact does not discount the structures of colonialism and settler colonialism, it represents a subversive force by some settlers who allied with some Indigenous people to resist colonial orthodoxy, sometimes leading to Indigenous resilience and persistence.

Over the past seventy-five years or so, the emphasis of historical archaeology has changed significantly. Much of historical archaeology's earlier emphasis on sites of White and Indigenous contact and White settler sites contributed to narratives of Native disappearance that perpetuated settler colonialism, marginalizing Indigenous people. More recently, historical archaeology has begun to foreground Indigenous people and their lengthy history before European settlement, focusing on the effects of waves of culture contact and colonial projects (e.g., Lightfoot 1995; Lightfoot and Gonzalez 2018; Oland et al. 2012; Silliman 2012). In this vein, the recognition that history transcends the colonial boundary is important in the Pacific Northwest. More recent explorations of the unique structures of colonialism and settler colonialism in historical archaeology, examined in this book, permit a more critical view of Indigenous presence and continuity (Montgomery 2022). The interplay of these forms of colonialism is nuanced, reflecting the abundance of mineral resources, timber, and fish, as well as agricultural lands, and the overall dearth of labor, which required substantial investment in Indigenous and non-White immigrant labor.

Many of the first historical archaeologists in the Pacific Northwest studied sites of the British American colonial past, particularly sites that were (or would become) historical parks commemorating early colonial settlements, forts, and battlefields. Major post–World War II public projects, including the construction of the interstate highway system and the damming of rivers for hydroelectric power, led to "salvage" archaeology that exposed many young archaeologists trained in precolonial archaeology to historical sites and their plethora of exotic manufactured goods. Today, historical archaeology is a crucial part of cultural resources management and academic exploration of colonial identities, capitalism, and technology. In short, historical archaeology has become a major factor in our understanding of the modern world, significantly contributing to the American experience, as the books in this series demonstrate.

About This Book

Through historical archaeological research and theories, this book examines places, landscapes, and sites in the Pacific Northwest to elucidate the American experience. I look at how belongings, features, and architecture assist, augment, and provide new ways of looking at past events. I also present very different ways of looking at people of the Pacific Northwest and their practices, exploring how deep and structural, inherent patterns were maintained, sometimes through racism, and how certain symbolic items were manipulated by people to serve their own ends. Finally, I address how individual actors and groups affect the culture(s) of the Pacific Northwest and how technology has dramatically changed both the environment and people over the past two hundred years.

How people of the Northwest represent themselves (intentionally and unintentionally) through activities and practices is a recurring theme. Technological attributes of material items also reflect the massive changes in the nature of the world in the late eighteenth and nineteenth centuries, vis-à-vis the industrial revolution. In essence, the Pacific Northwest is a microcosm of the American experience, and this book explores regional expressions of global processes in this unique place. It also explores how historical archaeology informs on the ways in which heritage places are remembered and interpreted, including perspectives on how material things can expand interpretation of the past for people who are marginalized, silenced, or ignored in traditional historical narratives, emphasizing the theme of cultural diversity.

Another significant theme of this book centers on the relationship of people to the natural environment. Arguments and issues of the environment, both scientific and political, are central to the history of the Pacific Northwest, and are at heart social struggles and not inherent to the natural world. Issues of sustainability—how we measure, maintain, or alter humanity's impact on the environment—is a central question that drives much of Pacific Northwest history. It is a human problem intimately related to the development and industrialization of the region, contrasting with the large expanses of land inhabited by relatively few people. I argue that to understand the modern Pacific Northwest, how we got from smaller populations, with almost unlimited resources, to larger populations, and limits to growth, is an issue central for historical archaeology. Further, understanding past human–environment relationships is critical to the formation of modern policies that intend to intervene in current human practices. This book strives to understand past patterns, specifically the decision-making processes foundational to major changes in human actions, the distribution of peoples across the region, and the redistribution of resources, products, and ideas. The efficacy of policies tied to global climate change and other environment-based problems should be based on our understanding of past policies and human cultural responses to those policies. As such, documenting the entanglement of people and their environments is necessary to fully understand the American experience in the Pacific Northwest.

The organizing principal for this book is that the Pacific Northwest is a place of confluence and conflict. Theoretically, this book seeks pragmatic and postcolonial interpretations, attempting to liberate the people today from prior colonial narratives. In this way, it couples with the New Western History and other post-processual, agency-based, materialist, and Indigenous conceptions of archaeology. Juxtaposing information from academic pursuits with that of cultural resources management illuminates the unique contribution of this region to the American experience. The chapters are arranged roughly chronologically, addressing the main temporal periods in which scholars have worked. This chronological orientation recognizes that patterns and processes present in one period often continue into the next, and it is difficult to understand the Pacific Northwest without understanding how the past formed the present. But the notion of time can be problematic, as Indigenous and other memories are long, and continuity is as much a part of the story as change (e.g., Schaepe et al. 2017; cf., Montón-Subías and Hernando 2018).

In chapter 2, I explore the region's historical archaeology roots and how historical orientations toward immigration, settler colonialism, economic pursuits, and trade influenced the academic field. I also discuss some of the significant trends in theory and cultural resources management that influenced practice. Chapter 3 focuses on historical archaeology tied to the earliest colonial experience in the Pacific Northwest, from early seventeenth-century Spanish contacts to competition between the British and American fur traders in the early nineteenth century. I explore the relationship of the environment to economic activities and early colonial settlements, connecting early settlement on major rivers to changes in the abundance of species and consequent impacts on both Fur Trader and Indigenous people.

The short but highly significant period of the later fur trade era is explored in chapter 4, a time of transition between about 1824 and 1849, and the period in which Christian missionaries first entered the region. I explore the extensive historical archaeology of later fur trade sites and the nuanced history of Protestant and Catholic missionaries. I also explore how Indigenous people and the non-White employees of the fur trade adjusted to changes brought about by colonialism. The archaeology of the rapid settlement and expansion of American settlers who crossed the Oregon trail is the subject of chapter 5. I investigate the role of the U.S. and British militaries in nation-building, and the attendant suppression and marginalization of Indigenous populations. While Native peoples and other minority groups suffered lasting impacts from this phase of settler colonialism, I show how historical archaeology has documented their resistance, persistence, and in the case of Indigenous people, their survivance.

The unfortunate history of archaeologists' exhumation of ancestral graves is considered in chapter 6. It is noted that the ways in which historical archaeologists look at burials and cemeteries has changed, but that studies of cemetery monuments and the discovery of unmarked human burials provide important information on settler and Indigenous social identity and beliefs, and can even assist in reconciling and healing past traumas caused by colonialism. The West as a locus of extractive capitalism, including the exploitation of agricultural land, fish, minerals, and timber, is the subject of chapter 7. Homesteads and ranches are seen as social and economic phenomena often significantly intertwined with other economic pursuits. The material remains of Asian American immigrants and their substantial roles in mining, fish processing, and logging is explored. I contrast how Asian traditions and belongings mixed with Western products to assist Asian American's survival in a racialized environment where "otherness" was exploited for political and economic gain. I also explore Indigenous people's participation in settler industries and how it served their communities' survival and persistence in the face of settler colonialism.

The dramatic changes associated with transportation and increased urbanization is addressed in chapter 8, including the historical archaeology of rural Depression-era communities, Civilian Conservation Corps (CCC) camps, the growth of cities, and the role of urban Chinatowns in the Chinese diaspora. I also survey the material remains of World War II facilities and archaeologists' relationship with living descendants and descendant communities to adjudicate "dark" heritage tied to both racism and environmental change in the twentieth century. I conclude the book in chapter 9 by discussing the few cases in the region where historical archaeology has addressed modernity, or the historical archaeology of the late twentieth and early twenty-first centuries. I then explore the roles of historical archaeology in interpreting the American experience for peoples of the Pacific Northwest, demonstrating the long legacy of public and community archaeology. I suggest there is an enduring role for historical archaeology in accurately and inclusively framing and exploring the American experience in the Pacific Northwest and its importance in recalibrating our understanding of American heritage for the twenty-first century.

2

Origins of Historical Archaeology in the Pacific Northwest

The Pacific Northwest has a long tradition of scholars and laypeople investigating archaeological sites of the colonial period. Roderick Sprague (1975) first summarized the origins of historical archaeology and its regional development, noting three phases. His contact-period "explorer" phase consisted primarily of the looting of Indigenous burials for crania and the recording of Chinese coins in buried contexts. The "pioneer" phase involved the examination of contact-period sites as part of larger precolonial archaeological investigations, primarily in the early twentieth century. Sprague's third phase included early park development after World War II, initiated by the work of Louis Caywood at Fort Vancouver. Sprague's earlier two phases are important in examining how nineteenth and early twentieth-century scholars engaged with the recent past, usually utilizing some form of scientific and anthropological precepts. The latter period corresponds with the development of historical archaeology as a distinct academic field. Summaries of fur trade archaeology in western Canada document the early dominance of museums and universities who commenced systematic work in the mid–twentieth century tied to historic site development and commemoration (Klimko 2004). In the 1970s, Canadian Federal and Provincial agencies were influential supporters of archaeology, with a shift to the private sector and agencies conducting most of the work in the 1980s and 1990s. The shift from the development and interpretation of historical sites to more anthropological questions centered on problem-oriented research included increasingly post-processual analyses, and even attention to Indigenous people's entanglements with fur traders (Klimko 2004: 168, 174).

The history of archaeology in the region, as these summaries suggest, parallels the mid-twentieth- to twenty-first-century progression of archaeology in North America. Like all science, the cultural milieu and theoretical and methodological traditions of the archaeologists impacted the ways in which they constructed and implemented research programs and designs (Trigger 2006). This evolution of ideas and methods, influenced in part by changing sociopolitical agendas, fundamentally altered the field, and while much research builds on past studies, new ideas, techniques, and orientations resulted in new understandings.

This chapter briefly explores the approaches, context, and limitations of historical archaeology in the Pacific Northwest (e.g., Carlson 2006: 199; Ross 2017b: 201–202; Smith 2004: 227). This background helps to frame why archaeologists chose certain sites and problems to explore, which objects they analyzed, how they interpreted the data they collected, and how they interfaced with the overall development and interpretation of regional and national histories.

Evolution of Historical Archaeology in the Pacific Northwest

Based on the overall development of historical archaeology and a few regional and site-specific reviews (e.g., Carlson 2006; Dixon 2014, 2020; Ross 2015; Wilson et al. 2020: 44), I follow Sprague (1975), defining five periods in the evolution of historical archaeology in the Pacific Northwest.

1. Contact Curiosity and Pioneer Identity (ca. 1870–1945)
2. Dams, Parks, and People (ca. 1946–1966)
3. Expanding the Reach of Historic Preservation (ca. 1967–1982)
4. Expanding Partners in Heritage (1983–1999)
5. Reconciling Heritage (ca. 2000–2022)

Period 1: Contact Curiosity and Pioneer Identity (ca. 1870–1945)

Sprague (1975) discusses this period ("Exploration") as one of early curiosity by settlers in their heritage and the exhumation of human remains from contact-period Indigenous cemeteries. Many early fur trade sites were visited and sometimes excavated in the early twentieth century. Basil G. Hamilton, a local newspaper writer and historian dug at Kootenai House (1807–1809) in 1910 (Heitzmann 2004, 2006; Moore 2012). Historian Robert Moulton Gatke tested the root cellar of Jason Lee's 1834–1841 Willamette Mission in the 1920s (Chapman 1983). As part of Ezra Meeker's tireless avocation to publicize and commemorate the Oregon Trail, many sites were surveyed and marked. In 1906, Meeker and locals incorrectly marked the site of Fort Hall in eastern Idaho. Luckily, the Shoshone-Bannock knew its correct location, and Meeker revisited in 1916, conducting uncontrolled testing for "confirmation" (Brown 1932: 362–367; Thomas 2008: 8). Belongings curated and collected by households also piqued interest in "pioneer industries." Locally made stoneware jars in collections in the Willamette Valley, for example, led to a detailed analysis to document the Barnett Ramsay redware potteries (Haskin 1942).

Professional archaeologists routinely excavated Native American graves during this time, some of which contained European-manufactured belongings dating to the period of colonial contact (e.g., Collier et al. 1942; Cressman 1933; Laughlin 1941; Lewis 2017; Smith and Fowke 1901; Strong et al. 1930). This exhumation of Indigenous human remains of the more recent period was collateral to goals of documenting "ancient" Native American cultures. Not only was there not much interest in the ethics of digging up ancestral graves, but the primary emphasis was also in describing an Indigenous history before colonial contact.

Period 2: Dams, Parks, and People (ca. 1946–1966)

Harrington's (1955) review of the field of historical archaeology notes the abundance of work on historical sites in North America after World War II, much of it geared to visitor interpretation, including in some cases full-scale reconstructions of forts, buildings, and villages. Harrington suggested that Colonial Williamsburg in Virginia was a model for historic preservation and site reconstructions elsewhere, foreshadowing reconstruction work at Fort Vancouver, Fort Langley, Fort Clatsop, and other fur trade sites of the Pacific Northwest. The role of historical archaeology in this period was to augment documentary records to create more authentic reconstructions and more accurate and realistic interpretations of daily life. Harrington specifically called out the archaeological work at Fort Vancouver, including both the discovery of remains of the fort's architecture and its collection of fur trade belongings, as crucial to the interpretation of the fur trade. He also noted historical archaeology's role in "salvage" projects tied to areas inundated by new dams and construction associated with the development of the interstate highway system (figure 2.1).

During this period, archaeology's focus on culture history was often couched in nationalist, colonial, and/or racist perspectives that extended into the past or as justifications for present conditions (Trigger 2006). Harrington (1955: 1121) specifically separated the study of "white sites" from aborigine studies, focusing on the "sites associated with the history of white men in North America." Cotter and Jelks (1957: 389) emphasized the "first industries" of Jamestown colonists as economic innovation and industrial development, distinguishing American colonies from England, leading to a "spirit of independence." At about the same time, Quimby and Spoehr (1951: 147) explored how "primitive people" adopted and modified European American

Figure 2.1. Examination of beaver trap fragments during the 1947 excavations at Fort Vancouver. *Left to right:* National Park Service Regional Historian Aubrey Nesham, National Park Service Archeologist Louis Caywood, Lee Breitenstein, George Vogel, and Eric Olson. Photo courtesy of the National Park Service.

and Indigenous belongings and were themselves modified by contact with "Western Civilization." Thus, the study of White colonial ingenuity and industrious was contrasted with termination narratives tied to the disintegration of Indigenous societies.

For those attempting to reconstruct the culture history of the Pacific Northwest, the direct historical method was often used to attempt to go from historically documented sites back in time to develop sequences of cultural traits. For example, Newman's (1959) excavations at the Netarts Sand Spit site (35TI1) recorded a contact-period Tillamook village to compare with earlier sites. Indirectly, the presence of Chinese porcelain in the assemblage raised enduring questions about early maritime contacts (see chapter 3).

A unique example of a culture history approach from southern Alaska is de Laguna's work, which used ethnography, archaeology, and history to explore the northern Tlingit, suggesting that "if combined and analyzed together, can give a deeper insight than any one type of material or methodology alone" (de Laguna 1960: 200). This pioneering work prophetically espoused techniques that many historical archaeologists embraced later (e.g., Deetz 1988). De Laguna's student Susan Kardas utilized these methods to conduct the first significant work in the Fort Vancouver Village in 1968–1969 (Kardas 1971).

In contrast, much of the earliest historical archaeology examining European American sites was couched in terms of American exceptionalism, focusing on the history of the colonizer. In its late nineteenth- and early twentieth-century form, American exceptionalism embodied a confluence of Victorian and Gilded Age values, espousing normative views of gender, race, and the evolution of civilization, with America as the newest and most highly developed (White) race and the lead proponent of progress (Chaplin 2003: 1432–1433; Matthews 2012). For example, Caywood (1954a: xi) identified the importance of Fort Spokane and his exploratory excavations there in terms of the "first permanent settlement of *white men* in Washington" (my emphasis), and portraying the significance of the fort to its "foundation for present-day trading and business development in the Inland Empire" (the region of eastern Washington and northern Idaho). Caywood primarily used artifacts to examine the lifeways of the fur traders (Caywood 1951: 8; 1954a: 47). The study of fur trade establishments also fit neatly into the documentation of earliest "frontier" conditions under the Turnerian hypothesis, whereby eastern European American populations drove a succession of "frontiers" where traders, hunters, and subsistence farmers ("pioneers") were succeeded by miners and farmers, and later cities and industrial development.

During this period, conservation of archaeological resources was subservient to heritage projects. For example, the reconstruction of fur trade forts often had significant adverse impacts on archaeological resources, such as at Fort Langley where much of the evidence of the earlier palisades was destroyed by the reconstruction (Steer et al. 1980: 46). The exceptional scale of projects associated with dam construction led to increased archaeology, including the archaeology of the historical period, but also to rampant relic hunting and traumatic impacts to Indigenous heritage and people who accompanied the inundation of river basins (e.g., Butler 2007; cf., O'Grady et al. 2022).

Period 3: Expanding the Reach of Historic Preservation (ca. 1967–1982)

Starting in the 1960s, North American archaeologists shifted significantly toward anthropological theory and the exploration of evolutionary processes over descriptions of culture history (e.g., Binford 1962, 1965). For historical archaeology, Hardesty (1981) explored the notion that "frontiers" should be considered in terms of ecological communities in transition due to external and internal forces, including colonization, competition, and technology. This purely processual conception focused on households as evolutionary units and processes of competition that made groups more heterogeneous while the ideology of Victorianism made them more homogeneous. Hardesty's view suggested that Victorianism as an ideology led to uniformity in behavior and consumption, countering the competition associated with individual, household, and community production (cf., Praetzellis and Praetzellis 1992).

Most practitioners in the Pacific Northwest, however, explored sites that demonstrated American or European colonization, following twentieth-century narratives of fur trade and early American settlement. In 1978, both the Lewis and Clark and Oregon Trails were designated national historic trails. Historical archaeology did not gain formal status until the mid-1960s, when scholars formed the Society for Historical Archaeology (Deagan 1982; Sprague 1975: 10). Louis Caywood and Roderick Sprague were founding members, publishing articles in *Historical Archaeology*'s first volume. The field in general rapidly progressed in the 1960s and 1970s, partly spurred by the American Bicentennial effort and its focus on historical sites of the colonial period, and partly tied to analyses that compared written documents and material culture to address human behavior and perception and how people manipulated and coped with their environments (Deagan 1982: 153). Dethlefsen and Deetz's (1966) exploration of gravestones in New England influenced early gravestone studies in the Willamette Valley and British Columbia (e.g., Francaviglia 1971; Philpot 1976). Deetz's (1996) structuralist-idealist approach to historical archaeology also influenced post-processual approaches to historical archaeology in the Pacific Northwest, particularly work on identity and inequality.

Coincident with the turn toward new ways of looking at the past, the U.S. Congress passed the critically important National Historic Preservation Act of 1966 (NHPA), which afforded protection to significant archaeological sites at least fifty years old or older in the United States (McManamon 2018). This created a catalyst for the exploration of historical archaeological sites, building on salvage projects of the previous decades. New institutions were formed that tied academic and governmental archaeologists together, including the State Historic Preservation Offices and the Washington Archaeological Research Center, to coordinate funding and data (Croes and Hackenberger 2022). Massive historical archaeology projects were conducted, including work at Fort Vancouver, Lake Roosevelt, San Juan Island, and elsewhere. Inspired by the NHPA, new state laws or enhancements of existing laws were enacted to protect Native American burials and archaeological sites in Idaho,

Oregon, and Washington (Cenarrusa 1984: 135–138; Griffin 2009; R. White 1975: 500–503).

Stanley South introduced processual and behavioral archaeology concepts to historical archaeology (South 1977, 1978). In the Pacific Northwest, archaeologists widely employed South's methods, sometimes seeking the Brunswick pattern of refuse disposal (e.g., Chance and Chance 1979: 109), or comparing sites using South's functional classification comparative method. South's Brunswick Pattern identified the practice of eighteenth-century British American colonists to discard refuse at the entryways of houses, shops, and forts, providing distinctive depositional contexts useful in exploring past behavior (South 1977, 1978). The functional classification typology was incorporated in projects throughout the Pacific Northwest, but somewhat haphazardly. In South's original arrangement, artifacts were classified by type and class into one of eight functional groups: Kitchen, Architecture, Furniture, Arms, Clothing, Personal, Tobacco Pipes, and Activities. South then compared the percentage range of assemblages of artifacts from sites to identify patterning that he felt represented "regularity in the by-products of human behavior," or a cultural expression that conformed to the frequencies with which refuse from activities was accumulated (South 1977, 1978). His method of comparing assemblages using functional groups identified two distinct patterns: a Carolina Pattern at colonial sites on the east coast, where assemblages were dominated by kitchen-related items, and a Frontier Pattern at interior sites where assemblages were dominated by architecture-related items. Some Pacific Northwest researchers embraced South's typology (e.g., Minor and Beckham 1984; Sauer 1995) and its direct offspring, the Sonoma State functional classification system (e.g., Rose and Johnson 2015; Tveskov 2021b; Tveskov et al. 2017). Many historical archaeologists employed a similar functional typology developed at the University of Idaho and first reported for 1970s excavations at Fort Colvile (Clark 2002; Roulette and Chapman 1996; Saastamo 1971; Chapman 1983; Sprague 1981: 252; Stilson 1990c). Sprague's (1981) classification was predicated on the desire to use artifact function to explore and define human cultural traits in the eighteenth and nineteenth centuries. He identified eight higher-level categories: Personal, Domestic, Architecture, Personal and Domestic Transportation, Commerce and Industry, Group Services, Group Ritual, and Unknown. These were used to characterize early colonial sites in the Pacific Northwest.

In some cases, the Sprague typology was modified to more closely match South's to attempt to extend the Frontier Pattern to the nineteenth-century Pacific Northwest (e.g., Minor et al. 1981; Minor and Beckham 1984; Nicholls 1986; Speulda 1988). To South, "frontier" meant far removed from the eighteenth-century centers of commerce with Great Britain, with his explanation for the pattern that the short length of occupation and distance from ports with ready access to commercial goods decreased the abundance of domestic items (South 1977, 1978). As the Pacific Northwest was even farther removed from the eastern United States and Canada, researchers felt the Frontier Pattern might operate in the region in the nineteenth century. Also of consequence, South's notion of "frontier" perpetuated anthropological and historical ideas regarding the expansion of nation-states into adjacent areas, essentially continuing the exploration of the Turnerian hypothesis of American frontier expansion (Ostrogorsky 1982).

While most explorations of the Frontier Pattern in the nineteenth-century Pacific Northwest identified an abundance of architectural materials that mimicked South's findings for eighteenth-century eastern frontier forts and settlement sites, explanations did not consider the eighteenth- and nineteenth-century technological advances in architecture and transportation that profoundly affected archaeological assemblages. In particular, the machine manufacture of nails, onset of steam-powered lumber mills that could produce lighter timbers for framing, and the increasing abundance of manufactured window glass together increased the availability and lowered the cost of architectural materials (Adams 2002; Cavanagh 1997; Garth 1947; Giedion 1941; Petersen 2000; P. Sprague 1981; Roenke 1978). New forms of framing and larger windows led to a generally greater abundance of architectural remains for mid- to late-nineteenth-century sites.

The other obvious critique of functional classifications is that the categories are not always mutually exclusive, and there is considerable room for interpretive variability (Bowyer 1992: 47). Issues of context are particularly acute as a square nail found at a colonial settlement might reflect the remains of a structure, while a square nail on a battlefield might reflect remains of the boxes used to carry ammunition and supplies. More recent applications of functional typologies use the classification of belongings as a launching point to compare assemblages, taking deeper dives into specific types of items.

Archaeologists' interest in formation processes, including refuse disposal, as well as embracing the scientific method, greatly influenced historical archaeology in the Pacific northwest. For example, work at Silcott, a small twentieth-century agricultural community in eastern Washington (see chapter 8), compared multiple data sets to address archaeological and historical bias (Adams 1977), examined the recent past and ethnoarchaeology (Adams 1973), and explored artifact breakage related to use patterns (e.g., Gaw 1975), refuse disposal (Adams 1975), and time lag in dated ceramic and glass vessels (Adams and Gaw 1977). Elsewhere, South's Mean Ceramic Dating (MCD) procedure was tested for the nineteenth century using trademarks on ceramics at San Juan Island sites with known occupations (Ferguson 1983c: 774–784). A related analytical tool developed during this time period was to focus on economic data and the potential to use items found at sites to document the origins of consumer products, exploring trends in national, international, and local markets, commodity flows, and consumer behavior (Adams 1977; Jones 1983; Riordan and Adams 1985).

Following in the footsteps of de Laguna (1960), Fladmark's excavations at the Richardson Ranch site in British Columbia used archaeology as an independent source of data to compare with the ethnographic and ethnohistoric record of colonial-period Indigenous sites (Fladmark 1973). He critiqued the then typical use of the ethnographic record as a source for analogy but stressed the unique ability of both sources of data to inform on each other. Elsewhere in the Pacific Northwest, historical archaeologists began overt comparisons of historical narratives with archaeological data (e.g., Mead and Womack 1975), and researchers began exploring Chinese American mining communities, but using then current anthropological models of acculturation and adaptation (LaLande 1981, 1982).

Period 4: Expanding Partners in Heritage (1983–1999)

The post-processual debate profoundly influenced historical archaeology, particularly in the exploration of the symbolic nature of belongings and structures, and increasing interest in the role of capitalism in examining inequality (Little 1994). Historical archaeology began to address global contexts and delved more deeply into the impact of colonialism on Indigenous peoples, influenced by Eric Wolf's (1982) *Europe and the People without History* and the Columbian Quincentennial (e.g., Little 1994; Paynter 2000a, 2000b).

In British Columbia, the Heritage Conservation Act was amended in 1994 to protect all archaeological sites predating 1846, the year in which the International Boundary was established, which served to protect many earlier fur trade and Indigenous sites but did not protect most historical archaeological sites (e.g., Muckle 2021; Parsley 2011; Ross 2015: 164–165, 180; Schaepe et al. 2020). Regardless, academics, park managers, and sometimes local archaeological societies in British Columbia continued to seek ways to explore a variety of important historical archaeology subjects.

Stanley South's ideas continued to inspire historical archaeology in the Pacific Northwest, primarily for American settler sites (e.g., Bowyer 1992;

Minor and Beckam 1984, 1988; Speulda 1988). Exploration of commodity flow and consumer behavior continued (Miss et al. 2000; Riordan and Adams 1985; Ross et al. 1995), and systems theory was sometimes evoked (Stapp 1990). The work of David Brauner and his students at Champoeg illuminated the lives of early fur trade families who had preceded the Oregon Trail migration and the study of Coast Reservation forts began to set a basis for exploring the military's involvement in settlement and control of Indigenous people (e.g., Bowyer 1992; Brauner 1989; Chapman 1993; Schablitsky 1996; Speulda 1988). Material science approaches were occasionally applied to historical archaeology questions, like Steele's (1989) metallurgical and metallographic analysis of non-ferrous Indigenous artifacts from 35TI1 (Netarts Sand Spit site) to determine if they preceded the maritime fur trade (his analysis suggested not) or Sullivan's (1986) Neutron Activation analysis (NAA) of kiln wasters from the Buena Vista pottery company.

Gravestone studies continued in the Pacific Northwest during this period, largely by non-archaeologists (e.g., Coates 1984, 1987; Hawker 1987; Meyer 1990, 1992). Historical archaeologists increased attention to oral histories to compare with documentary and material remains at more recent historic sites, such as fish canneries (Fagan 1993; Newell 1991). Increasingly, researchers explored Chinese Americans in mining, fishing, and urban settings, with some investing in post-processual, contextual approaches (e.g., Chen 2001).

Historical archaeology began to focus on Indigenous people as agents rather than victims of colonialism. Toward the end of this period, Kent Lightfoot and his students' work at Russian Fort Ross in northern California (e.g., Lightfoot 1995; Lightfoot et al. 1998) influenced many students in the Pacific Northwest. The work of the University of Oregon's Southwest Oregon Research Project is notable as an early academic collaboration with the Coquille Indian Tribe and that included the archaeology of the historic period (e.g., Erlandson et al. 1997; Tveskov 2000; see O'Neill and Tveskov 2008). Other examples include Marshall and Maas's (1997) novel exploration of the Indigenous adoption of ceramics at Nootka Sound and Bella Bella in British Columbia and the first Indigenous Archaeology project in 1993–1994 at McLeod's Lake at the Tsek'ehne Village site (Nicholas et al. 2008).

Period 5: Reconciling Heritage (ca. 2000–2022)

Since 2000, historical archaeologists increasingly attempt to address past practices of archaeology through directly confronting racism, colonialism, settler colonialism, and capitalism using multiscalar, landscape, and Indigenous approaches. Multiscalar analysis compares household, community, and international data linking individual sites with local and global phenomena (Orser 2010: 116–120). In the Pacific Northwest, these types of analyses include colonial fort sites (e.g., Horton 2014; Moore 2012; Wilson 2014, 2018), sites of Asian American immigrants (e.g., Campbell 2017a, 2017b, 2021; Carlson 2021; Ross 2013), and contact-period Indigenous sites (e.g., Byram 2002; Sobel 2012; Tveskov 2000, 2007). Academic interest has increased in explorations of capitalism's role in shaping the past, including studies of consumption, and emphasis on identity and social inequality (Campbell 2021; Ng and Camp 2014). Indigenous archaeology and studies of other marginalized groups in the Pacific Northwest have explored agency or taken a community-centered approach that questions traditional American narratives that use racial and ethnic tropes to sideline non-White people (Ames 2017; Carlson 2006; Connolly et al. 2022; Gonzalez et al. 2018; Gonzalez and Edwards 2020; Kretzler 2019; Nicholas 2006; Nicholas et al. 2008; Prentiss 2017; Rose 2020; Ross 2012, 2013; Smith 2017). A few researchers continue to explore world systems models but with Indigenous agency as a factor in the negotiation of the colonial "middle ground" (e.g., Moore 2012).

In this vein, postcolonial and antiracist projects are becoming more commonplace, challenging the historiography of the American West, and addressing diaspora, transnationalism, and the New Western History (e.g., Fong et al. 2022; Hann 2021; Lee 2020; Rose 2013, 2020; Rose and Ruiz 2014; Ross 2013; White 2017b). Theory has shifted away from acculturation and world systems theory toward more decolonized viewpoints that center Indigenous people's agency and practice, not as "customers" or "consumers" of goods but as agents that make decisions based on a variety of inputs, including colonialism (Cipolla 2021; e.g., Carlson 2017; Prentiss 2017: 5; Prince 2002b: 52; Sobel 2012: 1). Landscape level analyses are epitomized by work at homesteads, frontier forts, Indigenous landscapes, and massive twentieth-century work and incarceration camps (e.g., Camp 2016: 173–174; Nicholas 2006; Speulda and Bowyer 2002; Tveskov and Cohen 2014). Studies that engage with feminist and gender theory, while sporadic, include studies of colonial homes and male-only incarceration camps (e.g., Fitz-Gerald 2015; Manion 2014; Stone 2010).

Calls for greater coordination in research include better coordination of researchers and the development of standardized data collection (e.g., Camp 2021). Academic debates regarding archaeological education, practice, cultural resources management, and public archaeology are lively and relevant to current social justice issues, and perhaps even the evolution of the field (Harris et al. 2017; Hutchings 2021; Hutchings and La Salle 2014, 2015; Kopperl 2022; La Salle and Hutchings 2016; Martindale et al. 2016; Wessen 2022).

Figure 2.2. Excavation of an officer's quarters at Fort Yamhill with an Oregon State University field school, July 23, 2013. Photo courtesy of Daniel Klug.

In turn, the continuing influence of behavioral archaeology techniques to explore a variety of sites and infer past practices is apparent in studies that address refuse disposal behavior and the interpretation of site formation processes and consumer behavior, and is sometimes linked with post-processual theories and concepts like symbolic display of authority, practice theory, and Indigenous Archaeology (figure 2.2; e.g., Connolly et al. 2022; Cromwell 2017b; Eichelberger 2019a; Ruiz 2010).

Attention to graveyards and cemeteries has increased, including belowground studies by archaeologists (e.g., Connolly et al. 2010; Smits 2008) and gravestone studies by archaeology and history students (e.g., Boulware 2008; Drew 2010; Straus 2018). Exploration of the burial practices and cemeteries of marginalized groups include Chinese Americans and Basques (e.g., Abraham and Wegars 2003, 2005; Smits 2008; Fitzgerald 2018, Fitzgerald et al. 2021).

Public and community archaeology continues to evolve, including projects that engage with Indigenous people and other marginalized communities, and through connecting the public to archaeology in different ways (e.g., Butler et al. 2021; Parks and Merrifield 2021; Warner et al. 2014; White 2016; Wilson 2015; Wilson et al. 2022). In particular, Indigenous collaborations with archaeologists are becoming more common, led by work in British Columbia and Oregon (e.g., Ivy and Byram 2002; Losey 2000; Rippee and Scott 2023; Tveskov 2007; Yellowhorn 2002; Younker et al. 2001), and now including projects that address such thorny issues as residential schools, Western-style education, and the meaning of archaeological sites to Indigenous communities (Gonzalez et al. 2018; Harris et al. 2017; Kretzler and Gonzalez 2021; Moss and Wasson 2009; Nicholas 2006; Nicholas et al. 2008; Rahemtulla 2020; Simons et al. 2021).

Methods of Historical Archaeology in the Pacific Northwest

Historical archaeologists in the Pacific Northwest practice their craft in ways similar to other areas of North America and the world, but the unique social and natural environments and the history of regional academic and governmental institutions have influenced it. This section briefly explores archaeological resources as a subject matter and how historical archaeologists define, explore, analyze, and report them in the Pacific Northwest.

The Definition and Significance of Archaeological Resources

Most archaeological resources are below ground, but some are structural remains, including underwater shipwrecks, and some archaeological deposits are associated with the built environment, including buildings facilities, monuments, roads, and trails. Research designs, with well-defined problems and techniques, are necessary to collect data that determine the value of archaeological resources. However, archaeological resources also can have direct heritage connections to cultural groups, including Native American and minority populations. As a consequence, many individuals and groups have exceptional ties to archaeological sites, particularly those protected as heritage parks, landscapes, or monuments, through their unique histories and direct historical and descendant connections. Some view archaeological resources as intrinsic to their and their people's heritage, or even sacred. Thus, while archaeological resources are important to academic archaeologists and other specialists that depend on their study, these resources also may be highly important to culturally affiliated descendant groups and individuals.

The age of sites studied by historical archaeology in the Pacific Northwest is constrained by the problematic notion of how old a site has to be to be considered worthy of study. In the United States, most protections for archaeological sites begin once they cross the fifty-year threshold, and in some cases the threshold is set at a higher boundary, such as seventy-five or one hundred years (Griffin and Churchill 2003). As noted above, in British Columbia, the date for which archaeological sites are protected by law in the province is fixed at 1846, creating an absence of protection for most sites and a significant dearth of focus on archaeological resources after the fur trade era (e.g., Ross 2015: 164–165, 180; Schaepe et al. 2020).

Archaeological Techniques

Historical archaeologists typically develop some form of research design to explain the context and goals of their work, the research questions posed, and the means to answer them. For the Pacific Northwest, much of the development of background historical research relies on historical maps, like those of the U.S. General Land Office or the Sanborn Fire Insurance maps. The General Land Office conducted surveys in the 1850s through the late nineteenth century throughout the western United States to define land ownership. Notes for these surveys and plat maps, available through the Bureau of Land Management, contain abundant information on early American settlements and sometimes even show contemporaneous Indigenous villages and camps. Fire Insurance maps are used extensively by historical archaeologists in the Pacific Northwest to explore urban areas or significant industrial developments from the 1880s through 1940s.

Starting in the 1990s, near surface geophysical remote sensing, including ground-penetrating radar, magnetometry, and electromagnetic conductivity, became prevalent in the region and is now routine for many projects (e.g., Bell 1990; Harris et al. 2017; McDonald 2002; Tveskov et al. 2019). Likewise, the early use of geographical information systems (GIS) started with geographic interpretation of historical maps to put past places on the modern landscape (e.g., Thomas and Hibbs 1984) and visualization techniques, including the SYMAP program, to map artifact densities across sites (e.g., Chance and Chance 1985b: 227). This has given way to the routine use of GIS to register historical maps to modern features and to record excavation locations (e.g., Tveskov et al. 2019). Metal detectors are used routinely for battlefield studies and at other locations where the ground surface is covered in thick forest duff or otherwise not visible (e.g., Mack 2005; Muckle 2001; Tveskov 2020a).

Pedestrian survey is most commonly used to find sites, and if the ground is not visible, archaeologists will excavate a small sample of sediment in probes, often sieving the materials through metal screens to detect objects. Screening with 1/4-inch (6 mm) hardware mesh started sporadically in the 1960s and remained an option into the 1970s. By the 1990s, 1/4-inch and/or 1/8-inch (3 mm) mesh screens were more routinely used by archaeologists searching for small artifacts, including small pieces of lithic debitage, beads, and pins.

Archaeologists usually map sites with the global positioning system (GPS), and they are given a site number by the State or Province in which it is recorded. In British Columbia, the Borden system is used, which uses the Canadian National Topographic Series maps and a letter scheme tied to longitude and latitude to demarcate blocks of 10- × 10-minute areas and a unique number for the sites recorded within these blocks. In the United States, archaeological sites are commonly numbered using the system devised by the Smithsonian Institution for the River Basin Surveys, with a number representing the State, an alphanumeric code for the county, and a site number recorded within that county (Butler 2009). In Oregon, historical archaeological sites were given a different number, with an "OR" in place of the State number (and with duplicating site numbers). Oregon historical archaeological sites now are given a traditional Smithsonian number, but confusingly, many older reports cite the old number.

Grids are established on sites by archaeologists to record archaeological resources and facilitate reporting on where excavations occurred. The earliest grid system for historical archaeology in the Pacific Northwest was in 1947 at Waiilatpu Mission, which followed the system devised by J. C. Harrington for Jamestown, which was a 100-foot grid divided into 10-foot squares (Garth 1948). Prior to 2000, many excavations of historical archaeological sites employed English units, often measured with an English engineer's scale (tenths of a foot) in 10- × 10-foot or 5- × 5-foot excavation units. In some cases, historical archaeologists employed SI (metric) units for grids and excavation (e.g., Adams 1973; Chance and Chance 1979: 81; Chapman 1983; Ostrogorsky 1977: 6). Indigenous sites were more commonly excavated using SI (metric) units. Use of SI units is now routine in investigations of historical archaeology sites, typically 1 × 1 meter (excavation or test units) or 0.5 × 0.5 meter (quarter test units). In British Columbia, the Parks Canada archaeological system, the "Historic Sites Service Operations Method," was used to define specific "operations" to define areas of the site subject to examination below the site level (Parks Canada 2005). Sprague popularized the use of this system among his many students (and their students) south of the international border.

Artifact Analysis

The material culture of historical archaeology is well defined in the Pacific Northwest, by numerous analysts, and tied to national and global studies of the types of commercial products widely distributed throughout the world in the nineteenth and twentieth centuries. Many early studies focused on items associated with the fur trade and early settlement (e.g., Caywood 1955; Ross

1976), although more recent studies have scrutinized twentieth-century consumer goods. Early regional studies of ceramics include Chapman (1993), Ferguson (1983c), Ross (1977), and Sussman (1979). Analysis of pottery manufacturing of utilitarian ware in the Pacific Northwest include the work of Scheans (1984) and Sullivan (1986). Analysis of Asian ceramics was spearheaded by Ling (1982, 1983; Jones et al. 1979) and through the foundation of the Asian American Comparative Collection by Priscilla Wegars in 1982 (University of Idaho 2022). Southern Oregon University hosts a very useful online Chinese ceramic collection (Southern Oregon University 2018a). More recently, Ross (2009, 2011, 2013) and Campbell (2017a, 2017b, 2021), among others, have described Japanese ceramics (figure 2.3). Most modern ceramics analyses in the Pacific Northwest include the reporting of counts of sherds as well as minimum number of vessels (MNV). Miller's CC index, which ranks an assemblage's value based on the reported values of English pottery prices, which were fixed across companies, has been applied in studies exploring consumer choice (e.g., Cromwell 2006c; Roulette and Chapman 1996).

Other classes of artifacts studied by historical archaeologists include trade beads (Moura 1991; Quimby 1978; Ross 1990), buttons (e.g., Sprague 1998, 2002; Strong 1960, 1975; Sukau 2022), bottle glass (e.g., Carley 1982; Frescoln 1975; Simmons 2014), clay tobacco pipes (e.g., Pfeiffer 1981, 1982, 1983; Wynia 2013), tin cans (e.g., Bowyer 2002; O'Bannon 1983; Rock 1984, 1989; Southern Oregon University 2018b), and firearms and ammunition (e.g., Freeman et al. 2012; May 2018b; S. White 1975).

The analysis and interpretation of architectural items include the study of nails and other fasteners, window glass, and bricks. Because of the unique timing of colonial settlement and the transition from British to American distribution patterns across the southern portion of the region, architectural technology is particularly revealing. Gurcke (1987) conducted extensive research on bricks in the Pacific Northwest, helping to define earlier English, locally made, and imported types that became widespread across the Pacific Northwest (see Peterson 1989 for Victoria, British Columbia). More recently, Converse (2011) conducted INAA analysis on bricks from Fort Vancouver and locations in the Willamette Valley, England, and the Netherlands to explore local brick manufacturing in the "Oregon Country."

Karl Roenke determined that the thickness of fragments of window and other flat glass was useful for dating nineteenth-century archaeological sites, reflecting the technological changes associated with thinner, hand-blown crown glass used for window panes, to thicker, cylinder, and plate glasses (Roenke 1978, 1982, 1983). British tariffs that protected the thinner and

Figure 2.3. Japanese Sometsuke Senbori Gohan Jawan (rice/soup bowl with hand-painted cobalt and carved lines) collected from Minidoka National Historic Site, Idaho. Photo courtesy of the Asian American Comparative Collection, University of Idaho, catalog no. AACC-MIN-98-22.

lighter crown glass, plus the benefits of lighter weights for transportation by ship, resulted in thinner-paned windows. This pattern shifted in 1846, with British movement away from protectionism, and the settlement of the American boundary that favored importation of the thicker cylinder glass (Moura 1990c; Roenke 1978: 27–30). American settlement and the construction of railroads allowed rapid movement of glass from factories in the Midwest to the Pacific Northwest. Roenke compared distributions of glass thicknesses with the known dates of historical sites to develop a concordance that allowed one to measure a mode of window glass thickness to estimate the time period in which it was manufactured.

Roenke (1983) augmented his own system by suggesting that bimodal distributions of flat glass for a site might reflect structural additions, renovations, or a later structure. Stilson (1991a: 6.25–6.26) further questioned that variation around the measures of central tendency, particularly skewing, might also reflect aspects of structure renovation or the presence of a new structure. More recently, Connolly et al.'s (2009) window glass study at the Beatty Curve site questioned Roenke's system in more remote areas, examining a variety of techniques.

Archaeologists have explored nails and fasteners, particularly in transitional periods (e.g., Adams 2002). Like flat glass, hand-wrought nails from Great Britain were imported to Hudson's Bay Company sites until the mid-

1840s, although by then machine-made American nails were common elsewhere in the United States. The cottage industries that wrought British nails apparently were protected by the British government and its trade unions (Adams 2002: 70). Even those early English machine-made nails are distinctive as they continued to have hand-wrought heads. With the settlement of the United States/Canada boundary, most nails imported into the U.S. territory were American machine-cut. Wire nails became dominant in the region about 1900. Integration of fastener data with flat glass and other construction hardware allow detailed analyses of structure construction, maintenance, and abandonment (e.g., Mullaley 2011).

The study of these belongings within their sites and landscapes forms the fundamental data with which historical archaeologists explore the past. In the next chapters, I address the application of these methods to investigate the people and history of the Pacific Northwest.

3

Contextualizing Pacific Northwest Colonialism

In the early to mid–twentieth century, "colonial" in the United States signified both era and representation, including colonial revival architecture, early American furnishings, and the prominent display of American Eagle plaques that linked the occupants symbolically to the social, political, and ancestral origins of American culture (Rhoads 1976). Colonial revival was a design aesthetic that merged tradition and the progressive movement, countering modernization and appealing to the middle class (May 1991). Emblematic of American heritage, the historic preservation movement in the United States established National Park System sites, preserving buildings and communities (Tyler 2000). In the American West, advocates protected missions, forts, towns, and houses, and colonial was equated with heritage, though primarily a European American heritage.

The aesthetics of the colonial of the early to mid–twentieth century was a symbolic reflection on the past and a desire to live within an ancestral or heritage place. Connections with preserved heritage parks were part of the escape from the complexities of modernity in cities and suburbs to pasts that were simpler and more "natural." In the West, this was born out of American and Canadian settlement and a desire to commemorate colonial people. Discovering early explorer sites memorialized in camps and the graffiti of early traders is an important legacy of historical archaeology in the Pacific Northwest.

As shown in this chapter, the impulse to connect to the earliest contacts between Europeans and Indigenous peoples is strong, but the archaeological examination of sites of exploration, contact, and fur trade posts document the close connections between Indigenous places and the establishment of these settlements. Part of this is related to separating out "cultural" from "political" definitions of colonial, discriminating between state-driven and directed political colonization and the process of colonialism, whereby new systems of social and material relationships emerge (Beaule 2017: 6; Shepherd and Lawrence 2006: 69; Silliman 2020: 42). For example, the national policies and treaties that determined which colonial powers would be able to trade with

Indigenous people for furs in the Pacific Northwest and that led to the creation of mercantile colonial forts were motivated to secure near-monopolistic control over valuable Indigenous resources. On the other hand, the social interactions between fur traders and Indigenous people (and landscapes) created unique social and material relationships that dramatically affected Indigenous and colonial communities and created new connections between places and things.

In this sense, forts transcend both definitions, as they were purposefully placed in Indigenous lands, often at Native request, to provide easy access to exotic goods, while allowing fur traders to collect valuable animal pelts and other resources, including pemmican, deer, and elk hides. Each of these places is intimately tied to local landscapes and peoples, and the complex reactions of the Indigenous people to the influx of new stimuli of natural and social environments and material culture impacted both colonizer and colonized. These places of contact are embedded in the history, memory, and mythology of Indigenous and settler populations (e.g., Daehnke 2013; Tveskov 2007).

Environmental change affected decisions and agency in each region, with some of that change associated with overexploitation of fur-bearing and other economically important mammals or the introduction of new species, such as the horse. Changes in practices within the region are associated with disease, depletion of animals, social relations, and even the establishment and abandonment of fur trade posts. Even so, many Indigenous communities were not substantially changed during this early fur trade period. In some cases, such as at the Middle Village (see below), the fur trading was integrated into traditional and seasonal patterns. In other cases, fur traders were dependent on the Native American people to provide them with food.

In this study of forts within Indigenous landscapes, scholars have expended considerable effort to explain how colonial contacts affected Indigenous populations. Two fundamental theories have been raised since at least the mid–twentieth century. The *enrichment thesis* posits that the fur trade was "extremely favorable and stimulating for the Native communities involved" as it expanded their economies; introduced new tools and weapons; increased the exchange value of local commodities, such as salmon and beaver pelts; made the Indigenous trader wealthier; and gradually incorporated them into "a more advanced economic system" (Wike 1958: 1086–1087). In contrast, the *exploitation, or deprivation thesis* suggests that predatory commerce and contact with traders and other Whites led to worsening conditions associated with epidemics, dependency on trade goods, competition over land, increased inequality within tribes, over-exploitation of resources, and even the anxiety of impending contact (Cole and Darling 1990; Wike 1958). As we shall see, these theses continue to form a point of contention in understanding early contacts and the ways in which colonialism is theorized (cf., Acheson 1995; Sobel 2012).

This chapter explores how historical archaeologists explore early colonial history in the Pacific Northwest through their study of places tied symbolically to the land claims of Nation states, but also demonstrating how Indigenous people were central to the establishment of many of these places, intrinsic to their success or failure, and directly participating in the rich social relations that emerged. While these connections were ignored or misunderstood by many early researchers, the underlying indigeneity of these colonial places is central to the American experience in the Pacific Northwest. Neither exploitation nor enrichment can explain fully the entanglement of fur trade people with Indigenous communities, and as this book reveals, Indigenous people persisted on their landscapes, even as fur traders became more persistent in their presence and economic and social manipulation. Building on concepts of resistance, resilience, and persistence (Connolly et al. 2022; Oliver 2013; Panich 2013; Silliman 2020), the concept of survivance, which transcends both survival and resistance of Indigenous communities, is an important non-Western means to examine the creative ways in which Native people addressed colonialism (Cipolla 2021: 113; Kretzler 2019; Vizenor 2008).

First Contacts and Colonialism in the Pacific Northwest

The first direct contacts between Europeans and Indigenous peoples occurred through maritime trade along the Pacific coast, and sometimes accidentally through shipwrecks. Later, groups of explorers and fur traders made arduous journeys across the continent. Historical archaeology has influenced the discovery, exploration, and interpretation of these sites. Much of the evidence is gleaned from sites of Indigenous people, and while foreign products and colonial trading regimes consume much scholarly attention, less has been shown toward how these artifacts became the belongings of Native people.

Among early venturers to the Pacific Northwest, perhaps the most famous and controversial is Sir Francis Drake. While it is clear from primary sources that Drake sailed as far north as the Oregon Coast in 1579 during his circumnavigation of the globe, Darby (2019) reviews the evidence for an Oregon landfall at Whale Cove near Depoe Bay, or another Oregon harbor, refuting the traditional site at Drake's Bay in California (figure 3.1). Placing the location where the *Golden Hind* was careened in Oregon partly requires a conspiracy by the English crown to make a far southern claim to the lands of northern California, and with intentional obfuscation of the reported lati-

36 · The Historical Archaeology of the Pacific Northwest

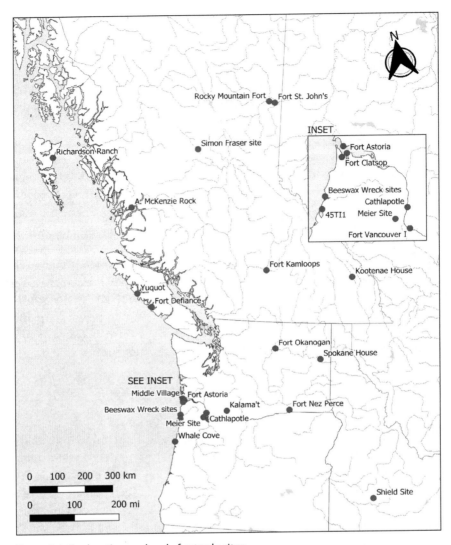

Figure 3.1. Exploration and early fur trade sites.

tudes. Analysis of the descriptions of Native American people in Drake's and the Anglican Priest Fletcher's accounts compares plausibly with later ethnographic descriptions of the coastal people of southwest Oregon, but the archaeological evidence to date is scant, essentially a ca. 1560 English shilling found on the beaches of Nehalem Bay and a ca. 1551–1552 silver shilling found in disturbed context in Victoria, British Columbia (Darby 2019: 78).

Shipwrecks are ubiquitous on the Pacific coast, and colonial records and oral traditions document early contacts among Asian, European, and Indigenous people. There has been a long discussion of Asian shipwrecks supplying iron for implements noted in the possession of Native Americans by European American explorers or found in archaeological sites in contexts that predate British and American colonial contact (e.g., Ames 2017: 369–375; Beals 1980; Keddie 1990, 2004; Quimby 1948, 1985).

The Beeswax Wreck

The most famous shipwreck in the Pacific Northwest is the Beeswax Wreck of Nehalem, Oregon. Newman (1959: 17) first noted over one hundred Chinese porcelain sherds from at least five vessels in the upper fill of a pit in a Native Tillamook plankhouse at the Netarts Sand Spit site (35TI1), on Netarts Bay, west of Tillamook, Oregon. Newman's interest in culture history suggested a "Developed Northwest Culture" related to the ethnographic Tillamook people, but the Chinese sherds were a puzzle, and Newman (1959: 32–33) hypothesized they came from a wrecked fur-trading vessel. Typological and chemical reanalysis of the porcelain dated them to the Late Ming (Wan Li, 1573–1617) or the early Ch'ing/Qing dynasties (K'ang Hsi/Kang Xi; 1662–1722), suggesting they came from a Spanish shipwreck, not later fur traders (Beals and Steele 1981: 26). Notably, Lewis and Clark commented on the presence of beeswax at Nehalem Bay, about 50 kilometers north of Netarts, along with observations that some Clatsop-Nehalem people had red hair and pale skin (La Follette and Deur 2018: 181–187). Beeswax was a substance unknown to the Indigenous people of the Pacific Northwest, but the Nehalem-Tillamook people collected it from the wreck, incorporating it into traditional uses, including sealing canoes, waterproofing clothing, lighting in lamps, and as medicine, and also trading it widely with other wreck materials across the region (Erlandson et al. 2001: 50; La Follette and Deur 2018: 182–183).

Chinese porcelain sherds were also found at two house sites and a midden in a Tillamook/Nehalem village site (35TI4) and from surface finds on the beaches near Tillamook, Oregon (Woodward 1986). The Indigenous inhabitants reworked some of these into projectile points and discarded other tools and stoneware sherds, fragments of metal, beeswax, and other imported artifacts that predated the nineteenth century (figure 3.2). Oral history of the Clatsop-Nehalem people includes an account of the first contact with the Beeswax ship crew, and ethnohistoric accounts describe the wide distribution of beeswax among Indigenous peoples and their trade to early settlers (Erlandson et al. 2001: 50).

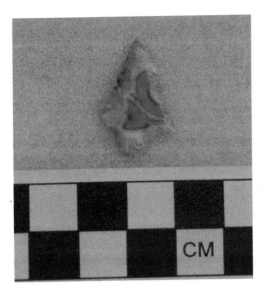

Figure 3.2. Blue on white Chinese export porcelain sherd remanufactured into a projectile point. The decoration appears to be Tiger Lily floral scroll motif (Kangxi) likely derived from the Beeswax wreck. This specimen was shown to the author on June 29, 2010, and is reported to have been collected from the lower Columbia River.

Since 2006, the Maritime Archaeological Society has collected local histories of beeswax, teak timbers from the shore and a sea cave, and other objects found in the area, examining the extensive colonial record of Spanish galleons lost at sea, and exploring archaeological evidence (La Follette 2022; La Follette, Deur, et al. 2018; Williams 2007, 2020, 2023; Williams et al. 2018). Geoarchaeological analyses confirm the potential of the A.D. 1700 tsunami to impact the remains of the wreck (Peterson et al. 2011; Williams et al. 2017). Williams et al. (2017: 159) suggest that this dispersal led to its widespread accessibility, feeding local traditions of shipwrecks, beeswax, and treasure trove. This likely also enabled the Nehalem-Tillamook people to more easily collect beeswax and other wreck materials from the beaches, resulting in increased local use and trade to other coastal groups.

Based on Spanish records and material evidence, the wreck is likely the 1693 wreck of the *Santo Christo de Burgos,* a galleon that sailed from Manila in the Philippines but never reached its destination of Acapulco, Mexico (Williams 2016; Williams et al. 2018). Inferring that the inscriptions carved into the beeswax were Spanish shipping marks, and expressing the importance of beeswax as a cargo for ecclesiastical purposes in New Spain, Williams et al. (2018: 195) discount prior hypotheses of a wrecked Chinese, Japanese, Portuguese, or even pirate ship. Comparing the oral traditions of the Nehalem-Tillamook and Clatsop people with the locations of wreck artifacts and traditions of later settler residents confirms contact by Indigenous people with the crew, with survivors leaving descendants within the Nehalem-Tillamook community (La Follette and Deur 2018). Interestingly, the oral traditions became embellished through time, becoming fodder for treasure tales, occasioning a tradition of treasure hunting on Neahkahnie Mountain. This injection of legendary, even mythological significance to the landscape led to conflicts among collectors, archaeologists, and Indigenous communities, and eventually statewide archaeological permitting requirements (Griffin 2009; La Follette, Griffin, and Deur 2018).

Scholars have documented the porcelain, stoneware, and earthenware ceramics from the shipwreck, including analysis of an extensive private collection with good provenience (Lally 2008, 2016; Litzenberg 2022). Most of the sherds date to the wreck of the *Santo Christo de Burgos,* but some of the porcelain fragments contain attributes consistent with an earlier age of manufacture (1520–1635) pointing to a possible earlier shipwreck, tempered by the uncertainty of knowledge of this period's Chinese ceramics and possible long lag times for storage vessels on galleons (Lally 2008: 97). The porcelain sherds came from plates, bowls, lidded cups, globular box-shapes, a vase or bottle, and even a figurine (Lally 2008: 37–42). Stoneware and earthenware storage jars, and perhaps some smaller containers, including bowls, dominated the rest of the ceramic assemblage, consistent with East and Southeast Asia manufacture, including at least one Chinese Dragon Jar (Litzenberg 2022: 83). The porcelain ceramics from the wreck were widely traded, as similar ceramics have shown up as far inland as the Cathlapotle site on the Columbia River near Ridgefield, Washington (Ames 2017; Cromwell 2017a; see figure 3.2).

The influence of these first direct visitors to the Northwest Coast was impactful, but localized and infrequent. Early contacts brought a few new materials into the region, some of which were traded widely and remanufactured into traditional forms. Likewise, the localized mixing of peoples led to offspring with mixed genetic heritage. These introductions, however, while leaving a rich mythology, did not fundamentally change Indigenous people. The materials were reused for traditional practices, like the manufacture of projectiles from Chinese porcelain or the use of beeswax for sealing, lighting, or medicinal purposes.

Exploration and Early Fur Trade

In the Pacific Northwest, maritime exploration was coincident with mercantile capitalists who sought animal pelts, particularly those from sea otters, and linking the Pacific Northwest globally with Europe and Asia. The fur trade was well developed in North America before traders reached the Pacific

Northwest by both sea and land (Barman 2007: 34–36; Jepsen and Norberg 2017: 36; Nassaney 2015; Schwantes 1996: 62–64). Fladmark (1973) identifies a period of intensive maritime fur trading (1774–1830) associated with contacts with the Haida of the Haida Gwaii (Queen Charlotte Islands), ending with the near extermination of sea otters. While the Russians were likely the first to see British Columbia, Spanish expeditions to the region by Juan Perez in 1774 and Bruno de Hezeta and Juan Francisco de la Bodega y Quadra in 1775 were designed to plant 12-foot wooden crosses along the coastline to claim the land for Spain. The first terrestrial contact by a fur trader was Alexander Mackenzie of the British North West Company, who in 1793 traversed the Peace River gorge and crossed the Coast Range to the Bella Coola Valley and the Pacific Ocean. On a rock at Dean Channel, Mackenzie marked his feat with ochre and bear's grease (Francis and Porter 2010). Within a few decades of the initiation of the maritime fur trade, terrestrial incursions led to trading forts and posts centered on the upper Peace River and Columbia River drainages, and a later maritime fur trade focusing on beaver pelts (Burley and Hobler 1997).

San Lorenzo de Nutka/Fort San Miguel (1789–1795) and Yuquot

Yuquot, on the southwestern edge of Vancouver Island, was one of the earliest places of European contact with Indigenous people. Captain James Cook visited the site in 1778, with John Meares (following other maritime fur traders) in 1788, and Estevan José Martinez claimed Spanish sovereignty in 1789, establishing a Spanish fort and gun battery called San Lorenzo de Nutka and Fort San Miguel. The Nootka Conventions, including the meeting between the Spanish Quadra and British Vancouver in 1792, averted war between the colonial powers, which led to the abandonment at Yuquot of permanent colonial settlements (Barman 2007: 21–31). Extensive excavations searched for early traces of explorers in the large midden at Yuquot, and for the Spanish battery on San Miguel Island (Folan 1969; Folan and Dewhirst 1970, 1980a, 1980b, 1981). Very few remains from the earliest colonial contact were found, but the midden of Yuquot contained abundant artifacts from the ca. 1875 period of intensive contact with European Canadians. One of the burials recorded in the central "abandoned" portion of the village, inferred to be the location of several Spanish troop quarters, contained Spanish plainware suggesting deposition during or shortly after the 1789–1795 Spanish occupation (Folan and Dewhirst 1980a: 56). Within the midden and the gun battery excavations, the archaeologists recovered Majolica vessels and Spanish or Mexican coarse earthenware, likely deriving from western Mexico (Lueger 1981; Weigand et al. 1981). The site of Meares Factory (trading post) and other

Spanish-related sites could not be examined because they were occupied by later houses and a graveyard.

The investigations at Yuquot are characteristic of early historical archaeology in the Pacific Northwest, whereby European and American sites of claims and conflict were emphasized, with archaeologists seeking belongings tied to British or Spanish people. The subtext of these archaeological projects, however, is also very important, as the investigators recovered many thousands of items from the massive Yuquot midden, reflecting the Mowachaht/Muchalaht people's over 4,000-year tenure of the site, and how the events of the late eighteenth century, while ushering in the colonial era, really had limited impacts on their ways of life, particularly after the global powers abandoned the region. The abundant material objects from Yuquot form a baseline for both precontact and colonial archaeological research, including objects of Indigenous and foreign manufacture that frame time periods long before colonial contact and after (Folan and Dewirst 1980a, 1980b, 1981). The researchers inferred cultural continuity until ca. 1871, when commercial manufactured products accompanied by European Canadian merchants and missionaries flooded the area with new things, ideas, and rules (Folan and Dewhirst 1980a: 345).

A similar maritime colonial site is Fort Defiance (1791–1792) on Meares Island on Clayoquot Sound, about 70 kilometers southeast of Yuquot. Robert Gray overwintered there with the *Columbia Rediviva* and built the Sloop *Adventure*, the first American ship constructed on the west coast. Gray is credited with "discovering" the Columbia River. Archaeologists documented archaeological remains of this site, including a hearth, forge, the stocks for the *Adventure*, and nearly 1,600 artifacts (Mitchell 1970; Mitchell and Knox 1972).

The Search for Fort Clatsop (1805–1806)

Besides the maritime fur trade, political and economic expeditions sought terrestrial routes across the Rocky Mountains to the rich fur-bearing streams of the Pacific Northwest. The Jefferson administration instigated Lewis and Clark's expedition to explore the Missouri River, cross the Rocky Mountains to the Clearwater River, and follow the Columbia River to the Pacific Ocean. Both scholars and the public embrace the expedition as legendary, with the journals seen as national treasures that bolstered U.S. claims to the Pacific Northwest while scientifically documenting the early nineteenth century west (e.g., Schwantes 1996: 53–62). The impacts and reactions of Indigenous people to Lewis and Clark are complex, particularly as their expedition hastened the colonial era, but some see common ground in the ways the explorers and

Indigenous peoples interacted and traded (Jepsen and Norberg 2017: 13–21; Ronda 1984).

Some of the earliest historical archaeology in the region searched for Fort Clatsop—Lewis and Clark's 1805–1806 overwintering fort on the northwest bank of the Lewis and Clark River, approximately 8 kilometers from Astoria, Oregon. The location of Fort Clatsop is based on oral traditions, including Native Clatsop descendants, and reminiscences that correspond well with known historical facts (Hussey 1958). William Clark's maps were too imprecise to accurately map the fort's location, but Byram (2005) convincingly argues that the 1852 U.S. Coast Survey map made by Richard Cutts conforms well with both the actual course of the Lewis and Clark River where the Fort was built and the strong testimonial evidence documented by Hussey (1958) that suggests that the National Park Service unit is at or near the historical fort's location.

In 1948, National Park Service archaeologist Louis Caywood conducted the first "exploratory excavations" to test the reputed location for the Oregon Historical Society with a large block excavation and five smaller trenches and blocks. Caywood (1948b: 209–210) felt that the lack of refuse (military-like tidiness), presence of four small "fire pits," a "barbecue pit" with "burned" rocks, charcoal, and animal bones, a "whittled stick," and a sawn piece of wood, along with the strength of the historical record, suggested that he had found evidence of the Lewis and Clark expedition. Schumacher followed with extensive excavations during three short intervals in 1956, 1957, and 1961, excavating over 600 cubic meters using laborers from the local labor office, and in 1961, a backhoe (Schumacher 1957, 1961). This work identified seventeen more "fire pits," two of which contained bones, including deer/elk and bird. In addition, later nineteenth-century historical artifacts from a settler's house were noted, and summarily discarded without analysis (Schumacher 1961). While Schumacher discounted Caywood's "whittled stick" as a natural feature (a "buckhorn," or non-decayed heart wood of a coniferous tree branch-trunk juncture) and felt that the "barbecue pit" was probably a modern feature, he concluded after the third season that the fire pits represented the remains of the expedition (Schumacher 1961).

Archaeology at Fort Clatsop was restimulated by the park's ramp-up for the Lewis and Clark bicentennial. Extensive remote sensing, including ground-penetrating radar, magnetic gradiometer, and electrical resistivity studies were conducted between 1990 and 2006, all of which discovered spatially discrete anomalies in the geophysical data, suggesting buried pits, trenches, and other subsurface features (e.g., Bell 1990, 1996; Kvamme and Reynolds 2003; Weymouth 2001). Between 1996 and 2006, nine separate archaeological investigations by Montana State University, Portland State University, University of Washington, and the National Park Service excavated nearly 90 square meters of site sediments in and around the ca. 1950 Fort Clatsop replica (Cromwell 2002; Kiers 1998; Stein et al. 2006; Wilson 2005; Wynia 2022). These excavations included small bucket auger tests and traditional test excavation units and unearthed abundant evidence of Schumacher's past trenching and artifacts from two settler houses, including the one discovered by Schumacher (e.g., Wynia 2022), but few artifacts that pre-dated the mid–nineteenth century. Tests for phosphorus and mercury concentrations to relocate the Fort's privies were also negative (Stein et al. 2006). Many human activities likely disturbed the site, such as uses by Clatsop people as a hunting camp, and nineteenth-century settler activities, including pit digging, plowing, mining clay for bricks and pottery, logging, manufacturing charcoal, and tourism (Hussey 1958; Wilson 2006). Close examination of one of Schumacher's fire pits suggest it was caused by a natural forest fire, and it is likely that natural processes created most of them, including the penetration of roots, forest fires, and the swell and swale forest topography (Stein et al. 2006; Wilson 2006). Since 1996, investigators have identified about twenty pieces of lithic debitage, a cobble tool, and a few other items that represent use by the Clatsop people. They have yet to find any incontrovertible remains of the Lewis and Clark expedition.

In spite of enduring public interest, the inordinate amount of work to relocate Fort Clatsop is out of proportion to its scientific value. The continuing colonial narrative of discovery, and almost mythical demarcation of American conquest, are central to the continuing search. In the context of changing Indigenous and settler landscapes and their disturbance of the site, however, Lewis and Clark's true contributions are revealed in the dramatic changes to the social and natural environments that they began, shaping the American experience in the Pacific Northwest.

Terrestrial Fur Trade Archaeology

The marking of places by explorers, like the large wooden crosses of the Spanish or the ochre and bear's grease of MacKenzie, were important to ritually "claim" places for European nations. In 1806, as the Lewis and Clark expedition was leaving the Pacific Coast, Northwest Company clerk Simon Fraser marked his name using red ochre on a cliff at Stuart Lake, near Fort St. James (Francis and Porter 2010). These sites, like the collective memory of Fort Clatsop or Fort Defiance, provide continuity to explorer narratives of colonialism. MacKenzie and Fraser were followed by groups of fur traders who traveled

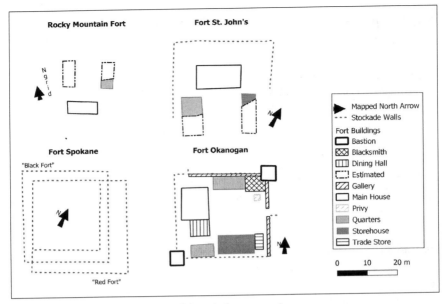

Figure 3.3. Plans of selected early fur trade forts to scale.

Native trails and water routes using canoes, horses, mules, and sometimes wagons and more substantial boats. These caravans of traders and trappers were generally termed "brigades" (cf., Innis 1930: 220), bringing British and American products to the Pacific Northwest for trade, and taking furs to suitable locations for shipment to England and the east coast of the United States. In the Pacific Northwest, another form of brigade sent parties of fur trappers across the region to spend winters collecting pelts, before returning to fur-trade depots (Chittenden 1901: 38; Mackie 1997: 60–64; Schwantes 1996: 69).

The region of both Mackenzie and Fraser's entry along the Peace River has seen considerable archaeological work. Fladmark (1985) first explored the Peace River area of British Columbia in the mid-1970s, funded through a proposed hydroelectric project (Burley et al. 1996). Archaeological remains of Rocky Mountain Fort, Rocky Mountain Portage House, and Fort St. John's are some of the earliest fur trade forts in the Pacific Northwest and reflect the earliest competition between the Northwest Company and John Jacob Astor's Pacific Fur Company, and later, the competition between the Northwest Company and the Hudson's Bay Company prior to their merger in 1821 (Burley et al. 1996; Fladmark 1985) (figure 3.3).

Rocky Mountain Fort (ca. 1794–1804)

Archaeological work at Rocky Mountain Fort noted remnants of the earlier post reoccupied by the Hudson's Bay Company, and the separate location of the rival Northwest Company "nuisance post" adjacent to the Hudson's Bay Company fort (Burley et al. 1996: 96–108). Burley and Hamilton (1991) report on the work at the earlier Rocky Mountain Fort, including excavations in 1986 and 1987. The absence of a palisade wall is attributed to the overall good relations with the local Dunne-za or Dane-zaa (Beaver Indians). A sparse assemblage other than glass beads is attributed to the "extreme distances" and conditions of "intense" trade with the local Indigenous people. Reflecting this, fort inhabitants commonly remanufactured trade goods into other items such as pendants, pins, and metal arrowheads (Burley et al. 1996: 57). The relatively abundant faunal remains suggest they also extracted grease from bison bone to produce pemmican, an essential food in the fur trade (Burley 1989; Nassaney 2015: 155).

The occupational and status hierarchy at these remote posts led to the intentional removal of food bone refuse from the Officer's House, which contrasted with abundant food bone refuse in the Laborer's Quarters and in midden areas around the post (Hamilton 2000). In remote over-wintering posts, symbolic differences in refuse disposal were created to reinforce the status hierarchy of the company and the authority of the clerk. These patterns in refuse disposal are seen elsewhere in the fur trade at remote outposts, where greater displays of status, including imposing architecture, gentlemen's attire, and specialized foods, were less available due to logistics and the distances from regional headquarters (Hamilton 2000).

Fort St. John's/Fort D'Epinette (1806–1823)

The later Northwest Company Fort St. John's was a somewhat larger palisaded fort with a "big house" (or "main house") that served as the Chief Trader's residence, store and mess hall, a "men's house," and other features (Fladmark 1985; figure 3.3). The fort was called Fort D'Epinette after the merger with the Hudson's Bay Company in 1821. The amalgamation of the Hudson's Bay Company and Northwest Company, and the decision by the Hudson's Bay Company to abandon the post, led to the "Fort St. John's Massacre" where Dunne-za people killed four fur traders. The abandonment of the fort and its burning created well-preserved and charred archaeological remains (Bedard 1990: 39; Burley et al. 1996: 79–96). The fort had a three-room main (or "big") house with two well-built sandstone fireplaces, flanked by a more crudely built "men's house," and a poorly preserved building interpreted as a warehouse and shop. Bedard (1990) explored the archaeological evidence to address whether the diverse population of the fort maintained distinct ethnic boundaries within its Indigenous and Métis employees and also tied to gendered activities. There was variation across space between the main and men's house, in particular in the frequency of Indigenous "folk industries," but the general presence of both European and Indigenous artifacts Beddard attributed to "the adaptive and elastic nature of the social and economic environment, as well as the presence of an established social rank structure within the fort" (Bedard 1990: 136).

Comparing animal bone assemblages at Rocky Mountain Fort and Fort St. John's, it appears the fur traders rapidly decimated bison and beaver populations, resulting in significant ecological effects (Burley and Hamilton 1991: 16; Burley et al. 1996: 93, 128–134). In part, these impacted the ability of the Dunne-za to support themselves and may have led to regional starvation along with the eradication of the most valuable animals essential to the fur trade. The killing of fur traders at the end of the post's history is correlated with the stress associated with animal resource depletion due to overexploitation, as well as the dependency of Dunne-za people on trade goods and credit (Burley et al. 1996: 124–134).

Kootenai House (1807–1809)

David Thompson of the Northwest Company established Kootenai House, the first fur trade post west of the Rocky Mountains on the Columbia River drainage near Invermere, British Columbia. This site was rediscovered in 1910 by Basil G. Hamilton, but not tested by professional archaeologists until 2005 (Heitzmann 2004, 2006; Moore 2012). The site was one of a number of "Kootenai Houses" established between 1807 and the early 1850s in British Columbia, Montana, and Idaho. Kootenai House contained three buildings with a palisade on three sides: a building with a room for the trader and Indian Hall, a Men's House, and a structure with a magazine, shop, and storehouse. Ground-penetrating radar survey and subsequent test excavations confirmed the presence of the palisade on three sides with the fourth wall formed by buildings (Heitzmann 2004, 2006). A variety of architectural styles are indicated, including saddle-notched and post-in-the-ground construction. The artifacts included sparse fur trade–era items similar to the Peace River posts, including a few ceramics, buttons, drawn and wound beads, a musketball, an iron arrowhead, gun flints, and wrought nails. Stone artifacts were found in the fort area that may be contemporaneous with or preceding the fort and concentrated in a pit house or storage pit depression to the north of the fort, which included a Pelican Lake Phase projectile point that clearly precedes the fort, dating to about 2,000–3,000 years ago.

Spokan House/Fur Trade Fort Spokane (1810–1826)

The first permanent terrestrial fur trade post in what would become the State of Washington was Spokan House, established by the Northwest Company in 1810. Louis Caywood excavated at the site of the later Pacific Fur Company (and Northwest Company and Hudson's Bay Company) Fort Spokane in 1950 (Caywood 1951, 1954a). Caywood's initial excavations discovered palisade walls (figure 3.3), a fireplace, a possible cellar depression, and fur trade artifacts that contrasted in style with those he unearthed at 1829–1866 Hudson's Bay Company Fort Vancouver (see chapter 4). Many stone and shell artifacts were present, suggesting that the Upper Spokane people (Snxwemi'ne) used the area for centuries prior to the fur trade era. Indigenous informants reported the Fort Spokane vicinity as nxwemi'ne/nxwəmɛ'ne ("steelhead trout place"), the primary village of the Upper Spokane people and a place of meeting, trading, gambling, food gathering, and fishing (Ray 1936: 122, 135). Three years of excavation followed, which detailed the structure of the post, which the three fur trade companies augmented, renovated, and maintained. The archaeological site contained three distinctive palisade lines, including a double palisaded fort designated as the "Black Fort" and an enlarged fort designated as the "Red Fort" (figure 3.3). The original Pacific Fur Company fort is represented by the outer stockade within the smaller (Black) fort, with the Northwest Company adding the interior row of palisades, while the Hudson's Bay Company expanded the fort into the outermost (Red) fort after the merger of the companies in 1821 and prior to its abandonment in 1826 (Caywood 1954a: 42).

As part of these excavations, the burial of Jacques Raphael (Jaco) Finlay was exhumed within the remains of the southeastern corner bastion (see chapter 6). A depression turned out to be the historically documented boat shed and saw pit of the fur trade fort. The burial of a Spokane person in the base of the pit suggested that either it had been reused by local people after the post was abandoned, or that the fur traders had modified an existing pit house and burial site (Caywood 1951). A historical Spokane cemetery was discovered east of the fort, and four burials were disinterred that together contained numerous trade goods, including one that held remains of three flintlock muskets (Caywood 1954a). As noted in chapter 2, and discussed in chapter 6, burial excavation by archaeologists was common prior to passage of the Native American Graves Protection and Repatriation Act of 1990 (NAGPRA).

Excavations by Washington State University at the site in 1962–1963 attempted to find the earlier 1810 Northwest Company Spokan House and conducted additional excavations within the stockade (Combes 1962, 1964). The exploratory excavations rediscovered a "large Indian burial ground" to the northeast of the fort on the northern edges of where Caywood had excavated burials. Screening of that and two other areas using 1/4-inch screens recovered many hand-wrought nails, Chinese and English ceramics, clay pipe fragments, glass beads, parts of firearms, and items of Indigenous manufacture, including projectile points. The material assemblage from fur trade Fort Spokane helped to establish differences in clay tobacco pipe styles between the Pacific Fur Company, Northwest Company, and Hudson's Bay Company that would help in the interpretation and dating of other fur trade sites (Pfeiffer 1981). Ceramics were dominated by Chinese export ware, including porcelain and stoneware, and a relative dearth of hand-decorated creamware, transferprinted pearlware, and European stoneware (Cromwell 2006a, 2018; cf., Chance and Chance 1979: 108). The Chinese ceramics likely came directly from Asia and likely were brought in by American merchants or purchased surreptitiously by other means to become part of this early fur trade assemblage. The presence of Chinese and English ceramics at early fur trade sites suggests adroit maneuvering by the British companies, including trade with Americans to avoid the East India Company monopoly on Asian goods.

Combes's recommendations for interpretation of the fort included the astonishing proposal to expose Indigenous burials and stabilize them for viewing by visitors (Combes 1964: 64), a suggestion that fortunately was never acted on. The proximity of contact-period Indigenous sites, including the cemetery, is a testament to the social relations between the fur traders and the Spokane people. While the archaeological work was couched in mid-century narratives and unapologetically unearthed Indigenous human remains, the actual evidence recorded from the fort points to a much more nuanced and entangled place where the fur traders became a part of, yet separate from, Indigenous communities.

Another important early site in the Pacific Northwest is Pacific Fur Company Fort Astoria, renamed Northwest Company/Hudson's Bay Company Fort George (1811–1848), the headquarters of all three companies in the West until the 1825 founding of Fort Vancouver. Test excavations in the summer of 2012 recovered a small sample of fur-trade era belongings from the memorial park (Wilson 2020). Ceramics and beads were similar to later fur trade assemblages at Fort Vancouver but included items consistent with the assemblage from Middle Village, a Chinook Village across the Columbia River from Fort Astoria that contained abundant early fur trade objects (Stokeld 2016; Wilson et al. 2009, discussed below). Hand-painted and plain creamware ceramics and relatively abundant Chinese export porcelain suggest that numerous artifacts date to the earlier fur trade period (Cromwell 2018; Stokeld 2016).

Fort Okanogan (1811–ca. 1831)

The Pacific Fur Company/Northwest Company Fort Okanogan was initially test excavated by Caywood (1954b), who located its stockade pickets. Fort Okanogan was established by Astor's Pacific Fur Company on the south bank of the Okanogan River, and then operated after 1813 by the Northwest Company. Both Alexander Ross and Ross Cox clerked at the fort and left useful journals detailing its establishment and business. After 1821, when the Northwest Company merged with the Hudson's Bay Company, buffalo hides became an important product, shipped northward, but after 1829 the post became primarily a rest/repair stop for the fur brigades sending furs to Fort Vancouver, and around 1831 the post was moved to a location on the north bank of the Columbia River (Caywood 1954b; Grabert 1968).

Caywood's initial work was the outcome of a long legal process that started with the first fort's centennial and led in 1922 to a congressional act that removed the sites from the Colville[2] Tribes' reservation (Benson et al. 1987). This undoubtedly reflected a desire to preserve the colonial fort sites while discounting any views or input of the Colville people. Earl Swanson (1957) returned to test the site in 1957 using aerial photography to locate its outline and also nearby pit house depressions. His excavations relocated stockade pickets and portions of interior buildings. Besides fur trade objects, including concentrations of clay pipe remains at inferred popular smoking areas, he noted abundant Native American artifacts associated with the fort and nearby pit houses. Like other early fur trade posts, Fort Okanogan was established in an existing ancient cultural landscape, and its archaeology is inextricably linked to the Okanogan people, who requested that it be built close to four named winter villages at or near the mouth of the Okanogan River (Grabert 1968; Ross 1849: 145; Walters 1938: 85–86).

Extensive excavations of Fort Okanogan during the Wells Reservoir salvage project in 1963–1964 located stockade walls and evidence of galleries on two sides, bastions, a main house site with two fireplaces, and adobe plastered walls, a trading store and warehouse, blacksmith shop, and dwelling (Grabert 1965, 1968; figure 3.3). A possible tanning pit was located outside the fort. Hand-wrought nails dominated the assemblage with relatively few

---

[2] Note that "Fort Colvile" with one "L" is named after Andrew Wedderburn Colvile, who sat on the Hudson's Bay Company Committee, while the Tribe (and many place-names) have added a double "LL" to become "Colville."

machine-cut (both fully machine-headed and British wrought styles). Other items included creamware, transferprinted whiteware, and European stoneware ceramics. Similar to Fort Astoria and Fort Spokane, Chinese export porcelain and Chinese stoneware comprised altogether nearly a quarter of the assemblage (Cromwell 2018; Grabert 1968). Trade goods included needles, awls, thimbles, scissors, buttons, fishhooks, brooches, rings, straight pins, brass and copper kettle fragments, buckles, iron projectile points, and thousands of glass beads. Evidence of pre- and post-contact use by Indigenous people included stone projectile points, stone scrapers, bone objects, steatite pipes, tinklers manufactured from trade copper, and abundant lithic debitage. Grabert suggests that the low intensity of Indigenous occupation suggested seasonal camping, rather than a permanent or semi-permanent village, perhaps used by visitors who did not live in one of the four local villages.

Benson et al. (1987) excavated tests and conducted data recovery excavations during a drawdown of the reservoir in 1983–1984. Analysis focused on areas east and west of the fort, identifying a late precontact component that surrounded and was stratigraphically below the fur trade component. Analysis of faunal remains within fur trade–era trash dumps reflected "an eclectic diet" consisting primarily of horse, salmon, and rabbits/hare (Benson et al. 1987: 53). In 2011, during a time of state budget cuts, the park was transferred back to the Confederated Tribes of the Colville Reservation, and the Fort Okanogan Interpretive Center now explores the intertwined history of Native peoples and the fur trade from an Indigenous perspective.

Two other important fort sites include Fort Nez Percé/Fort Walla Walla (1818–1860) located at the confluence of the Walla Walla and Columbia Rivers, and Fort Vancouver I (1825–1829), which was established north of the Columbia River in modern Vancouver, Washington. Extensive excavations at Fort Walla Walla (Garth 1951, 1952a) focused on later Hudson's Bay Company–era deposits, and in contrast to the extensive archaeology at the second Fort Vancouver, only limited subsurface survey as part of a public archaeology project has sought (partly successfully) to locate Fort Vancouver I (Clearman 2020; see chapter 9).

Initial Indigenous Adjustments to Colonialism

As noted above, most excavations of early fur trade forts recovered substantial numbers of Indigenous belongings, and often the fort sites are located on landscapes integral to Native lives. Early historical archeologists usually noted these belongings, often in considerable detail, as these were often the first archaeological studies of any kind in the region. Besides learning how the fur traders lived and established trading regimes, the effects of the fur trade on Indigenous peoples were a continuing fascination for many of the earlier researchers. Historical archaeology up until at least the 1980s fell within the acculturation framework of Western anthropological scholarship, characterized as changes in cultures that occur as a result of culture contact, but usually outlined as an asymmetrical assimilation of normative and monolithic Indigenous cultures to equally normative and monolithic Western and American cultures (Cipolla 2021: 110–111). Acculturation theory supported terminal narratives for Pacific Northwest Tribes, while more recent research recognizes more nuanced Indigenous responses to colonialism.

Inadvertent effects of colonialism elsewhere in North America introduced two distinctive and profoundly important biological agents to the Pacific Northwest, starting before direct colonial contact, in what researchers have called the "protohistoric" period. The first of these was the horse, which likely entered the plateau ca. A.D. 1690 through the Shoshone-Bannock people and then spread northward over the next twenty to forty years (Ewers 1955: 71; Grabert 1973: 111–112; Haines 1938: 435). Horses are documented in the southern Puget Sound area by the late eighteenth century, and in the Willamette Valley by at least 1814, but were likely never very important in coastal areas (Silverstein 1990: 540; Suttles and Lane 1990: 492). In contrast, the horse greatly expanded the transportation capabilities of plateau people, allowing for seasonal migration across large distances for hunting, gathering, trading, and warfare. Indigenous people moved seasonally on trading and hunting trips between the Great Plains and California. The horse became highly significant for Southern Plateau people, signifying wealth and status, and even sacred importance (Ewers 1955; Stern 1993: 41–48; Walker 1965; Walker and Sprague 1998: 139). When explorers and fur traders noted the Plateau people, they documented herds of over 1,000 horses (Ewers 1955: 31–32). Horses allowed increased mobility, including farther travel with heavier loads. Increased raiding and military activity between groups led to larger tribal gatherings and more pronounced wealth and status differentiation (Walker and Sprague 1998).

The archaeology of the importance of horses to Native people is reflected in petroglyph sites that date to the introduction of the horse, with images of horses and riders like the Shield Site (10GG318). Merrell and Johnson (2011) infer that the Shoshone pecked these images in the Bennett Hills of central Idaho (about 50 km east of Mountain Home). Another important horse site is *kalama't* (yellow pond lily in Sahaptin) in the Cascade Range within the Gifford Pinchot National Forest (Kirk and Daugherty 2007: 117; Mack 1997). This site, also called the Indian Race Track, was where Yakama people gathered to race horses during the huckleberry harvest that took place in the mountains in late summer and early fall. The race track is visible as a distinct depression, 3 meters wide and over 300 meters long, with nearby remains of camping sites and huckleberry processing features.

The second biological agent to hit the Indigenous people of the Pacific Northwest was disease. Campbell (1989) hypothesized a sixteenth-century introduction of small pox into the Plateau, supporting the concept of an early North American pandemic (e.g., Dobyns 1993, cf., Jones et al. 2021). Less controversial is the evidence for a series of smallpox infections on the Northwest Coast by the late 1770s, likely spreading from coastal contacts, the northern plains, and/or possibly from Alaska (Boyd 1990, 1994, 1996, 1999). Mortality figures from this early period likely exceeded 30 percent of the population. Small pox returned ca. 1801–1802, 1836–1838, 1853, and 1862–1863 (Boyd 1999). With increased European and American interaction, other diseases, including measles, malaria, and dysentery, had a devastating impact on Indigenous people. It is estimated that malaria killed about 90 percent of the people of the lower Columbia River between 1830 and 1833, during the epidemic described as the "fever and ague" (Boyd 1975, 1990, 1999). The impacts of these biological agents, the horse and disease, recur across the historical archaeology of the Pacific Northwest, impacting the social and natural environment for Indigenous people and affecting what early fur traders and explorers encountered.

Richardson Ranch Site and the Haida Gwaii

Some of the earliest historical archaeology in the Pacific Northwest that focused primary attention on Indigenous people rather than fur trade forts was in British Columbia. Fladmark (1973) explored one of three Haida house sites on the eastern edge of Graham Island in the northern portion of the Haida Gwaii. Fladmark equates the very large house with the ethnographically described Nagi I' L xagit—k! a'-idAngAns ("the house Chiefs peeped at because it was too great to let them come near") built by Nestacanna, within the region of Tl-ell.

A 20-meter-long, 2-meter-wide trench, excavated longitudinally across the house, discovered a central hearth, interior house posts, remains from food preparation and storage activities, storage pits, and a burned wooden box (Fladmark 1973). Two people were buried in a single red cedar box within the high-status end of the house, likely at its abandonment. Belongings recovered from the excavation included Native-manufactured bone tubes, and other worked bone items, hammerstones, abraders, pigment stones, wooden boxes, lithic debitage, and painted pebbles. Introduced items included glass beads, materials of copper and brass, whiteware (likely creamware), hand-painted whiteware, and transferprinted pearlware, clay pipe fragments, gunflints, lead shot, buttons of metal and glass (probably ceramic prosser buttons), cast-iron pot fragments, a gun barrel fragment, and other items. Many of the European-manufactured items and non-utilitarian Indigenous items were found in the higher-status end of the house, consistent with the well-documented status differentiation of Pacific Northwest Native households.

The large archaeological collection of argillite items within the house reflected manufacturing and use of tobacco smoking pipes in simple, functional, elbow-style, European forms. This suggested that the Haida were creating new argillite forms for local community use, possibly learned from Métis stone carvers, and that this preceded the well-known manufacturing of argillite for the external market (Fladmark 1973: 75–77).

At a larger scale, cultural adjustments in settlement patterns and social relations in the Haida Gwaii during the fur trade era suggests that the Haida were neither enriched, with an elaboration of existing cultural patterns due to the influx of new products (the "enrichment thesis") or exploited by the fur traders, demoralizing their culture and making them dependent (the "exploitation thesis") (Acheson 1995: 288). The Kunghit Haida on the southern portion of the Haida Gwaii shifted from small, nucleated, year-round settlements to large multilineage villages, with senior-ranking chiefs aggregating power through control and acquisition of fur trade goods over previously more independent chiefs (Acheson 1995). This adjustment was exacerbated by violence between the Haida and fur traders and the decline in population associated with introduced diseases (Acheson and Delgado 2004). The "surprisingly commonplace" attacks against Europeans involved the recovery, maintenance, and enhancement of chiefly status. With the depletion of fur-bearing animals, the Haida, who had become increasingly reliant on the fur trade, shifted to supplying potatoes and argillite carvings to European Canadians. Argillite carving, in particular, is seen as a social negotiation of relationships with European colonizers (Mullins and Paynter 2000). After the depletion of sea otter populations in the 1820s, carved argillite was used by the Haida as a replacement product to sell to European Canadians and Americans. Carved tobacco pipes and depictions of Europeans and colonial structures, including forts and watercraft, were altered to use cosmological motifs and other traditional forms in the 1870s. These were marketed to increasing numbers of Canadian and American consumers, forming a part of the negotiation of colonial power relations (Mullins and Paynter 2000). Far from showing the dilution of Indigenous traditions, these belongings are better seen as active outcomes of the changing relationships between Haida producers and the

Canadian and American consumers. These outcomes speak to the continuing native presence on the landscape reflecting ongoing Indigenous narratives tied to material culture.

Thompson's River Post/Fort Kamloops (1811–1841) *Secwepemc* Kamloops Village

The 1993–1999 excavations at the *Secwepemc* Village at the Northwest Company/Hudson's Bay Company's Thompson's River Post/Fort Kamloops were located at the confluence of the North and South Thompson Rivers, tributaries of the Fraser (Carlson 2000, 2006). This post was central to moving people and furs from the northern New Caledonia District to the Columbia District around 1825, after the merger of the Northwest Company and the Hudson's Bay Company. Actively collaborating with the Kamloops Indian Band, archaeologists revealed that the *Secwepemc* Village was established as a result of the establishment of the fur trade post. Comparing a fur trade structure within the fort area with areas of smaller and larger pit houses, all roughly contemporaneous, suggested that the people of Kamloops lived in traditional houses oriented to the river, stored salmon and other foods in traditional underground caches, likely conducted feasting in large pit houses, and were organized in an egalitarian society that ran counter to the hierarchical British fur trade company. While certain trade objects were acquired, particularly metal substitutes for stone, and basket items and beads, crystal, and copper items with ceremonial and symbolic meanings, much of the traditional elements of the culture were maintained (Carlson 2000, 2006). In fact, the fur trade colonists depended on the Indigenous people for dried salmon and other foods. This project helped to reframe colonial narratives, recognizing Indigenous persistence on the landscape.

Ktunaxa (Kutenai) Fur Trade Landscape

A similar study compares the archaeological data from the Northwest Company's Rocky Mountain House (1799–1821) and Kootenai House (discussed above) to examine the early nineteenth-century fur trade between the Niitsitapi (Blackfeet) and Ktunaxa (Kootenai) and European Americans (Moore 2012). Using animal bones recovered from these Northwest Company posts compared with ethnographic and ethnohistorical data, it is clear that until the merger of the Northwest Company and Hudson's Bay Company, each Indigenous group negotiated the capture and trade of food and furs in culturally specific ways. This included the Niitsitapi maintaining a taboo on hunting beaver, which resulted in fur trade posts placed on the periphery of their lands and focus by Indigenous hunters on less spiritually damaging bison for hides and pemmican. Likewise, the Ktunaxa who had no such prescription, influenced the establishment and movement of posts in their territory, expanding beyond harvesting and trade in small mammals, including beaver and muskrat, to create a niche market in deer hides more consistent with their cultural traditions. Fur traders made in-the-field adjustments to cater to the different Indigenous groups, including addressing intergroup rivalries, while attempting to maximize profits from a variety of fur and food products (Moore 2012).

Meier and Cathlapotle (Chinook Ancestral Sites)

On the lower Columbia River, two extensively excavated Upper Chinookan plankhouses in the Portland Basin suggest that the Indigenous people of the region continued traditional lifestyles in the early fur trade era while intentionally engaging with traders to integrate new European and Asian products into existing local conceptions of prestige and competition (Ames 2017; Banach 2017; Cooper et al. 2015; Cromwell 2017a; Kaehler 2017; Sobel 2012). The Meier site (35CO5) is a single large plankhouse near Scappoose, Oregon, dating to between A.D. 1400 and ca. 1810–1820, while the Cathlapotle site (45CL1) is a large plankhouse village near modern-day Ridgefield, Washington, dating to between A.D. 1450 and ca. 1832 that was documented by early explorers, including Lewis and Clark. Both sites were excavated by Portland State University between 1987 and 1996.

Early maritime contacts are reflected in Chinese "Kraak" sherds, one modified into a scraper, at Cathlapotle, and another two sherds at Meier, that appear to date to the late seventeenth century. An iron adze found at Cathlapotle stratigraphically appears to originate from the same contexts (Ames 2017: 369–375; Cromwell 2017a). The integration of these objects into site deposits suggest the widespread trade in foreign objects from early contact shipwrecks, including probably the beeswax wreck.

The introduction of later fur trade objects at both sites includes a variety of ferrous, cupreous, and lead-based metal objects, glass beads, ceramics, and vessel glass that were likely integrated into the existing cultural activities of the villages, fitting within extant Indigenous worldviews and landscapes (Banach 2017; Cooper et al. 2015; Cromwell 2017a; Kaehler 2017). Unlike the Richardson Ranch site, discussed above, no evidence indicated that any one household or household segment (household areas centered on hearths within larger plankhouses) dominated the access to trade goods (Ames 2017). This suggests that prestige was not necessarily tied to the abundance of fur trade items, with each household separately participating in the fur trade, employing a variety of strategies to produce items for trade, such as animal pelts and clamons (elkskin armor) (Ames 2017). Many of the container glass forms at the sites were fragments of alcohol bottles, suggesting that fur traders attempted to manipulate Indigenous people with spirits to create favorable exchanges and make them dependent. The reuse of bottles to make flaked tools, and its relative scarcity, suggest that the Chinook people resisted this manipulation and integrated these new materials into traditional forms, following Native practices and perceptions (Simmons 2014, 2017). Modification of glass ranged from 12.5 to 35.1 percent of the glass assemblages (including biproducts—glass debitage) at both sites, with 8 to 18 percent of the total glass assemblages comprised of glass tools, including projectile points, scrapers, saws, and knives (Simmons 2017).

Traditional Indigenous artifacts also exhibit changes associated with the fur trade. Increases in bone tools at Meier, and hide scrapers at Cathlapotle, appear to be related to the increased production of clamons traded to resell to Indigenous (and warlike) people farther north (Ames 2017: 37). Comparison of introduced and traditional items at Meier, Cathlapotle, and another upriver Chinook village site, Clahclellah (45SA11), suggest flexible, nuanced, and regional patterns that challenge the enrichment thesis (Sobel 2012). Certain traditional trade good patterns, such as that tied to obsidian used for stone tools, were disrupted and changed by the introduction of metal tools. While some elite goods increased, the trade of other types of exchanged items was interrupted. Abandonment of these sites was likely slow and gradual, reflective of long-term regional declines in Indigenous populations, rather than a single catastrophic event (Ames 2017; Ames and Brown 2019). In fact, the continuing connections of Tribes to the Cathlapotle and other landscapes and the continuing contested nature of some of these connections (e.g., Daehnke 2013) suggest that Indigenous people never fully vacated the sites. Their landscapes continue to form important narratives of survivance.

Middle Village (*qíqayaqilxam*)

While Lewis and Clark famously paused their expedition at "Station Camp" on the north bank of the Columbia River to explore the surrounding territory and decide where to stay for the winter (Nicandri 2010), extensive archaeology at the site found abundant historical artifacts associated with *qíqayaqilxam*, the Chinook "Middle Village" (Wilson 2012; Wilson et al. 2009, 2017). While nothing material could be definitively associated with the Lewis and Clark expedition except perhaps a portable inkwell similar to those carried by the expedition, the village contained well-preserved remains of traditional summer plankhouses that held traditional belongings of the Chinook people, including stone arrow points, fishing net weights, abraders, and lithic debitage,

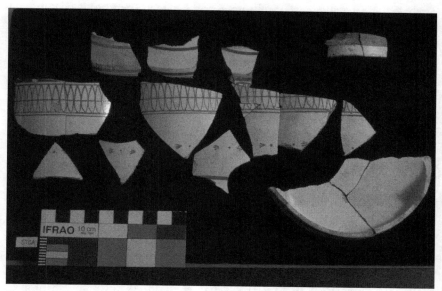

Figure 3.4. Hand-painted English creamware tea caddy recovered from Middle Village (qí'qayaqilxam). Photo courtesy of the National Park Service.

combined with abundant fur trade items, including musket balls, bottle glass, glass and copper beads, argillite pipe fragments, creamware, and Chinese porcelain. The introduction of fur trade items in traditional plankhouse spaces reflect continuing traditional lifeways but also an entanglement with Europeans and European Americans (figure 3.4).

Documentary evidence places the Middle Village at the location of the village noted by Robert Gray and others who visited the mouth of the Columbia River during the maritime fur trade era (Wilson 2012). This was the place named "Chinook," which was the core of Chinook territory recorded by explorers and fur traders. It is likely the summer village of the famous Chinook headman Concomly, and the abundance of fur trade items found in one of the houses suggests his summer residence (Wilson et al. 2009; Wilson 2012). The village developed as a direct response to the fur trade, starting ca. 1788, although Chinook oral traditions suggest a much longer occupation. In comparison to other contact-era Chinook sites, both in the interior (e.g., Meier and Cathlapotle), and in coastal estuarine settings, traditional stone tools and other items are present at Middle Village but are quite low in number (Wilson et al. 2017). In contrast, fur trade items are much more diverse and in much higher densities than for other contact-era sites, suggesting a chiefly assemblage. Employing ethnographic and ethnohistoric data, combined with the archaeological evidence, my colleagues and I suggest that the site was embedded within the traditional seasonal round of the Chinook, but in this case was dedicated to trading with Europeans and European Americans. In this system, wealth items could be accumulated and exchanged as middlemen with other Indigenous groups in the interior for other high-prestige items, notably enslaved Native Americans (Hajda 2005; Wilson et al. 2017).

The move of the Hudson's Bay Company headquarters to Fort Vancouver in 1825 recognizes perhaps that the Chinook at the mouth of the Columbia River had become too wealthy, controlling trade with interior groups, like those of the Cathlapotle site, and that the Hudson's Bay Company felt it was necessary to move the headquarters post inland (Wilson et al. 2017: 134). Combined with the death of two of Concomly's sons in 1825, and exacerbated by the onset of a significant disease outbreak (inferred to be malaria) in 1830, the Chinook abandoned Middle Village. That it was never fully abandoned or forgotten is represented in the continuing tribal connections to the site and its Indigenous landscape and is reflected in the resulting design of the national park unit (Finegan 2019). In the next chapter, I address how the Hudson's Bay Company fur traders and Christian missionaries more intensively impacted both the environment and the Indigenous peoples of the Pacific Northwest.

4

The New York of the West

In March 1836, Narcissa Whitman and her husband Marcus left Pittsburgh, Pennsylvania, on a 3,200-kilometer (1,988 miles) journey to convert the Indigenous people of the Pacific Northwest (Addis 2005). Nearly six months later, on September 12, 1836, they reached Fort Vancouver, after traveling by steamboat, horse, wagon, and boat. On reaching the fort, Narcissa remarked, "We are now in Vancouver, the New York of the Pacific Ocean" (Whitman 2002: 36). Whitman's comparison of Fort Vancouver to New York was an exaggeration but also foreshadows the dramatic social and ecological changes that came to the region during this time, shaped by commerce, religion, technology, politics, and racism. Historical archaeology has explored this transitional period between 1829 and 1849 in the United States (later in Canada), focusing on the later fur trade era and the role of missionaries in setting the stage for American and Canadian settlers. Indigenous groups adjusted, adapted, and persisted in the face of this next wave of colonialism.

Much of the early historical archaeology of the later Hudson's Bay Company fort sites like that at Fort Vancouver, Fort Langley, Fort Nez Percé, and at missions like Waiilatpu, were tied to venerating the colonial past—reinforcing a narrative that valued Christian missionaries and applauded the business interests that "opened" the land for settlement. By the 1970s, more scientific approaches began to focus on documenting the material culture of these sites to explore chronology, characterize the commercial products of the fur traders and missionaries, and compare assemblages using their inferred functions. Much of the work at larger Hudson's Bay Company forts was tied to reconstructions associated with national centennials and heritage production that often failed to account for the contributions of Indigenous people. More recent work explores in more depth colonialism's impacts on Indigenous peoples, documenting resistance to colonialism and Indigenous peoples' persistence in the face of the double onslaught of mercantile capitalism and Christianity.

The Later Fur Trade

Hudson's Bay Company Governor George Simpson and Chief Factor John McLoughlin brought major changes in the organization, economy, and social pursuits of the Pacific Northwest fur traders. First, they built bigger posts, notably Fort Victoria, Fort Langley, Fort Nisqually, Fort Colvile, and Fort Vancouver (figure 4.1). Many of the smaller Northwest Company forts were abandoned, relocated, or sometimes expanded to address the new needs of the company and its diversified pursuits. Industries at smaller posts continued

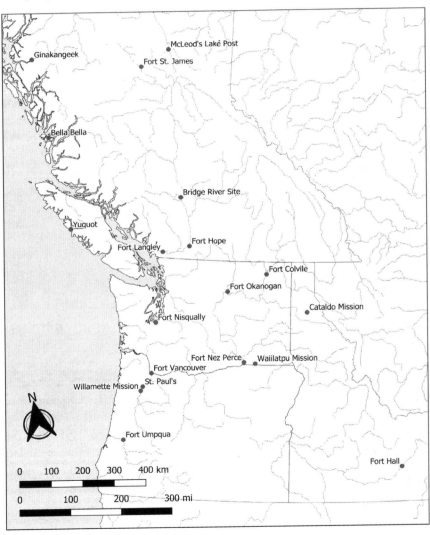

Figure 4.1. Later fur trade and mission sites.

to address repair of equipment and survival, including woodworking, boat-building, and blacksmithing, but at larger posts, the fur traders manufactured items for trade and engaged in greater industrial development (Ross 1975a). The increased activities of the Hudson's Bay Company within the Pacific Northwest did not go unnoticed by U.S. visitors, and their reports back east encouraged missionary activities and, eventually, the Oregon Trail migration.

Smaller Hudson's Bay Company Posts

Many of the same posts employed by earlier fur traders continued in service, while some new posts were established, like Fort Rupert, to help in coal mining at the northern end of Vancouver Island (Simonsen and Judd 2020). As noted in chapter 3, the Fort St. John's massacre led to the abandonment of Fort D'Epinette and the Upper Peace River area in 1824 (Burley et al. 1996: 124–134). Fort George (Astoria) was abandoned at the establishment of Fort Vancouver in 1825, although it was reoccupied within a few years (Hussey 1957; Morris 1937). Likewise, the Hudson's Bay Company abandoned Fort Spokane to Jacques Finlay and his family in 1826 for a new post called Fort Colvile at Kettle Falls (Caywood 1954a: 5–9).

Fort Okanogan reoriented as a rest/repair stop for the fur brigades, sending animal pelts to Fort Vancouver, and the post was moved from the Okanogan to the Columbia River bank ca. 1831, as it had a deeper draft for boats. Caywood (1954b) recorded a small stockade with two bastions and excavated five buildings, including a sod-roofed adobe trading post and storehouse, a two-room adobe Clerk's residence, and a possible dairy or kitchen. The house yielded manufacturing debris of sawed steatite modeled after Hudson's Bay Company imported clay pipes. Interestingly, Caywood noted belongings in the upper floor levels, including beads, a bone awl, mussel shells, animal bones cracked open for marrow, a bird-bone flute, and a projectile point, which suggested reuse by Okanogan people after the fort's 1860 abandonment. Like earlier fur trade posts, these later traces suggest continuing use of the landscape by Native people.

New fort sites were established to facilitate transportation and trade. For example, Fort Umpqua (1836–1852), near Elkton, Oregon, supported Hudson's Bay Company trapping parties heading south toward California or north toward the Willamette Valley. Archaeological testing of a trash deposit discovered many artifacts consistent with the Hudson's Bay Company fort, including Copeland pattern transferprint ceramics, container, window, and mirror glass, glass beads, hand-forged and machine-cut nails, and shot, buckshot, and percussion caps (Schlesser 1975). Fort Hall (1834–1856), located on the banks of the Snake River, was established by Nathaniel Wyeth during his second expedition, becoming a Hudson's Bay Company fort trading to Indigenous people as well as emigrants on the Oregon Trail (Brown 1932; Grant 1940; Schwantes 1996: 77–79). Archaeological testing collected a small sample of belongings and mapped surface features (e.g., Cromwell 2006b; Thomas 2008).

McLeod's Lake Post (1805–1953)

McLeod's Lake Post (GfRs 3), which was established on the northern portion of McLeod's Lake in 1805, continued long after the Hudson's Bay Company took over. The first post flooded in 1823, but the Hudson's Bay Company moved to higher ground, continuing there until 1953 (Quackenbush 1990: 6). Quackenbush explored changes in the post over this long period, revealed through the documentary record and an archaeological sample. Consistent with other Hudson's Bay Company posts in Canada, prior to 1870, fur traders focused on profit under the oligarchical "Club Law" of the fur trade, leaving little impact on Indigenous lifeways and with fur traders living roughly within the rules that governed the local Sekani people. In contrast, with the introduction of "Crown Law" after 1870, Hudson's Bay Company employees could more easily leave for other employment in a freer market and the greater local competition led to a symbolic fort-like look to lure customers. The earlier (pre-1900) component contained abundant flaked stone tools and debris and a greater reliance on fish, compared with the later (post-1900) dominance of European Canadian products and increased presence of domesticated animals. The changes associated with the intrusion of both church and state to assimilate Indigenous people led to changes in relations between the Sekani and the fur traders, as well as concomitant changes to the structure and products associated with the post (Quackenbush 1990).

In 1993, the Tsek'ehne village site (GfRs 2) adjacent to McLeod's Lake Post became the first Indigenous archaeology project in the Pacific Northwest (Yellowhorn 2002: 259–314). Focused on the creation of heritage tourism to promote job creation, Yellowhorn trained an Indigenous crew to test the village. The belongings they found represented the long-term Sekani presence, ranging from stone and bone items to modern children's toys. The work contributed to the development of the heritage park at McLeod Lake and, along with McLeod's Lake Post, reveal the long-term impacts of the fur trade in the less populated areas of British Columbia.

A similar case is present at late nineteenth-century/early twentieth-century Fort St. James, on the southern end of Stuart Lake, which was the central trading post of the New Caledonia District (Harris 1972: 6–12). Historical archaeology reveals the Hudson's Bay Company's continuing influence on Indigenous people into the late nineteenth and early twentieth centuries (Harris 1972, 1974). Klippenstein (1992), using documentary and anthropological data, notes the changing role of Carrier First Nations peoples at Fort St. James, similar to that at McLeod's Lake Post, with a shift from provisioning of food to direct labor. Clearly, the fur trade and the influence of the Hudson's Bay Company extended much longer in Canada because of the low populations, and resultant differences in settler colonialism, even after it became part of the Canadian Confederation in 1871 (Barman 2007: 104–105).

Fort Nez Percé/Fort Walla Walla (1818–1860)

The Northwest Company established Fort Nez Percé a central supply post between Fort George on the Pacific Coast and Fort Spokane. Alexander Ross called it the "Gibraltar of the Columbia" due to its thick, sawed plank pickets and strong bastions, galleries, and armaments. After the Hudson's Bay Company took over, it continued to support local trappers, but in 1825 began to serve as the outfitting post for the Snake River brigades at the abandonment of Fort Spokane. The Hudson's Bay Company built a larger stockaded fort, followed by a smaller adobe fort, both usually referred to as Fort Walla Walla. Archaeological excavations in 1949–1950 discovered packed occupation levels ("floors") that dated to the later Hudson's Bay Company period (Garth 1951, 1952b). One floor was dated to the accidental burning of the fort in 1842, and one to 1855 when the abandoned fort was burnt by Indigenous combatants in the Yakima War. Another floor dated to the reuse of the Fort by the U.S. Army (ca. 1856–1860) and the burning of buildings within the fort area in 1880 when it was part of the business section of Walula City, a steamboat landing and boomtown that supplied the Idaho gold mines. Excavations focused on the later adobe fort, including testing a bastion, the main house dwelling, trading room and kitchen, the "men's quarters," powder magazine, and storehouses. A cellar in the northwest corner of the fort contained at least forty-nine reconstructible whiteware vessels believed to have been intentionally destroyed when the post was abandoned at the start of the Yakima War (Garth 1952a: 42). In one of the storerooms, Garth recovered charred remains of peas, beans, coffee, corn, potatoes, hazel nuts, peach pits, chicken bones, and eggshells. Salted pork remains were found in a cask in a cellar. While the excavations by Garth explored in depth the colonial ties to the place and supported the settler narratives associated with the fur trade and later development during the gold rush, the work largely ignored the Walula people and even the *Gardin*, or Home Guard Indians, who were associated with its establishment and contributed to its success (Stern 1993, 1996). Like other important fort sites, Fort Nez Percé/Fort Walla Walla was established in an underlying Indigenous landscape.

Major Hudson's Bay Company Posts

Some of the most intensive archaeological excavations in the Pacific Northwest have occurred at the larger Hudson's Bay Company posts. These posts and the evidence recovered from them embody the diversification of the Hudson's Bay Company into many new economic pursuits, including agriculture, fishing, and lumbering, and more intrusive relations with Native Americans.

Fort Colvile (1825–1871)

The Hudson's Bay Company established Fort Colvile at the Columbia River salmon fishery of Kettle Falls, within the territory of the Shwayip/sxoie'łpᵘ. Named after Andrew Wedderburn Colvile, who sat on the Hudson's Bay Company committee, the fort's purpose was tied to the reorganization of the district and in Simpson's desire to economize, including improved transportation, increased agriculture, and benefits from being close to the salmon fishery. It was a "major station" in the communication route between York Factory on Hudson Bay and Fort Vancouver, and a central post of the annual fur brigades on the Columbia River (Chance 1973: 1). While the site has been inundated since the 1940 construction of the Grand Coulee Dam, it is exposed during drawdowns of Lake Roosevelt. University of Idaho conducted extensive excavations at Fort Colvile in 1970–1971, and 1976–1978 and also studied contemporary Indigenous sites with colonial-period assemblages, including the nearby Fishery site (45ST94) and Dune Site (45ST119) (Chance 1972, 1973, 1986; Chance and Chance 1977, 1979, 1985b; Stout 1973).

Classification of the 1971 assemblage from the Chief Trader's House was the first use of the Sprague typological system, finding abundant commerce and industry items (Saastamo 1971). Archaeological work between 1970 and 1978 included the complete excavation of the Chief Trader's House and sampling of the Trading Store, Fur Store, Indian Hall, Men's House, and Officers' Quarters. Archaeologists uncovered numerous cellars, privies, a meat house, and servants' quarters. The long-occupied post contained abundant ceramics, nails, and window glass that helped define chronological sequences of historical artifacts (see chapter 2). Other analyses explored three blacksmith's shops, discovering an increase in iron waste later in time, associated with increased access to the market, and a decrease in copper and brass material, tied to less demand for trade jewelry and other "bright" objects (Chance and Chance 1985b). The persistent plan of Fort Colvile suggests a conservative Hudson's

Bay Company model that showed little change in orientation or use of space over forty-five years (Chance and Chance 1985b).

Ethnohistoric and ethnographic data verify that the Hudson's Bay Company attempted to maximize profit over the long term, but maintained relations with Indigenous people in idiosyncratic ways, based on who was in command of the post, their religious predilections, and ambitions (Chance 1973). The Hudson's Bay Company sought Indigenous people as allies and as wives, encouraged and supported the adoption of agriculture, and promoted peaceful relations between Native groups using existing tribal political systems (Chance 1973). The Hudson's Bay Company marketed European goods while maintaining stable prices for Indigenous trade when European demand for furs fluctuated. They also used Christianity, British morality, and work habits, as means to control Indigenous people with the goal to improve trade and justify their monopoly (Chance 1973: 132). Decreasing collection of beaver and otter pelts, and increasing bear pelts, suggest an exhaustion of animals in the district associated with the Hudson's Bay Company's "fur desert" policy—to not trap sustainably in areas that might become U.S. territory.

At the end of the fur trade era, the racially diverse former employees and their families settled in the Colville Valley, but as Whites entered the region they were racialized, and their history became invisible or Americanized (Barman and Watson 1999). As these families were composed of French Canadians, Orkney Islanders, Native Hawaiians, Métis, and Indigenous people, their community was discounted by White settlers as mixed or non-White, evolutionarily inferior, and subordinate to Whites. The extensive historical archaeology of Fort Colvile provides an important window onto the underlying cultural importance of the Kettle Falls fishery to the Colville people, their continuing adjustments to address colonialism, and the relationship of the place to human–fish connections (e.g., Hutchinson and Hall 2020).

Fort Langley I (1827–1839) and Fort Langley II (1839–1888)

Established two years after Fort Colvile and Fort Vancouver, Fort Langley became one of the most important Hudson's Bay Company posts in the Pacific Northwest. Established on the Fraser River, the first post, Fort Langley I (DhRp-37), was moved in 1839 to a new site, the current location of Fort Langley National Historic Site. The site's preservation is centered on the November 19, 1858, proclamation of British Columbia as a colony during the height of the Fraser River Gold Rush (see chapter 7).

In 1956, "uncontrolled testing" by the architect in charge of the reconstruction (Peeps 1958), was followed by professional excavations in the 1970s and 1980s (Porter and Steer 1987; Porter et al. 1995; Steer et al. 1980). Porter et al. (1995) summarize the construction history, suggesting that the 1827 fort was moderate-sized (120 × 135 ft.), dedicated to the collection of animal pelts and processing salmon. By 1833, agriculture became important, and in 1839, the second post was established in an area with improved docking. The Hudson's Bay Company expanded the new fort to the south in four phases to a maximum extent of 670.5 × 202.5 feet (Porter et al. 1995: 55; Steer et al. 1980: 46–50). At the second Fort Langley, the Hudson's Bay Company cured (salted) salmon, packed cranberries, conducted dairying, produced agricultural crops, built boats, and wrought iron for trade and other implements (Porter et al. 1995: 4). Excavations identified palisade lines and gallery support posts, and collected samples of structures and artifacts to relocate the historical stockade and building locations, supporting reconstruction and park interpretation (Porter et al. 1995; Steer et al. 1980: 1). Excavations at a Native Hawaiian dwelling, the "Kanaka House,"[3] found numerous cellars, many overlapping, and four separate rooms or compartments with associated cache pits (some formed by buried barrels), and the base of a hearth/fireplace. The pits contained glass beads, clay tobacco pipe stems, lead shot, and buttons. These European-manufactured quotidian items did not reflect Native Hawaiian traditions, likely because all employees acquired goods from the Hudson's Bay Company Sale Shop (company store). The work identified items typical of other Hudson's Bay Company assemblages (Porter et al. 1995: appendix B; Steer et al. 1980: 76).

Fort Nisqually I (1833–1843) and Fort Nisqually II (1843–1869)

The Hudson's Bay Company established the first Fort Nisqually in 1833 on the southern edge of Puget Sound within the Nisqually cultural landscape of *Sequalitchew,* and between Fort Langley and Fort Vancouver (Chance 1990). While the fur traders sought animal pelts among the people of Puget Sound, the primary purpose of Fort Nisqually was to establish a farm and cattle/sheep ranch. Fur traders grew potatoes, peas, wheat, corn, oats, barley, and apple trees and raised Spanish cattle and imported sheep (Chance 1990; Stilson 1990a: 2–3). Later, after the establishment of the Puget Sound Agricultural Company (PSAC), a subsidiary of the Hudson's Bay Company entirely focused on agriculture, the fort, as its headquarters, was moved about .8 of a kilometer inland to be closer to arable land.

Archaeology at Fort Nisqually began after DuPont sold the property to the Weyerhaeuser Company in 1976. Faced with both environmental and historic preservation opposition to their plans for a forest products export facility,

---

3   "Kanaka" is a Hawaiian language term for "human being" that was applied to Native Hawaiians and other people from Polynesia.

Weyerhaeuser instead developed Northwest Landing, a planned housing development (Creighton 2004; Kirk 1991). The private ownership and development of the land created troublesome historic preservation complications that impacted the nature and intensity of archaeological research. Creighton wrote her doctoral dissertation to document the conflict between historic preservation advocates, the State of Washington, the Nisqually Tribe, and the Weyerhaeuser Company (Creighton 2004). Capuder's (2013) Indigenous perspective critiques both the housing development and the archaeology associated with it, suggesting that ancestral grave sites, sacred sites, and sites of cultural and historical significance were desecrated under a form of colonial structural violence (see also Moura 1990a: 17–19). The historical archaeology is extensive, though with a few exceptions is relegated to cultural resources management's gray literature (cf., Kirk and Daugherty 2007: 127–132).

At Fort Nisqually I (45PI55), the archaeologists identified palisade lines and bastions, the positions of interior structures, and an assemblage of belongings, including a privy filled with items from the elite managers of the post (Kirk 1991: 25; Kirk and Daugherty 2007: 127–132; Moura 1990a). Pacific Lutheran University tested Fort Nisqually II (45PI56) in 1988 to collect data in support of a rehabilitation of the 1930 replica at Point Defiance Park in Tacoma (Stilson 1990a, 1990b). Contract archaeologists conducted the most extensive excavations outside of the fort areas along Sequalitchew Creek, labeled by researchers as "Nisqually Village," and were threatened by a new roadway (Stilson 1990c, 1991a, 1991b). Archaeologists excavated six house sites on either side of the creek, all of which were built in the 1840s and 1850s to house the racially diverse Hudson's Bay Company employees, including many Native American women who married the French Canadian and Métis workers (Stilson 1991a). Many Nisqually, such as the dairyman Sciousin, were local, while other workers included people from Snohomish and Puyallup. The excavations revealed a diversity of French Canadian (Red River Frame) styles, including *poteau sur sole* (post-on-sill) and *pieux en terre* (pile-in-ground) buildings with measurements in both French Canadian toise (about 1.95 m) and English feet, and evidence for rebuilding, remodeling, and additions. Besides a dearth of typical trading items, the shift to agriculture is documented through comparison of the faunal remains from the 1833 fort to Nisqually Village (Moura 1990b, 1992; Stilson 1990c). The earlier fort site exhibits a diversity of wild and domesticated animals, including deer, elk, cattle, and sheep, consistent with the development of agriculture during a time when fur trading was still present. By the time of the PSAC and Fort Nisqually II, the diet of the inhabitants of Nisqually Village was dominated by the poorer cuts of meat from the farm, processed into soups and stews. While deer and elk are still present, and there are some bird, swine, and fish bones, the assemblage contains mostly cattle and sheep. For both the earlier fort and the later village, the evidence suggests intensive processing to extract bone marrow. The historical archaeology of Fort Nisqually, although controversial, contains valuable studies of the belongings and lifeways of the families affiliated with the later Hudson's Bay Company posts. The work provides a useful contrast to other large Hudson's Bay Company forts and connects closely to the histories and persistence of fur trade and Indigenous families.

Fort Vancouver (ca. 1827–1866)

Fort Vancouver was the center of British colonial control and culture, and the Hudson's Bay Company entrepot of the Pacific Northwest. The fort was moved to a mostly flood-free lower prairie in 1829, and from this vantage, Fort Vancouver conducted far-ranging activities tied to the fur trade, including managing and supplying its numerous trading posts, maintaining a maritime trading fleet, and outfitting annual fur "brigades" of employees and their families who would trap throughout the region during the winter (Hussey 1957). Like other large Hudson's Bay Company posts, it was diversified to include a large-scale agricultural enterprise, or "great farm," that provisioned these far-flung operations, putting hundreds of acres under cultivation, orcharding, raising thousands of head of cattle, sheep, hogs, and horses, managing a dairy farm, curing (salting) salmon, and conducting a retail trade with employees, missionaries, explorers, and eventually thousands of American immigrants (Erigero 1992; Hussey 1957; Wilson and Langford 2011). A water-powered lumber mill employed a sizeable community about 8 kilometers upriver that shipped wood to other places on the Pacific Rim, including California and Hawaii (Erigero 1992; Hussey 1957). The large Fort Vancouver stockade contained warehouses to hold furs and trade goods, blacksmith, carpenter, and harness shops, as well as administrative offices and dwellings of the Chief Factor, traders, clerks, and other elite "gentlemen" and their families (Erigero 1992; Hussey 1957; Wilson 2018).

Like other fur trade posts, Fort Vancouver was closely entangled with Indigenous people, including resident Native groups living near the fort, visiting groups who gathered at the fort to socialize and trade, and a resident community inside the fort and its surroundings who were part of the fur trade post's operations and their families (Deur 2012: 42). Further, the colonial population included Native Hawaiians, Métis, east-coast and Canadian Native peoples, French Canadians, and numerous workers from across the British Isles, including Orkney Islanders, Welsh, Irish, Scots, and English. Most of these people lived in a village physically segregated from the fort by agricultural fields (Erigero 1992; Hussey 1957; Taber et al. 2019; Wilson 2014, 2018). When the Brigades returned to deliver animal pelts, the village population would swell to as many as a thousand people. Descriptions of the village suggest there were forty to sixty houses, with outbuildings, corrals, fenced gardens, roads, trails, and other features (Hussey 1976: 217–218; Thomas and Hibbs 1984: 45–47; Wilson and Langford 2011). The St. James Catholic Mission (later Cathedral) was established on the northern end of the village in 1844–1845 with a church that could accommodate five hundred people. The Hudson's Bay Company also established the first school for the children of the fur traders and orphaned Native Americans (Erigero 1992; Hussey 1957). Like other fur trade posts, the documentary record of this racially diverse community is highly biased and contradictory, clouded by American nationalism and overt racism that sought to marginalize, deemphasize, and erase the contributions of the British and their Indigenous allies (cf., Barman and Watson 1999; Wilson 2014). Historical archaeology therefore is instrumental to bring a more nuanced history back to Fort Vancouver, as well as other fur trade-era posts (Taber et al. 2019; Wilson 2015; Wilson et al. 2022).

Archaeological excavations at Fort Vancouver span seventy-five years, with initial work by Caywood relocating remains of the stockade and many of the interior structures, followed by many archaeologists who further documented the stockade and conducted massive excavations to facilitate reconstruction and assist in National Park Service interpretation (Caywood 1948a, Wilson et al. 2020). Work in the Fort Vancouver village and waterfront included both academic and cultural resources management projects (Wilson et al. 2020). Literally thousands of units were excavated across the site to document structures and collect samples, yet this represents only a small fraction of the over 81-hectare site. More recently, multiscalar analysis seeks to summarize some of this work, integrating new information to explore issues of colonialism, identity, and nationalism (Wilson 2014, 2018).

Like many of the Hudson's Bay Company's forts, Fort Vancouver was spatially structured, in this case with homes and administrative buildings concentrated in the northern and northeastern areas within the stockade, and warehouse and retail trade functions in the southern and western portions (figure 4.2). While not militarily strong, a variety of physical cues, including clapboard-clad painted structures for offices and the Chief Factor's residence, formal gardens, and 18-pound cannon, symbolically reinforced the power of the Hudson's Bay Company (Nelson 2007; Wilson 2018: 101–109). The fort was intentionally placed in the landscape, surrounded by pastures, agricultural fields, and gardens, with the village and Catholic Church at a distance (Wilson 2018). A waterfront complex contained wharves, boat-works, a

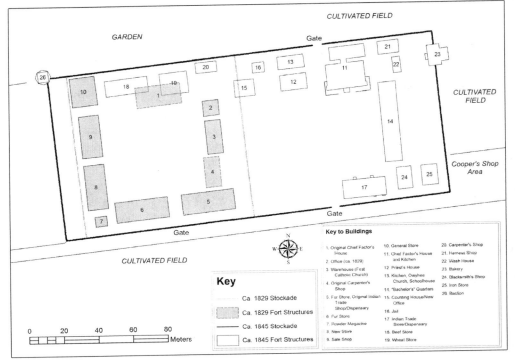

Figure 4.2. Plan of Fort Vancouver ca. 1829 and 1845.

salmon salting store, and a malaria hospital, the latter of which contained evidence of nineteenth-century medical practices, including bleeding, smudging, and the more productive treatment of cinchona bark and quinine (Carley 1981).

The many people of the village lived primarily in French Canadian–style houses constructed using the French Canadian *toise* unit in post-on-sill, pile-in-the-ground, and *pièce-sur-pièce en queue d'aronde* (dovetail notched) styles (Garth 1947: 221–222; Kardas 1971; Mullaley 2011; Thomas and Hibbs 1984). The spatial distribution of nails, window glass thicknesses, and other evidence suggests a period ca. 1845 of renewed maintenance in the village, including reroofing, during the maximum reorientation of the Hudson's Bay Company to pursuits other than strictly the fur trade (Mullaley 2011). Concentrations of clay tobacco pipes near hearths and in an exterior area central to the community suggest socializing that crosscut the lines of race and possibly gender (Wynia 2013). Pollen from the fort's extensive garden compares with samples from the village, indicating that many of the same exotic plants found in the formal garden controlled by McLoughlin were also grown in the village, and connoting an actively maintained space (Dorset 2012; Wilson 2018). The presence of ceramic and glass gastroliths, formed by domesticated birds swallowing small gravels to aid in digestion, suggests the widespread use of domesticated fowl by households regardless of ancestry (Taber et al. 2019). Other spatially discrete patterning exists, including the presence of dog burials, fenced areas, and other attributes of a complex landscape (Wilson 2014).

Ceramics recovered from the village indicate that in spite of low wages and markups that favored the gentlemen, the inhabitants acquired prodigious numbers of ceramic vessels in mostly the same styles as the elites, over 50 percent of which were transferprinted whitewares, including tea cups and tea pots (Cromwell 2006c, 2017b; Holschuh 2013). Sartorial artifacts suggest that British orthodoxy in dress was adjusted by the villagers (Sukau 2022). For example, evidence of conformance with British dress styles and hygiene by gentlemen living within the stockade contrasts with greater variation in designs and an absence of hygiene items in the village. The village population conformed to the basics of Western-style dress, augmenting it with ornamentation, and forming an internal means to address social standing and identity within the employee community (Sukau 2022). Glass was modified into tools, suggesting some continuity with Indigenous stone tool traditions, perhaps even resistance to British hierarchy (Simmons 2014: 116–117). The archaeological evidence from the village suggests a complex yet distinct population that maintained their homes, grew exotic plants, socialized using tobacco and tea, and otherwise conducted activities that crosscut the British status hierarchy and its rigid prescriptions (Wilson 2014, 2018). While concepts of hybridity and creolization have been critiqued (Palmié 2016; Silliman 2015), it is clear that people and families within the village used British products and practices creatively to practically reside, adjust, and even signal their association with the fur trade.

The demise of the Hudson's Bay Company post was tied to the American immigration over the Oregon Trail and the establishment of the U.S. Army fort that occupied the same landscape. The introduction of new merchants, the gold rush of early 1850, treaties that pushed Native American people to reservations, and the enforcement of American tariffs challenged the British Colonial system and their economic power (Chapman 1993; Deur 2012: 147; Steele 1975; Steele et al. 1975). The Hudson's Bay Company moved its headquarters to Victoria in 1845, and the U.S. Army increasingly inhabited spaces vacated by the fur trade company (Wilson 2014). The mixed-race employees dispersed, with some moving to Canada, some settling on landscapes with White immigrants, and some removed to Indian reservations (Deur 2012;

Wilson 2014). While the archaeological evidence suggests a shared cultural identity among these people, similar to the Métis of Canada, the disruption of American settlement and the historical paths of people illustrate "acts of residence" or practices that endured the entanglement of identities and Indigenous persistence after the fur trade era (Wilson 2018, see chapter 5).

Missionaries and Missions

Tied intimately to the colonial projects of both Great Britain and the United States, the missionaries of the Pacific Northwest brought Christianity, literacy, commercial goods, and Western-style agriculture to Native American people, simultaneously preparing a pathway for American colonization. Attempts at Indigenous cultural change and assimilation have been likened to cultural genocide, with its concomitant racialization leading to dispossession (Barman 2007: 168–169; Jepsen and Norberg 2017: 59–77; Tinker 1993; Whaley 2006). The missionaries represent a leading edge, like that of the fur traders, in introducing new ideas, people, retail products, and disease vectors, and their daily lives and work imprinted on the American experience in the Pacific Northwest (Schwantes 1996: 98). Historical archaeologists have explored a few of the missions of this period, and their work illuminates the variability in mission practices and effects on Indigenous peoples. Their role in nation-building was also variable, with some more interested in pushing national objectives and assisting in colonial settlement, while others were more focused on evangelizing Indigenous communities.

Willamette Mission (1834–1841)

Authorized by the Board of Managers of the Methodist Episcopal Church, Jason Lee and his party of missionaries accompanied the second Wyeth expedition west to assimilate Indigenous people employing a racial and religious ideology that focused on their transformation (Whaley 2006). Encouraged by McLoughlin to settle in the Willamette Valley, Lee and his brother Francis and their party established a mission about 97 kilometers (60 miles) south of the mouth of the Willamette River on the southwestern edge of French Prairie. About a dozen retired French Canadian fur trappers and their families were farming there at the time (see chapter 5). Eventually, three buildings were constructed, serving as residence, school room, and chapel. Both Indigenous and French-Canadian farmers' children attended the school and religious services. Additional structures were added, including a barn, kitchen, hospital, storehouses, and shops (Bewall 1982; Chapman 1983: 18–25). The cemetery, used for missionaries and Native American children "charges," was located close by. Established during the malaria epidemics of the 1830s, many of the children died in the early years and, in 1841, the entire Mission was moved to Mill Creek on Chemeketa Plain, where a mill was built along with a school, parsonage, and house, the future site of Salem, Oregon.

Historian Robert M. Gatke tested the site in the early 1920s, exposing a possible cellar and related mission belongings, but professional archaeology did not occur until 1979–1980, when Oregon State University recovered nearly 10,000 items. In the main excavation block, the archeologists found remains of a fireplace, a hearth associated with the kitchen, and a gravel pavement or "floor" (Chapman 1983: 55–59). Based on documentary and archaeological evidence, the first two buildings were likely saddle-notched oak log cabins, with the third a French-Canadian style. Nails and post holes around the gravel floor suggested a covered outdoor area associated with the three connected buildings.

The belongings from Willamette Mission included domestic and personal items tied to food storage, preparation, and use, personal grooming, clothing repair and construction, hunting, and protection. Slate tablet and pencil fragments reflect school activities, while traditional artifacts were limited to eleven stone projectile points, a scraper, flakes, and obsidian nodules. The relative dearth of Indigenous cultural material was deemed a "reflection of the missionaries' zeal for rapid assimilation," or perhaps the Hudson's Bay Company's prior impact on Indigenous people (Chapman 1983: 254). While many of the Mission belongings were similar to types found at Fort Vancouver, many others were clearly not purchased from the British, suggesting the missionaries intentionally sought alternative American sources (Chapman 1983: 260). This is consistent with their development of a warehouse at Oregon City and a retail store for goods at the mission, arguing through their actions for U.S. dominance (Chapman 1993: 22, 29–30). The ultimate failure of the Mission and unceremonious removal of Jason Lee, partly for use of mission funds for speculation, did not prevent the revival of his memory and veneration in the early twentieth century (e.g., Scott 1906, see chapter 6), or his reinterpretation in the early twenty-first (e.g., Lewis 2014; Whaley 2006). The site of the mission remains an Oregon State Park, and the historical archaeology provides useful information on the activities of the missionaries and their Indigenous charges.

Waiilatpu Mission (1836–1847)

Perhaps the most notorious of the Christian missions, Presbyterian missionaries Marcus and Narcissa Whitman established Waiilatpu amongst the Cayuse people in a cultural landscape and village of the same name. As noted earlier in the chapter, the Whitmans emigrated west in 1836 at the behest of the American Board of Commissioners for Foreign Missions, a consortium of protestant religions that supported missions in foreign countries. Waiilatpu Mission was developed to proselytize to the Cayuse, pushing them to adopt European American–style agriculture, literacy, religion, laws, and medicine (Addis 2005; Stern 1996: 42–78). Within a few years, the flood of American emigrants on the Oregon Trail led the Whitmans to shift toward religious, medical, and material support for the predominantly White settlers traveling through. Conflict with the Cayuse erupted in late 1847 when Americans, sick with measles and dysentery, overwintered at the Mission and measles spread. The Whitmans were killed on November 29, 1847, and those women and children who remained alive were enslaved until the Hudson's Bay Company ransomed them. This "massacre" ushered in decades of conflict between Americans and Indigenous people (Garth 1948: 117–118; Stern 1996: 168–346). In the development of the American narrative of the Pacific Northwest, the Mission became iconic of American settlement, with the missionaries becoming "martyrs" and Whitman evolving into the man who "saved Oregon" by taking on the Hudson's Bay Company, Catholics, and Indigenous people in an unapologetic reading of the American colonial project (Addis 2005).

Archaeological excavations at Waiilatpu were some of the earliest historical archaeology in the region, associated with one of the first national park units preserved besides Fort Vancouver (Garth 1948, 1949, 1952b; Kirk and Daugherty 2007: 133–139). In dramatic juxtaposition, material remains from the Missionaries and Cayuse people were found on floors that tie directly to the historical events that led to the killings and aftermath. National Park Service archaeologists and their crews identified the adobe walls, hearth remains, and cellars of a First House, "T-shaped" Mission House, Mansion House, the remains of a pile-in-ground Blacksmith Shop and corral, and the base of the grist mill (Garth 1948, 1949, 1952b). Garth extrapolated the construction and furnishing of the buildings, interweaving historical and archaeological information, finding hard-packed "occupation floors" that were tied to the Whitman Mission, reoccupation by Indigenous people after they had burned the Mission buildings, reoccupation again by volunteer soldiers during the first Cayuse War when the site briefly became "Fort Waters," and finally subsequent destruction by Indigenous people. Some of the belongings within the ruined Mission House tied directly to the Whitmans included medical items from Dr. Whitman's practice, such as peg-style porcelain false teeth, medicine bottle fragments, a thermometer tube, the handle of a surgical knife, a small bronze weight for scales, and an intact bottle with a stopper containing iodine (Garth 1949: 306–308). The archaeologists found curios from Dr. Whitman's

Figure 4.3. Silver spoon (15 cm long) recovered from the Mission House at Waiilatpu. Courtesy of National Park Service, Whitman Mission National Historic Site, WHMI 161.

natural and cultural history collections, including crystals, petrified wood, a bone needle, and a basalt spear point. A pewter and silver spoon each contained the initials "S.C.P." inferred to be Stephen and Clarissa Prentiss, who were Narcissa's parents (figure 4.3). Personal and domestic items provided information on the types of furnishings at the Mission, and sheep shears, a bone shuttle for weaving, homespun cloth, and the skull of a sheep provide confirmation of the mission's pastoral activities. Charred wheat, beans, peas, corn, squash, peach pits, and the bones of cattle and other domesticated animals corroborated domestication activities recorded in period documents. Ceramics found near the pantry were dominated by the same Copeland- and Garrett-style ceramics found at Hudson's Bay Company posts, with the more expensive transferprinted patterns prevalent and few undecorated types.

In contrast, the occupation floor located on top of the roof fall after the houses were burnt contained glass beads, dentalia, clam-shell beads, stone pipes, bone fragments of cattle, deer, and other animals, long bones broken for marrow, stone tools, gun flints, ceramic sherds, and other European-manufactured items tied to the Indigenous reoccupation of the ruin (Garth 1948: 123, 1952b: 8). The abundance of square nails in hearths found on the mud stratum associated with the fallen roof were inferred to be from the burning of mission boards from the houses (Garth 1948: 123). Wagon parts found in the ruins are consistent with documentation that the Cayuse piled wagons into the houses before they burned them (Garth 1949: 309). The archaeologists also relocated the gunsmithing materials of W. J. Berry lost during the destruction of the Mission, including numerous gun hammers for percussion-type firearms.

The archaeology of Waiilatpu is astounding for the many intimate possessions of the Whitmans and others found in the houses, and in the colonial products that reflect developments tied to the Oregon Trail migration. While Garth's original work bolstered settler narratives of the massacre and Oregon trail hardships, within its strata are materials that directly speak to the intensive struggle of Indigenous people to defend their homelands against the colonizers.

St. Paul at French Prairie (1839–1849)

Retired French Canadian fur trapper families who settled at French Prairie (see below), petitioned for a Catholic priest as early as 1834, the same year that Jason Lee established Willamette Mission, and even built a log church by 1836 (Poet 1996). It was not until 1838, however, that the Bishop of Quebec sent out Francis Norbert Blanchet and Modeste Demers, who arrived at Fort Vancouver late in the year, holding the first Catholic Mass within the kitchen/schoolhouse behind the chaplain's house (soon renamed the priest's house). In January 1839, Blanchet held mass at the French Prairie log church, which he named St. Paul's. The Mission de Willamette (Willamette Mission) included the 1842 construction of a boy's school, St. Joseph's College, and in 1844, a girl's boarding school, called Sainte Marie de Willamette, established by Belgian nuns who came at the behest of the Jesuit missionary DeSmet (see below). In the same year, DeSmet built St. Francis Xavier about 1.6 kilometers west of St. Paul as the administrative center for Jesuit activities in the Pacific Northwest (Chapman 1993: 12–13). The Catholic priests built a brick church in 1846 that still stands in St. Paul (figure 4.4). Both boarding schools served the children of the multiracial French-Canadian families, generally French-Canadian fathers and Indigenous mothers. In some cases, orphaned Indigenous children were taught at the schools, and even some Methodist children attended. It is likely that the son of a powerful tribal chief, "Pierre Cayouse," was taught at the school (Stern 1996: 377). With the exception of the brick church, both schools and the Jesuit operations ended shortly after the news of the California gold rush depopulated much of the Willamette Valley, with farmers heading south to seek their fortunes, ruining the prospects for educating local children. By 1852, both schools and the Jesuit Mission were closed, and the nuns relocated to Oregon City, Oregon, and California.

Archaeologists from Oregon State University sought the first log church as part of the French-Canadian Archaeological Project, but testing revealed artifacts in a wood-cribbed cellar and well, inconsistent with St. Paul's hum-

Figure 4.4. Church of St. Paul, in St. Paul, Oregon, constructed in 1846. A scale model of the 1836 log church is to the right of the church.

ble beginnings (Brauner 1989). Window glass thickness data from the cellar (35MA260/ORMA67) suggested it dated to 1845–1855, after the construction of the brick church. Poet (1996) felt that the cellar was part of the girl's boarding school and wrote her thesis making this assumption, but a relocated 1851 map of St. Paul suggested that the site was actually associated with St. Joseph's College. Hill's (2014) reanalysis of the assemblage confirmed a more domestic and male-dominated assemblage, with abundant ceramics, glass, animal bone, and other items. Importantly, few objects could be construed as Catholic, or even ideological, although the emphasis on ceramics and other goods readily available at Fort Vancouver suggested alignment with British colonial interests. Hill suggests that the relatively low socioeconomic status of the priests, their limited market access, along with ethnicity and gender considerations, created a distinctive archaeological assemblage. A unique type of Chinese ceramic and distinctive flow blue ceramics were distinguished at the mission property, indicating imported items brought out by the Catholic priests and missionaries or tied to a unique religious network for acquiring consumer products (Hill 2014).

Cataldo Mission (1846–1877)

The Jesuit Order of the Catholic Church also heeded the call to Christianize the Indigenous people of the Pacific Northwest, reportedly from the fourth delegation of Flathead people who had come to St. Louis in 1840. Father Pierre-Jean DeSmet entered the region in 1841, and with his Jesuit brothers established a number of missions west of the Rocky Mountains and on the headwaters of the Columbia River, as well as in the Willamette Valley. One of these was at Cataldo, where Father Joseph Joset established a temporary chapel in 1846 and a substantial and still-standing Mission church after 1850, called the Coeur d'Alene Mission of the Sacred Heart (Schroer et al. 1976). The Jesuits followed the reduction (Spanish *reducción*) system whereby missions were placed in proximity to Indigenous communities receptive to Christianity, and located near agricultural lands where they could raise crops and domesticated animals. Priests simultaneously sought to aggregate Native Americans into "neophyte" colonies surrounding the Mission church, preaching against heterodox practices like gambling and polygamy, establishing agrarian practices, and indoctrinating children to Christian beliefs and Western-style education (Weaver 1977). While the Franciscan version of this system had intensely damaging effects on Californian Indigenous peoples (e.g., Lightfoot 2005; Lightfoot et al. 2013), and earlier Jesuit versions produced devastating impacts on other colonized groups, such as the Chamorro (e.g., Montón-Subías et al. 2020), the Jesuits in the Pacific Northwest were too few in number, the Pacific Northwest too vast, and the Coeur d'Alene people less amenable to giving up their ways of life, and a middle ground of "cooperation and mutual tolerance" was formed (Woodworth-Ney 1996: 71).

The first historical archaeology at Cataldo Mission was a 1957 survey for a natural gas pipeline that recorded the nearby Coeur d'Alene Encampment (10KA3) (Tuohy 1958). Extensive historical archaeology occurred as a result of American bicentennial restoration efforts initiated in 1973 (Fielder and Sprague 1974; Weaver 1976, 1977). Archaeological work in 1973–1974 included excavations to explore the Church's post-on-sill structure built on a field-stone foundation, areas within the church, and outbuilding areas adjacent to the church, including the barn, dwelling for the Jesuit brothers, pre-1864 parsonage, blacksmith and harness shops, and Coeur d'Alene habitations (Fielder and Sprague 1974; New 2013: 65–80; Weaver 1976, 1977). Related to the restoration work, burials of three priests were discovered during construction of new foundations inside the church. The full Cataldo collection was not curated and analyzed in detail until 2005–2007 (New 2013), and no analysis has compared the Coeur d'Alene Encampment and Cataldo sites.

The historical archaeology suggests a close correspondence between the Coeur d'Alene people and the mission (New 2013; Weaver 1977). An abundance of medicine bottles is likely associated with stress caused by Western diseases on the Coeur d'Alene people and alcohol bottles attributed to a "regular or average presence of alcohol at the mission" likely related to its use in Holy Communion (New 2013: 106). The relative austerity of the missionaries is suggested by ceramics that include a substantial number of inexpensive Chinese Bamboo pattern porcelain bowls, some transferprinted earthenware vessels, but also many that are minimally decorated, which New (2013: 107–112) contrasts with the abundant finely decorated ceramics of the Methodist Missions. The historical archaeology supports the documentary records suggesting that the missionaries had some important effects on the Coeur d'Alene people, including the introduction of Christianity and agriculture, but that the Indigenous people did not readily relinquish their lifeways and cultural identity.

Indigenous Sites of the Later Fur Trade Period

Until recently, few studies explored Indigenous places from the later fur trade period. Some connections were made between Native Americans and mission sites, some tied to dramatic historical events like at Waiilatpu, and some, like Cataldo, tied to long-term and enduring relationships between missions and Indigenous communities. The Yuquot midden contained extensive European and Canadian commercial products dating after 1871, suggesting market penetration of Nuu-chah-nulth communities after the establishment of the Confederation of Canada and introduction of missionaries (Folan and Dewhirst 1980a: 345). Collections from the Old Songhees Village site (DcRu-25 and DcRu-123), on the western side of Victoria Harbor, include numerous artifacts tied to the close association between Indigenous people and Hudson's Bay Company and later Canadian colonists until 1911 (Bown 2016). While primarily tied to salvage and cultural resources management projects, the recovered items include traditional objects like bone points, sandstone abraders, carved argillite fragments, and beaver tooth gaming pieces, as well as abundant imported commercial artifacts—dark olive glass bottles, clay tobacco pipes, English transferprinted whitewares, and Chinese porcelain (Bown 2016).

Coastal Sites in Northern British Columbia

Old Bella Bella (Qelc) on Denny Island near Namu, British Columbia, was established ca. 1835 after the construction of Fort McLoughlin (1833–43), literally creating a space between Heiltsuk traditional practices, including the well-documented gift-giving potlatch ceremony, and the later colonial period (Hobler 2000: 6; Lynch 2015). Based on historical, archaeological, and ethnographic data, the Heiltsuk changed their settlement pattern from dispersed summer camps to nucleated communities around Fort McLoughlin, with later impacts of introduced diseases and a shift to wage work. In this later period, federal restrictions on Indigenous people included amendments to the Federal Indian Act in 1880 prohibiting assembly, the banning of the potlatch in 1885, licensing of commercial fishing in 1888, and expansion of the residential school system in the 1890s (Pegg 2018). Hobler (2000: 16) suggests, however, that dramatic shifts in housing and responses to colonial attacks on cultural institutions like the potlatch "should be seen in the light of the long-standing Native tradition of settlement flexibility in which different locales and different architectural forms are in use over the course of a year." Analysis of ceramics suggest a shift from bowls and communal serving dishes in bright colors used for display and serving in the potlatch to more diverse forms, in individualized place settings, and increased plain whitewares. This occurred as the community shifted to smaller frame houses from large communal houses, and as the missionaries and government began to attack traditional lifeways (Marshall and Maas 1997). This shift in ceramic forms did not necessarily mean a shift in tradition, however, as cups and saucers became gifts tied to attendance at prohibited potlatches, such that some households are reported to contain over two hundred cup-and-saucer sets (Marshall and Maas 1997: 279–281).

Likewise, analysis of ceramics from late nineteenth- and early twentieth-century dwelling sites of the Mowachaht/Muchalaht people of Nootka Sound, including Yuquot, contained abundant soup bowls and cups and saucers in bright banded and sponge wares (Marshall and Maas 1997). Like the ceramics at Old Bella Bella, the Mowachaht/Muchalaht people likely used these brightly colored ceramics in ceremonial display and as gifts at potlatches. Based on historical records, it appears that many of the ceramics were "set aside and curated, not to be mixed with the common utensils of everyday life" (Marshall and Maas 1997: 285). Thus, at both Old Bella Bella and Nootka Sound, the social context of ceramics use was the dominant determinant of what types of vessels to purchase, and how they were used, suggesting a continuity of Indigenous traditions related to cultural persistence into the early twentieth century. Lynch's (2015) more recent analysis of the adoption of other European Canadian products at Bella Bella provides a nuanced interpretation of the effects of fur traders and missionaries on the Heiltsuk for other categories of belongings.

Martindale and Jurakic (2006) suggest that the reuse of broken glass bottles as tools at the Ginakangeek village on the Skeena River was a means for Tsimshian people to "distinguish themselves from European values" as a material gesture to reclaim aspects of precontact culture and maintain Indigenous identity. Bottle fragments were refashioned into knives, scrapers, and other forms. These practices emerged during the 1870s, as the village material assemblage became increasingly dominated by European goods in the form of metal, glass, ceramic, and other items. Similarly, the highly conservative nature of the community of Kimsquit, at the head of the Dean Channel, further south is reflected in a very slow adoption of European Canadian technology, including trade goods refashioned into technologically and ideologically useful implements and Western house styles that co-existed with traditional plankhouses (Prince 2002a, 2016). Experimentation with house forms and the slow adoption of Western-style houses until the early twentieth century on the Dean and Bella Coola River valleys suggests Indigenous agency, accommodation, and negotiation in an entangled colonial situation (Prince 2016).

Interior British Columbia Sites

Farther south, archaeologists studied the *Ts'qó:ls* village (DiRi 1) on the east bank of the Fraser River near 1848 Hudson's Bay Company Fort Hope, sampling two historic-period *Stó:lō* pit houses between 2002 and 2005 (Arnold et al. 2017). Modern *Stó:lō* people reported that the houses were occupied by known individuals, *Sexyel* (Captain Charlie) and Patrick Joe. *Sexyel* was a prominent member of the community and a well-known hunter, doctor/curer, and leader. Artifacts from his ca. 1860–1880 house suggest he maintained regular access to imported European and Canadian commercial items. Overlapping hearths and the likely presence of a wood-burning stove, stakes associated with grilling salmon, and other traditional tools and items include slate knives, ground stone tools, hand mauls, and simple flaked stone tools. These belongings contrast with imported trade items, including glass beads, shell buttons, metal objects, and glass bottles for beverages and oils (Arnold et al. 2017). The small sample from Patrick Joe's house yielded fewer trade items, suggesting the higher status of *Sexyel,* whose house contained more exotic European and Canadian manufactured goods.

The mid–Fraser River Canyon is far removed from the coastal or even interior fur trade posts, and excavations of a moderate-sized contact-period pit house (Housepit 54) at the Bridge River site (St'át'imc ancestral site) focused on fur trade impacts in an area where Indigenous people were less exposed to direct colonization (Prentiss 2017). Archaeology of the final occupation of the Bridge River site in 2012 examined the Indigenous St'át'imc people in the mid–nineteenth century (ca. 1830s–1850s). Notably, this excavation and its overarching longitudinal project was a collaborative partnership between the Bridge River Band (Xwísten) and the University of Montana. Excavations of Housepit 54 uncovered roof, floor, and midden deposits, and evidence for distinctive "room-based" activity areas within the large circular subterranean house. The archaeologists found postholes, a cache pit, and a central hearth (Prentiss 2017). In contrast to the large number of traditional stone artifacts, they recovered only fifty-one European trade goods from the house, less than 1 percent of the entire assemblage, including drawn glass beads, jingle (or tinkler) cones, metal arrowheads, a trade ring, a horseshoe, and a machine-made bone button. Local steatite was used to manufacture beads, pendants, traditional tubular and European-style tobacco bowl pipes, and a female "baby" figurine (Prentiss 2017: 249).

Compared with earlier precontact housepit floors from a nearby village, the Housepit 54 assemblage suggests that many precolonial practices continued, including egalitarian household and intrahousehold organization, and collector-based subsistence (Smith 2017). Based on an increase in deer bones and hide scrapers, as well as the high value of deer hides, Smith (2017: 240–243) posits intensification of deer hunting that may have increased emphasis on hunting and deer meat as a prestige item later in the fur trade period. Prentiss (2017: 254) suggests the occupants collected and prepared traditional foods, constructed a traditional-style house, and in many ways persisted in traditional lifeways, while taking advantage "of new and alternative strategies for survival and success."

Indigenous Sites South of the International Border

Historical archaeologists have excavated fewer Indigenous sites associated with the later fur trade south of the international border. At Fort Okanogan, there was no clear intensive aggregation of Indigenous peoples at the post or formation of a new fur trade community, possibly because local villages were nearby, but also due to the rapid decline in beaver populations and the depopulating effects of disease (Grabert 1973: 121). However, the examination of the nearby mat lodge village (45OK91) found few Indigenous artifacts, and mostly European or American manufactured goods, including possible blacksmithing remains.

Chance's (1973: 132) ethnohistoric analysis of the Hudson's Bay Company's effects on the Colville people suggests that the Hudson's Bay Company sought Native Americans as allies, fostering agriculture and peace, and keyed into the political systems of the Native groups. The Hudson's Bay Company also strove to increase Indigenous people's appetite for European goods, maintaining stable prices, and using Christianity, European morality, the education of children, and emphasis on protestant work habits to improve trade. Chance (1973: 135–136) felt that the Colville's response to the Hudson's Bay Company was a successful "assimilation" until the influx of American immigrants tied to the Oregon trail, the 1854 gold rush, and related Indian Wars. Certainly by 1870, substantial numbers of Native American people of the upper Columbia River, including the Colville, Spokane, Pend d'Oreille, Sanpoil/Nespelem, and Okanogan, conducted some Western-style agriculture, including harvesting of wheat, potatoes, and the raising of horses, cattle, and chickens (Chance 1973: 106–115). Likewise, the diverse former employees of the Hudson's Bay Company stayed in the Colville Valley, setting up farms and continuing agricultural practices (Barman and Watson 1999). The fur trade families, however, were marginalized by the large influx of American settlers, who espoused the ideology of manifest destiny, while utilizing nationality, social status, religion, and race to separate, and then actively forget the original fur trade communities (Barman and Watson 1999). Chance's conceptions of assimilation, therefore, are problematic due to the racialized and entangled colonial environment, which included resident cultures that adopted some colonial practices and the fur trade community that was embedded with Native peoples. As Barman and Watson (1999: 151) note, the descendants have not forgotten their fur trade heritage and unique connections to these places, keeping "alive their families' contribution to the settlement history of the Pacific Northwest."

In the next chapter, I explore Oregon trail sites, and how American immigration further changed the relations between Nations and people. This also continued the dramatic effects on the environment started in the fur trade era.

5

American Conquest

Between May 10 and October 13, 1849, Brevet-colonel William Wing Loring with five companies of the Regiment of Mounted Riflemen, accompanied by 700 horses, 1,200 mules, and 171 wagons, marched from Camp Sumner near Leavenworth, Kansas, to Fort Vancouver and Oregon City along the Oregon Trail. On arrival, Loring wrote:

> It is gratifying to state that the expedition has reached its destination safely after one of the longest marches that has ever been made, a distance of over 2,000 miles across a country—a large portion of which approaches a waste and much of it mountainous—where the command was compelled to feel its way along. The whole [is] a wilderness, at no point of which supplies of any description can be had. (Loring 1940: 341)

Major Osborne Cross, the quartermaster on the expedition reported:

> The land from the base of the Cascade mountains to the junction of the two rivers [Columbia and Willamette] will bear comparison with any in the states. Grain is raised in this country in great abundance, consisting of oats, barley, and wheat . . . Vegetables of the finest kind grow without the least trouble . . . (Cross 1940: 269)

Emblematic of both the arduous journey that American emigrants took to cross the Oregon Trail and the rich agricultural lands that drew them, both Loring and Cross speak to how the settlers viewed much of the Pacific Northwest as a waste devoid of timber and grazing but filled with "numerous bands of Indians" along its rivers, and an agricultural trophy at the end of the trail (Boag 1993; Loring 1940: 341). The material remains of the American invasion over the Oregon Trail led to profound changes in social relations and the environment in the Pacific Northwest. What may have been simmering resentments over the later fur trade and missionary projects to assimilate Native American communities boiled over into overt warfare that lasted episodically throughout the 1850s, 1860s, and 1870s. In this chapter, I explore the historical archaeology of Oregon trail sites and communities related to the largely American emigration, and then address forts and their role in U.S. and British nation-building, development, and the suppression and marginalization of Indigenous populations.

The Oregon Trail and Settlement (1840–1880)

Settlement of the Willamette Valley by fur traders turned farmers began as early as 1830, and at least by 1834, the Wyeth and Lee expedition of fur traders and missionaries identified a trail suitable for wagons across the Rockies. In 1841, the Hudson's Bay Company convinced 115 people in twenty-three families from the Red River area of Canada to emigrate on a route that crossed the Rocky Mountains near Banff and then down the Columbia and up the Cowlitz River to Puget Sound (Houston et al. 1997; Jackson 1984). The waves of American emigrants did not start in earnest until the "Great Migration" of 1843 (Unruh 1979: 5). Usually starting in Independence, Missouri, and ending at Oregon City, Oregon, a distance of 3,106 km (1,930 miles), only thirteen made the trek in 1840, but 875 arrived in 1843, followed by thousands in subsequent years (Unruh 1979: 118–119; NPS 1981: 1). Fueled by promoters and propagandists, the emigrants undertook the long and arduous journey for many reasons, including seeking relief from financial, legal, romantic, and health-related difficulties, patriotism associated with manifest destiny, a desire to minister to Indigenous people, the increasing unrest associated with the enslavement of African Americans in the east, and simply an instinct to head west (Gibson 1985: 133; Unruh 1979: 90–93). The mythology of "vanishing Indians" tied in part to disease-caused declines in Native populations, and the opportunity for speculation of up to 640 acres of farmland per person helped fuel the rush to what was likened to a "Garden of Eden" (Boyd 1999; Brauner 1989: 26; Spores 1993; Whaley 2010: 174–175).

The trail split in what would become Idaho to take emigrants to California at the Raft River Crossing, and later in 1849 at Hudspeth's Cutoff at Soda Springs, 77 kilometers west and 103 kilometers east, respectively, of Fort Hall (figure 5.1). Before that, at Fort Bridger, Wyoming, a branch took Mormon settlers to the Great Salt Lake. Stan Young and John Latschar of the National Park Service surveyed the route and its branches, identifying 125 sites and site complexes, and seven cross-country segments (NPS 1981). While neither was an archaeologist, they recorded the remains of many trail features (NPS 1981).

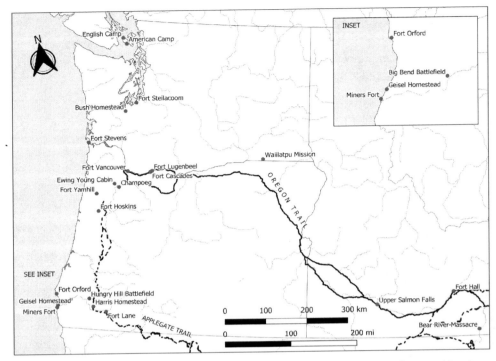

Figure 5.1. The Oregon and Applegate trails, showing early settlements, Army forts, and battlefields.

The most notable physical traces of the Oregon Trail are the characteristic depressions, ruts, swales, tracks, scarring, vegetative differences, rock alignments, and eroded trail features (figure 5.2). Natural landmarks, obstacles, and essential natural resources for the emigrants include trailside springs, mountain ascents and descents, valleys, rock formations, and river crossings. Many of the campsites contain archaeological remains, including fur trade and U.S. military forts, mission sites, Indian war battlefields, "massacre" sites, wagon train destruction sites, and emigrant graves (Beckham 2012; NPS 1981). Many of these sites on public lands have been surveyed, documented, and sometimes archaeologically tested (e.g., Brauner et al. 1998).

Indigenous connections to the Oregon Trail are represented in fort, battlefield, and massacre sites associated with conflict. One of the more horrific places is the Bear River Massacre site, where on January 29, 1863, California volunteer infantry and cavalry killed between 224 and 400 Shoshone men, women, and children at their winter village (Barnes 2008; Bearss and Wells 1990; Schindler 1999). The California soldiers were sent in retaliation

Figure 5.2. A remnant swale from the Barlow Road route of the Oregon Trail on Mount Hood, Oregon, in September 2016.

for the deaths of miners and Oregon trail emigrants in southeastern Idaho. Utah State University and the Idaho State Historic Preservation Office used documentary records, metal detector survey, and magnetometry to define the location of the village and massacre, recording a bridle ring and a number of lead bullets amongst numerous later-period items (Cannon et al. 2014).

Some places along the trail yield materials scavenged and reworked by Native Americans into useful implements (Crabtree 1968; Croney 2008; Willson 2008). Crabtee, the noted flintknapper, reported an Oregon Trail camp site near the Upper Salmon Falls power plant, where debris associated with repairing harness, wagons, and water barrels was scavenged and refashioned by local Indigenous people into knives, metal projectile points, and ornaments (Crabtree 1968: 38).

Some suggest that the many thousands of American emigrants accompanied by mules, oxen, horses, and cattle created significant environmental impacts to regions along the trail, including devastation of plant communities and game animals used by Native Americans, exacerbating economic conflict and undermining Indigenous lifeways (e.g., Hutchison and Jones 1993: 115). Others counter that the 53,000 emigrants and 360,000 stock crossing the Oregon Trail over twenty years had only localized and temporary impacts given the lateness of the season in which the wagon trains passed, and that hunting of game by emigrants was limited because of the need to keep the wagons moving (Webb 2013). Regardless, sustained contact was ultimately devastating to Indigenous populations. While many Oregon Trail emigrants maintained productive trading relations with Native Americans (Hutchison and Jones 1993;114–116; Unruh 1979: 156–167), the spread of disease and the presence of so many strangers led to conflicts, such as that at Waiilatpu Mission or the Bear River Massacre. Likewise, the impacts of settlement led to the rapid introduction and spread of new plant and animal species, the alteration of streams and wetlands, and the eradication of wildlife (e.g., Bunting 1995).

French Prairie and Champoeg (ca. 1829–1861)

Champoeg is tied symbolically to the settlement of Oregon and the creation of a provisional government (Scott 1931), but also as a place where fur traders turned to farming (Atherton 1975b: 103; Brauner et al. 1993: 30). The role of the French-Canadian farmers and their Indigenous wives was substantial in the successful establishment of Christian missions, and later American settlement in the Willamette Valley, although their history is obscured by later anti-British and anti-Catholic biases (Brauner 1989; Chapman 1993). The Pacific Fur Company's short-lived Wallace House (1812–1814) near Salem, Oregon, and the Northwest Company's Willamette Post (1813–1824), a fur-trading site about 5 kilometers upriver from the meadows of Champoeg (called *Campment du Sable*), preceded settlement (Barry 1941; Brauner 1989; Chapman 1993: 103; Jetté 2007). While evidence shows that Indigenous Kalapuyan people spent time in the area, and that the Hudson's Bay Company continued to use the area as a base for its southern fur expeditions, Champoeg did not become a significant colonial settlement until 1830, when retired fur trappers began to inhabit French Prairie, the broad, lowland area along the Willamette River (Brauner et al. 1993).

Scatters of artifacts, often in modern agricultural fields, are the primary remnants of the earliest colonial homesteads. Oregon State University relocated, surface collected, and tested some of these sites, and analyzed avocational collections with good provenience (Brauner 1989; Chapman 1993). *Campment du Sable* became a gathering place associated with the settlements that grew into the town of Champoeg, which became a shipping center for wheat from the Willamette River sent down to Fort Vancouver (Nicholls [Speulda] 1986: 22–35). As Americans began to flood the Willamette Valley, but prior to the full impact of the Great Migration, a provisional government was determined by vote in Champoeg on May 2, 1843.

Archaeological excavations at the Champoeg townsite (35MA186) within Champoeg State Park began in 1971 with periodic work subsequently utilizing students from three universities and archaeologists from state agencies and the private sector (Atherton 1975a, 1975b; Brauner 1989, Brauner et al. 1993; Nesbitt 1972; Nicholls 1986; Rose and Johnson 2018: 11–38; Speulda 1988). The Oregon College of Education (now Western Oregon University) first surveyed portions of the site, mapping concentrations of surface artifacts, and excavating at the Dr. William J. Bailey house that burned in 1853 (Nesbitt 1972). Historical records on land transactions, the census, and the platting of the site allowed correlation of historical documents with block and lot locations to artifacts from surface survey and test excavations (e.g., Atherton 1975a). Most recently, pedestrian and subsurface survey, and human remains detection dogs, have explored much of the park area, clarifying the boundaries between historical and precolonial sites and identifying potential areas of human burials (Rose and Johnson 2018; Taylor et al 2017).

Detailed analysis of artifacts excavated in 1973–1975 from four areas, including a hotel and carpenter's shop, explored South's Frontier model adapted to Sprague's (1981) typology (Nicholls [Speulda] 1986; Speulda 1988). This confirmed the abundance of architectural materials (most American machine-cut nails and window glass) compared to the relative dearth of domestic items. Excavations in 1990 and 1991 explored a number of sites associated with structures at Champoeg, including the ca. 1839–1842 home of Andre Longtain, the ca. 1858 David Weston blacksmith shop, the Edward Dupuis store and stage stop, and the Pettygrove warehouse (Brauner et al. 1993). West of the townsite, archaeologists tested the ca. 1841–1843 site of the Hudson's Bay Company's warehouse, store, and dwelling (35MA263) on the northwestern fringes of the park (Brauner 1987).

Extensive work has been conducted at the Robert Newell farmstead (35MA41), discovered in 1996 in a plowed field on the southeastern edge of the platted townsite (Rose and Johnson 2018). Newell was a retired fur trader and farmer who emigrated from Fort Hall with one of the first American groups to settle in the Willamette Valley. Magnetometry and testing relocated the house, and Oregon State University hosted five field schools between 2002 and 2014 (Cromwell et al. 2000; Manion 2006, 2014). The archaeology delineated a large hearth and house floor and extensively sampled the outlying areas around the structure (figure 5.3). Manion (2006, 2014) inferred that the house was built by John Ball in 1833, likely assisted by his neighbors, using a French-Canadian pile-in-ground style of architecture with wattle-and-daub chimney, similar to those at the Fort Vancouver village. It was then reoccupied by employees of Nathaniel Wyeth, and subsequently by the families of William Johnson and Robert Newell (Manion 2006, 2014). The primary occupants of the house, however, were women and children, as the men were often away, and women likely created most of the structured archaeological remains (Manion 2014). Besides concentrated areas of refuse around the door, hearth, and items buried into its floor, the archaeologists found children's toys and slate tablet and pencil fragments concentrated in an exterior yard that also contained gastroliths from domesticated fowl. Teaware sets in a variety of patterns suggest that, like at Fort Vancouver, the British tea ceremony was important to the women of these households. Mixed European American dress items and glass beads suggest mixed clothing styles, and flaked stone fragments are likely tied to Indigenous practices. The large hearth at the Newell site included an impressive Western-style baking oven. Overall, a gendered space is indicated, with active participation of women and children (Manion 2014: 192). The complexity of the mixed-race Champoeg households, where women came from a variety of tribal backgrounds, had little influence on the types of ceramics and other items found at the sites, suggesting a fur trade "culture" (McAleer 2003).

Two other important early settlements tested by historical archaeologists are the Ewing Young–Sidney Smith Cabin Site (ca. 1835–1850) and the ca. 1844 George Bush Homestead, on Bush Prairie, near Olympia, Washington (Krotscheck and Sonenshine 2018; Speulda et al. 1987). Ewing Young, a trapper and entrepreneur, arrived in Oregon in 1834 with a herd of Mexican horses, following disastrous exchanges with the so-called "Rogue Indians" (see Whaley 2010: 28–29). As a wealthy man with property, Young's death in 1841 is seen by many as one impetus for the establishment of the territorial government (Young 1920; Scott 1931). Archaeological investigations relocated Young's cabin site between 1984 and 1987, recovering an important comparative collection (Speulda et al. 1987). Bush was among the first African American immigrants to the Oregon Country, but testing at his home-

Figure 5.3. Excavations at the Newell House at Champoeg, showing brick concentrations, paths, and a brick floor in July 2014.

stead identified limited remains from his initial farm and considerable later disturbance (Krotscheck and Sonenshine 2018).

U.S. Army Forts and Battlefields

The U.S. Military arrived in the Pacific Northwest in 1849 after the conclusion of the Mexican War (1846–1848). Their first post, called Camp Vancouver, was established on the meadow above the Hudson's Bay Company's Fort Vancouver, and just north and east of the Hudson's Bay Company Cemetery (Sinclair 2004). Company "L" of the First Artillery under Brevet-Major John S. Hatheway came first by ship after crossing the Isthmus of Panama, and as noted above, the Regiment of Mounted Riflemen crossed on the Oregon Trail. In 1850, the post's name became Columbia Barracks, in 1853 it became Fort Vancouver, and in 1879 the Army renamed it once again to Vancouver Barracks. From this initial headquarters fort and quartermaster's depot, other military posts were established throughout the territory, some to ensure the safety of emigrants and others to ensure the safety and containment of Native Americans. Conflicts between Natives and settlers spread throughout the region, and many wartime posts were established. In some cases, fur trade posts such as Fort Walla Walla were reoccupied, but in many cases the Army established new posts, often using the same names as the fur trade posts though they were in different places (e.g., Fort Umpqua).

Many of the first military posts were established in the 1850s during the latter stages of the Cayuse War (1847–1855), which began at Waiilatpu. The U.S. Army conducted military actions, establishing military posts during the Yakima War (1855–1858), and related Puget Sound (1855–56) and Coeur d'Alene Wars (1858). In southern Oregon, the Rogue River War (1855–1856) led to the development of both military and settler forts. In British Columbia, the Fraser Canyon War (1858) was an impetus for the intervention of the Columbia Detachment of the Royal Engineers (see chapter 7).

Military posts have a central role in understanding the settler colonial processes and American experience in the Pacific Northwest. Interest in frontier forts by historical archaeologists has a long history, and often the heroic role of settler narratives driven by Manifest Destiny and "rugged individualism" attracted archaeologists to these sites (Tveskov and Rose 2019). The actual stories behind these places, and the people and relationships they formed, however, goes well beyond normalizing the colonial enterprises of the United States and Canada. More recent studies address the military's role in violence, alienation, social inequality, institutionalized racism, and environmental impacts on Indigenous peoples, and often illuminate ambiguous relations between settlers and soldiers (Barnes 2008; Tveskov and Cohen 2014, Tveskov and Rose 2019).

U.S. Fort Vancouver (1849–2012)

Fort Vancouver was the largest nineteenth-century military post in the Pacific Northwest, serving as the U.S. Army's headquarters for the Columbia District. The soldiers who served at Fort Vancouver were a diverse group, with substantial numbers emigrating from Germany, Ireland, and England, but usually led by American-born officers. The landscape of the post included (1) the quartermaster's depot in its southwestern corner at the main government wharf, (2) a main post area, and (3) an attached command for the Ordnance Department's Vancouver Arsenal on its eastern edges. The initial construction of the barracks and officers' quarters was wooden notched-log construction, and the commander's quarters, now referred to as the Grant House, is the only remaining standing structure from this earliest period. Over the history of the post, literally hundreds of structures were constructed, remodeled, and replaced.

For nearly fifty years, archaeologists have explored portions of the Vancouver Barracks site (45CL162) and other adjoining places, uncovering artifacts spanning precontact to the mid–twentieth century (Wilson et al. 2020). Cultural resources management drove most of the archaeology related to Vancouver Barracks, including substantial studies for highway work (Chance and Chance 1976; Chance et al. 1982; Carley 1982; O'Rourke et al. 2010; Thomas and Hibbs 1984). Other archaeology has assisted in the rehabilitation of infrastructure, historical buildings, and the military landscape (e.g., Cromwell et al. 2009; Cromwell et al. 2014; Horton and Wilson 2015; Langford and Wilson 2002; Thomas 1998). These studies documented military features and conducted detailed analyses of material culture chronology and typology (see chapter 2). Only a few researchers, however, have conducted academic research projects, including the exploration of ceramics found at the Sutler's Store and comparisons of Sutler's Store, Officers' Row (45CL160), and enlisted men's barracks (Horton 2014; Hosken 2023).

Field schools by Portland State University/Washington State University in 2007–2008 conducted some of the most extensive excavations on Officers' Row and the Vancouver Barracks (Horton 2014). Preceded by magnetic and GPR surveys, students excavated 50- × 50-centimeter shovel tests and 1- × 1-meter test units at an officers' quarters, kitchen, and yard, as well as an enlisted men's barracks, kitchen, and laundresses' areas. Documentary and archaeological remains explored the experiences of junior commissioned officers, noncommissioned officers, laundresses, and enlisted men who lived within a highly structured social and built environment (Horton 2014). The Army system intentionally created, transmitted, and enforced Victorian ideology through three levels of cultural space: the built environment, the household (barracks and officers' quarters), and the individual. Objects such as buildings, food, clothing, and personal objects distributed symbolically encoded information that communicated the military's cultural values. For example, the superior position of the officers' quarters to the enlisted men and laundresses reinforced the subservience of the latter, and the formal maintained parade ground with large flagstaff reinforced Victorian notions of gentility, cohesiveness, and masculinity within the highly gendered space. The evidence for chickens raised near the barracks kitchens (eggs and chicken were luxury foods) and alcohol bottles suggest some negotiation of these dominant ideologies by soldiers (Horton 2014).

In the central portion of Vancouver Barracks, archaeologists encountered the remains of the mid-nineteenth-century Sutler's Store (ca. 1850–1870), uncovering remnant pickets conforming to historical drawings of the facility, a privy filled with artifacts representing the Sutler's Store daily operations, and a mid-nineteenth-century sheet midden (Horton 2014; Hosken 2023). The archaeologists recovered more than 60,000 ca. 1850–1860 period artifacts. The presence of French-manufactured ceramics allowed Hosken (2023) to compare the retail operations of sutlers with soldiers' and officers' consumption, inferring how American nationalism is imperfectly reflected in ceramics that differed substantially from Hudson's Bay Company inventories.

Two other important early U.S. military posts tested by historical archaeologists are Fort Steilacoom (1849–1868) southwest of Tacoma, Washington, an important location during the Puget Sound Indian War, and Fort Stevens (1863–1947), one of the few coastal fortifications built in the West during the American Civil War (Avey 1986; Harrison 1979, 1988, 1990; Larson and Moura 1984; Uldall and Rooke 2016). Both posts exhibit considerable disturbance from later uses, but archaeologists have exposed some intact remains from both sites.

Rogue War Battlefields and Fort Lane (1853–1856)

Some of the most extensive historical archaeology of this period is tied to the Rogue War in southern Oregon. The Rogue War grew out of the chaos, lawlessness, and racial enmity arising from gold rushes in California and Oregon (Beckham 1971; Tveskov 2017, 2020a; Tveskov and Cohen 2014: 197; Utley 2003: 40–41). Influenced by the early colonial violence perpetrated on the Indigenous people of the Rogue Valley, including that of Ewing Young, bad relations only continued after the discovery of gold (Tveskov 2020b: 16–17; Tveskov and Cohen 2008: 16–17; see chapter 7). Violence between miners and Indigenous people led to the August 24, 1853, Battle of Evan's Creek, resulting in the negotiation of the 1853 Table Rock Treaty establishing the Table Rock Reservation along the Rogue River (Tveskov 2020b: 47–57). The U.S. Army created Fort Lane the same year to monitor that reservation. A year earlier, the Army established Fort Orford on the southwest Oregon coast to protect miners and settlers.

Unfortunately, violent clashes between Indigenous people and miners continued, leading to the October 8, 1855, incident where James A. Lupton, a delegate to the Oregon Territorial Legislature, led a band of "exterminator" vigilantes in attacking three Takelma Villages on the southeastern edge of the reservation (Tveskov 2015: 21–23). The Indigenous response to the Lupton Massacre was predictable, including reprisal attacks that spread across southwestern Oregon, including open warfare among many of the Indigenous groups, settlers, and the U.S. Army (Beckham 1971). Miners at the coast were besieged at a makeshift fort (Miners' Fort) in February 1856 after the U.S. military lost the Battle of Hungry Hill (October 25 to November 1, 1855) (Tveskov 2015, 2017). The Battle of Big Bend (May 27–28, 1856) ended the war, with many of the remaining Indigenous people displaced to the Grand Ronde Reservation, over 320 kilometers (199 miles) north (Tveskov 2018).

Historical archaeology by Southern Oregon University has demonstrated how the landscape of the Rogue War in southern Oregon "embroiled civilians as well as combatants in a complicated and ambiguous series of events that saw indigenous people fighting a guerilla campaign against the settlers and the U.S. Army" (Tveskov 2018: 4). Southern Oregon University researchers relocated the site of the Harris family cabin, whose men and boys were killed by Takelma and Shasta people on October 9–10, 1855, but whose women survived the attack. Tveskov (2020b: 3) argues that this event was fundamental in the later pioneer narrative used to explain the war, including a besieged "captivity narrative" that placed the ordeal of women at the center of the rationalization for settler colonialism. The historical, material, and anthropological record places the events of this action and the wider events of the Rogue War into context, juxtaposing the rationale for Indigenous retaliation against settlers with the landscape, events, and settler actions of this first phase of the Rogue War.

A small, nondescript roadside park on Highway 101, about 11 kilometers north of Gold Beach, provides another seminal place in the settler mythology of the Rogue War. Test excavations recovered the burned belongings of the John Geisel family, whose men and male children were killed on February 26, 1856, and women held hostage at the place formerly known as Elizabethtown (Tveskov et al. 2017). Besides fasteners and other hardware associated with the burned home, personal and domestic items include a spring scale; leaded pressed glass dish fragments; whiteware plate, saucer, and cup fragments; transferprinted sherds from dishes; glass beads; and buttons. These items, consistent with the belongings of a mining family, were partially melted, deformed, or burnt, likely in the fire that consumed the cabin. The project also sought to relocate other later nineteenth-century graves at the makeshift graveyard/former settlement, including, reportedly, the remains of fourteen Indigenous men killed by vigilantes in 1858, immediately after the Rogue War—retribution for the Geisel family massacre (Tveskov et al. 2017). The monumentation and preservation of the park is explicitly tied to the deaths of the Geisel family, for which the park is named, ignoring the reprisal massacre of Native Americans.

Silencing of the Indigenous voice of the Rogue War is not confined to the Geisel Monument. The obfuscation of the Battle of Hungry Hill (also known as the Battle of Grave Creek Hills), one of the first military engagements of the Rogue War, fits into a later nineteenth- and early twentieth-century frontier narrative where accounts mythologized the bravery of volunteer soldiers, or were simply silent (Tveskov 2015, 2018). Southern Oregon University and Indigenous researchers examined documentary and archaeological evidence from the poorly known battle (Tveskov 2015, 2018). At Hungry Hill, "Queen Mary," a daughter of Takelma leader Joseph Lane ("Tyee Joe"), defeated a superior American force of dragoons and volunteers. The documentary research indicates a significant U.S. defeat, partly related to technological issues of the trooper's firearms but also to the superior bravery and tactical skills of the Indigenous defenders. Later nineteenth-century narratives on the bravery of volunteers were more closely related to claims for federal payments and a desire to focus on the heroics of the combined American force at the expense of the historical reality of the ineffectiveness of both regulars and volunteers (Tveskov 2017).

On February 22, 1856, the lower Rogue River and southern Oregon coast people joined their Takelma and Shasta neighbors in revolt. After Gold Beach was overrun, over 120 settlers and a few Indigenous people were besieged in a small 35- × 21-meter earthen breastwork fort with bastions, called Miners' Fort (35CU241), near modern Otter Point State Park. Notably, Indigenous women who sought refuge with their settler husbands also played a crucial role in ransoming the survivors of the Geisel Massacre. Ironically, the besieged settlers segregated themselves by race and social class, with White women and their families, including the freed Geisel women, in the larger, northern cabin, and Indigenous women and their families in the southern cabin. Paradoxically, the single African American settler was killed by Indigenous fighters while trying to forage away from the fort. The fort was relocated using remote sensing and sampled to assess its extent and integrity (Tveskov 2021a; Tveskov et al. 2019). The agency of Indigenous women inside Miners' Fort is suggested by the discovery of a traditional camas-roasting hearth in the southern cabin. The abundance of lead shot and musket balls speak to the desperation of the settlers, and the hunger of the group is suggested by the relative dearth of any but the most highly fragmented and calcined animal bones (Tveskov 2021a; Tveskov et al. 2019). Miners' Fort embodies the complexity of the war revealed by historical archaeology and ethnographic context, contrasting with narratives that simplified the story and memorialized only White settlers.

While excavations at Fort Orford suggest that much of the site was destroyed by development of the modern city (Aikens et al. 2011: 273), Fort Lane is much better preserved and has been the subject of extensive archaeological study (figure 5.4). Fort Lane both preceded and formed a central operations center for the Rogue War. First tested by Goebel (1995), more extensive archaeological work has been conducted by Tveskov and colleagues. Using phenomenology and landscape-level analyses, historical archaeology has explored the significance and interpreted the ambiguity of the fort site and its role in settlement, suppression of Indigenous people, and the onset of modernity (Tveskov and Cohen 2008, 2014; Tveskov and Johnson 2014; Tveskov and Rose 2019). This small post hosted fewer than one hundred troopers of the First U.S. Dragoons and was abandoned in 1856 after the end of the Rogue War, following the incarceration and removal of Indigenous people to the Coast Reservation. As the first military post established in southern Oregon, Fort Lane was important on multiple levels, representing both a symbol of the "tyranny of the Federal government" over intrepid settlers and an arena for negotiating new social identities through interactions with soldiers, settlers, and Indigenous people (Tveskov and Cohen 2008, 2014; Tveskov and Rose 2019: 45). Excavations at the officers' quarters, barracks, kitchens, and outbuildings demonstrate the global connections to the post, with items transported from manufacturing and distribution centers of the Industrial Revolution over thousands of kilometers to San Francisco, and thence to southern Oregon. The development of a hierarchy of military status, examined through documentary and material records, describes the formulation of officer's identities in ways that would extend beyond their posting at Fort Lane. For example, George Crook was a lieutenant at the post, going on to serve on Ulysses S. Grant's staff during the Civil War, and afterward prosecuting the war against Crazy Horse and Geronimo in the southwest. Tveskov suggests that time at Fort Lane was a crucible for the formulation of a Western identity. Further, the ambiguity of relations with Indigenous people and settlers was reformed after the fact into a heroic Manifest Destiny narrative.

After the Battle of Hungry Hill, many of the Indigenous people retreated to fortified refuges in the rugged Rogue River Canyon. The Battle of Big Bend (35CU229) was fought between Indigenous forces under Tyee John of the Shasta and troops of the 1st Regiment of Dragoons and the 4th Infantry who had relieved Miners' Fort earlier that year (Applen 1997; Tveskov 2018, 2020a). A reinforced company of dragoons was besieged on a ridge near the Big Bend of the Rogue River before being relieved by a force of Infantry. Together, the troops drove the Indigenous combatants away from the battlefield. Studies by

Figure 5.4. Excavation of the enlisted men's barrack at Fort Lane with a Southern Oregon University archaeological field school, July 2012. Photo courtesy of the Sociology and Anthropology Program, Southern Oregon University.

Oregon State and Southern Oregon Universities recovered over one hundred items, including lead shot, conical rifle bullets, percussion caps, fragments of nipple picks used to clear the hole of a percussion firearm nipple/cone, a musket ball extractor, a ramrod, and lead slag (Applen 1997; Tveskov 2020a). The archaeologists also recovered a Zachary Taylor effigy pipe. Tveskov uses the spatial locations of these items, combined with the historical records, to reconstruct the battle (Tveskov 2020a).

The context of the war and its end is symbolized by the Tseriadun site, which is much older than the battles of the Rogue War, dating to at least 7,000 years ago. This site contains the earliest dated shell midden on the Oregon Coast and the remains of a later plankhouse village of the Athapaskan-speaking Qua-to-mah people. It demonstrates the long presence of Indigenous people on the landscape, but also the impacts of settler colonialism tied to the Rogue War (Cohen and Tveskov 2008). For just a short time between October 1855 and the summer of 1856, about 1,500 Native Americans were incarcerated there prior to their exile to the Coast Reservation. The sparse scatter of artifacts from that time includes black glass, five glass beads, and a

Queen Victoria effigy pipe bowl, an item that conveys the meanings behind "civilizing" the southern Oregon Native people, in this case embodied in their banishment.

Other landscapes of conflict explored by archaeologists include Fort Cascades (1855–1861) and Fort Lugenbeel (1856–1861) in the Columbia River Gorge, about 64 kilometers (just under 40 miles) upriver of Fort Vancouver (Beckham 1984). Historical archaeology at these posts, which were attacked, besieged, and relieved in Spring 1855 during the Yakima War, revealed structural remains and concentrations of belongings with significant impacts from the later Flood of 1894 (Minor and Beckham 1984, 1988).

San Juan Island Sites of the "Pig War" (1853–1874)

The historical archaeology of the San Juan Islands illustrates in a microcosm the nineteenth-century conflicts among nations arising from colonial settlement; lands that were solely Indigenous were appropriated for Hudson's Bay Company agricultural enterprise, and then to American settlement. That the killing of a pig (the namesake for the war) could have sparked a conflict between Great Britain and the United States, and resulted in a decades-long joint occupation of San Juan Island by both nations, is uniquely part of the American experience in the Pacific Northwest. Historical archaeology explores the complex story of fur traders and Indigenous people, the daily lives associated with two small military posts, and the role of American entrepreneurs in settlement (Sprague 1983).

The "war" was the last act of the dispute over the boundary of the United States and Great Britain. While in 1846, the 49th parallel was decided as the boundary between the two nations, the prolonged dispute over the San Juan Islands was due to the exception for Vancouver Island, which was retained in its entirety by Great Britain, and over which one of the three channels between this island and the mainland represented the international boundary (O'Gorman 1983). In 1853, Americans incorporated the San Juan Islands into Whatcom County, part of the newly formed Washington Territory. In response, Hudson's Bay Company Chief Factor James Douglas, also the Governor of Vancouver Island, established a sheep farm in the southern portion of the largest (and namesake) island. Attempts to levy taxes on the Hudson's Bay Company's sheep at Bellevue Farm by American customs inspectors were largely rebuffed, but with the 1856 discovery of gold in British Columbia (see chapter 7) and the consequent settlement of the Islands by Americans returning from the gold fields, friction culminated in the principal events of the dispute. As noted above, the sole casualty of the war was a Hudson's Bay Company pig, slaughtered in 1859 by an American settler named Lyman Cutler.

Figure 5.5. View of the Blockhouse, Parade Ground, and Garden at English Camp on San Juan Island.

Under the direction of Brigadier General William S. Harney, a company of American soldiers under Captain George E. Pickett occupied the Island under the guise of watching for Indigenous people from British Columbia, who would both raid colonial settlements and farms and visit relatives at tribal and settler villages. Pickett, who in just four years, and now a general, would command the ill-fated charge by the Confederates at the Battle of Gettysburg, imposed U.S. law on the Island. In response, a fleet of five British warships with over 2,000 men, including six hundred Royal Marines, stood directly off the Island, dwarfing the small but reinforced contingent of 461 American soldiers (Tyler 1976: 17). General Winfield Scott negotiated with Douglas the joint occupation of the island. Between 1860 and 1874, San Juan Island contained soldiers of both nations. In 1872, Kaiser Wilhelm I of Germany arbitrated the case in favor of the United States (O'Gorman 1983).

University of Idaho conducted extensive historical archaeology on San Juan Island for the National Park Service between 1970 and 1977, collecting over 300,000 artifacts (Sprague 1983). Students excavated at English Camp (45SJ24), the post for the British Royal Marines, in the northern unit of the park (figure 5.5), the Hudson's Bay Company's Bellevue Farm (45SJ295),

American Camp (45SJ300), and San Juan Town (45SJ290) in the southern unit. At the same time, excavations associated with precontact Native American sites were undertaken by University of Washington, becoming an important and well-reported archaeological project (Kenady 1973; Stein 1992, 2000; Taylor and Stein 2011). While the historical archaeology is limited to a series of University of Idaho manuscript series reports and two large summary volumes, these represent important and influential research (Sprague 1983).

Besides a documentary analysis of the location of the "pig" incident, excavations from 1973 and 1975 at Belleview Farm included tests of eight dwelling sites, a kitchen, a well, and the flag pole (Rossillon 1983; Sprague 1973). Excavations at English Camp, undertaken in 1970 and 1971, included exploration of areas underneath the historical commissary and barracks to aid in their reconstruction. Because the camp was placed on top of an Indigenous village and shell midden, the archaeologists uncovered abundant Native belongings including human remains of precolonial Native American people. They found a Salish-style longhouse underneath the commissary building. The students and staff collected artifacts from the beach, and excavated at the Officer's dump, plus at a range of building sites associated with the Royal Marine post.

American Camp was excavated in 1974–1976, with excavations at officers' row and the laundress quarters, hospital, barracks, sutler's building, and stockade. Research explored the documentary records of soldier's lives, describing the ammunition, clothing hooks, buckles, buttons, insignia, and other uniform accoutrements (Masich 1983a, 1983b). Nearby San Juan Town was surveyed in 1971, and excavated in 1972, exploring five depressions along the central roadway from the Hudson's Bay Company pier on Griffin Bay (Tyler 1976, 1983). The sites included a likely hotel, saloon or alcohol storeroom, a drug store, and a number of dwellings that dated to the Pig War period (Roenke 1983: 807; Tyler 1983). The intimate relationship of the town to the U.S. military post is correlated with the "surge of activity" associated with the sale of liquor, land sales, and prostitution, but when the camp was abandoned, the town also vacated to Friday Harbor (Frescoln 1975: 72).

Artifact summaries for the San Juan sites contributed to the growing data on material culture of the mid–nineteenth century, including studies of nails from English and American Camps (Bischof 1983); ceramics (Ferguson 1983a, 1983b, 1983c, 1983d, 1983e); bricks (Gurcke 1983); buttons (Roddy 1983); clay tobacco pipes (Pfeiffer 1983); hinges (Suckling 1983); and flat glass (Roenke 1983). Frescoln (1975) compared the bottle glass between English Camp and San Juan Town, noting the dominance of alcohol bottles at both the British Royal Marines garrison and the town that catered to the U.S. military. Perhaps not surprisingly, an exceptional number of Lea & Perrins Worcestershire Sauce bottles were found at the Officers' Quarters and Barracks at English camp, but quite a number of perfume bottles also were recovered at the Barracks, suggesting that women visited from San Juan Town. Czehatowski (1983) described the bottles from the American camp, confirming there the overall pattern of abundant alcohol consumption, particularly evident in the officers' quarters' privy.

The ceramic sherd assemblages from the San Juan sites were primarily earthenware, with the decorated wares dominated by transferprint designs (Ferguson 1983c). Components at the sites were identified using South's mean ceramic date formula, using maker's marks to assess date ranges, including later use of sites by settlers and caretakers (Ferguson 1983c: 775–784). Differences in taste (but also likely market access and nationalism) was responsible for the distinct differences in the American and British assemblages, with the occupants of English Camp and Belleview Farm owning large quantities of transferprint, shell edge, lusterware, and mochaware, with lower quantities of these types at American sites. American sites yielded higher proportions of hand-painted, glazed, and gilded wares (Ferguson 1983c: 769). While most of the decorated ceramics were manufactured by English potteries, American brands were more prevalent at the American sites. In contrast, numerous stoneware ale bottles at English Camp originated from the nearby Laumeister and Gowen brewery in Victoria (Ferguson 1983d). The Royal Marines at English Camp appear to have acquired Chinese and Japanese "quality" ceramics during their postings in Asia, including a few ceremonial bowls, tea cup, and rice and wine bowls (Ling 1983).

A novel analysis used behavioral and economic archaeology to explore how changing population size affected local, regional, and national/international markets associated with the materials found at the San Juan Island sites (Jones 1983). Until at least 1860, international markets dominated the assemblages, with most of the goods delivered directly by Hudson's Bay Company ships from England. During the Pig War period and after (1863 to 1888), regional trade grew important, after which national and international brands again dominate as the population of the Islands and west coast cities increased significantly after 1890 (Jones 1983: 862–867).

The historical archaeology excavations on San Juan Island complemented other contemporaneous large-scale projects, in particular those at Fort Colvile and Fort Vancouver, in describing and preliminarily interpreting nineteenth-century material culture, documenting Hudson's Bay Company sites, and exploring both British and American military camps. Sprague (1983: 872) suggests that explorations of the "Indian Camp" at Bellevue Farm (as well as the precontact sites) was an important future direction that "would lend an additional facet to the relationship of the native population to the Hudson's Bay Company and perhaps also to the American troops." Unfortunately, this significant lack of investment in Indigenous people, in particular the role of the Lummi, Clallam, and Saanich people, is the most glaring gap in understanding the Pig War from a historical archaeology perspective. Sprinkled throughout the reports are anecdotes regarding the importance of the relationships of Native American people to the settlement of the San Juan Islands and the war. For example, O'Gorman (1983) discusses the significance of raiding by "Northern Indians," including dictates to families at nearby Port Townsend to return "Northern Indian" mothers and wives to their northern villages, as these visiting Indigenous relatives were deemed causal to the conflict (O'Gorman 1983: 38). Tyler (1976: 18) briefly described the killing and robbing of a Haida man at San Juan Town as evidence of its "lawlessness," which resulted in the use of the American military to keep the peace. The occupation of the island by American settlers was bound to the population of miners returning from the Fraser River Gold Rush, suggesting that relationships tied to the extraction of mineral resources, and underlying Indigenous resistance, are at the heart of the conflict between Great Britain and the United States. Since the large studies in the 1970s and 1980s, cultural resources management work has sporadically explored many of the historical sites (e.g., Horton 2010, 2011a, 2011b; O'Rourke 2009; Wilson 2004).

Indian Reservation Forts and Communities

The new American Indian policy of the 1850s used the treaty process to place Indigenous people on Reservations, often in areas far from their homelands and the fertile agricultural lands coveted by American settlers (Tveskov and Cohen 2008: 2; Utley 2003: 35–63). The U.S. government "designed reservations as vehicles toward cultural erasure and implemented policies that compelled individuals to adopt settler practices and beliefs" (Kretzler 2019: 3). Military posts prevented Indigenous people from leaving reservations and guarded against settler encroachment. Fort Lane, discussed above, was one of these places, that then formed a base to prosecute the Rogue War and the exile of southern Oregon Native people. Archaeologists have tested a number of reservation-era forts, including Fort Umpqua (1856–1862), the southernmost military post guarding approaches to the Coast Reservation (Beckham 1990; Eichelberger 2014); Fort Simcoe (1856–1922) in central Washington on the Yakama Indian Reservation (Nagaoka 1990; Weeks 1962); and Fort Sherman (1878–1905) in Coeur d'Alene, Idaho (Sims 1982; University of Idaho 2021).

Besides Fort Umpqua, two other forts, Fort Hoskins and Yamhill, were built immediately after the Rogue War, in 1856, to guard the passes that led to the newly formed Coast Reservation. Historical archaeologists have explored Fort Hoskins and Fort Yamhill extensively, and together they provide a good set of examples of mid-nineteenth-century military forts in the Pacific Northwest. At this time, the frontier army was largely distrusted by American settlers and was spread very thinly across the west in seventy-four small posts in 1855, and 138 by 1857 (Bowyer 1992: 16; Rickey 1963: 26–28; Utley 1984: 40–41). The success of forts, whose role was to "protect" and "civilize" Indigenous people on Reservations, was uneven at best, but they form an intrinsic part of modern tribal history, albeit not usually a triumphal one. While Fort Umpqua was abandoned, Forts Yamhill and Hoskins continued to be garrisoned by volunteer troops from California, Oregon, and Washington (Eichelberger 2019b: 57). In some cases, Tribes have monitored or cooperated in archaeological projects. Most recently, Indigenous archaeology has been used to explore more than just the military posts to examine the early reservation settlements (Kretzler and Gonzalez 2021).

Fort Hoskins (1856–1865)

An enduring research question for nineteenth-century forts is how their spatial organization supported the hierarchical structure of the military, exploring how status, authority, and ideology is reflected in material culture differences between the enlisted men and officers. Fort Hoskins (35BE15) overlooks a bend in the Little Luckiamute River, about 16 kilometers northwest of Corvallis, Oregon. Research by Oregon State University has explored differences in personal and domestic items between officers and enlisted soldiers using the Sprague functional typology, and South's pattern analysis, to illuminate symbolic differences in military status, authority, and duty (Bowyer 1992). Historical documents suggest that the daily lives of the soldiers were similar to other American settlers, including land-clearing projects, constructing buildings and roads, and growing food. The small size of many U.S. Army posts required considerable effort to maintain and repair them, and also to feed the troops, leaving little time for training. Documentation of women at Fort Hoskins, including wives, laundresses, and visitors, contrasts with, and likely affected, the daily lives of the soldiers (Schablitsky 1996).

Excavation data from 1976 and 1977 compared officers' quarters, privies, and a dump with enlisted men's barracks and privies (Bowyer 1992). The officers' assemblage was dominated by domestic items, while the soldiers' assemblage contained more personal and military items, including many alcohol bottles and tobacco pipe fragments. The officers' assemblage held a greater variety of personal jewelry and grooming items, and objects related to recreation and pastimes. While part of this patterning was due to the presence of women and children in officers' houses, importantly, Bowyer (1992) explored the quantity of items, controlling for excavated space, noting that while similar quantities of artifacts were present in both officers and enlisted men's spaces, the officers and their families contained a much higher ratio of items to people, with only about one officer (with family members) to every twenty-eight soldiers.

Fort Yamhill (1856–1866)

Between 2004 and 2013, Oregon State University conducted archaeological field schools at the northernmost fort of the Coast Reservation, Fort Yamhill (35PO75), situated above Cosper Creek, on a height just north of the South Fork of the Yamhill River, about 1.6 kilometers east of the Grand Ronde Indian Agency. The Confederated Tribes of the Grand Ronde Community of Oregon (Grand Ronde) are the modern-day descendants. Work has surveyed and tested much of the site (e.g., Eichelberger 2011, 2014, 2019a, 2019b), and while recognizing the importance of the sites to the Tribe, has primarily collaborated with Oregon State Parks and Recreation. The fort's purpose was to monitor, police, and isolate the Coast Reservation inhabitants, supervising traffic in and out, preventing incursion by White Americans, and supporting the Indian Agents program to "civilize" through agricultural instruction and "cultural reformation" (Eichelberger 2019: 57; Kretzler 2019: 116–117).

Students excavated officers' quarters, the company kitchen, and the post bakery to explore food acquisition, preparation, and use at this remote post, far from the "Commissary of Subsistence" at Fort Vancouver. Analysis of over 1,000 animal bone and teeth fragments, combined with historical records, indicates that the standard ration was supplemented with local produce and animals from nearby farms and a garden and through hunting and fishing (Eichelberger 2011). Commissioned officers had access to more expensive and perishable items, including ham, dried fruit, milk, coffee, sugar, molasses, and superior whiskey. In addition, commissioned officers tended to have greater access to chicken and meat from beef forequarters.

In-depth analysis compared captains with subaltern lieutenants at both Fort Yamhill and Fort Hoskins to examine rank-based status inequality, finding that the increased authority and economic status of captains led to larger yards, more outbuildings, special architectural features, like bay windows, and quarters farther from barracks, stables, and the blacksmith shop (Eichelberger 2019a, 2019b). Captains had the best overall views of the post, although like at Fort Vancouver, all commissioned officers maintained superior topographic positions compared with enlisted men. Likewise, captains purchased more items overall, and those tended to be of higher social and economic status, with greater numbers of expensive porcelains, gilded and transfer-printed ceramics, cut glassware, matched dish sets, and a much wider range of dining vessel forms, suggestive of a "formal and genteel dining behavior associated with high status" (Eichelberger 2019b: 363). With some exceptions, captains had larger quantities and higher-preference butcher cuts for pork, beef, and venison, than lower-ranked officers. They controlled more high-end alcohol, including champagne, had specialized glassware to drink it out of, and smoked tobacco from fancier tobacco pipes of porcelain and hard rubber. Captain's quarters also contained more expensive gilt and nonregulation buttons, insignia, weapons, and accoutrements that could represent trophies, mementos, or souvenirs, or perhaps an ability to break from some military dress regulations. They contained more medical items, grooming items, and personal adornment items, and more and higher-quality toys for their children. The evidence suggests that higher-graded and -ranked officers used their increased compensation to consume leisure products and engage in conspicuous consumption (Eichelberger 2019a, 2019b).

Some of the most recent work in the vicinity of Fort Yamhill has shifted focus from the White European American soldiers and officers to the Indigenous people who they were protecting and oppressing. Between 2015 and 2018, archaeological field schools from University of Washington partnered with the Grand Ronde Tribe to explore survivance, placing Indigenous interests and participation in the foreground of the work to condition how the archaeological project was constructed (Gonzalez et al. 2018; Gonzalez and Edwards 2020; Kretzler 2019; Kretzler and Gonzalez 2021). Kretzler (2019), in particular, employed multi-phase, low-impact methods to explore the Umpqua and Molalla encampments in the valleys around Fort Yamhill directly after establishment of the Coast Reservation. For the Umpqua encampment, which rested on a terrace above the Yamhill River, the field school employed aerial photography, auger survey, and metal detection, finding over 350 belongings. These were characterized by mixed periods and included tin can fragments and porcelain from the later nineteenth and twentieth centuries, and glass beads and lithic debitage associated with the earlier reservation-era encampment. The site of the Molalla Encampment is at the contemporary Pow Wow grounds on the edge of Cosper Creek, near Fort Yamhill. Using aerial photography, ground-penetrating radar, controlled surface collection, auger testing, and fifteen larger test units, the students and staff found a few fur trade–era glass beads, while a worked amethyst glass fragment is suggestive of lithic tool practices extending to glass materials in the later nineteenth century (Kretzler 2019). Wire nails and ceramics, including later nineteenth- and twentieth-century styles, dominated the assemblage, and most artifacts date to the Dawes Act allotment and post-allotment period (1890–1940), associated with the construction of Western-style structures. A few objects were tied to the modern Pow Wow grounds, including modern tent stakes, contemporary food remains, modern plastic and glass beads, and a friendship bracelet.

Substantial numbers of lithic debitage at both the Mollala and Umpqua encampments suggest that early reservation period people continued production of expedient stone tools. Fire-cracked rock suggests the presence of traditional hearths, and resource procurement likely included both wild plant gathering and animal husbandry. The traditional expedient tools were likely essential during the early (and difficult) reservation period, but also may have "reiterated connections to historically meaningful, storied landscapes off-reservation" (Kretzler 2019: 292). The University of Washington's work at Grand Ronde is important, as it shifts focus from predominantly White military communities to the communities that the forts were built to control. Like the work by Southern Oregon University, collaboration with Indigenous communities allowed raising of important questions that bring a Native American presence and authority to the work (see chapter 9).

The historical archaeology of early settler communities and U.S. Army forts reveal the nuances associated with Indigenous–White relations and provide a materialist window on the imposition of Victorian structures on the social, Indigenous, and fur trade landscapes. In the next chapter, I turn to the exploration of these processes associated with the commemoration of death and treatment of the dead.

6

Death, Burial, and Commemoration in the Pacific Northwest

Forbes and Maria Pambrun Barclay's headstones rest at Mountain View Cemetery in Oregon City, Oregon (figure 6.1). Barclay, a Scottish immigrant, was the surgeon at Hudson's Bay Company's Fort Vancouver between 1840 and 1850, and later became an important citizen of Oregon City, including school superintendent, mayor, and an investor in the Oregon City Woolen Mills (Lange 1935; Lomax 1931). Many things are notable in examining the graves of this Oregon couple. First, like many Victorian-era monuments of the West and elsewhere (Curl 1975; Francaviglia 1971: 507; Hawker 1987), the iconography is decidedly classical Greek and Christian. The broken column signifies untimely death and is a masonic symbol, consistent with Barclay's participation in Multnomah Lodge No. 84, the first masonic lodge in Oregon. The people of Oregon City purchased through subscription an Italian marble monument on a base of Oregon City basalt. The epitaph inscribes his profession, place of origin, and his honoring by the townspeople (figure 6.1). Maria's headstone is in the form of a book, representative of the bible, and on her epitaph is her relationship to Forbes, place of origin, and a biblical verse (figure 6.1, inset). These grave markers embody the esteem this family held amongst their peers, their associations with Christian and Masonic beliefs, and their extensive social networks. The *Oregonian* newspaper published lengthy obituaries extolling their contributions to the pioneer period. Like other important early settlers, their deaths are tied to a pattern of veneration that began in the year of Forbes's passing in 1873 with the creation of the Oregon Pioneer Association, and coinciding with widespread economic downturns in the economy (Boag 2014). It continues today with the preservation of the Barclays' home by the National Park Service.

While many things are represented on these grave markers, many others are absent. Not revealed is that Maria was part Cree and that both she and her husband spent much of their lives at Hudson's Bay Company posts literally surrounded by Native American people, Native Hawaiians, and people of mixed descent. Ms. Barclay is represented as a wife, but the stone is moot (as

Figure 6.1. Headstones of Forbes and Maria Barclay at Mountain View Cemetery, Oregon City, Oregon.

is her husband's) on her many children, including those who died in infancy (although some are memorialized in the family plot), and her many female connections across the Oregon territory. The Barclays' history crossed two distinctive immigrant worlds—that of the British colonial fur trader and that of the American settler. The statements of their life reflected in their cemetery monuments are strongly tied to the latter, contrasting equally strongly in the silences of the former, and the underlying Native American origins of Maria's family. In this case, the monumental art envisages the social and economic values of a U.S. colonizer, silencing their longer histories and denying any form of Indigenous persistence.

Since the beginnings of the discipline, historical archaeologists have known that cemeteries and grave markers contain valuable information about people (Baugher and Veit 2014). Gravestones and monuments are spatially constrained, material statements of what those who installed them believed about death, and what they wanted others to know about the deceased, their families, and their communities. As Baugher and Veit (2014: 2) suggest, grave markers, "are the ultimate historical artifact: they are part material culture and part document." However, the anthropological and historical study of the deceased and the sacred places where they are interred and memorialized is highly sensitive and controversial. In particular, the study of human remains in burials is a Western cultural endeavor that started with some of the first settlements on the East Coast of North America, and continued by archaeologists and other scholars throughout the eighteenth, nineteenth, and twentieth centuries (Baugher and Veit 2014: 18–24). These excavations of burial places disproportionately targeted Native Americans, the poor, and disenfranchised. In the Pacific Northwest, like other places in North America, there is a long tradition of excavating and studying burials of precontact Native Americans to explore time–space systematics and subjects like status and wealth, identity, and custom (e.g., Brown 1971; Kroeber 1927). For some who hold strong and close beliefs about the dead and ancestors, these former and sometimes ongoing academic practices are hurtful, sacrilegious, and traumatic. In this chapter, I discuss the historical archaeology of burials and cemeteries in the Pacific Northwest. In doing so, my aim is to respect the deceased whose remains and monuments are studied, and indirectly, their families and those who are otherwise connected to burial places by heritage, belief, and emotion. An anthropological examination of cemeteries often addresses historical processes and trends in burial customs and how people are remembered. In some cases, as discussed below, archaeological work can help to heal divisions and trauma caused by past events and actions. In this chapter, I seek to mediate, however imperfectly, between those who are interested in the history and heritage of the people who reside in the Pacific Northwest and those who revere burial places for their religious and ancestral values.

Changing Studies of Cemeteries in the Pacific Northwest

Much of the scholarly work on cemeteries, and in particular grave markers, has taken place on the east coast of the United States. Baugher and Veit (2014) in fact do not mention the Pacific Northwest except for studies of Chinese American grave markers and cemeteries. Like other areas of North America (Baugher and Veit 2014: 126), the study of nineteenth- and twentieth-century grave markers in the Pacific Northwest has been conducted by a variety of scholars besides archaeologists, including historians, folklorists, cultural geographers, and art historians.

A fundamental transition in Western-style burial practices occurred during this period in the Pacific Northwest, from burying grounds associated with missionaries and graveyards at fur trade posts, and isolated burials along major routes of travel, to family graveyards on farms (Coates 1987: 12; Connolly et al. 2010; Francaviglia 1971: 505). The rural cemetery movement, which began in the eastern United States in the 1830s (Baugher and Veit 2014: 128–133; Sachs 2013: 21–26), did not emerge in the Pacific Northwest until the mid–nineteenth century, often correlated with rapidly expanding cities (e.g., Hawker 1987: 19). The rural cemetery, starting with Boston's Mount Auburn, integrated burials with natural features and vegetation in park-like settings to create a refuge from rapidly industrializing cities (Sachs 2013). Straus (2018: 27) posits that the timing of colonial settlement of the Oregon Country led to an "odd conceptual place" between burying ground, rural cemetery, and commercial park cemetery. Emulation of the great cemeteries of the East, and the rehabilitation and ritual reburial of certain Oregon pioneers, was tempered by the abundance of rural spaces and a desire to create a "well maintained and beautifully landscaped escape *from* the wild" (Straus 2018: 64). By the late nineteenth century, many of the patterns seen across the United States and Canada (Baugher and Veit 2014) appear in the Pacific Northwest.

Excavation of Contact-Period Native American Graves

Like elsewhere, archaeologists in the Pacific Northwest have exhumed, examined, and collected the human remains of Indigenous people and the objects, belongings, and offerings deposited in their graves. The primary motivation for this work was to better understand burial traditions of Native American people, and yet, as noted above, excavation of graves is highly controversial, heightened by the past practices of archaeologists who were not always self-reflexive or sensitive to the concerns of descendant groups (see Baugher and Veit 2014: 18–24). Native American graves were routinely excavated without sanction by descendant communities throughout the region until the passing of NAGPRA in 1990 (e.g., Collier et al. 1942; Cressman 1933; Laughlin 1941; Lewis 2017; Smith and Fowke 1901; Strong et al. 1930; Woodward 1977). While the emphasis of most of this work was on Native American burial practices prior to contact with European Americans, primarily to address ques-

Figure 6.2. Phoenix buttons recovered from the Fort Vancouver village. *Upper left and bottom*, FOVA10931, *left*, FOVA10932, *right*, FOVA10933. These belongings were *not* found in a grave or burial context. Photo courtesy of the National Park Service.

tions of culture history, some burials contained European-manufactured objects left as offerings to or the possessions of the deceased. The archaeologists studied these to establish a baseline to compare with ethnographic studies. For example, Strong et al. (1930: 64–65) collected historic-period belongings from graves they excavated on Miller's Island in the Columbia River at the mouth of the Deschutes, including metal buttons, copper beads, bracelets, rings, pendants, wire, iron artifacts, and glass beads. One burial contained a phoenix button, which suggested to these early twentieth-century excavators that the grave was less than a hundred years old (figure 6.2). Phoenix buttons are flat and ball-shaped cupreous buttons with the image of a phoenix, a regimental number, and the words *Je Renais de Mes Cendres* (I am reborn from my ashes). William Bushby of London apparently manufactured the buttons for King Christophe of Haiti, but they were likely never delivered (Sprague 1998; Strong 1960, 1975). While phoenix buttons are found rarely across most of North America, Nathanial Wyeth brought them to the lower Columbia River in large numbers and traded them to Indigenous people from Fort William on Sauvies Island around 1832–1833. The inventory was later purchased by the Hudson's Bay Company and traded widely throughout the Columbia District through Fort Vancouver and its subsidiary posts.

The early archaeological excavators of graves rarely commented on descendant communities except as informants. With respect to burial cairns of southeast Vancouver Island, the San Juan Islands, and Whidbey Island, Smith and Fowke (1901: 55) suggest that "the Indians have no historic tradition as to their origin." In contrast, Lewis (2017) uncovered a newspaper report on the resistance maintained by members of the Grand Ronde Reservation to the excavation of a cemetery mound in the Tualatin area of the Willamette Valley. A. M. Brumback of McMinnville College excavated the mound with students in 1900, collecting belongings, including at least one phoenix button. Another news story suggested that Indigenous descendants actively tried (unsuccessfully) to prevent desecration of this cemetery.

Some work was necessitated by the construction of dams that threatened to inundate burial areas (e.g., Chance and Chance 1985b: 227–236). Sprague's (1967) examination of the ca. 1850–1910 Palus burial site (45FR36-B) was conducted at the request of the Nez Perce Tribe because the cemetery was threatened by the creation of Lake Sacajawea and construction of Lower Monumental Dam. Comparison of eighty known contact-period and later historical burial sites on the Plateau suggested that burial practices changed rapidly during the protohistoric and early colonial periods, associated with a variety of styles (Sprague 1967: 213–215, 1968). By 1850, the Palus, and other Indigenous people of the Plateau, adopted many Western-style practices, including dominant use of wooden coffins, but with abundant grave offerings. Of the 249 burials (260 people) in the Palus burial site, only twenty-one were not buried in wooden coffins (Sprague 1967).

Another wide-ranging study examined copper tube beads, pendants, and other copper items in Indigenous burial sites across the Pacific Northwest using morphological and trace element chemical analyses (Stapp 1984). The analysis suggested that the primary sources of copper in the region were from the maritime fur trade, with most post-dating 1790, when the trading at the mouth of the Columbia ramped up. Burials within the Lower and Upper Columbia River regions contained the highest numbers of copper artifacts, likely associated with the two Indigenous trading centers at The Dalles and Kettle Falls. Copper tube beads, pendants, and bracelets were found in male, female, adult, and children's burials, suggesting that certain important men and their families were able to accumulate copper wealth. Changes in Indigenous cultures associated with the introduction of horses and increased fur trade contacts likely influenced the shift toward increased copper wealth (Stapp 1984).

While some early archaeologists engaged with Tribes and First Nations (e.g., Folan and Dewhirst 1980; Sprague 1967), it was not until Native Americans began actively protesting archaeological fieldwork in the 1960s and '70s, that archaeologists began documenting their efforts at tribal outreach and partnering, including those in the Pacific Northwest (e.g., Sprague 1974). With the advent of NAGPRA, it became a requirement for agencies to consult with Tribes on the excavation of human remains, funerary offerings, other sacred objects, and objects of cultural patrimony on Federal lands, and to work toward repatriating the collections of skeletal materials and related objects held in federally funded museums to culturally affiliated descendants (Baugher and Veit 2014: 25–29; Sprague 1993; Stark 2016). Given the quantity of materials exhumed and collected, the repatriation process continues as old collections are reanalyzed and curators address more recent regulations associated with culturally unaffiliated remains.

Early Colonial Burials

Most fur trade burials were located within or near the forts, with the burial of Jacques Raphael (Jaco) Finlay an exceptional example. Finlay was the son of a founder of the Northwest Company, James Finlay, and a Chippewa woman. Jacques was educated and served as a clerk for the Northwest Company, building Spokan House in 1810 (Watson 2010: 53, 373–374; see chapter 3). After the merger of the Northwest Company and Hudson's Bay Company, he was a freeman (independent trader), although he worked for the Hudson's Bay Company at times. His final days were spent at Fort Spokane, remaining there after the Hudson's Bay Company moved to Fort Colvile in 1826. Finlay died on May 20, 1828, and at his request was buried in one of the fort's bastions. Caywood (1954a: 20–23) describes Finlay's burial, which was uncovered during the 1951 excavations. A wooden coffin manufactured with nails was placed under some large flat rocks just six inches below the ground surface. Jacques was laid out with his head to the southeast and buried with five smoking pipes of various materials, along with a bone comb, a piece of writing slate, a hunting knife and sheath, fragments of a pair of spectacles, an iron cup, and three metal buttons associated with the remains of a coat. That it was Finlay's grave is documented in the historical record, and this was one reason why later travelers found the bastion still standing after Spokane people scavenged the rest of the fort for firewood, but respected the burial place (Caywood 1954a: 8–10). After his remains were stored at a local museum for over twenty years, Finlay's descendants (from a prodigious family that started with 3 wives and 19 children) requested his reburial, and he was reinterred at Fort Spokane in 1976, but the eighty-eight funerary items recovered were not repatriated to family members until 2015 (Courchane nd; O'Brien 2015). For those sites that became villages, towns, and cities, often the early fur trade graveyards were lost within the street grid of rapidly expanding urban areas. For example, the early Fort Astoria/Fort George Cemetery was absorbed into the street grid east of the fort's location, resulting in inadvertent finds of human remains and reports of burials (Penner 1993).

In contrast to the extensive archaeological excavation of Indigenous burials, researchers have noted that Oregon Trail pioneer burials are understudied (Binder 2011: 2; Blatt et al. 2017; Straus 2018: 6–7). Binder's (2011) review of nineteenth-century burial practices in the eastern U.S., and Oregon-California Trail diaries and letters, countered the myth that the emigrants were exposed to such high rates of death along the trail that they became detached from it, leading to expeditious disposal of the body in hasty and shallow graves. Her research suggests that "emigrant deaths could not be separated from the ritualized mourning practices of the nineteenth century" (Binder 2011: 55). Death along the trail was often associated with ceremonies, singing, and the placement of grave markers. Caskets were made from available materials, including storage boxes, pieces of furniture, or tree trunks cut into boards or hollowed out to hold the body. The bodies were usually wrapped in bedsheets, quilts, or other fabric, and markers were constructed from wooden boards, sandstone slabs, and in one case, an iron wagon wheel hoop (Binder 2011: 46–48). Commonly, emigrants noted a fear of disturbance by wolves or even Indigenous people scavenging the dead person's clothing. Sometimes emigrants hid graves by running wagons over the site or keeping the oxen paddocked over them.

A famous Oregon Trail grave site is of the pioneer woman's grave on the Barlow Road segment on Mt. Hood (figure 6.3). A rock cairn marks the site that rests on the south side of old Highway 35 at the western base of Barlow Pass just south of the East Fork of the Salmon River. Discovered by workers in 1924 while constructing the Highway 35 Mount Hood Loop, they exhumed from a wagon box the remains of a woman, which they reburied nearby, constructing a cairn of rocks to mark the site. While virtually nothing else is known about this woman, her discovery, anonymity, and reburial coincided with increased publicity about memorializing the Oregon Trail, striking a nerve that continues today. Because of its proximity to the Portland metropolitan area and the improvement of the highway that followed the Barlow Road, many who traveled and recreated on Mt. Hood have visited the site, and it has been maintained and interpreted since its discovery. A wooden cross was placed in 1924, later replaced by a bronze Daughters of the American Revolution (DAR) plaque (1936), a large, rustic, wooden marker (1930s),

Figure 6.3. Unknown Pioneer Woman's Grave with modern grave offerings on Mt. Hood, September 24, 2016. Memorial plaque in inset.

a second DAR bronze plaque to replace the first (1982), and a sequence of interpretive markers, most focusing on Barlow's history of establishing the route (U.S. Forest Service 1991). The significance of this monument is not in its scientific value to historical archaeology or as a means to address gender, health, or Oregon Trail burial practices, but in its simple monumentality and the reverence that continues to be afforded to Pioneer settlers in the American West. Visiting hikers continue to place offerings at the grave site, continuing a centuries-old emotional connection by many to Oregon Trail emigrants.

One of the few published forensic examinations of Oregon pioneers explored the burial practices and human remains of a settler family in western Oregon, in the southern portion of the Willamette Valley (Connolly et al. 2010). Exposed during the construction of a hospital in Springfield, Oregon, archaeologists excavated twelve grave sites within the forgotten burial ground. The family cemetery dated to between ca. 1854 and 1879, and while only four intact burials were found, many grave items and even human remains were found in the other grave sites. Forensic and documentary analysis of the Springfield human remains suggests high infant mortality and adults who died in their forties and fifties, with the matriarch dying at seventy-two.

Connolly et al. (2010: 39) tie infant mortality to the "difficult realities of life on the frontier," partly explained by the scarcity of health care. Increasing ornamentation in the burials is somewhat delayed from patterns recorded in the east. The increased elaboration expresses the Victorian idea of the "beautification of death," and the simplicity of earlier burials is likely due to the isolation of the settlers on a "remote frontier" (Connolly et al. 2010: 43–44). This simplicity diverges from the increasing availability of mass-produced funerary items in later burials tied to national trends in protestant Christian burial practices. Connolly et al.'s (2010) work is important as they seek to explain why the graveyards and cemeteries in the Pacific Northwest, and other areas of the Western United States and Canada, developed differently from the East. A more youthful population and limited access to commercial markets and health care in the early decades of settlement appear to have altered the character of the early settler communities and their burial practices.

In the Pacific Northwest, collective memory of the stressful period of warfare between Indigenous people and American settlers is tied to the establishment and memorialization of the dead. The 1856 massacre of John Geisel and his three young sons at the former mining encampment of Elizabethtown became the impetus for a small community graveyard that became a state park in 1930 (Tveskov et al. 2017). As noted in chapter 5, the remains were burned in the homestead by Indigenous combatants, and the headstone, placed shortly afterward, reads: "Sacred to the Memory of John Geisel. Also, his three Sons John Henry & Andrew. Who were Massacred by the Indians Feb. 22, A.D. 1856. Aged respectively 45. 9. 7. & 5 years." Sadly, the nineteen Indigenous men and boys massacred in 1858 at the same graveyard in retribution for the killings are unmarked (Tveskov et al. 2017).

In contrast to the Pioneer Women's grave on Mount Hood, the burials of two anonymous women at Walters Ferry (10CN140), on the Snake River south of Nampa, Idaho, illuminate issues of gender, health, and work in the late nineteenth century (Blatt et al. 2017). Walters Ferry was an important crossing tied to the Boise–San Francisco stage route. The individuals were interred in wooden coffins made with machine-cut nails and wood screws, oriented north–south with the crania toward the river. Swallows had disturbed portions of the coffins, found in shallow graves (80 and 120 cm below surface). Osteobiological measurements suggest that both were European women, one over thirty and the other between thirty-nine and fifty-nine years old. Grave items included rivets and iron loops, China (prosser) and plastic buttons from clothing, red ribbon, and the remains of mid-calf leather boots with gray woolen socks. Fragments of a newspaper clipping were from an article dating to no earlier than December 25, 1888. The investigators suggest the clothing was "masculine, work-worthy" and both women's skeletons exhibited disease and trauma, including fractured ribs, bone spurs, a crushing injury to one of the women's feet, chronic infection, and degenerative diseases, suggestive of the hard-working lives of European American women in the late nineteenth century (Blatt et al. 2017: 16).

Dental hygiene is another health-related issue of nineteenth-century settlers. Exhumation of four individuals from the ca. 1880–1903 Sandpoint, Idaho, cemetery included a child, a young adult, a middle-aged adult, and an older adult. Except for the child, all contained numerous dental caries, and all exhibited calculus and abnormal bone loss around the tooth cavities. The middle-aged and older individuals exhibited dental wear suggesting routine clay tobacco pipe smoking (Brown 2014).

Grave Marker Studies in the Pacific Northwest

Researchers in the Pacific Northwest have sporadically studied grave markers. Richard Francaviglia, a cultural geographer, explored five Oregon cemeteries in the southern portion of the Willamette Valley, comparing them to cemeteries in Minnesota, Wisconsin, and New York (Francaviglia 1971). His analysis indicated that the cemeteries were miniaturized versions of the architecture, settlement patterns, and landscapes of the communities of which they were a part. All of Francaviglia's cemeteries were developed by White protestants from the American Midwest who primarily emigrated to the Willamette Valley between the 1850s and 1880s. Defining nine categories of markers and considering spatial organization, Francaviglia contrasted the change in styles and size of headstones through time over four periods:

> Pioneer Period (1850–1879) dominated by American gothic revival styles, including tablet, block, and pointed arch forms, limited ornamentation, and simple inscriptions, with grid patterns.
> Victorian Period (1880–1905) characterized by ornate architectural styles and patterns introduced from the eastern United States, including classical architectural styles, obelisks and columns, wrought-iron enclosures for family plots, and the peak of separation of rich from poor in space and elaboration.
> Conservative Period (1906–1929) characterized by a change toward simple geometric forms, like the rounded scroll, slant pulpit, and block forms. The height of the monuments decreased, and there was less distinction in class or wealth.

Modern Period (1930–1970) continued the simplification of markers and a shift toward greater emphasis on the landscape, with raised top monuments becoming lower, and with more markers flush to the ground. The graveyards shift away from the grid style to more curved roads and paths.

Francaviglia, like Deetz (1996), suggested that deeply ingrained cultural structures (*genre de vie*) reflect the overall plan of the cemeteries and their markers. The Willamette Valley cemeteries were similar to those in the Midwest and eastern United States, but lagging in time.

In contrast, the diverse environment and settlement in southern British Columbia resulted in greater diversity in cemetery landscapes (Coates 1987: 12; Philpot 1976). A reconnaissance of fifteen smaller cemeteries (fewer than 1,000 graves per cemetery) across the lower portion of British Columbia, with sampling of grave markers in ten cemeteries that dated between 1850 and 1925, confirmed Francaviglia's pattern of peak monumentality in the late nineteenth century and a shift toward less elaboration after 1915 (Philpot 1976). While only the Ross Bay Cemetery in Victoria approached the Victorian ideal landscape, small cemeteries from agrarian communities on the lower Fraser River Valley and Saanich peninsula contained more "settled" burial grounds. These exhibited more of the elaboration associated with the Victorian ideal in both cemetery landscape and burial ritual, with physical separation of rich and poor. Cemeteries in the interior, associated with mining boom and bust cycles, were less elaborate because the towns did not last long, the large numbers of young men who lived in them were far from their families, and those who died and their surviving friends had less ability to pay for elaborate ceremonies (Philpot 1976). Notably, the modern appearance and experience of visiting these cemeteries also differed, suggesting that the better-kept cemeteries in agrarian areas resulted from the stability of the communities. The burial grounds of the interior were not well tended because their descendants were not local and the turnover in settlers led to neglect and erasure of social memory (Philpot 1976).

Study of the Pioneer Square and Ross Bay cemeteries of Victoria, British Columbia, exhibit a shift in form from classical and Egyptian revival, Gothic, and Picturesque-inspired natural forms, to more eclectic, mixed forms of the High Victorian style in the latter part of the nineteenth century (Hawker 1987). The dramatic increase in monuments is correlated with the increase in population after the gold rush of 1858, and the dramatic increase in shipping and commerce as the city developed. Many of the later nineteenth-century monuments of Ross Bay exhibit the impact of catalogs, pattern books, and imported, mass-produced headstones. Further exploration of larger urban centers in British Columbia suggests that the shift from burial grounds within the city to larger civic cemeteries on the outskirts of the city was due to changing conceptions of aesthetics and sanitation during the time of the miasmic theory of disease (Coates 1984, 1987). The shift from more elaborate Victorian burials to smaller markers and eventually flat markers in these urban cemeteries is associated with contemporaneous critiques of the Victorian era, as well as changing perceptions of health and death. With the introduction of germ theory and modern medicine, life expectancies increased. People began to loathe living adjacent to cemeteries due to their now depressing emphasis on death, and the likelihood that residents might happen upon what was now an uncomfortable burial ceremony. The shift toward more park-like settings with easier-to-maintain monuments is perhaps associated with shifts in twentieth-century economics and conceptions of land value. Exploring the decrease in death rates attributed to modern medicine, Coates (1984: 33) notes that "where individuals were once content to entrust their fate to God, increasingly, their medical fate became their own responsibility."

The nineteenth-century burial ritual in British Columbia (and likely elsewhere in the Pacific Northwest) created cohesion among family members, and selected community members, while emphasizing social distinctions tied to class (Coates 1984: 61–62). Religious and ethnic distinctions created in the earliest cemeteries, however, were maintained through the early twentieth century, with Chinese, Japanese, East Indian, and other ethnic and racial classes relegated to the least desirable parcels (Coates 1987). The emphasis on uniformity of monumentation and de-emphasis of death led to the modern trend toward cremation and a shift from the celebration of death in the Victorian cemeteries of major cities toward an intellectualization of death, including the hiding of death, while emphasizing direct individual connections to the deceased.

Farther south, surveys of hundreds of "pioneer" cemeteries in Oregon confirm increased Victorian elaboration found elsewhere but also demonstrate the attention paid to hazards attendant upon Oregon settlers, including accidents and violence, but also celebrating the Oregon Trail experience (Meyer 1990). For example, many graves list typhoid or small pox as causes of death for adults, and scarlet fever and diphtheria for children, with in some cases as many as six children dying within a few months of each other (Meyer 1990: 95). Death by violence associated with Indigenous people is included on some monuments, such as the Geisel grave site noted above, and many define their occupant's state of origin and the iconic covered wagon as emblematic of the deceased's emigration credentials. More recent mid- to late-twentieth-century grave markers of loggers also emphasize hardships and dangers, in this case of the logging profession (Meyer 1992). Imagery, inscriptions, and materials (carved wood) reflect the primarily male logging profession, including elements such as hard hats, "corked" boots, axes, chainsaws, and even truck rigs, along with logging-related epitaphs on the gravestones. These masculine visual representations of equipment, and activities of logging with their related epitaphs, have been termed "occupational folklore," suggesting they "serve to reinforce the pride, self-identity, and worldview associated with members of this occupational folk group" (Meyer 1992: 64).

Religion and ethnic identity are other important considerations in explaining grave markers. Historical archaeology of two Catholic cemeteries associated with St. Paul, Oregon, explore how religious iconography and attention to family is demonstrated on pre-1905 grave markers (Boulware 2008). At St. Paul, one of the earliest settler communities on French Prairie, ethnic identity is subservient to Catholic identity, but Irish American immigrants emphasized more ostentatious grave displays than earlier French Canadian/Métis families (Boulware 2008: 108). While motif, markers, and inscriptions reflect Catholic ideology, they also contain inscriptions that trumpet pioneer origins (Boulware 2008: 66). Differences in elaboration and display of Irish American versus French Canadian/Métis markers suggest that in the rapidly settled Willamette Valley, the French Canadian/Métis population was increasingly isolated and marginalized as non-White "others" affiliated more closely with Native American populations, while Irish American settlers intentionally exploited Victorian ideology to compete with their French Canadian/Métis neighbors (Drew 2010).

Researchers have explored the documentary record of early cemeteries of Portland and Salem, Oregon, contrasting the veneration of pioneers and movements to rebury pioneers in Salem's rural cemeteries, with neglected and poorly managed cemeteries for the poor and disadvantaged, including the State Asylum and Willamette Mission cemeteries (Straus 2018). The 1904 exhumation of Jason Lee from Stanstead, Quebec, Canada, where he had been buried in 1845, and his triumphal reburial in 1906 at Salem's Jason Lee cemetery after journeying 4,800 kilometers (2,982 miles), reflected the culmination of the reinterpretation of Lee as a colonizing force. Notably, about the same time that Lee was buried in Quebec, Anna Maria Pittman Lee and Cyrus Shepard were moved from the Mission Bottom cemetery to Salem, but leaving all the deceased Native American children behind.

Portland, Oregon's earliest cemeteries were very haphazard and poorly managed, with many grave sites lost through time. Early graveyards quickly became absorbed into the city under rapid urbanization and poor city management, leading to inadvertent discoveries of human remains in the older portions of Portland, and land disputes over the old Portland city cemetery (Straus 2018). Private interests more successfully developed the 1855 Lone Fir and 1879 Riverview cemeteries. The connection of larger, more formal cemeteries by nongovernmental interests, such as Salem's Odd Fellows rural cemetery, and urban development, including the advertising of "civilized" western cities, is also tied to veneration of Jason Lee and settler colonization (Straus 2018).

Race and Ethnicity in Cemetery Studies

Minority and disadvantaged populations did not necessarily follow the dominant patterns in burial practices in the Pacific Northwest. While the studies noted above suggest many similarities in burial practices across the region, especially for the more settled areas, some groups did not conform to these patterns, and their burial practices are distinctive. Abraham and Wegars (2005: 158) suggest that Chinese cemeteries and grave markers are "silent monuments memorializing Chinese contributions to the growth and development of the West." However, Chung and Wegars (2005: 13) suggest that Chinese burial practices also reinforced American nativist views that the Chinese were so radically different from White America that they could not assimilate into the American culture, thus justifying anti-Chinese racism. Historical archaeologists and other researchers have explored how Chinese traditions adapted and evolved in the Pacific Northwest, and the role of how transnational practices helped to justify racism and the exclusion of Chinese immigrants. Further, they have shown the variability in expression of Chinese burial practices and how some resisted racism, carving out a space for Chinese Americans in Pacific Northwest cemeteries.

Most Chinese emigrated from southeastern coastal China from Guangdong Province at the Pearl River delta, and their burial practices are predominantly those of southeastern China (Abraham and Wegars 2003; Barth 1964; Pasacreta 2005). Abraham and Wegars's (2003) survey of overseas Chinese burial customs identified the physical remains of Cantonese burial rituals in Idaho, eastern Oregon, and elsewhere in the United States and Australia (see Abraham and Wegars 2005; Pasacreta 2005). They note depressions associated with Chinese cemeteries related to exhumation of remains for return to home villages (see Chen 2001: 41; Pasacreta 2005). While many Chinese were exhumed, some individuals remained buried, particularly women and children, who were typically not considered part of the lineage, and were not believed to afford benefits to the living from reunification with their ancestors. The orientation of Chinese burials did not conform to European American patterns but often followed the topography of the land or were oriented north–south (Abraham and Wegars 2005: 162). In contrast to the park-like and groomed landscapes of the rural cemeteries and their successors, Chinese cemeteries were kept more "natural" or "untended" as the living avoided burial grounds except for specific annual ceremonies (Abraham and Wegars 2003: 61). In the nineteenth century, Chinese Americans placed markers with the names of the deceased, their date of death, and their home village, for the convenience of those who would ritually disinter the remains to prepare them for transportation to China. Often these were a family name affinity or regional association, the latter of which was later combined into the Chinese Consolidated Benevolent Association (Abraham and Wegars 2003: 55, 2005: 159; Chung and Wegars 2005: 17–18). Historical archaeologists have documented wooden markers; bottles with wooden slats; linen or paper strips with the deceased person's name; and sometimes even inscribed bricks buried with the individual (Abraham and Wegars 2003: 61, 2005: 167–169).

Chinese immigrants in Victoria, British Columbia; Warren, Idaho; and elsewhere in the Pacific Northwest may have practiced *feng shui* to establish burial site locations (Abraham and Wegars 2003: 61, 2005: 162–164; Couch 1996: 194–200; Fitzgerald 2018: 65, 71; Lai 1974; Pasacreta 2005). While a complex concept, *feng shui* uses geomancy to place burials in auspicious locations based on relationships to geographic features, including smooth forms, and avoiding straight lines, including routes of water courses and roads. They tend to rest on slopes or terraces with views surrounded by mountains and hills (Lai 1974). Part of the purpose of *feng shui* is to channel good energy, while preventing malevolent spirits from finding the graves.

In the far southeastern corner of British Columbia, in East Kootenay, a study documented the Chinese burial ground in the Wild Horse Creek Provincial Historic Site, adjacent to Fisherville, an 1864–1865 gold rush settlement subsequently reinhabited by Chinese miners (Pasacreta 2005). The broad-ranging study explored the history and prescriptions for Chinese death rituals in China, and compared them with documentary and archaeological evidence from Chinese cemeteries across southern British Columbia, Hawaii, Tahiti, and New Zealand. Confirming the importance of *feng shui* in the layout of Chinese graveyards and the amplification of funeral rites due to the increased fear of inauspicious spirits or ghosts in foreign lands, the wealth of merchants is also showcased in many overseas contexts (Pasacreta 2005). At Wild Horse Creek, evidence of offerings to the deceased included the remains of a wooden altar, wooden burial markers, and a pale fence that surrounded the cemetery. In association with grave depressions, the archaeologist found fragments of Winter Green[4] porcelain bowls and Chinese brown-glazed stoneware containers that likely represented the remains of food and beverage offerings (figure 6.4). Apple trees associated with burial pits also may reflect the remains of offerings that became volunteer landscaping (Pasacreta 2005). Metal detecting and magnetometry suggest the likely presence of intact burials between grave depressions that Chinese Canadian bone collectors missed or ignored.

In the twentieth century, Chinese burial customs changed due to attenuation of transpacific shipping during the Japanese–China conflict, World War II, and the Cold War, and variations in ritual, including the introduction of Western-style headstones in non-Chinese cemeteries with Chinese, Chinese and English, and solely English inscriptions (Abraham and Wegars 2003, 2005). Other cemetery features include memorial shrines, bone houses, and burners used for paper offerings to assist the deceased in the afterlife (see Abraham and Wegars 2005: 169–172).

Analysis of 2,755 Chinese Canadian grave markers in Victoria and Vancouver, British Columbia, combined with documentary evidence suggests considerable diversity in burial practices in twentieth-century British Columbia, with evidence for both individual and group agency (Chénier 2009). Chinese Canadians developed unique responses to racism in urban environments during the time of Chinese exclusion in British Columbia. In Victoria, six markers in the Ross Bay Cemetery and 353 in the Victoria Chinese Cemetery suggest a shift from patterns using benevolent association cemeteries and networks to repatriate bones to China, toward practices that emphasized more local ties with other Chinese Canadians (Chénier 2009; Lai 1987). Some of the grave markers were nonstandard as well, emphasizing individual agency and using burial spaces to foster relationships of the deceased with their families, religious congregations, other city residents, and other Chinese Canadians. Analysis of 2,396 Chinese markers in the Mountain View Cemetery of Vancouver revealed that, in earlier times, the majority of Chinese Canadians were repatriated after death to China, but that a significant minority still were buried and whose skeletal remains were not repatriated. These markers often exhibited more than just the name, ancestral village, and date of death but included marital and lineage ties, and some of the most ostentatious markers were placed closest to the public altar (Chénier 2009). After it was no longer possible to repatriate human remains to China, even the more conser-

---

4   Archaeologists have often identified this ceramic as celadon, but it is more accurately identified as Winter Green (Choy 2014)

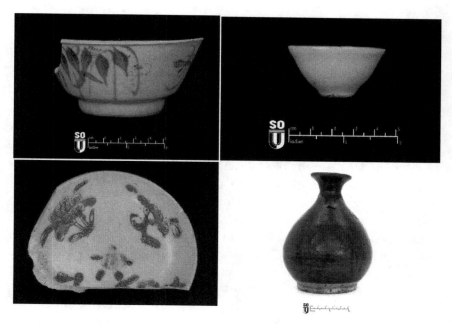

Figure 6.4. Typical Chinese ceramics found at sites in the Pacific Northwest. *Upper left*: Bamboo pattern rice bowl (artifact 13.09-2816); *upper right*: Winter Green liquor cup (artifact 13.09-3838); *lower left*: Four Seasons Flowers dish, rim dimension 8.5 centimeters (artifact 13.09-1596); *lower right*: Chinese, Brown-Glazed Stoneware liquor bottle (Artifact PC-001). All but PC-001 are from Jacksonville, Oregon. None of these belongings was found in a grave or burial context. These images are part of the Chinese Material Culture Collection in the Southern Oregon University Laboratory of Anthropology and made available by Southern Oregon University Hannon Library.

vative Chinese created a uniquely Chinese Canadian space that is evident in the uniformity of its markers.

In the United States, excavation of the former Chinese block of the Lone Fir cemetery in Portland, Oregon, led to the analysis of 403 artifacts recovered from disturbed contexts associated with early twentieth-century Chinese American graves (Smits 2008; Strauss 2018). The excavations were conducted on behalf of Multnomah County, the local neighborhood association, and Portland's Chinese Consolidated Benevolent Association, as it was believed that intact burials remained. This block was associated with both Chinese Americans and mental health patients. Artifacts recovered from the disturbed contexts included numerous Chinese porcelain ceramics, including Bamboo pattern rice bowls, Winter Green pattern–serving vessel and tea cup fragments, and Four Seasons pattern tableware (figure 6.4). The investigators also recovered Chinese brown-glazed stoneware liquor bottles and food storage vessel fragments. Other artifacts included a Chinese medicine vial and lock. British and American ceramics included whiteware vessel fragments, including transferprinted whiteware, decalcomania whiteware, and porcelain. Fragments of coffin hardware, including coffin handles, were also recovered, as well as other artifacts consistent with burials and burial offerings. The archaeologists recovered fragmented headstones, with inscriptions in both English and Chinese, and at least two specific headstones with Chinese men's inscriptions. On discovery of an intact burial, no additional excavations were undertaken and the project was terminated.

The Chinese Americans in Portland, like those of urban areas of British Columbia, "selectively appropriated European- and American-made elements and assigned them new meanings as objects used in Chinese funeral rituals" (Smits 2008: 119). Consistent with documentary records and other scholar's analyses, Portland's Chinese community was simultaneously engaged in "economic, social, and political affairs" in Portland and their home villages in China, actively preserving "traditional Chinese customs and selectively incorporated European and American elements in funeral rituals as they actively forged transnational identities as Chinese Americans" (Smits 2008: 111). After discovery of the intact burial, a building and parking lot placed on the block were removed, and by 2021 a cultural heritage garden was planned to honor the Chinese American cemetery as well as the mental health patients (Wallace 2021).

Historical archaeology also was used to relocate and interpret Salem's Chinese Shrine at the Oddfellow's Rural Cemetery as part of a study of its poorly known Chinese community (Fitzgerald 2018; Fitzgerald et al., 2021). Chinese Americans were buried in the cemetery between 1874 and 1925, and documentary evidence indicates the disinterment of men and their repatriation to China. Using a city-planning framework tied to the Salem Landmarks Commission, the historical archaeology project engaged Chinese American residents, the historic preservation community, and city parks representatives to help guide the project in a meaningful and sensitive manner. A concrete pad with three holes and a broken marble tablet composed the remains of the Chinese shrine, similar in construction to a shrine found in Marysville, California, and more ancient villages in southeastern China (Fitzgerald 2018: 70, 72–73). Artifacts found in association with the shrine included a Winter Green porcelain sherd and Chinese brown-glazed stoneware, consistent with offering vessels found at other sites (e.g., Pasacreta 2005; Smits 2008). The shrine was not oriented to the Oddfellow's cemetery grid but rather to the Willamette River, with Mount Hood to the east, suggestive of *feng shui* (Fitzgerald 2018: 65, 71). Community outreach culminated in a Buddhist blessing over the shrine, and the discovery of two discarded Chinese headstones that had been curated by a neighbor. Public archaeology was used to address the history of a poorly known but significant part of the City's history, and to begin a dialogue with the City of Salem about the interpretation and preservation of its Chinese American past.

Another distinctive minority population in Idaho and eastern Washington and Oregon are the Basque, who emigrated to the Pacific Northwest from northeast Spain and southwest France. Brooks (2021) explored Basque headstones in Jordan Valley, Oregon, and Emmett, Idaho, finding Basque symbols that represent a revitalization of Basque heritage in the late twentieth and twenty-first centuries (Brooks 2021).

Native American Graveyards

In Indigenous graveyards of the colonial period, we come full circle, from studies of ancient cemeteries of Native Americans who inhabited the landscape before settler colonialism, and the occasional examination of contact-period graves, to the historical archaeology of more recent burial grounds of Indigenous people. In a classic study, Blackman (1973) documented the replacement of burial practices among the Haida from above ground burial to inhumation, and from carved wooden memorial columns and grave posts to tombstones. She discusses the reinterpretation of meanings and the functions of Christian burial practices, including the erection of headstones imported from Victoria, in terms of Indigenous beliefs, and how potlatching was incorporated into the burial ceremony, sometimes with the inclusion of missionaries (albeit unwittingly).

Likewise, investigation of nineteenth-century Christian headstones of the Tsimshian people of the Nass and Skeena River valleys of British Columbia exposed missionaries' roles in reshaping burial traditions, but also documented the maintenance of Indigenous art forms and adaptation of cemetery markers to maintain family status symbolism (Hawker 1991). Shifts from wooden crest (totem) poles to stone grave markers is partly tied to missionaries' and colonial administrators' attacks on Indigenous traditions like potlatching, secret societies, traditional medicine, and the introduction of residential (boarding) schools, but the headstones also exhibit cultural persistence through Native symbols, including animal and traditional art forms. The shift to Victorian symbols on headstones, largely manufactured in Victoria, British Columbia, but sometimes modified by Native artists, were repurposed to meet local social needs while adapting to Christian religious ideology. People were buried in the cemetery based on their matrilineal clan, and the elaborateness of the marker denoted their traditional status. Some markers are stone representations of crest poles, while others include crest symbols to denote the special traditional rights of the deceased and their families. The missionaries tolerated these adjustments, compromising religious ideology to address at least these Indigenous cultural forms.

Prince (2002b: 63) suggests that the rapid addition of European Canadian coffins and hardware, building material, headstones, crosses, and funerary objects in the Kimsquit cemetery (ca. 1850–1927) were adapted to "uniquely native contexts in accordance with deeply entrenched values." European Canadian goods, like pots and pans, left at the grave site for the use of the deceased, traditional grave houses that used Western-style architecture, and erection of ancestral crests and potlatch-related items alongside headstones, suggest both resistance to the prohibition on potlatching and other Indigenous traditions, and the agency of the community to maintain important cultural traditions, also seen in architecture and belongings (Prince 2002a, 2002b, 2016).

In a similar vein, microhistory of cemeteries associated with *Stó:lō* and Métis communities addresses how Catholic orthodoxy in the form of the Oblate doctrine became entangled with Indigenous systems of understanding and memorializing the deceased (Gambell 2009). Catholic missionaries "disciplined" space (Foucault 1995) using cemeteries to exert the power of colonizer over the colonized, creating conditions where unbelievers and unbaptized children were buried separately from their families, and re-introducing the practice of inhumation. Yet Indigenous peoples memorialized, adapted, and resisted this spatial control. Modern-day descendants visiting the *Shxwōwhámél* cemetery, on the lower Fraser River valley pointed out a nearby cedar tree likely used formerly for tree burials. This suggests either that the cemetery was placed on a former traditional burial ground, or that the tree has been "repurposed" to serve as a symbol of traditional culture (Gambell 2009: 61–62). Chiefly status is marked on some cemetery monuments, and oral history suggests that ritual consumption of materials was expended in feasting grave rituals of high-status individuals, while avoidance of cemeteries by *Stó:lō* people at dusk reflect traditional Indigenous belief systems (Gambell 2009). The cemetery serves as a reminder to *Stó:lō* people of the devastation of introduced diseases and the process of separating nonbelieving kin from converted Catholics.

In a decided turn from the practices of the twentieth century, archaeologists are beginning to collaborate with Tribes in locating burials of deceased children tied to the Canadian residential schools. The Canadian Truth and

Reconciliation Commission (TRC) documented the cultural genocide attendant on Indigenous peoples in Canada, including abuses associated with residential (boarding) schools. Archaeology has emerged as a significant decolonizing tool in identifying, documenting, and preserving the burials of children tied to the schools (Montgomery and Supernant 2022). Among the many genocidal policies that the Canadian government and their nongovernmental instruments implemented to assimilate Native American people into the Canadian dominant culture, perhaps the most emotionally and spiritually harmful was the separation of children from their parents, and the practices employed to eradicate Indigenous culture and identity (TRC 2015a: 4). Furthermore, Indigenous children in the residential schools died at a much higher rate than school-aged children in the general population, their deaths were often unrecorded, and the cemeteries where they were buried were "abandoned, disused, and vulnerable to accidental disturbance" (Hamilton 2021; TRC 2015b: 1). At least eighteen residential schools operated in British Columbia between the late nineteenth and late twentieth centuries (TRC 2015b: 139–151).

Increasingly, near-surface geophysical remote sensing using ground-penetrating radar, electrical conductivity, magnetometry, and other scientific methods are being combined with engagement and collaboration with Indigenous communities to find ancestral graves (Hamilton 2021: 36–38; Rogers 2001; Wadsworth 2020; Wadsworth et al. 2021). For example, at the Kuper Island Indian Residential School on Penelakut Island in the southern Gulf Islands, archaeologists assisted Indigenous communities to relocate the school cemetery (Harris et al. 2017; Simons et al. 2021). Considerable attention was given to not just the scientific means of grave site discovery but also to the ways in which the scientists collaborate with the community and the community's reactions and social and spiritual responses to the work. Harris et al. (2017) contrast the collaborative work to relocate the school cemetery with the pain and anguish of the descendants of children who died in one of the more notorious schools. Ground-penetrating radar, combined with vegetation clearance, discovered graves of the staff and children who died at the school. The discovery of unmarked graves through archival and archaeological methods was counterbalanced with the need for self-examination by the researchers, and "a willingness to acknowledge and find meaning in the spiritual truth of Indigenous knowledge" tied to the Penelakut community (Harris et al. 2017: 17). The Penelakut sought more than just the locations of the graves but also to find healing for the children who had died and their descendants who felt strongly their ancestors' suffering. Simons et al. (2021) note that archaeologists face many issues in working with the Coast Salish, and with descendant groups in general, including the need to build trust and to avoid appropriation, while addressing the underlying spiritual and social aspects of the work.

The historical archaeology of cemeteries can help reconcile differing narratives of settler and Indigenous history, leading to a more nuanced interpretation of these places. For some, this can even be therapeutic, healing some of the disruptions associated with colonial practices. Exposing historical silences and relocating hidden grave sites perhaps provides some solace to descendant communities and individuals seeking connections with their ancestors. Fundamentally, interpretation and commemoration of cemeteries should address the needs and concerns of descendants, including Native American communities, Native Hawaiians, Chinese Americans, local community members, and others, including even occupational classes, the military, and their dependents. Such commemoration should include greater dialogue with descendant communities, like the work by Fitzgerald (2018; Fitzgerald et al. 2021) at the Oddfellow's Rural Cemetery in Salem, Oregon. The exploration of larger cultural patterns in the interests of descendant communities is an important shift for historical archaeology in the Pacific Northwest.

7

Slugs of Gold

The Historical Archaeology of Pacific Northwest Industries

William Earl crossed the Oregon Trail from Iowa in 1845, spending his first winter on the Tualatin Plains west of Portland. His brother Robert, his mother, and he settled on three land claims south of the Santiam River, establishing a homestead near Mill Creek, a tributary of the Santiam River, about 13 kilometers east of Albany, Oregon (Chapman 2014; Roulette and Chapman 1996). Robert, who left a diary, stated: "we made a plow and we plowed—point a Short barr & we made the wole out of a twisty pice [of] oak then we went to breaking prairie one of my brothers Stoped in french prair[ie] to work for wheat for Seed we [ploughed?] 20 acres for wheat and garden we built cabon [cabin]" (Earl in Harrison 1993: 28).

From these humble beginnings, William Earl became one of the wealthiest farmers in Linn County, diversifying his economic pursuits during the period of early settlement (Chapman 2014; Roulette and Chapman 1996). He took trips to the gold fields of California in 1848 and 1849, selling supplies, which allowed him to purchase two hundred head of cattle. He then took a trip in 1851 to southern Oregon to the mines in Josephine County, establishing a trading post and stock ranch, and in 1857 took food to sell in Yreka, California. He partnered with another man to build a sawmill on or near his Willamette Valley claim in 1853. These ventures resulted in a prosperous farm, where by 1852 he owned 606 acres and raised wheat, horses, cattle, and pigs. He was in the top 4 percent of wealth earners in the county according to the 1854 tax assessment (Roulette and Chapman 1996: 7–12 to 7–14). After his 1851 trip, it is reported that his children played with $50 slugs of gold.

Unruh (1979: 7) noted the very different motivations of those emigrating to the California gold fields seeking a stake to bring back to their homeland, versus those who planned to stay and farm. However, like the Earl household, the American settlement of the Pacific Northwest is dominated by the interconnectedness of domestic, commercial, and industrial enterprises, with many instances of farmers leaving for the gold fields or enlarging their existing repertoire of economic activities to augment incomes and improve their economic standing. Ranching and farming supported the gold rushes, and the labor needed for production of livestock, agricultural crops, and industry leaned heavily on Indigenous and other racial minorities, including the Chinese and Japanese.

Agriculture, including ranching, fish canning, mining, and logging, impacted tremendously the natural environment, leading to the introduction of new species, exhausting soil nutrients through unsustainable agriculture, depleting once abundant fish runs, reordering entire stream courses through hydraulic mining, and clear-cutting stands of trees. Chinese and Japanese immigrants, as well as the Indigenous populations, contributed to these industries. While racist laws, combined with structural and overt violence, tried to constrain non-White populations, giving advantage to White settlers; in many cases, these populations formed the fabric of settlements, resisting, persisting, and adapting in spite of concerted prejudice and violence.

This chapter explores the economic pursuits of settlers in the Pacific Northwest from the mid–nineteenth century to the early twentieth century, and their impacts on the social and natural environment. In a few cases, historical archaeology has addressed nineteenth-century manufacturing, like the iron furnace at Lake Oswego (Kuo and Minor 2016) or potteries in the Willamette Valley (Haskin 1942, Peterson 2008; Schablitsky 2007:33; Scheans 1984; Schmeer 1987; Sullivan 1986). Most work, however, has explored the major industries of farming, ranching, fishing, mining, and logging.

Agriculture

The Oregon Provisional Government defined land rights for settlers to one square mile (640 acres, 259 ha). After resolution of the international boundary, the U.S. Government invoked the Donation Land Claim Act of 1850 to accommodate earlier land claims and allow each new White person to claim 320 acres (130 ha), and double that for couples. In order to accommodate this transfer of lands, the U.S. General Land Office imposed a two-dimensional Euclidean space, the U.S. Public Land Survey System, on prior cultural landscapes, crossing mountains, valleys, and prairies to make a suitable grid for American settlement (Speulda and Bowyer 2002). The Willamette Meridian demarcated areas into 6-square-mile townships defined in townships north-south and ranges east–west from the origin point in the Portland West Hills (now called the Willamette Stone). Each township was then divided into 36-square-mile sections numbered 1 to 36. A similar system was imposed on Idaho, and a Canadian version was imposed on western Canada, including British Columbia (Cameron 2009; Dennis 1892). Ironically, the U.S. treaties designed to extinguish title to Indigenous lands allowing for White settlement were not concluded or ratified by the U.S. Congress prior to the recording of thousands of settlers' claims for hundreds of thousands of prime acres (Robbins 2022). Some treaties were never ratified, and the settlers, disregarding the necessity for official title, seized "sprawling land claims" and conducted "a lively trade in selling and swapping sections of claims that they legally did not own" (Whaley 2010:195). After the Donation Land Claim Act, the U.S. Congress enacted a series of homestead acts through the early twentieth century to encourage even more American settlement (Sekora and Ross 1995: 10–6–10–10; Speulda and Bowyer 2002).

Homesteads are significant rural landscapes, often including a house or cabin, accompanied by outbuildings, and activity areas related to farming, orcharding, woodlots, or pastures (Speulda and Bowyer 2002). The settlers also were highly influenced by American consumerism and mass marketing, and this pattern appears within a decade or two of establishment of the new communities. Prior to about 1854, the Hudson's Bay Company supplied most of the household goods to settlers, but after this, American merchants began to dominate the market (Roulette and Chapman 1996: 7–7 to 7–12). Even at isolated religious communities, like the German-American colony at Aurora in the Willamette Valley, consumer assemblages are overshadowed by products manufactured in eastern factories, suggesting the influence of capitalism even on farms that avoided extravagant practices (Minor et al. 1981: 127–128). By the early 1860s, retail markets developed, and general mercantile stores supplied farmers with goods, including architectural hardware, dishes, and other products, also serving as stage stops, post offices, and the center of social networks (e.g., Hill 2019).

William Earl Homestead (ca. 1846–1865)

Excavations at the William Earl site (35LIN459) discovered a plow zone assemblage with intact house footing, likely from the two-story house that Earl built in 1848 after his marriage to Louisa (figure 7.1; Chapman 2014; Roulette and Chapman 1996). While the Earl enterprise started in a primitive fashion with a handmade plow, the family actively embraced the Victorian ideals of the "woman's sphere" and "cult of domesticity," purchasing the most expensive decorative ceramics (Roulette and Chapman 1996: 7–59). Thousands of ceramic sherds represented twenty-one distinctive table plate patterns from a dozen manufacturers, and twenty teaware patterns, many of them not the same style, and sometimes by different manufacturers. Even in earlier periods, when the Earls had an important reason to invest in the farm, they purchased expensive dishes, accelerating these purchases as the farm developed (Roulette and Chapman 1996). Eight different pressed glass patterns, and an

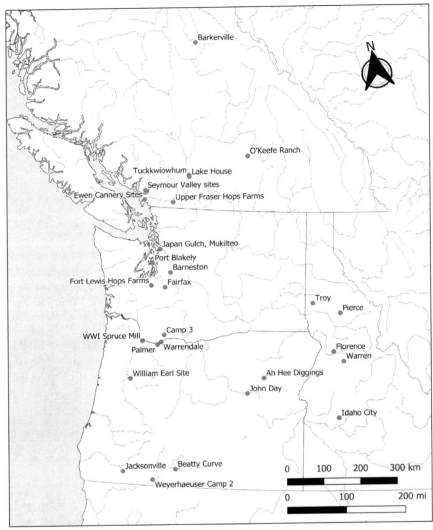

Figure 7.1. Sites associated with Northwest industries.

abundance of containers used for pepper sauce, pickles, ground pepper, catsup, and olive oil also suggest luxury items to communicate to guests their wealth and status. Ceramic and glass marbles, small white porcelain teaware or doll's dishes, and slate tablet fragments speak to socialization of children.

Even with markups on the frontier, the Earl assemblage CC index, or rank of the assemblage's value based on the English potter's fixed prices, is greater at 2.17 (2.49 for the later assemblage) than comparable rural assemblages in the East, and is comparable to the gentlemen's households at Fort Vancouver from a decade earlier (CC Index = 2.71 for the Chief Factor's house and 2.81 for the Bachelor's Quarters) (Chapman 1993; Cromwell 2006c: 160, 184; Roulette and Chapman 1996: 7–61). The uneven and chaotic nature of land "claiming" and the underlying Indigenous presence is noted in the diary of Robert Earl. Recollections of hundreds of Indigenous people traveling through the valley are juxtaposed with the Earl's violent removal of Santiam people—driving them "out of the country and they neve[r] come back again" (Earl in Roulette and Chapman 1996: 7–5).

Hops were first grown at Hudson's Bay Company's Fort Vancouver, and many early settlers grew some for medicinal or domestic purposes (Dorset 2012: 75–76; Erigero 1992: 218; Kopp 2016; Nelson 1963). The first commercial hops growing in the Puyallup Valley are attributed to Jacob Meeker, an Oregon Trail emigrant (the father of Ezra), followed by experiments by others at Buena Vista, Oregon, in 1867, and Eugene, Oregon, two years later (Kopp 2011; Nelson 1963; Shaw et al. 2009). The soils, precipitation, and climate were exceedingly good for hops in the Pacific Northwest, and farmers could achieve returns 2.5–6 times that of Europe or New York State. Hop farms over 100 acres contained specialized hop kilns, cooling, storage, and baling facilities, while smaller farms might have all of these operations in one building (Shaw et al. 2009:18).

Hops harvesting in September was extremely labor intensive, and farmers recruited labor from Indigenous, Chinese, Japanese, and other groups (Kopp 2011, 2016; Shaw et al. 2009:14). Oliver (2013) suggests that *Stó:lō* people's participation at hop camps in the Fraser Valley became part of the reconstitution of their Indigenous social networks and identities during the colonial period. Hopyards developed in the Fraser Valley in the 1870s by White settlers, but as the farms were close to Native villages, Coast Salish were hired as laborers, particularly during harvest time. Hops picking became part of the *Stó:lō* seasonal round, and while hop camps formed part of the new settler landscape, they also became "one of the few places where large groups could routinely exchange information and express opinions" during the period when potlatches and winter dances were banned or discouraged (Oliver 2013: 107). Similar gatherings of Native American people in the Puget Sound and Willamette Valley also provided access to traditional lands by Native Americans, as well as opportunities for socializing off reservation (Kopp 2011: 426–428, Kopp 2016: 64–68). These places were tied to ancient prairies in the Willamette Valley and canoe landings on Puget sound, affording opportunities to dance, gamble, race horses, sell baskets and photographs to White tourists, and construct and use traditional sweat lodges.

O'Keefe Ranch (1867–ca. 1923)

Located on the northern end of Lake Okanagan near Vernon, the origins of the O'Keefe Ranch began with Indigenous Sqilxw people who for millennia had lived in the same location, called *Nk'maplqs* (Acheson 2022). Cornelius O'Keefe conducted a number of cattle drives with partners in 1866–1867 to supply the gold fields of British Columbia, the latter of which followed the old Hudson's Bay Company trail to the north end of Okanagan Lake. On June 20, 1867, O'Keefe and Thomas Greenhow settled at *Nk'maplqs,* and in the late 1860s, O'Keefe married (under Indigenous law) a Sqilxw woman, Alapetsa, also known as Rosie, and had two children. He later abandoned her, remarrying sequentially two Irish Canadian women, and raising an additional fifteen children (Acheson 2022; Sauer 1995).

Ranches, like the O'Keefe Ranch, were ground zero in the settlement of eastern British Columbia, providing competition to American cattle raisers in Oregon, and establishing many of the economic ventures and social institutions of the region (Sauer 1995). Greenhow and O'Keefe each claimed 160 acres, but through water rights controlled many hundreds of acres upstream (Acheson 2022). The O'Keefe Ranch was the terminus of the wagon road from Kamloops into the Okanagan Valley, a stage stop, and contained the first post office in the area. After the mining boom, the railroad provided new routes to market, and by the end of the 1880s, O'Keefe and Greenhow had secured 20,000 acres and 2,000 head of cattle. This patriarchal capitalist system effectively removed ownership from the Sqilxw (as Indigenous people couldn't claim lands), ignored centuries-old traditions of resource collecting, and established "Reserves," while employing Indigenous people as labor in Western-style placemaking (Acheson 2022).

Test excavations at the ranch recovered nearly 11,000 belongings, most of which came from a dump (1903–ca. 1906) and two privies, one used post-1885 by the later O'Keefe family, and the other used by Chinese workers ca. 1923. Commercial goods found in the dump and privy assemblages suggest that the late nineteenth-century deposits were dominated by British and Canadian goods connected to Canadian trade protectionism. The later twentieth-century deposits contained a broader range of products from England, Scotland, Germany, Canada, and the United States, correlated with relaxed tariffs and a stronger Canadian economy between 1896–1911 (Sauer 1995). The eight to twenty Chinese Canadian workers included cooks, gardeners, and laborers (usually 2–3 at any one time), but very few belongings originated in China (Sauer 1996). Historical records suggest that the Sqilxw served as cowboys and ranch hands. While Sauer (1995: 178) suggests that Sqilxw cowboys were assimilated to European goods by 1877, Acheson (2022) documents oral traditions and other evidence to support the persistence of Sqilxw people and their resistance to the colonial narrative that silenced their communities and connections to place. Indigenous women and Native cowboys connected the intertwined Indigenous and settler landscapes of the ranch with oral traditions to maintain an identity that contrasted with the White-dominant ranch community.

Fishing and Canneries

Since time immemorial, Native American people collected, dried, and traded salmon and many other fish. For example, Byram (2002) documents the long history of Indigenous use of fish weir structures and basket traps on the Oregon Coast, and their continuing use into the late nineteenth century in southwest Oregon. American immigrants, however, brought both technological and market innovations that dramatically changed the nature of the fisheries. Early European American commercial fishing activities in the 1830s and 1840s produced salted and barreled salmon at the Hudson's Bay Company's Fort Vancouver, Fort Langley, and at Nathaniel Wyeth's operation on the Columbia River (Cobb 1921: 25–26; O'Bannon 1983: 13–14). The first Columbia River cannery was established in 1866 at the Hapgood, Hume and Company cannery at Eagle Cliff, Washington, and by 1883, there were forty canneries on the lower Columbia River served by over 1,000 fishing boats (Cobb 1921: 28; Fagan 1993; Gile 1955; Harrison 2008; O'Bannon 1983: 23–32). Likewise, in British Columbia, small salmon factories and camps were established by 1871 in the tidal estuary of the Fraser River, but by the early twentieth century there were over two hundred canneries within the dense forests along river banks and rocky beaches of the British Columbia coast (Newell 1987, 1991). Increased competition, regional economic downturns, and other regulations to preserve the fishery, led to the closing of many of the canneries by the mid-twentieth century (Fagan 1993).

Canneries did not conform to typical industrial factories, as they were operated seasonally, and in British Columbia were often very remote. Analysis of late nineteenth- and early twentieth-century fire insurance maps documents the spatial arrangements of over 144 canneries in British Columbia, revealing that the large cannery buildings were most commonly built on pilings on the foreshore, with other support buildings nearby (Newell 1987, 1991). Indigenous people from many tribes, Chinese Americans, Japanese Americans, Scandinavians, and other European-Americans lived in shacks, huts, cabins, and bunkhouses, linked by boardwalks to the main cannery building (Newell

1987: 10). The primary archaeological remains of canneries are the pilings and refuse dumped next to bunkhouses or dumped on the beaches or off the piers.

Ewen Cannery (1885–1930)

The Ewen Cannery was established on the Don and Lion Islands of the Fraser River, about 20 kilometers southeast of Vancouver, British Columbia. Don Island was host to a permanent community of Japanese fishermen from Miyagi prefecture, about 160 kilometers north of Tokyo, and numbering at maximum seventy to one hundred people. Lion Island contained the cannery complex, including a large Chinese bunkhouse that could accommodate up to one hundred seasonal workers. Ross (2009, 2010, 2011, 2012, 2013, 2017a, 2017b) explores these two island cannery communities through concepts of transnationalism and diaspora to address cultural change and persistence. Using documentary sources and archaeological remains, Ross's work represents the most detailed and theoretically sophisticated historical archaeology of Asian workers at canneries.

Comparison of the two sites suggests that food and beverage items were dominated by Asian-style meals, with communal meals for both Japanese and Chinese. Large numbers of imported Asian table wares and other ceramics supported traditional meals of rice, miso soup, and pickled vegetables on Don Island, and rice and vegetables often served with fresh pork, and preserved foods from China on Lion Island (Ross 2011). Each of the communities used some Western-style ceramics, often for serving dishes, glass tableware, and Western-style condiments. Foods included traditional canned and preserved foods, combined with fresh foods, particularly in the case of the Japanese fishermen. Food was acquired from local merchants, and through hunting, fishing, cultivating, and gathering wild and domestic plants and animals. Interestingly, the inhabitants of both sites consumed Western alcohol, but also imported some Asian types (Ross 2010). Both Asian and Western-style medicines were prevalent, and the people of both communities adopted Western-style domestic and work clothes (Ross 2013). The Japanese fishermen on Don Island were more entrepreneurial, including brewing of sake, and the production of soy sauce, miso, and fresh vegetables for sale. The Japanese also exhibited greater consumer choice, possibly because they lived in a year-round community and were not subject to a labor contractor. The Chinese bunkhouse on Lion Island exhibited more limited pursuits and consumer choice, but with more evidence for recreational games and opium consumption—and, as noted above, more reliance on preserved foods, possibly related to the labor contractor's retail importing business.

Ross (2013: 184) suggests that product consumption was affected "by proximate influences of the adopted country but also from abroad through family connections and merchant networks." Impacts on consumption included the community's sex and age composition, ability to purchase goods individually or reliance on labor contractors, proximity to stores, and other factors. The consumption on both Island's communities was "as much a product of contextual factors in the home and host countries as of the ethnic or cultural identities of their occupants" (Ross 2013: 191). The migration process, combined with opportunities and pressures of British Columbia, both streamlined and transformed traditions from the homeland into symbolic markers of ethnicity: "Overall, it appears both groups of Asian migrants maintained strong diasporic identities rooted in the homeland but exhibited behavior suggesting that many established transnational connections with both home and host countries . . ." (Ross 2013: 195). Other important studies of canneries include Bay View (1873–1930) and Warrendale (1876–1930) on the Columbia River, with the latter containing analyses of Chinese cannery workers and a novel micro-archaeological analysis (Fagan 1993; Gehr 1975; Reese 1989).

Mining

The discovery of gold in California spread prospectors and entrepreneurs out across the region, transforming landscapes in their path, and impacting the social, economic, and natural environments. As noted above, many homesteaders participated in the gold rushes, as miners, merchants, and suppliers of cattle and grain, and many, like William Earl, became wealthy. Supply of gold rush districts and settlements created opportunities for farming, ranching, lumbering, and road building in nearby suitable areas, often leading to interaction and friction with Native Americans, Chinese Americans, Native Hawaiians, Mexican Americans, and others who became intrinsic parts of mining communities (e.g., LaLande 1981, 1982; Rose 2009, 2013; Rose and Ruiz 2014). Mining rushes in the Pacific Northwest began on tributaries of the Rogue River in southwestern Oregon, including Jackson Creek, Josephine Creek, and the Applegate River (Atwood and Gray 2003; Ericson 2012; LaLande 1981: 23). These were followed by 1858 mining rushes to the Fraser River, and eventually to the Cariboo region in British Columbia, on the Clearwater River at Oro Fino City by mid-1861, and the same year spreading to Elk City, Florence, and Warren to the south (Stapp 1990: 52–56). Prospecting in the Blue Mountains of northeastern Oregon found gold in Griffin Gulch southwest of Baker City, resulting in the 1862 boomtowns of Auburn and Canyon City (Lindgren 1901: 563–564; Steeves 1984). Gold was found in the

Boise Basin of Idaho, including Idaho City, and in Oregon's Owyhee Mountains (Hardesty 2010: xiii). Most early mining consisted of placer mining by individuals and small groups, often giving way to hard-rock and hydraulic mining, requiring substantial (sometimes foreign) investment, and leaving a variety of archaeological deposits associated with discovery, extraction, and processing (LaLande 1981: 312–321, 1985; Hardesty 2010: 29–107). Mining settlements rapidly boomed, necessitating freighting of entire assemblages of material culture, and with equally rapid regional social and economic adjustments (Ostrogorsky 1982). Much of the mining archaeology in the Pacific Northwest has focused on the Chinese as a distinct community, whose documentary record is so biased on the European-American side it has been likened to cultural amnesia (Hann 2021), and on the Chinese side is less accessible to researchers through language and cultural barriers.

Jacksonville and Southern Oregon Mining (1851–1884)

The December 1851 gold discovery on Jackson and Daisy Creeks, tributaries of the Rogue River, led to the first gold rush in the Pacific Northwest. Jacksonville (initially "Table Rock City") was platted in 1852 within James Cluggage's and James Poole's claims, and within less than a year grew to a County seat of about nine hundred people housed in 150 to 200 frame structures (Ross and Owens 1979; Rose and Ruiz 2014). For a short time, Jacksonville was Oregon's most populous city, serving as the center of settler commerce and transportation in southwestern Oregon until 1884, when it was bypassed by the railroad (McKithan 1977; Rose and Johnson 2016).

Historical archaeology has explored numerous sites within and near Jacksonville (e.g., Bastier and Rose 2016; Goebel 1995; LaLande 1981, 1982, 1985; Popper 2020; Rose 2020; Rose and Johnson 2015, 2016, 2022; Rose et al. 2014; Ruiz and O'Grady 2008; Schablitsky and Ruiz 2009; Winthrop and Winthrop 1983). Some deposits contain quintessential gold rush items, including mining pans, red ware and effigy smoking pipes, glass tumblers, shot glasses, and numerous fragments of alcohol bottles, suggestive of the male-dominated early days of mining (Rose and Johnson 2015). Kanaka Flat, about 1.5 kilometers southwest of Jacksonville, contained a documentary and oral history record suggesting that numerous Native Hawaiians, Native Americans, African Americans, Portuguese, and Whites fostered mixed-race and sometimes long-lived households (Rose 2009, 2013). The presence of Indigenous women of Rogue River, Umpqua, and Shasta heritage conforms with the continued persistence of Indigenous women on the southern Oregon landscape (e.g., Tveskov 2007), revealing a community that contrasts with its notoriety as a place of lawlessness, drug and alcohol abuse, gambling, and prostitution depicted by White settlers and their biographers (Rose 2009, 2013).

Chinese Americans arrived in Jacksonville as early as 1851, establishing a Chinese quarter on the edge of the central business district by 1860 (LaLande 1982: 24–25). Rose and Ruiz (2014) discuss the interests of White Americans in mining towns, including Jacksonville, to marginalize and denigrate other racial and ethnic groups, including laws to exclude some from owning property, becoming citizens, prohibitions on testimony against Whites, and prohibitions on interracial marriage. The Chinese Exclusion Act of 1882, the Sweet ruling in the fall of 1889 that prohibited Chinese from owning mining claims, the Geary Act of 1892, along with the accompanying violence perpetrated on Chinese Americans is seen throughout the Pacific Northwest (e.g., Stapp 1990: 362–367; Stapp 1993: 11; Wegars 1991: 59–127; Withee 2021: 372). Institution of local taxes targeting non-White businesses, such as Chinese laundries, and the statewide poll tax on ethnic minorities, as well as overt aggression documented in local newspapers, are other ways in which White hostility was maintained against racial minorities (Rose and Johnson 2016: 19–21). While some settlers were tolerant and protested acts of aggression or maintained business relationships with Chinese Americans, the overt creation of a non-White "other" category of citizens was intrinsically tied to maintaining the power of White businessmen (Rose and Ruiz 2014).

Domestic and personal items found in refuse deposits indicate that Jacksonville residents participated in Victorianism, with evidence for the cult of true womanhood, including children's socialization—revealing "the early roots of the town's stability despite its beginnings as a transient mining community," but also the demonstrated marginalization of Chinese Americans distinguished by the virtual absence of Chinese-origin artifacts within the main town deposits (Schablitsky and Ruiz 2009: 85). Excavations by the University of Oregon and Southern Oregon University explored areas fronting Main Street within the Jacksonville Chinese Quarter (35JA737), finding prodigious numbers of belongings, including many Chinese-manufactured items. Animal bones suggest that the Chinese maintained food traditions, with pork, chicken, turkey, duck, and geese prevalent (Ruiz and O'Grady 2008). Excavation of just four 1- × 1-meter excavation units recovered over 24,000 artifacts plus faunal and macrobotanical remains from a portion of a "Chinese Shanty" shown on the 1884 Sanborn fire insurance map (figure 7.2; Rose and Johnson 2016; Rose 2020). The *in-situ* assemblage of items from the catastrophically burned structure represented either a small family or an informal business or store, including numerous tools, writing items, and wom-

Figure 7.2. North wall profile of two units excavated into a Chinese dwelling site in Jacksonville, Oregon. The length of the profile is 2 meters; the depth is approximately 150 centimeters. Photo courtesy Southern Oregon University Laboratory of Anthropology.

en's and children's belongings. Distinctive activity areas included an outdoor kitchen area with patio, brick hearth, wok, cleaver, handled pan, seeds, hazelnut shells, and faunal remains. The Chinese inhabitants consumed a variety of wild and domesticated local and imported foods, including Chinese olive and Szechuan pepper (Popper 2020: 322–323). Debris related to recreational gambling was preserved under burnt shelving, including a coin purse, Winter Green tea cup, Asian and American coins, a stack of melted U.S. quarters, and liquor bottles (Rose and Johnson 2016). The evidence suggests that at a time when Chinese Americans were increasingly subject to racist violence and exclusionary laws, this structure was well stocked with a variety of "nourishing and flavorful foods," a large assemblage of Chinese dishes, some British and American ceramics, tools from a variety of skilled trades, artifacts of literacy including slate pencils and items used in calligraphy, toys suggestive of the presence of children, and even a small picture frame. Residents "were able to fully express their transnational identity by negotiating a home life created from the best of both worlds" with imported European, Chinese, and local American products (Rose 2020:183).

British Columbia Mining and Barkerville

Reports of gold in British Columbia date to the 1840s, and the Hudson's Bay Company made serious explorations in 1850 after the start of the California Gold Rush (Marshall 2018: 19–24). Gold was discovered on the international boundary in 1854 during the move of Fort Colvile to Fort Sheppard, leading to discoveries on Sheep Creek and China Bend (Litzkow 2018). Likewise, the governmental survey for the international boundary found gold along the Similkameen River in 1859, leading to a short-lived rush to Okanagan City (Evenson 2016: 19–20). Prospectors mined gold along the Columbia River in a series of finds between Rock Island Creek near Wenatchee, Washington, and the Pend Oreille River on the international border, continuing throughout the nineteenth century (Evenson 2016; Huntting 1955; Litzkow 2018). By 1870, most of these latter locations became dominated by Chinese placer miners, and there is a notable documentary record regarding Chinese stores and large Chinese mining placer camps, but few that are not currently inundated under reservoirs (Evenson 2016).

Gold discovery on the Fraser River was communicated to San Francisco, and in the Spring of 1858, miners flocked to British Columbia. By June, over 10,000 people had arrived, with between 30,000 and 100,000 people estimated by the end of that year (Marshall 2018: 121–122). The earliest finds were on the Lower Fraser River between Hudson's Bay Company Forts Hope and Yale, with Hill's Bar one of the best-known placer deposits. While Indigenous people were a significant portion of the initial mining work force, immigrant gold-seekers quickly flooded the region. Like other western gold rushes, the diverse population represented White American citizens, Europeans, and Chinese, primarily coming from California. Inevitable clashes between White miners and Indigenous people resulted in open warfare in the Fraser River Canyon in late summer 1858, leading to a miner-created treaty by late August (Marshall 2018: 170–179; Pegg 2018: 82–84). The same year, and as a result of the gold rush, British Columbia was founded as a colony at Fort Langley.

Since 2009, Kwantlen Polytechnic University has explored the impact of mining on the Indigenous communities of the Fraser River Canyon, including work at a miner's roadhouse called Lake House (DkRi-85), two ancient Indigenous housepit villages with contact-era components, Kopchitchin (DlRi-74) and Tuckkwiowhum (DlRi-3), and culturally modified trees on Lake Mountain (DkRi-74) (Pegg 2018; Pegg et al. 2011, 2013). The Lake House site contained typical mining items associated with a bunkhouse and large tent, including square nails, lead-soldered tin cans, mule and horse shoes, liquor bottle glass, tobacco pipe fragments, and even the remains of a carpet bag (Pegg 2018: 71). The Indigenous villages contained contact-period assemblages associated with the Fraser River War and its aftermath. At Kopchitchin, blue and green glass beads, a William Astons button, tobacco pipe fragments, and other items from both British and American sources were found in contexts that suggested the village was burned during the war. In contrast, at Tuckkwiowhum, the assemblage from the two pit houses was dominated by Western market items likely brought into the site on the Cariboo Wagon Road (Pegg 2018: 41). Exploring the clash between Indigenous practices and miners, tree-ring data on Lake Mountain suggests a low point of cedar harvesting in the 1850s coincident with the gold rush, but rebounding in the 1860s and 1870s, possibly reflective of new commercial opportunities associated with the construction of the Cariboo Wagon Road (Pegg 2018). After this, Canadian restrictions on Indigenous people resulted in curtailed cedar harvests. Documentary evidence to accompany the archaeological and tree-harvesting data suggests that the Nlaka'pamux resisted colonial domination, both defying Federal authorities while embracing economic opportunities that arose with the expansion of the mining-related transportation system.

The Cariboo Wagon Road was built between 1860–1865 by the Royal Marines, extending to Barkerville, 644 kilometers from its origin at Fort Yale (Boyle and Mackie 2015:80). Barkerville was the principal town of the Cariboo mining region, and at its maximum was about 6,000 people. A Hudson's Bay Company store (1861–1885) supplied both European and Chinese Canadian miners and merchants, restauranteurs, tradesmen, and Indigenous trappers (Boyle and Mackie 2015). Perhaps the most important archaeological work at Barkerville is with the Chinatown (Chen 2001; Ross 2015). Chinese were a significant force in the Cariboo mining area, with between 5,000 and 8,000 Chinese Canadians living there at the peak in the late 1860s. Excavation of the *Chih Kung T'ang* building site by Simon Fraser University in 1993 included a surface collection and excavation underneath the main structure (Chen 2001; Shields 2008). *Chih Kung T'ang* (志公堂, *ji gūng tòhng*) or the Hong-men society (洪門, *hùhng mùhn*) was formed in southern China as an organization to resist the Qing Dynasty, becoming important on the western mining frontier to provide room and board and help its members find jobs, but also fostering gambling, prostitution and opium smoking (Chen 2001: 320–342). Excavations recovered thousands of belongings and faunal remains dating from ca. 1877 to the mid–twentieth century, over 30 percent of which were Chinese manufactured, including opium smoking items, abacus and fan tan (gambling) beads, dominos, and many food remains (Chen 2001: 23–24; Ross 2015: 169).

From Chinese account books translated from the Barkerville archives, other archival materials, and the archaeological record, Chen (2001) described the Chinese Canadian community. In the earliest mining period, merchants and labor brokers dominated, but in the 1870s, as the gold rush declined, the Hong-men societies took on many of the community's social functions. Chen found that people shared co-residence in the north Cariboo, often coming from the same family, area, and community in China (Chen 2001: 375–376). Her conclusion is that the Chinese immigrants to British Columbia and elsewhere established "Colonies of Tang" (唐殖民地) based on ancestral ties to the Tang Dynasty (A.D. 618–907) that allowed external trade and emigration through the port at Guangzhou to southeast Asia. This ancestral concept was recorded on wooden boards with paper scrolls in the Barkerville archives that would have been displayed in stores or clan association rooms. This concept of an ancestral colony was an important Chinese Canadian worldview and replicated Chinese values of family, clan, and place of birth through settlement patterns and practices (Chen 2001: 256–257, 378). While more recent scholarship recognizes fluidity, situational and context-dependent conceptions of culture and identity (e.g., Ross 2015: 181–182), there is an authenticity to the notion of a historical and ancestral heritage that resonates, particularly given current attention to Indigenous cultural persistence.

Historical archaeology has explored how other groups, including Irish and Indigenous Canadians, carved out unique spaces in the British Columbia gold fields (e.g., Jorgenson 2015; Smith 2004). Gold rush opportunities attracted Indigenous people to the Barkerville area tied into traditional seasonal rounds (Jorgenson 2015). During the gold rush, Dakelh, St'at'imc, Tsilhqot'in, Haida, and Coast Salish visited and lived at or near Barkerville, occupied in picking berries, hunting, and supplying salmon and eulachon to the miners. Indigenous people supported White and Chinese Canadian miners as packers and couriers, in laundry services, and through prostitution. They labored in mines fitting opportunistic mining and wage labor activities into other more traditional seasonal activities (Jorgenson 2015).

Idaho and Northeastern Oregon Mining

The gold rushes of 1861 and 1862 brought numerous people to Idaho and northeastern Oregon. Within a year or two, Chinese Americans followed the European American miners, in some cases dominating the populations in the later 1860s and 1870s (Fee 1993; Stapp 1993; Steeves 1984:65; Wegars 1996). Besides the Hong-men societies, the Chinese "company" or *gūng sī* (公司), first established in West Borneo in the mid–eighteenth century, formed another model for many Chinese enterprises in the Pacific Northwest (Chen 2001: 100–104, 300–302; Hann 2021: 354–357). These profit-sharing organizations were often led by merchants and investors, with "brothers" who worked under a mine "master" and often did not receive a wage, distinguishing them from Western models of capitalism.

Archaeologists have conducted significant work near Pierce, Idaho (Longenecker and Stapp 1993; Stapp 1990, 1993); the Lower Salmon River, Florence and Warren, Idaho (Fee 1993; Sisson 1993; Turnipseed et al. 1994); the Blue Mountains of Oregon (Chapman and Ozbun 2002; Hann 2021; Heffner 2015; Jaehnig 1997; Lee 2020; Mead 1996; Myers 1999; Rose and Johnson 2020; Schablitsky and Connolly 2005; Schablitsky et al. 2006; Steeves 1984; Wegars 1996, 2002; Withee 2021); the Boise Basin (Jones et al. 1979; Ostrogorsky 1982); and other places (e.g., Evans-Janke 2007; James 1995). From this research combined with that from Jacksonville and Barkersville, a pattern in Chinese mining sites emerges. In most cases, Chinese are documented as present within a few years of the gold strikes (usually the early 1860s), but commonly excluded from owning mining claims (as were Native Hawaiians and other racialized minorities). Within a few years, however, when White miners wanted to unload their less productive claims, Chinese and other minorities were allowed to purchase or lease them (e.g., Stapp 1990: 57–59; 1993: 9–11; Steeves 1984: 160–161; Turnipseed et al. 1994). In many cases, *gūng sī* organized Chinese American mining early on, but in some cases individual entrepreneurial claims became prevalent (Stapp 1990). Chinese Americans became significant minorities of mining communities, sometimes the dominant population, but due to racist exclusion laws and diminishing returns were driven from the mining districts by the early twentieth century (Fee 1993; Jones et al. 1979; Stapp 1990, 1993; Steeves 1984: 160–161; Turnipseed et al. 1994; Wegars 1996, 2002).

Chinese Canadian site settlement patterns in the Barkerville region are similar to U.S. patterns (Chen 2001; Ross 2015). Larger Chinatowns were incorporated into the town, while some places were physically separated from the White population. Each larger Chinatown contained a cemetery, sometimes incorporated within the White cemetery but sometimes separate (see chapter 6). In smaller towns, a Chinese quarter was present, and Chinese Canadians were also present in separate quarters at larger White-owned mining camps. In some cases, larger Chinese mining camps and smaller individual cabin sites are present (Chen 2001: 35–50). In most cases, Chinese mining camps were connected to nearby Chinese communities in larger local towns and to larger regional Chinatowns in major population centers (Chen 2001; Jones et al. 1979; Wegars 1996, 2002).

Details of mining camps include considerable variation in architectural remains, including the use of dugouts, rock shelters, tent platforms, bermed-earth structures, and log cabins, often in association with U-shaped "wok" ovens (Jaehnig 1997; James 1995; Mead 1996; Myers 1999; Sisson 1993; Stapp 1990, 1993; Striker and Sprague 1993; Wegars 1996, 2002; Withee 2021). Myers (1999) suggested that many of the architectural styles of Blue Mountain Chinese mining camps are consistent with traditional southern China rammed earth structures *hāng tǔ* (夯土) and rectangular two-saddle, side-notch log cabins, with the entrance in the gable end, that approximate traditional *jinggan* or *jǐng jià fáng* (井架房) architecture. The layout of some Chinese mining camps may have conformed to the principles of Feng Shui, facing streams, marshy areas, or curved mining ditches with steeper terrain behind (e.g., Mead 1996). Fee (1993) documents terraced gardens in some locations to produce food for personal consumption and sale to other miners.

Overall, the evidence suggests that food was plentiful and Chinese miners were far from destitute (e.g., Longenecker and Stapp 1993; Rose 2020). Chinese-manufactured items at these sites include a range of typical porcelain serving and food bowls, and saucers in Winter Green, Four Seasons, Bamboo, and Double Happiness patterns (see figure 6.4; Hann 2021; James 1995; Jones et al. 1979; Longenecker and Stapp 1993; Mead 1996; Stapp 1990: 208–213; Striker and Sprague 1993; Wegars 1996, 2002; Withee 2021). Historical archaeologists have documented Asian foods, including Chinese olive (*Canarium album*), *gǎn lǎn* in Cantonese (橄欖) (Wegars 1989). The preferred meat tends to be pork, with beef and wild game more scarce (Jones et al. 1979; Longenecker and Stapp 1993; Stapp 1990). Documented beverages include tea, Chinese whiskey and wine, and European and American liquor, likely served in Chinese tea and liquor cups (Hann 2021; James 1995; Stapp 1990; Wegars 1996, 2002; Withee 2021). Nearly every site contains opium paraphernalia (e.g., James 1995; Jones et al. 1979; Mead 1996; Stapp 1990; Turnipseed et al. 1994; Wegars 1996, 2002). Chinese American and Canadian miners wore Western-style miners' clothing and footwear (Hann 2021; Mead 1996; Stapp 1990; Wegars 2002; Withee 2021), and Chinese-style gambling is suggested from the ubiquitous Chinese coins and gaming pieces (James 1995; Jones et al. 1979; Mead 1996; Stapp 1990; Turnipseed 1994). Chinese miners celebrated traditional and American-style festivals, including Chinese New Year, the Hungry Ghost Festival (*Zhōng yuán Jié*, 中元节), and American Independence Day (e.g., Chen 1972: 105–108; Fee 1993: 67–69).

While the large numbers of Chinese miners sometimes led to friendly and symbiotic relationships, including the instance of Whites guarding Pierce Chinese claims (Stapp 1990: 382–383), the control of these mining districts and mining towns was under laws that protected White interests enforced by local sheriffs. Some resistance to this authority is documented through attempts to avoid territorial taxes, refusal to register under the Geary Act, and perhaps even the killing of a White merchant that led to the extrajudicial lynching of three Chinese near Pierce City (Stapp 1990: 268, 363–366). Systematic violence against Chinese miners includes the hanging of a man for stealing a pair of boots (Fee 1993: 73) and the May 1887 massacre of thirty-four Chinese miners at the hands of Whites in Hells Canyon on the Snake River (James 1995: 16; Nokes 2006, 2022).

The Kam Wah Chung (金華昌, *gām wàh chēung*) Company building at the site of the John Day Chinatown is one of the best-preserved Chinese stores in the American West, and includes a Chinese herbal medicine business, general store, labor contracting office, post office, social center, temple, and residence for the Chinese American mining community (Donovan 2005). The building was locked in 1947, with all of its contents intact, until it was developed as a museum in the 1970s. Its collections are an exceptional assemblage of Chinese and American items dating to 1880–1940 (Heffner 2015: 136).

Archaeological work in the 2.1-hectare John Day Chinatown archaeological site (35GR2086) included ground-penetrating radar and test excavations in 2005 and 2018–2019 (Rose and Johnson 2020; Schablitsky and Connolly 2005; Schablitsky et al. 2006, 2007). Historical archaeology has revealed at least eight other buildings surrounding the Kam Wah Chung store, including a temple and residences. Belongings include typical imported Chinese items, mixed with European and American ceramics, canning jars, and buttons. A comparison of documentary and archaeological remains from Kam Wah Chung, Chinese mining sites on the Malheur National Forest, and Jacksonville, Oregon, demonstrates the variation in experiences of Chinese American miners (Lee 2020). Analysis suggests that the framework of laws that racialized Chinese Americans was operationalized in communities like John Day to impact Chinese miners' market access and consumption choices. The variety of responses to these policies are diverse, including the use of Chinese organizations and merchants to mitigate racism (Lee 2020).

Logging and Lumbering

Logging, or the acquisition of trees and their transport to a mill, is distinguished from lumbering, which involves acquisition and manufacture of forest products. The actions of logging and lumbering created many Pacific Northwest communities, significantly contributing to some of its most urbanized areas, such as Portland (originally called Stump Town) and Seattle,

Figure 7.3. Steam donkey on display at Camp 18 Restaurant, Elsie, Oregon.

which housed the original "skid road" (or skid row). Logging and lumbering's long, complex, and controversial history provides a fertile ground for historical archaeology (Barman 2007: 121–124; Clark 2002; Gregory 2001; Jepsen and Norberg 2017: 155–171; Schwantes 1996: 215–222).

Indigenous people of the Pacific Northwest had a well-developed woodworking tradition, including elaborately carved dugout canoes and monumental-sized wooden plankhouses (Ames and Maschner 1999; Ames and Shepard 2019; Boyd et al. 2015). The first British lumber mill was established about 10 kilometers upstream of Fort Vancouver on a small tributary of the Columbia River in the winter of 1828–1829 (Hussey 1957). Prior to about 1890, logging in the Northwest was small-scale, with most timber harvested near the shoreline and shipped to California lumber yards (Clark 2002: 90–91; Finger 1972; Gregory 2001: 11–12; Hills et al. 1996; Schwantes 1996: 217). Skidding, the means to get felled trees to transportation hubs, was limited to oxen, mules, or horses (Gregory 2001: 14–15; Rajala 1989: 169). By the 1880s, loggers employed high wheels—carts with wheels 8 to 10 feet (2.4 to 3 m) in diameter pulled by oxen or horses to convey sometimes very massive logs under its frame. The invention of a steam engine mounted on a sled, or "steam donkey," combined with the advent of mass-produced wire cable in the early twentieth century, allowed loggers to pull logs to central assembly areas (figure 7.3; Hills et al. 1996; Mack 2005: 31–33; Rajala 1989: 169; Sekora and Ross 1995: 10-65 to 10-67). These were replaced by gasoline-powered tractors starting in the 1920s. Wooden flumes and splash dams used water and gravity to move logs from ponded areas out of mountain areas to lower elevation mills. Log chutes used gravity, animals, or steam donkeys to move logs along prepared routes (Davis 1997). The "high lead logging" technique used steam donkeys and a "spar tree" rigged with steel rope to transport logs over obstructions, allowing nearly year-round logging (Bass 2017: 48–50; Miss et al. 2000: 111–112; Rajala 1989: 171).

Lumber companies rapidly moved to areas serviced by transcontinental railroads, ushering in a new era of logging, and providing substantial impetus for population growth between 1880–1920, with increased exports to the east coast and foreign ports (Clark 2002: 89–92; Gregory 2001: 12–13; Henning and Henning 1990). Starting with President Harrison in 1891, U.S. Federal "forest withdrawals" resulted in a rush by logging companies to get at those properties not yet reserved, including sometimes the use of "dummy entrymen" to claim properties on behalf of timber companies (Mack 2005: 4–10). Before World War I, many logging camps were smaller, temporary, single-bunkhouse camps characterized by log architecture, very crowded conditions with rough wooden bunks and straw, few bathing facilities, and menus focused on legumes (Conlin 1979; Rajala 1989, 1996).

Historical archaeology has explored many sites related to logging and lumbering (e.g., Bass 2017; Clark 2002; Connolly et al. 2011; Davis 1997; Gregory 2001; Haught-Bielmann 2018; Hills et al. 1996; Mack 2005; McIlrath 2002; Miss et al. 2000; Paullin 2007; Sekora and Ross 1995; Wilson 1999; Woodward 1975). Contrasting with narratives of logging ruggedness, by the late nineteenth century, even remote places in the Pacific Northwest were serviced by national markets, and archaeologists sometimes find very fancy Victorian products in the houses of owners, managers, and skilled workers at mill sites (Haught-Bielmann 2018; Warner 2017; Woodward 1975). Many of the homes in these logging communities were frame houses with glass windows, illuminated with kerosene oil lamps, containing doors with decorative ceramic doorknobs, and sometimes even telephones. Archaeologists find abundant consumer items, including transferprint and plain white earthenware dishes, decorative teacups and saucers, pressed glass dishes, and silver flatware from American or Canadian firms. Sometimes expensive clothing items, including gold-plated collar buttons and watch chains and parts, speak to the refinement of dress by some late-Victorian loggers when not at work. Domestic activities include food storage, represented by glass canning jars and stoneware crocks, and at some sites children's socialization is represented in belongings, including alphabet plates, children's tea sets, ceramic dolls, marbles, and slate fragments and pencils. Even for those who lived in ethnically distinct communities, there appears to be more of an emphasis on items that signaled elite, American socioeconomic status, such as lamps with fancy crystals, or that maintained a Victorian-gendered space over items that signaled ancestry (e.g., Haught-Bielmann 2018; Warner 2017).

By the 1910s, greater numbers of immigrants worked in lumber mills and logging camps, including people from eastern and northern Europe and Japan (McIlrath 2002: 6, 15). By the early twentieth century, logging camps were largely male, with only a few female cooks or waitresses. As a consequence, archaeological remains often reflect patterns dominated by the adult male gender, with limited evidence for other genders and even less evidence for children except at the biggest camps and mills (e.g., Mack 2005). Tinned enamelware dishes and graniteware coffee pots replace fancier ceramics found in managers' and mill owners' homes. Assemblages are dominated by tin cans from foods brought to the camp, but often supplemented with fresh meat and fruit. All of the sites contain substantial numbers of commercial remedies, no doubt associated with the difficult working conditions (e.g., McIlrath 2002: 35; Mack 2005; Woodward 1975).

While some of the late nineteenth-century sites, like Palmer in the Columbia River Gorge, contain a surprising lack of alcoholic beverage containers (Woodward 1975), others, like the early twentieth-century Camp 3 of the Wind River Lumber Company in Washington, contain gin and whisky flasks, and most contain abundant smoking items, including tobacco tins and tabs from Copenhagen, Prince Albert, and Lucky Strike brands (Mack 2005). Archaeologists tend to find simple workmen's clothing, grooming items like hard rubber combs, bone toothbrushes, mirror glass fragments, and straight razors (Mack 2005; Woodward 1975). Logging tools include blacksmithing gear, saw teeth, iron dogs (hooks), and chain links (cf., Mack 2005).

This period of logging changed forever in 1917, at the outset of U.S. involvement in World War I, when the Army ordered an astonishing 100 million board feet[5] of aircraft-quality spruce (about a billion board feet considering waste) (Crosman 2011; Rajala 1989, 1996; Tonsfeldt 2013; Tonsfeldt and Atwood 2003: 75–97; Williams 2018). Spruce was essential for manufacturing aircraft frames, which were then covered in fabric. Due to labor shortages and a massive region-wide strike (Rajala 1989, 1996; Tonsfeldt 2013:5–7), the U.S.

---

5   A board foot is a volumetric measure of lumber 1 foot long × 1 foot wide × 1 inch thick (30.5 × 30.5 × 2.5 cm); 1,000 board feet is a pile of lumber 10 feet long, 4 feet wide, and 2 feet high (3 × 1.2 × .6 m).

Army nationalized the logging industry, recruiting 25,000 soldier-loggers for the "Spruce Production Division" to work at logging camps and lumber mills, including a specialized mill for precision cutting at Vancouver Barracks. Labor reforms associated with the operation, including imposition of military wages, Army housing and food standards, and an eight-hour work day, largely remained standard in logging camps after the war (Tonsfeldt 2013: 134–136). Archaeological remains of the Spruce Production Division include camps, railroad grades, and the material evidence of the Spruce Mill itself, an enormous facility with a massive tent city to house its thousands of workers (e.g., Wilson et al. 2016).

Post–World War I Logging

After World War I, a common model of logging camps developed in the Pacific Northwest, housing considerably more people, from 150 to 600 loggers and their families (Bass 2017: 35–36; Clark 2002; Gregory 2001; Rajala 1989). By the 1920s, many logging camps contained stores, electric lights, showers, and recreational opportunities. Part of this heightened concern for the worker was the presence of larger, more capitalized logging companies, the expansion of railroad logging, and greater attention to sanitation, which overall improved the logger's bargaining position (Rajala 1989). Narrow-gauge logging railroads allowed transportation of the workers, and modified rail cars, and reusable "skid cabins," which could be moved on flat cars from camp to camp, allowed larger, longer-term camps (Hills et al. 1996). Camps were linear, usually running along the main trunk of the railroad or a nearby spur line, and sometimes elevated above the ground on stilts (e.g., Connolly et al. 2011). Development of family camps was promoted over male-only camps to create more stable communities with loggers less likely to cause labor unrest. As a consequence, many camps also had school facilities. The women of these families contributed cooking, laundering, and child-raising, usually unremunerated.

Large camp structures have been described at a number of larger logging camps in southern Oregon, including a Shevlin-Hixon camp, the Hub Camp, and Weyerhaeuser Camp 2 (Clark 2002; Hills et al. 1996). Documentary evidence for the Great Depression–era Camp 2, about 19 kilometers west of Klamath Falls, Oregon, indicates distinctive bachelor ("men's camp") and family camps with a developed "brass row" for managers, each separated from industrial areas (figure 7.4). Related to the companies' paternalistic interests in controlling information, reading rooms became common at the larger camps, and logging newspapers, such as *Camp and Mill News*, were developed to level the worker/operator distinctions and promote fellowship

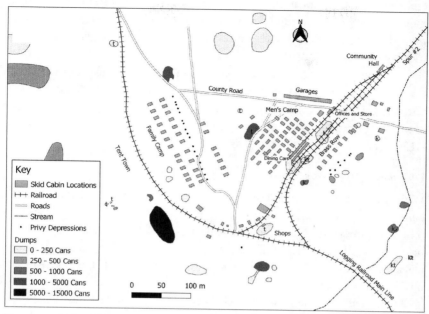

Figure 7.4. Map of the Weyerhaeuser Camp 2 showing archaeological and historical features (derived from Hills et al. 1996: figures 1.2, 6.1, 6.4 and table 6.2).

between bosses and loggers (Rajala 1989). Company picnics and company baseball teams were similar company strategies.

The archaeological remains of railroad logging include grades with associated wooden ties, spikes, bolts, and other hardware, usually with the rails removed for salvage or reuse, borrow pits, and logging camps (Clark 2002:96). Camps are organized around the dendritic and hub-and-spoke nodes of the logging railroads, and a landscape approach is necessary to understand and address the spatial organization of the sites and features. At Weyerhaeuser Camp 2, for example, tin can dumps, privy depressions, and some low rock walls correlate with Brass Row, Men's Camp, and Family Camp. Based on documentary and archaeological evidence, a "tent town" was established on the outskirts where loggers could live for free. Refuse disposal is correlated with housing areas and activity spaces, with smaller items like tobacco tins, glass fragments, and pottery sherds left around household activity areas at skid cabin sites as sheet trash. Most large, bulky items, including copious meat, fruit, vegetable, and milk tins, were deposited in dumps. Tin can dumps lie on the periphery of the main living and working areas and between physical (and probably symbolic) boundaries between different areas of the camp (see figure 7.4). Co-location of the single men's living quarters and the dining hall likely helped to curtail labor organization, a physical constraint to single men already sandwiched between the families of the managers and the family loggers (Hills et al. 1996). Family areas contain domestic items besides the ubiquitous tin cans, including cosmetics and toiletries, home food canning jars, laundry and household maintenance items, and decorative table and teawares. In contrast, concentrations of tobacco tins suggest locations of men's socialization, associated with the men's camp and the camp shop area (Hills et al. 1996).

Japanese American Logging Sites (1890s–1930s)

While concern about Japanese material culture accompanied the interest in Chinese American sites (e.g., Stenger 1993), only a few archaeologists explored Japanese American sites or material culture in the Pacific Northwest prior to the 1990s (Ross 2021). Since 2000, considerable archaeological work has focused on Japanese settlements, or *Nihonmachi* (日本町) (Aranyosi 2017a, 2017b; Ross 2021).

Associated with the 1867 Meiji Restoration in Japan, Japanese began emigrating to the Pacific Northwest, largely as replacements for Chinese American labor (Aronyosi 2017; Carlson 2017: 30, 2021: 696; Fiset and Nomura 2005: 5). By 1900, there were more than 10,000 Japanese immigrants in the region, and in British Columbia, 25 percent of the lumbering workforce were Japanese Canadians (Fiset and Nomura 2005:5; Muckle 2017:128). By 1910, more than 22,000 Japanese Americans were working in Oregon and Washington sawmills (Campbell 2021: 719).

Historical archaeology of early twentieth-century Japanese sites include Japanese Canadian logging sites in the Seymour Valley, British Columbia (Muckle 2001, 2008, 2012, 2017, 2021), and Japanese American communities at mill towns, such as Barneston, Washington (Carlson 2017, 2021); Japan Gulch, Mukilteo, Washington (Campbell 2017b, 2021); Fairfax, Washington (Taylor 2020); and the Yama and Nagaya communities at Port Blakely, Washington (Aranyosi 2017a, 2017b; Daugherty 1992; Hartse 2017; Hartse and Hannah 2021; White and Heideman 2008). At mill towns, Japanese workers were segregated from White populations, often living in housing situations that included bachelors, married men living alone, and families (Campbell 2021; Carlson 2017: 33–34; Hartze 2017; Hartze and Hannah 2021; Muckle 2017, 2021). The ceramics assemblages contain imported Japanese porcelain rice bowls, dishes, pickle plates, tea and sake cups, and sometimes teapots (Aronyosi 2017a, 2017b; Campbell 2021; Carlson 2017; Muckle 2017, 2021).

Researchers suggest the Japanese engaged in traditional cooking and dining customs, but Campbell (2021: 729) infers that their selection of consumer items may have signaled personal taste, "class ambition, socioeconomic status, and knowledge of modern non-traditional Japanese cuisine." For example, some Japanese ceramic decoration styles, including regional landscape-style teapots, contain subtle social commentaries on westernization and Japanese colonial ambitions (Campell 2021: 729–734).

Other types of belongings include food and cooking oil cans, pharmaceutical and alcohol bottles, including Western whiskey, and locally brewed beer, as well as imported Japanese beer and sake (e.g., Muckle 2017, 2021). Some of the communities contain Japanese-style bathhouses (Aranyosi 2017a; Carlson 2017, 2021; Muckle 2017, 2021), and other exterior features include outhouses, chicken yards, gardens, and in the case of Yama, a community cistern. The material assemblages usually contain evidence for Western-style clothing, including leather work boots, boot polish cans, talc shakers, combs, and jewelry. At Yama, socialization of children is represented in children's toys, including fragments of a miniature tea set and a ceramic doll, while in some communities, like Barneston, the documentary record suggests that Japanese American children learned at integrated public schools during the day and at Japanese schools in the evenings (Carlson 2021).

Similar to Japanese fishing camps, there is evidence of cultural persistence, but also practices that threaded the spaces defined by racism and social control. White managers employed paternalistic systems to control labor in their mills, using ethnic/racial tensions to keep groups separated, preventing the emergence of strong unions, and often relegating Japanese workers to the most menial and dangerous jobs (Carlson 2021; Taylor 2020).

Importantly, many Japanese American leaders and even the Japanese government pushed for Western assimilation (Carlson 2021: 690). Special bookman or foreman liaisons were used to help smooth over racial tensions and to shape "model" Japanese villages (Campbell 2017b: 65). At Yama, Hartse and Hannah (2021: 681) suggest a rapidly shifting and transient community through time formed a "critical center for the Japanese of the region" (Hartse and Hannah 2021: 681). Systemic racism in Canada and the United States, combined with Meiji elites who responded to negative racial stereotypes with social prescriptions, required novel responses by Japanese immigrants (Hartze 2017). The development of family communities with both Buddhist temples and Christian churches, as well as well-connected community leaders (*nushidōri*), suggests that Japanese men and women creatively engaged White community members. Resistance is inferred from continued acquisition of

Japanese ceramics in the face of pressure to purchase Western-style dishes from local sources, and as noted in the subtle commentaries of the selection of some of these ceramics (Campbell 2021).

Indigenous Persistence

Like at earlier missions and forts, many of the archaeological sites associated with the development of nineteenth- and early twentieth-century industries in the Pacific Northwest contain the material remains of precolonial Native Americans. Indigenous people also were intimately intertwined with extractive industries and formed major actors in many of the events and actions of the colonial businesses (Ewonus and Ewonus 2019). Native Americans also continued to persist on their landscapes (e.g., Byram 2002; Ewonus and Ewonus 2019; Nesbitt 1969, 1970; Tasa et al. 1993; Tveskov 2000, 2007). The Beatty Curve site (35KL95) is one example. About 64 kilometers northeast of Klamath Falls, Oregon, on the land of the former Klamath Indian Reservation, archaeologists excavated the remains of a small 1872–1920s cabin and its surrounding activity areas, including a likely dome-shaped mat lodge or wickiup and ramada (Connolly et al. 2022; Ruiz 2010). Connolly et al. (2022:2) use archaeology, oral history, and the concept of persistence and resilience to explore how the Klamath and Modoc people who lived at the Beatty Curve site addressed settler colonialism. U.S. Indian Agents built the cabin for James Barkley, a Klamath tribal leader, to push Western-style architecture and ideology. Outfitted with a cast-iron stove and containing Western-style eating utensils, butcher knives, a graniteware coffee pot, and other typical domestic dishes and ranch belongings, it looks much like other settler houses (Ruiz 2010). Cartridges and gun parts speak to hunting, and children's toys and Western-style educational items, including marbles, slate pencils and tablets, and a child-sized shoe, suggest that young people were receiving Western-style education and clothing. Decorative buttons, jewelry, hat pins and decorative hair combs suggest the presence of women, indicating that commercial culture was "increasingly pervasive at all socio-economic levels, extending even to Native Americans on the remote Klamath Reservation" (Ruiz 2010: 123).

However, the Beatty Curve site has many attributes that distinguish it materially from logging and mining camps and settler homesteads, including the discovery of evidence for the wickiup-like structure, inferred as a traditional mat-floored house (Connolly et al. 2022:6; Ruiz 2010: 120). Grinding tools found around the cabin suggest continuation of traditional food preparation and consumption, consistent with Agency records and oral history, including the gathering of pond lily "wocus" and other seeds, fruits, and roots. Traditional hunting and fishing also continued but was augmented by firearms, spring traps, and metal fishhooks. Wild animal bones included elk, deer, pronghorn antelope, beaver, and waterfowl. Fish bones suggest catching of suckers, chub, steelhead, and chinook salmon. Even among the domesticated animal bones, which included cattle, horse, swine, sheep, goat, and poultry, the evidence suggests butchery on site, with little evidence of commercial meat cuts or packaged foods. Surprisingly, there were very few tin cans, suggesting little reliance on prepackaged foods, quite unlike most logging and railroad camps found in the region. Oral history and archaeology suggest use of both introduced and wild food items.

The buttons found at Beatty Curve are abundant and diverse, representing prosser buttons in plain, printed, color and pie-cut styles, two- and four-hole shell (pearl) buttons, and highly decorative buttons, including classic Victorian mourning buttons. The archaeologists also recovered glass beads and metal cone-style tinklers, both premade and handmade; and repurposed tobacco tags used as tinklers. A cache of sixty-two obsidian needle tinklers in the remains of a bag, post-dating 1896, was found at the ramada where large numbers of the decorative buttons, beads, and metal tinklers were also found (Connolly et al. 2022: 8; Ruiz 2010: 119). Needle tinklers are long, thin fragments of obsidian that dancers attached to their clothing, making a sound when they clapped together. The occupants of Beatty Curve apparently used ornate buttons as an expression of wealth and identity, with Western-style buttons mixed with beads and tinklers used in regalia and button blankets. The caching of obsidian tinklers may represent resistance to attempts by the Indian Agents to end traditional healing and shamanism. The Beatty Curve site demonstrates in many ways cultural persistence in the traditional reinterpretation of Western-style spaces, while continuing traditions that reinforced Indigenous resilience (Connolly et al. 2022).

8

Transportation and Urbanism at the Onset of Modernity

Silcott, Washington, now inundated under the waters of Lower Granite Lake, was a small community, not particularly significant economically and inhabited by common farming folk (figure 8.1). The historical archaeology of Silcott in the early 1970s departed significantly from heritage sites associated with forts and colonial communities, focusing on scattered homesteads near the confluence of Alpowa Creek and the Snake River, about 16 kilometers from Lewiston, Idaho. While the community started as a ferry, stage station, and hostel in 1860, by the 1880s, wheat farming and fruit orchards were predominant (Adams 1973, 1975). Silcott was gone by the 1930s, ruined by construction of a new road to Lewiston, the onset of the Great Depression, and several hard freezes that killed the fruit crops. For the archaeologists of Silcott, the sites they explored were essentially "modern," being only about forty to sixty years old, and numerous people could still speak directly about their life there.

Expansive review of abundant early twentieth-century documents and oral history accompanied the recovery of archaeological remains from a general store, domestic home sites, and dumps. The archaeologists conducted novel analyses of consumer product distributions, tests of archaeological and informant methods, and even explored transient labor (Adams 1973, 1975, 1977; Adams and Gaw 1977; Gaw 1975; Riordan 1977; Riordan and Adams 1985). Silcott's community was connected to and affected by changing transportation systems and commercial goods, leading to shifts from general stores to retail outlets in larger communities facilitated by roads and railroads. This tied rural communities to larger markets, providing greater opportunities for businesses and the increasing urbanism of the major cities.

In this chapter, I explore the late nineteenth- and twentieth-century technological and social innovations that accompanied improved transportation and the creation of new urban areas. I also consider the materiality of Chinese, Japanese, African, and Native American communities up to World War II, the twentieth-century racism that confronted them, and the government's

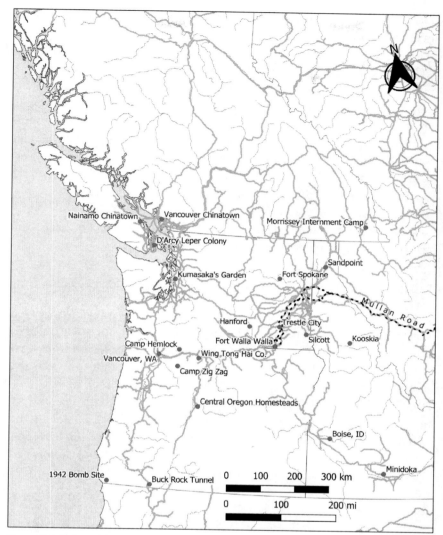

Figure 8.1. Railroad networks and archaeological sites.

role in isolation, incarceration, and attempted assimilation of these people. Historical archaeology has addressed climate, economic, and technological effects on the people of the late nineteenth- and early twentieth-century Pacific Northwest. Fluctuating climate and the Great Depression had significant roles in the failure of many homesteads in eastern regions, while major changes in transportation brought new people and created larger urban areas. While elites prior to World War I imposed Victorian ideology to "civilize" the landscape, this gave way to cheaper, mass-produced products and mismatched ceramics at small farms and poorer urban communities. Government policies impacted where people homesteaded and how they weathered the Great Depression and imposed new community structures in the form of CCC and World War II camps. Historical archaeology has explored the disciplines embodied in these camps and resistance to work by their inhabitants. Notably, many of the sites from World War II were studied because of ongoing environmental damage from hazardous landfills and major cleanup projects.

Historical archaeology also has started to document the practices and lifeways of Chinese, Japanese, and African Americans in the Pacific Northwest in urban areas, work camps, military bases, and the shameful incarceration of Japanese during World War II. Historical archaeology shows how these communities maintained distinctive places in the identity of the Pacific Northwest, carving out traditional and nuanced landscapes and practices, while resisting and surviving institutionalized and overt racism.

Failed Homesteads of the Twentieth Century (ca. 1900–1930s)

Development of the eastern, more arid portions of the region was much slower and later than in the west. The earliest settlements were associated with cattle grazing to support the gold rushes, and homesteaders did not arrive in many areas until the railroads were built and wheat production took over from ranching (Sekora and Ross 1995: 10–13 to 10–15; Thomas et al. 1984: 20). Historical archaeologists have explored small, failed homesteads, documenting roads, cleared fields, rock walls, fence lines, orchards, small stands of deciduous trees, and remains of structures, including houses, barns, and root cellars (Speulda and Bowyer 2002:83; Thomas et al. 1984). Across eastern Oregon and Washington, wetter, more agreeable conditions in the 1910s shifted to drought in the 1920s, combined with increased industrialization and urbanism, the effects of World War I, and finally the Great Depression, resulting in many abandonments (Speulda and Bowyer 2002; Thomas et al. 1984: 20, 179).

Homesteading occupants were often diverse in composition, including bachelors and families, but historical records often are misleading in specifying household composition or even homestead occupation dates (Speulda and Bowyer 2002: 84–86). Artifacts suggest that male-only households purchased wider varieties of prepared foods, with female-headed households buying such ingredients as baking powder, lard, and spices. Gendered objects include clothing items and children's clothing and toys (Speulda and Bowyer 2002). In this regard, homesteads reflect a variety of patterns, each containing distinctive belongings, and structured uniquely based on household size, family structure, and initial socioeconomic status. In the end, the potential of free land and governmental programs that encouraged homesteading could not compete with changing natural and social environments, making it impossible for many small farms and ranches to succeed in the arid West.

Changing Transportation and Communities

Steamboat landings and ferries were critical aspects of early transportation systems, which utilized river transportation and roads to carry people and supplies. Small communities surrounding ferry landings, however, gave way to railroad communities and towns. Some of the earliest roads were constructed in association with the military, many facilitating gold mining, such as the Cariboo Road in British Columbia, or the Mullan Road that linked Walla Walla, Washington, to northern Idaho and Montana (Freeman 1954). Archaeologists have explored the remains of ferry sites and steamboat landings (e.g., Carley and Sappington 1984; Thomas et al. 1984), railroad towns (e.g., Carley and Sappington 1984; Cavender 2018; Warner 2014; Weaver 2014), and railroad construction and operations camps (e.g., Akin et al. 2015; Christian et al. 2021; Wegars and Sprague 1981). Some work has characterized small communities that span the late nineteenth and early twentieth centuries, often associated with saloons, boarding houses, hotels, restaurants, post offices, shops, and schools.

Short-term trash accumulations, household and tin can dumps, ash deposits, privies, and cellars from construction and workmen's camps for the railroad often contain primarily male-dominated assemblages. For example, belongings recovered from the 1913–1914 Trestle City (Joso Trestle) Construction Camp (45FR51) suggested that workmen consumed beer, wine, whiskey and gin, smoked and chewed tobacco, played cards and gambled, treated ailments with national remedies, and played or listened to music (Wegars and Sprague 1981: 49–50). Abundant tin cans and food bones attest to prepared meals, mostly served on plain whiteware ceramics manufactured in England or the midwestern United States.

Many of the workers for railroad construction in the nineteenth century were Chinese Americans, and their camps represent an important element of transportation-related archaeology. Surface collection of short-term work camps of Chinese Americans in northern Idaho and western Montana allowed Akin et al. (2015) to examine the varied use of Asian coins lost during construction of the Northern Pacific Railroad. Chinese *wen*, Vietnamese zinc *dong*, and Japanese *mon* were used for gaming, talismanic and decorative uses, and possibly as traditional medicine (cf., Akin et al. 2015; Keddie 2019).

The technology associated with constructing railroads through the mountains and reliance on Chinese labor is epitomized by the failed Buck Rock Tunnel (1883–1885) near Ashland, Oregon (Christian et al. 2021). The tunnel was part of the Oregon and California Railroad (O&C), which tied Portland with the Southern Pacific Railroad in California. Because it was never completed, the archaeological remains demonstrate late nineteenth-century tunnel construction techniques, including remnant "heading and bench" excavations. The archaeological remains of the related camps are similar to others in the western states, with a stacked-rock wok oven, prepared tent pads, and associated Chinese ceramics (Christian et al. 2021).

Sandpoint, Idaho (1880–1935)

A major railroad hub, Sandpoint, Idaho, is representative of larger Pacific Northwest communities built on the transcontinental railroads. Plans to construct a bypass that would cross the original townsite resulted in Idaho's largest archaeological data recovery excavation (Cavender 2018; Warner 2014; Weaver 2014). Over 560,000 items were recovered, tracing through documents and belongings the emergence of the railroad town, and uniquely exploring the remains of Sandpoint's "restricted district."

The confluence of the 1883 Northern Pacific, the 1893 Great Northern (now the Burlington Northern and Santa Fe), and the Spokane International Railway, combined with the development of the 1899 Sand Point Lumber Company (later Humbird Lumber), significantly expanded the frontier community of about one hundred people in 1886, to about 3,600 people by 1910 (Cavender 2018; Weaver 2014). Expansion resulted in a push for greater respectability, and the restricted district was created from the southern portion of the original townsite, with saloons, brothels, and other businesses. Prohibition in 1916 drove out the saloons, eroding the influence of the red-light district, and by 1921 the brothels were gone.

Railroads provided Sandpoint's residents global access to consumer goods, with items delivered from thirty-six states within the United States and sixteen countries (Warner, Swords, and Haught-Bielmann 2014). There was a mixture of locally produced items amid the deluge of imported goods, with approximately 45 percent of the medicines and pharmaceuticals locally produced, competing with nationally marketed remedies (Cavender 2018:23). The primary contributions of the excavations at Sandpoint are tied to explorations of the restricted district, including the lives of prostitutes and the small Chinese American community. Prostitution was one of the more common and open elements of western towns in the late nineteenth and early twentieth centuries (Simmons 1982, 1989), and some of the most extensive remains of prostitution in the Pacific Northwest to date have illuminated the daily lives of the prostitutes at Henderson's Brothel, as well as at an adjoining higher-class Hermann's Bordello (Warner and Bard 2014). Not surprisingly, alcohol bottles were common at both sites, representing 67 percent of identifiable bottles, with wine and champagne the most common, including "Mumms" French champagne. Likewise, tumblers, stemware, and glasses for cordials, shots, and pilsner beer were recovered. Interestingly, faunal remains suggest mixed cuts of beef, with steaks and other high-quality meat cuts contrasting with inexpensive ones. Apparently, everyday moderation was tempered with sporadic splurges, possibly on a lumber mill or railroad payday (Warner and Bard 2014).

Toys and children's clothing attest to the presence of the prostitute's children in the brothels. Victorian bric-a-brac was also noted, including tongue-in-cheek angel statues, see-no-evil monkeys, and a cupid doll among the possessions (Cavender 2018; Warner and Bard 2014). Four men's wedding bands likely represent items stolen by one or more of the prostitutes. There were also products marketed for the treatment of venereal disease and a urethral syringe and parts for treating male syphilis (Warner and Bard 2014; Warner, Martin, and Brown 2014).

Perhaps the most distinctive site within the "restricted district" was a Chinese laundry that formed the "Chinatown" of Sandpoint (Warner, Kisling, and Swords 2014: 55). The Chinese quarter was very small compared to mining camps and towns, forming a separate enclave, with residents serving as cooks, laundrymen, and servants (Warner, Kisling, and Swords 2014). Similarities to other Chinese American sites include Asian-origin ceramics, opium smoking paraphernalia, gaming pieces, and Chinese medicine vials (Warner, Kisling, and Swords 2014). Porcelain included a prodigious number of Japanese wares, including Geisha Girl wares, which were manufactured and marketed to Western stereotypes of the Japanese (Camp 2014). The laundry owners may have intentionally displayed these wares and the exoticism of Asia to potential White American customers, or perhaps to cater to the numerous Japanese laborers associated with the nearby lumber mill (Camp 2014: 76). Chinese porcelain includes Winter Green, Four Seasons, Bamboo, and Double Happiness, but with greater diversity than in mining and logging camps, which often are dominated by the cheaper styles (Camp 2014: 78).

The hundreds of glass vessels were primarily European-American products, including condiments, sauces, extracts, flavorings, and spices, including Western-style ketchup, Worcestershire sauce, and grape juice, and locally distributed milk in bottles. Alcohol was dominated by American and British brands, as were pharmaceutical bottles, with only thirteen identified as

Chinese. The animal protein consumed in Sandpoint's Chinese community contrasts with other Chinese American sites, with beef dominant, perhaps related to restaurant workers taking home leftover foods (Warner, Kisling, and Swords 2014).

Consistent with its function as a laundry, hundreds of buttons, most of Western origin but some of traditional Chinese design, were recovered. Glass gaming pieces, dominated by white glass pieces, suggest *fan tan* gambling, as do Chinese and Vietnamese coins (Camp 2014: 80–84). Nesting brass turtles, a jade bracelet, and a glass bird feeder represent other belongings found at the site that hint at Chinese identity in this tiny Chinese American enclave (Cavender 2018; Warner, Kisling, and Swords 2014).

Urbanization

One of the outcomes of the construction of railroads was increased urbanization and dramatic changes to urban landscapes. There have been numerous and extensive urban archaeology projects in the Pacific Northwest, most of which relate to large transportation projects associated with highways, urban rail lines, and sometimes the redevelopment of historical blocks. Unfortunately, the results of these projects are largely relegated to gray literature or have not been fully reported, and there are no synthetic books or journal volumes. While it is impossible to address all the projects in larger urban areas, I explore as exemplary some of these projects in two moderate-sized cities: Vancouver, Washington, and Boise, Idaho.

Vancouver, Washington

The American settler Henry Williamson filed the first land claim for what would become the City of Vancouver in 1845, west of Fort Vancouver, and platted the townsite of "Columbia City" with William Fellows in 1848. By 1854, Pete Fergusson opened the first commercial structure, a saloon, on Main and Second Street, and the widowed Esther Short, who had squatted on Williamson's land claim, built the Pacific House Restaurant nearby (Beckham 2006; Minor 2006: 95–100). The population of Vancouver was quite small until the twentieth century, with only 3,545 inhabitants in 1890, but jumping to 9,300 in 1910 after the Spokane, Portland & Seattle (SP&S) Railroad was built (U.S. Census Bureau 1910). Vancouver Barracks continued to influence the growing city, with military personnel representing 15 percent of the city's 1910 population. By 1940, the population grew to 18,782 people, and with construction of the World War II shipyard, the town boomed to 95,000 residents (Roulette et al. 2010:10). The city now houses about 195,000 people and is one of the largest cities in the state of Washington.

In spite of the extensive archaeological excavations at Fort Vancouver/Vancouver Barracks, few historical archaeology projects were undertaken within the downtown of the American city prior to early twenty-first century redevelopment. Archaeologists monitored historical Blocks 24 and 25 (45CL514) in one of the oldest parts of Vancouver, on the western border of Vancouver Barracks (Minor 2006). The project identified a brick-lined dry well, cellars, refuse and ash deposits, concrete footings, and the remains of a ca. 1928 Chinese laundry, suggesting that "abundant and well-preserved archaeological remains are present beneath the older portions of the City of Vancouver" (Minor 2006: 110).

Since then, archaeologists have recorded numerous sites, usually associated with a building lot or block of the city, and often correlated with Sanborn fire insurance maps, finding brick and concrete foundations, historical debris, pit features, fence lines, and trash pits from houses, stores, saloons, and shops (Minor et al. 2010; Roulette and White 2005, 2011; Roulette et al. 2018). Excavations at the blocks south of Esther Short Park explored a residential area associated with the Victorian era between ca. 1870 and 1920, examining individualism, medical freedom, and personal hygiene; dining habits, industrialized foodways, modern ideas of material consumption and disposability; and childhood (Roulette et al. 2018: 3–5 to 3–6). The work on historical Block 55 examined features associated with life during the Great Depression in the 1930s and 1940s (Roulette and White 2011). More recently, archaeologists have explored the blocks south of the railroad tracks in the area of the Vancouver Waterfront development, examining neighborhoods split from the Vancouver downtown area by the construction of the SP&S Railroad (Roulette et al. 2018).

Using economic scaling of ceramics as a measure, Roulette et al. (2018) compared lower middle- and working-class neighborhoods. Prior to construction of the railroad, the neighborhood north of the tracks contained middle- and upper-middle-class households. While many of these families continued to reside in Vancouver into the twentieth century, by 1920 urban infill was largely complete and there were fewer owner-occupied homes, with increased numbers of lower-class and working-class lodgers and renters. By the time of the Great Depression, matched ceramic and glassware sets were uncommon, perhaps similar to the "hodge podge" of patterns noted by Gaw (1975) at Silcott. Earlier in the Victorian era, houses south of Esther Short Park contained abundant evidence for matched ceramic sets and considerable wealth displayed in clothing items (Bush 2006; Roulette et al. 2018). The depression-era households contained an abundance of canning jars and lids and a dearth of tin cans, suggesting a mentality of "making do," with an overall dearth of alcohol remains likely associated with both the temperance movement and economic factors (Roulette and White 2011). Also of interest, the residents of Block 55 continued to dump refuse on their lots in spite of city prohibitions, contrasting with the more settled households just across the park (Roulette and White 2011).

A related study explored fish use in Vancouver using data from the six blocks south of Esther Short Park (Taber 2018). Historical records show that by the turn of the twentieth century, nonnative fish were promoted more than native fishes, with native salmon, steelhead, and sturgeon filling the role of a low-valued staple food. Introduced fishes, such as nonnative trout, shad, bass, and catfish, were more expensive. The archaeological remains suggest that the lower- to middle-class households selectively purchased fish, often lower-cost varieties and parts, including fish heads. It appears that the acceptance of Victorian ideals and access to higher-cost market purchases was at best sporadic. Out of proportion to the huge fishery that is the Columbia River, fish was only periodically consumed in Vancouver. Importantly, Taber (2018: 133–134) notes that the industrialization of the banks of the Columbia River changed the abundance and safety of fish in its waters, such that fish caught off the pier that could be eaten in the late nineteenth and early twentieth centuries are much less abundant and safe to eat due to pollution.

Boise, Idaho

Some of the earliest urban archaeology in the Pacific Northwest was conducted in Boise, Idaho, during urban renewal in the late 1970s and early 1980s. Since then, archaeological work has continued intermittently, including academic research by the University of Idaho. Volunteers established military Fort Boise in June 1863 during the American Civil War to provide protection to the Boise Basin Gold Rush, with Boise established as a support community, booming during the gold rush period to about 2,000 people by the mid-1860s (Goodwin 2018; Jones 1980; Ostrogorsky 1977). Boise persisted, serving as a supply center for the gold rush, and also catering to Oregon Trail emigrants and Boise River Valley farmers. It eventually became the largest city in Idaho and its capital. By 1887, the Oregon Short Line Railroad arrived, and by 1890 there were 4,000 inhabitants. Lumbering activities increased the population in 1920 to 21,000 (Jones 1980; White 2017:37), and it now contains nearly 240,000 people.

Archaeologists from University of Idaho conducted testing to explore the eight-block downtown redevelopment area, exposing foundations, cellars, and lenses of trash from an 1880–1906 Chinese American house, the Egyptian Theater and earlier saloon site, and other areas (Jones 1980). The Chinese American site recovered over 11,500 items, with abundant Asian artifacts, including Chinese porcelain and Brown-glazed stoneware, along with many other typical Chinese belongings (Jones 1980).

Elites of Boise

Contrasting with the Boise Chinatown, a number of archaeological excavations explored the elite White settlers, including the 1890s–early 1900s refuse-filled well of the Cyrus and Mary Ellen Jacob house (10AA636) (Goodwin 2014, 2018; Warner 2017); the 1885–1889 Arthur DeWint and Mary Haviland Hallock (Molly) Foote House site and dump (10AA96) (Jones 1982; Knudson et al. 1982; Longenecker 1992); and Fort Boise's (10AA161) 1871–1890 Surgeon's Quarters (May 2018a, 2020). The belongings recovered from these sites reflect the occupants' desires to acquire commercial goods while participating in Victorianism. All contained ceramics that suggested matching dish patterns in multiple vessel forms, including tea cups, cream pitchers, sugar bowls, table plates and bowls, serving platters and bowls, multiple sizes of tureens, and specialized dishes such as muffin and twiffler plates. Plain white as well as blue, black, and brown transferprinted wares are represented, primarily manufactured in Staffordshire, but with some American, French, Chinese, and Japanese examples. Canning jars and lids from the sites suggest home preserving of foods. Alcohol bottles reflect the serving of ale, wine, champagne, and whisky (Goodwin 2014, 2018; Jones 1982; May 2018a).

Hygiene products and medicine/remedy bottles are well represented at all the sites, including the remains of toothbrushes, toothpaste containers, mouthwash, shaving cream, perfume bottles, perfumed water, shoe polish, and hair grower. The Jacobs' house reportedly hosted the first residential bath tub in Boise, a zinc-lined tub installed off the kitchen (Goodwin 2014, 2018). Patent medicine bottles, bitters, and pharmaceutical/prescription bottles include local drug stores and national remedies for consumption, cold, cough, digestive and urinary disorders. Children's play and socialization is represented by glass and ceramic marbles, German-manufactured porcelain doll heads and arms, and children's tea sets. The presence of Indigenous belongings in the same context at Fort Boise suggests curiosity about an Indigenous past, or perhaps a perceived "enemy," and firearms-related items found in the same context suggest the socialization of children to hunting and shooting, both of which reflect the uniquely Western form that mixed both sense of place and Victorianism in its educational pursuits (May 2018a, 2020).

The elite households of Boise were tied into national and global markets for consumer products, including products imported from the eastern United States, Europe, and east Asia (Goodwin 2018; Jones 1982; May 2018a, 2020; Warner 2017:314). The Jacobs' house possessed Boise's first piano, hauled by wagon from Kelton, Utah (Goodwin 2018; Warner 2017). These assemblages and the documentary record suggests that Victorian values were conflated with the acquisition of commercial goods, but likely tempered by the settlers' conception of wilderness and the desire to domesticate it (Warner 2017). Elite women espoused the Victorian cult of domesticity, not just to reflect eastern values but to impose these Victorian meanings on western landscapes. Business connections established enterprises that promoted local industry, enabling Boise to prosper, and their participation in social and political activities, at least for the Jacobs, "created a domestic sanctuary that reflected their relative wealth and social position" (Goodwin 2018: 59).

River Street Neighborhood

Historical archaeologists explored a different kind of community in the River Street neighborhood, explicitly addressing structural racism in Boise's turn-of-the-twentieth-century "black neighborhood" (White 2016, 2017a, 2017b). The urban experience is quite different from smaller towns and work camps, with more complex social interactions and a more highly developed racialization process. The study of River Street sought to form a history of African Americans and other non-White people in urban Boise (White 2017a: 18).

With the construction of the railroad that connected Boise to the intercontinental railroad lines, the River Street neighborhood was developed and quickly populated by working-class Basque, Serbian and Greek immigrants, and later by African and Japanese Americans. River Street was stigmatized as a place for non-White "others," and among the few places in Boise where African Americans could purchase a house (White 2017a; 2017b). Archaeologists used shovel probes and formal excavation units to study the block associated with Erma Hayman's house, a long-term African American inhabitant (White 2017a). Excavation of yard areas recovered over 12,000 highly fragmented items, including furnishings, professionally butchered animal remains, chicken bones and eggshells, health items, and toys. The presence of souvenirs and bric-a-brac, including "small fragments of painted ceramic vessels, porcelain figurines, Asian porcelain vessels, and colored press-molded glass," suggest that households were asserting their middle-class economic status through consumption (White 2017a: 193–194). Evidence of men's fashionable clothing contrasts with frugality represented by remains of vegetable gardens, home canning, and raising of chickens. Literacy items including pencil leads and erasers correlate with oral histories that expressed the importance of homework in African American households. Related to Boise's Basque history, the remains of a handball court, or *fronton*, was discovered within the block. The archaeological project helped to build community understanding of Boise's "other" neighborhood, counteracting a century of racialization and exclusion, and exposing the lives and aspirations of its inhabitants (White 2016, 2017a, 2017b).

Urban Chinatowns

Increasing racialization of the Chinese and associated anti-Chinese violence in the late nineteenth and early twentieth centuries led to higher concentrations of Chinese Americans in urban areas, especially in Vancouver, British Columbia, and Portland, Oregon (Maddoux 2019: 127; Roulette et al. 1994: 8). Winter influxes of off-work Chinese miners and cannery workers, and business connections between urban and rural Chinese communities, suggest that urban Chinatowns were crucial centers in the Chinese American experience, linking isolated rural places with major entry points, and providing connections to Chinese homeland communities.

Historical archaeology has addressed the maintenance of identity and the racialization of Chinese American people in urban Chinatowns (e.g., Rose et al. 2021; Ruiz et al. 2021). As noted in chapter 7, anti-Chinese legislation began as soon as Chinese Americans started to arrive in the West, often accompanied by violence, but the Chinese Exclusion Act of 1882 dramatically changed the situation, as it suspended Chinese immigration and made Chinese Americans ineligible for naturalization (Lee 2020; Rose et al. 2021: 415–419). Likewise, the Canadian government imposed a "head tax" on Chinese immigrants in 1885, making for similar effects in British Columbia (Ross 2017b: 202). The experience of the Chinese in larger urban communities, especially after 1880, represents one of the more difficult aspects of the American experience in the Pacific Northwest. While there are some earlier examples, much of the work of urban Chinese sites has occurred since 2000.

Urban Chinatowns in British Columbia

Ross (2015: 175–176) notes the limited work on urban British Columbia Chinatowns, largely because of the lack of federal or provincial heritage legislation (e.g., Parsley 2011). Lim's 1996 pioneering excavations in Vancouver, British Columbia's Chinatown, dispelled myths about "underground tunnels," prostitution, and the composition of the neighborhood (Lim 2002). Volunteers from the local branch of the Archaeological Society of British Columbia and students from Vancouver Island University tested the third Chinatown site in Nanaimo in 2011. This early twentieth century Chinatown outside of city limits contained a 400-seat Opera house and many businesses, but most of the community was destroyed in a 1960 fire. Parsley (2011) describes landscape features and belongings found during probing and testing of the site. Similarly, excavations at the site of the Sung Lee/Cum Sing Laundry in Portland, Oregon (ca. 1884–1920), found substantial evidence of Chinese American practices in one of the largest Chinatowns on the west coast (Roulette et al. 1994; Wernz 2001; see Maddoux 2019: 94–96). Archaeology at the 1891–1924 D'Arcy Leper colony, while not a Chinatown, focused on the lives of Chinese Canadians with Hansen's disease, exploring racism and the maintenance of social inequality in British Columbia (French 1995, 1996).

The Wing Hong Hai Company (1889–1926)

Historical archaeology in the small Chinatown of The Dalles explored Chinese American resistance to racial exclusion laws. The Dalles served as an important transportation route for Indigenous communities and Oregon Trail emigrants; as access to the gold fields of British Columbia, Washington, Idaho, and northeastern Oregon; and as a wayside, providing cattle, other foodstuffs, equipment, labor, and entertainment to the boomtowns. It was a much smaller community, however, and although in the 1870s the majority of miners in Oregon were Chinese Americans, the population of Chinese in The Dalles was not large. At its height in the 1880s, about 17 percent of the population was Chinese Americans, concentrated in fourteen buildings on First Street (French 2016: 24–28). By 1900, there were 120 Chinese Americans, including laborers, cooks, cannery workers, gardeners, laundrymen, loggers, merchants, and domestic servants, but within a decade the population dropped to forty-eight.

The Wing Hong Hai company was a laundry and mercantile business owned by a group of Chinese men all with the Lee surname (French 2016: 36). Historical archaeologists excavated five 1- × 1-meter test units in the back yard of the building to prepare a porch, recovering an astounding 20,000 artifacts related to the business (figure 8.2). Analysis of these artifacts along with research into the U.S. government records on the partners and their workers provide a unique counterpoint to other Chinese businesses. Rose et al. (2021) explore how the evolution of racist exclusionary laws privileged a "merchant" status in the Chinese American communities that allowed transnational and social mobility. Examining the Wing Hong Hai company, they note that the

Figure 8.2. Eric Gleason exhibiting one of the test units behind the Wing Hong Hai Company building in The Dalles, Oregon, October 15, 2011.

end of the lucrative laundry business in 1908 allowed the owner Lee Yuen Hong to "perfect" his merchant status under the racist law.

Archaeology exposed a basalt cellar wall associated with the rear of the building, which had originally been enclosed as part of the wash house (French 2016). Analysis of the associated belongings suggest multiple functions, including items that may have been associated with products on the store shelves, including Chinese- and Western-style medicine bottles, combs, toothbrushes, beads, jewelry, remains of inlaid boxes, Western-style tobacco pipes and fragments, opium smoking paraphernalia, watches and watch parts, and hundreds of fragments of brass tea tins. Laundry-related items include numerous safety pins and pin parts in ferrous metal and brass, including tacks, bluing balls, and 294 buttons (sew-through prosser, shell, and collar types). French (2016: 91–92) and Maddoux (2015: 122) suggest that these could be mercantile products on cards, and/or reused as gaming markers to try to circumvent Oregon gambling laws.

Over a thousand ceramic fragments accounted for at least seventy-eight Chinese and twenty-three European or American vessels. Chinese Brown-glazed stoneware was dominant with soy sauce jars, wide-mouth jars, sake or tiger whiskey jars, lidded containers, crocks, and bottles. Chinese porcelain included Four Seasons, Bamboo, and Winter Green types and three Japanese-style spoons. The European-American ceramics included at least twelve holloware and seven flatware vessels, all dating to between 1880 and 1935. Porcelain doll parts may have been sold in the store or possibly represent repair of dolls in the laundry.

Along with the buttons, numerous gaming pieces were recovered, including seventy-six white and black glass fan tan gaming pieces and 138 coins of which the vast majority are Vietnamese Dong. Thousands of bones and bone fragments were recovered but only three seeds/pits from fruit. Also associated with the business functions was a brass top for a "call bell" that likely once graced the counter, and some distinctive grooves in the floor that could have been the pivot point for an ironer.

The Wing Hong Hai Company served its community as an organization, providing connections to Chinese associations and other Chinatowns, and ultimately Chinese homelands (French 2016: 115–116). Traditional gaming in the store created a "transnational space to thwart authority," with Lee Hong asserting his agency to maintain an ethnic identity while assisting in the economic survival of his family (Maddoux 2015: 122–125). Lee Hong navigated the racialized landscape of the Pacific Northwest, circumventing exclusionary laws and racism that targeted Chinese Americans (Rose et al. 2021).

The extant archaeological work on urban and rural Chinese communities clearly indicates that the Chinese organizations, including merchants, Hong Men societies, surname groups, benevolent societies, and temples and churches, were crucial institutions to assist Chinese Americans navigating the racist legislation and racial violence of the late nineteenth and early twentieth centuries. These institutions provided supplies including tablewares, clothing, and preserved and fresh foods to Chinese mining, agricultural, cannery, and other communities, as well as providing work and support (Fong et al. 2022; Horrocks 2019; Maddoux 2019; Rose et al. 2021). Recent archaeology has gone a long way toward dispelling the Western myths of Oriental exoticism, creating an antiracist place for Chinese American history in the Pacific Northwest—but there is much more to do.

Military Posts

After the battles of Little Bighorn in 1876, White Bird Canyon in 1877, and other contemporaneous Indian War defeats, the U.S. Army began to emphasize military training, including target practice and maneuvers (Rickey 1963: 99–106; Walker 1978). The introduction of the intercontinental railroad allowed aggregation of soldiers at larger forts, permitting an economy of scale that facilitated training time while maintaining facilities. At places like Vancouver Barracks, Fort Spokane, and Fort Walla Walla, a period of growth and development accompanied these changes through the early twentieth century. For example, in 1879, Vancouver Barracks became the Department of the Columbia headquarters, building a new commanding officer's quarter on the west side of the Parade Ground (Sinclair 2004). Renovation of some of the older barracks and officers' quarters, as well as new construction, was associated with an expansion in the number of troops that could be housed. Substantial excavations have yielded mostly descriptive reports on late nineteenth- and early twentieth- century Vancouver Barracks (e.g., Carley 1982; Chance and Chance 1976; Chance et al. 1982; Cromwell et al. 2014; O'Rourke et al. 2010; Thomas and Hibbs 1984). Likewise, archaeologists have reported on 1880–1929 U.S. Military Fort Spokane (e.g., Chance 1981; Chance and Chance 1985a; Combes 1965; Sands and Buchanan 2020; Wilson 1998).

Fort Walla Walla (1857–1930)

U.S. Military Fort Walla Walla was established in 1857, reactivated in 1873–1910, and reactivated again briefly during World War I. In 1975, Walla Walla Community College, and in 1976, Washington State University, excavated large samples of the post dump (45WW33), recovering over 32,000 artifacts (Hussey 1975, 1984; Riordan 1985). Sporadic studies of military artifacts and additional cultural resources management projects collected more data, some resulting in significant issues with orphan collections (e.g., Oliver 2014).

Historical archaeology at Fort Walla Walla pioneered the study of African Americans in the Pacific Northwest, comparing dump deposits associated with the 1st Cavalry, a White American Regiment stationed at Fort Walla Walla in 1909 and 1910, with the 9th Cavalry, an African American Regiment stationed at the fort between 1902 and 1904 (Riordan 1985). The economic and social status of the troops based on historical records was contrasted with the number of items and economic value of belongings, revealing that social status was "inextricably linked" to the value of materials (Riordan 1985: 2). Using glass bottle and ceramic maker's marks, military cartridge headstamps, unit insignia, and other artifact attributes, a fine-grained analysis of excavated dump deposits defined assemblages associated with each of the units. The comparison demonstrated the material record of racism in the U.S. Army, with refuse from the African American 9th Cavalry containing lower relative numbers of items associated with uniforms including insignia and buttons, horse-related items, and also lower-valued ceramics, including fewer numbers of high-quality porcelain and decorated earthenware vessels (Riordan 1985). Consistent with the historical record of discrimination against African American soldiers, this disinvestment in equipment contrasts with the substantial role that these troops played in both the Indian Wars and Spanish American War (Riordan 1985).

World War I Sites and the Morrissey Internment Camp (1915–1918)

Besides sites associated with the Spruce Production Division, including the Spruce Mill at Vancouver Barracks, archaeologists have studied the World War I Morrissey Internment Camp in southeastern British Columbia. This camp was used for prisoners of war from Germany, the Austro-Hungarian, and Ottoman Empires, including civilians and even some Canadian citizens. Documentary research and excavations explored food quality and coping mechanisms of prisoners (Beaulieu 2019, 2020, 2022). Arts and handicrafts documented through archival images and local citizens' collections illustrate how the prisoners adapted to the boredom and confinement of incarceration. Likewise, artifacts recovered from the site, including pro-Irish items (supported by Germany), and even an escape tunnel and stockpiled foods, reflect passive and direct resistance to the Canadian government (Beaulieu 2019, 2022). Perhaps most troubling, the decrease in quality of animal protein is documented in bone remains at the site, correlated with prisoner's complaints in smuggled letters to the Swiss embassy that the food was of poor quality, inconsistent with the 1906 Hague Convention (Beaulieu 2020).

Civilian Conservation Corps (CCC) Camps

The Pacific Northwest, like most areas of the United States and Canada, suffered significant economic distress during the Great Depression, with many losing jobs, homesteads abandoned, increased houselessness, and political radicalization, but the experience also is identified as a platform for increased U.S. Federal aid and as a stepping stone for future growth (Jepsen and Norberg 2017:232). The Civilian Conservation Corps (CCC) began during the Roosevelt administration, which stimulated local economies through environmental conservation work, educating and employing men aged eighteen to twenty-five. The program tried to prevent unemployed and transient youth from becoming radicalized by alternative political forms to democracy (Mawhirter 2013: 8–16). Led by the War Department, Departments of the Interior, Agriculture, and Labor all cooperated in setting up camps, with about two hundred of them in the Pacific Northwest. Young men conducted forestry and agricultural projects, road and trail maintenance, and forest fighting (Jepsen and Norberg 2017:239–240; Tuck 2010). Vancouver Barracks was a regional headquarters and hosted dozens of camps.

Camp Zig Zag (1936–1942), on Mt. Hood National Forest, about 64 kilometers east of Portland, was a typical CCC camp run by U.S. Army and Forest Service personnel, assisted by local craftsmen, known as "Local Experienced Men." Four bunkhouses housed 170–200 enrollees, with classrooms, an educational building, a recreation hall, kitchen and mess hall, officer's quarters, infirmary, shop building, and truck shed (Tuck 2010). The life of the enrollees was highly structured, with "reveille" in the morning and "retreat" in the evening, and enrollees were encouraged to take at least three hours of classwork a week from a variety of vocational courses (Tuck 2010).

Archaeologists tested Camp Zig Zag in 2007 with metal detectors and test units, recovering over 8,000 items (Tuck 2010). Oral histories, the documentary record, and archaeology detailed the social cohesion of the camp, which contrasted with evidence for internee resistance to authority (Tuck 2010). Military issue belongings, including dishware and dental care products, along with camp layout and routines, strengthened and structured the community to discipline the enrollees into perfect soldiers (*sensu* Foucault 1995; Tuck 2010; cf., Mawhirter 2014: 27–28, 69). In contrast, fishing gear, photography equipment, and even harmonica fragments found at the camp reflect individualized strategies for enrollees' personal freedom and relief from control. Bottle fragments of alcohol, including beer, wine, and gin, though low in number, reflect defiance of the no-alcohol policy. Mawhirter (2014:69) argues that the rigid military structure suggested by Tuck (2010) was much more fluid and flexible in the CCC, and that the "discipline, order and cleanliness" instilled by the Army was needed "to insure the health, wellbeing and orderly administration of the camp." However, the military structure of the camps, so unlike conditions at home where families were under tremendous financial stress, or the unstructured time of houselessness, did have important influences on the internees. Oral histories and the documentary record suggest that many internees later enlisted during World War II, and that their time in the CCC was tied to their success in the military (Jepsen and Norberg 2017: 240; Mawhirter 2013: 71; Sinclair and McClure 2003; Tuck 2010: 10). Other CCC camps that have been explored include Camp Hemlock on the Gifford Pinchot National Forest in Washington, Camp Reehers in Washington County, Oregon, and the Cove Creek CCC dump in central Idaho (Mawhirter 2013; Tuck 2010: 67–77).

World War II

One of the few World War II battlefield sites in the Pacific Northwest is the September 1942 Japanese bombing site in the forested Coast Range east of Brookings, Oregon, though material remains are scant (LaLande 2005). Historical archaeology has addressed some U.S. home-front activities in more detail, finding extensive remains associated with the excavation of a shipyard dump, the Manhattan Project at Hanford, Washington, and the incarceration of Japanese Americans.

Vancouver Shipyards (1942–1946)

As noted above, Vancouver, Washington, was a small city in the first half of the twentieth century, before booming during World War II, with many working in Kaiser's Vancouver Shipyard, one of three shipyards in the Portland-Vancouver area (Roulette et al. 2010; Sinclair 2005). Between 1942 and 1946, workers there built Liberty Ships, Baby Flat Tops, and LSTs, peaking in late 1943, when 39,000 employees worked three shifts.

The Kaiser Shipyard site (45CL927) was identified in 2006 as an industrial landfill containing ca. 1943–1946 shipyard debris. Archaeology focused on the environmental remediation of this landfill, and because it contained hazardous materials, the work collected artifacts selectively, and much of the effort was geared to confirming its age and origin tied to cleanup liability (Roulette et al. 2010). Millions of objects from shipbuilding, other shipyard operations, and shipyard workers were noted, with about 1,800 items collected, including industrial trim and scrap pieces of plate and sheet metal; electrical and plumbing fixtures; tools; blueprints, war bonds, paper punch cards; glass bottles; and some domestic ceramic items. Also found were pieces of welded and cut metal that appear to represent craft or art projects (figure 8.3); faunal materials; and other personal items (Roulette et al. 2010). Diagnostic artifacts, combined with aerial photographs, provided clear evidence of the waste's World War II shipyard origin.

Cosmetic items included a lipstick tube; two metal compacts that probably contained rouge, eye shadow, or face powder; cologne bottles; a Revlon makeup bottle; and cold cream jars, many of which were likely from female shipyard workers (Roulette et al. 2010: 47). The mid-twentieth-century expression of femininity was likely carried into the shipyard workplace by cis-gender women who were taking on traditional men's roles. Roulette et al. (2010: 49) infers resistance to work in the beer, whiskey, and wine bottles found in the dump and the possible misappropriation of company time and materials through art projects crafted from steel. The historical record con-

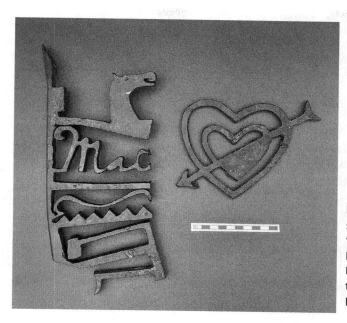

Figure 8.3. Kaiser shipyard welding "practice" artifacts, FOVA239114 and FOVA239115. Courtesy of the National Park Service.

firms alcohol consumption on site, particularly during times of layoffs near the end of the war. While recycling and salvage was important during World War II, large amounts of useable metal were recorded, suggesting a disconnect between official policies and the reality of shipyard waste disposal.

A related archaeological project is attempting to document the extensive Vanport shipyard community in northeast Portland, which contained a sizeable African American population (David Ellis, personal communication). Another contemporary landfill (the "burning pits") in Hanford, Washington, is associated with the "Atomic Boomtown" of the 1943–1945 Hanford Construction Camp, the temporary city for workers associated with the Manhattan Project. These workers built nuclear reactors, chemical separation structures, and a fuel fabrication facility, leading ultimately to the plutonium bomb that the United States dropped on Nagasaki, Japan, on August 9, 1945 (Gosling 1999: 32; Smith et al. 2012; Stapp and Longenecker 2009: 103–105; Wilson 2008). Even in a government facility under intensive secrecy controls, workers resisted institutional control policies, shown in the recovery of a union pin and 143 alcohol bottles pulled from the dump. As an essentially dry camp, alcohol consumption was supposed to be limited to group settings, with drinking in personal/private settings not allowed. The alcohol bottles found in the landfill were likely smuggled from nearby towns (Smith et al. 2012).

World War II Incarceration Camps

Japanese Americans became important in many Pacific Northwest industries, particularly in the early twentieth century (see chapter 7). Jobs were often the dirtiest and most dangerous, and owners used Japanese American's disinclination (or inability) to join unions to form a hedge against labor agitation (Carlson 2021: 687). Quotas on the number of Japanese who could immigrate to Canada were imposed as early as 1908, and the 1913 Alien Land laws of California, 1921 in Washington, and 1923 in Oregon, prevented ownership of property (Burton et al. 2000; Carlson 2021: 35–36; Ross 2017b: 202). Racialization took on the form of either the "yellow peril," or how immigration from Asia threatened Canadian and American culture, or as a "model minority," denoting ideal examples of immigrant assimilation and advancement—and these competing tropes often existed simultaneously (Carlson 2021: 690).

The bombing of Pearl Harbor by the Japanese Navy on December 7, 1941, resulted in the United States formally entering World War II, and led early the following year to Executive Order 9066, which incarcerated about 100,000 Japanese Americans living on the west coast of the United States (Camp 2016). The Wartime Civilian Control Agency (WCCA) coordinated incarceration, moving Japanese Americans to "assembly centers" prior to completion of "relocation camps" (incarceration camps) by the War Relocation Authority (WRA) (Burton et al. 2000; Burton and Farrell 2001). The WCCA incarcerated 7,628 Japanese Americans at the Western Washington State Fairgrounds near Puyallup, Washington, and another 4,290 at the 11-acre Pacific International Livestock Exposition Pavilion near Portland, Oregon (Burton et al. 2000). Incarcerated Japanese had to abandon all their possessions except what they could bring by hand. After incarceration at these temporary "assembly centers," the imprisoned Japanese Americans were moved to incarceration camps in remote areas with low populations. Two of these in the Pacific Northwest are Minidoka and Kooskia.

Minidoka

The windy, sage flats of the Snake River plain formed the setting for the Minidoka Relocation Center, a 33,000-acre incarceration camp about 24 kilometers northeast of Twin Falls, Idaho (Burton et al. 2000; Burton and Farrell 2001). Construction by the WRA started in June of 1942, with Japanese Americans arriving from assembly centers by early August. The camp rivaled the largest city in the region, Twin Falls, radically increasing the footprint of Japanese Americans. During its operation, the Minidoka Camp incarcerated 9,400 people housed in over six hundred buildings, surrounded by 5 miles

(8 km) of barbed wire fencing and eight guard towers. This city of incarcerated Japanese Americans ultimately housed 13,000 people (Burton and Farrell 2001).

Japanese Americans lived in standardized "barracks," 20 × 120 feet, each containing six rooms (or "apartments") of varying sizes to accommodate the variety of families and groups of single men or women. Walls between units extended only to the eaves, and each apartment was heated by a coal, wood, oil, or natural gas heating element, a single drop light, army cots, blankets, and mattresses (Burton et al. 2000; Burton and Farrell 2001: 9–12). A total of thirty-five residential "blocks" each contained twelve barracks, a mess hall, recreation hall, and an H-shaped structure housing a laundry and men's and women's lavatories. The incarcerated Japanese were allowed to set up services and businesses and developed a system of self-government. A variety of stores and services were created, and the incarcerated built two elementary schools, a high school, a health clinic, and two fire stations. The size of the camp required a large infrastructure, including wells, sewage disposal plant, and city dump/landfill. A cemetery was established, and a railroad spur and warehouse served the camp (Burton and Farrell 2001: 13).

The incarcerated were allowed to apply for work outside of the camp, and by October 1942, 1,700 people left to work in nearby potato and beet fields. Ultimately, wartime Japanese Americans worked in canneries, lumber mills, agricultural fields, and constructed irrigation canals, developing 740 acres of farmland at the camp, and raising garden vegetables. Japanese Americans also resisted incarceration by forming a labor union to protest unfair wages and resisted the draft. Other Japanese Americans joined the 442nd Regimental Combat Team, which fought as a highly decorated, segregated Japanese American unit in the European theater.

The archaeological survey of the Minidoka Internment National Monument (now Minidoka National Historic Site) recorded over two hundred features, including rock alignments, foundations, and other structural remains. The main entrance contains standing basalt and concrete walls of the Military Police Building and a Reception Building with a large stone fireplace and the nearby remains of an ornamental garden (Burton et al. 2000; Burton and Farrell 2001). The archaeologists recorded numerous concrete footings of structures, basalt rock alignments, a root cellar, remnants of the security fence, paths, roads, and a tin can dump. Gardens at the camp represent a form of agency and even resistance by the incarcerated Japanese Americans. Tamura (2004) argues that traditional Japanese garden landscapes created at Minidoka and other incarceration camps buffered the bureaucratic structured camp layouts. Their design and maintenance provided a hedge against the trauma of incarceration, representing "symbols of immeasurable fortitude within landscapes of shame and tragedy" (Tamura 2004: 2–3). The formal entrance garden at Minidoka was designed to advertise "loyalty and patriotism," carefully constructed behind an "honor roll board" of Japanese American soldiers with a large mound whose shape and configuration of basalt boulders represented an eagle. This overt challenge to incarceration was meant to promote Japanese Americans as loyal and patriotic. Other gardens at Minidoka and elsewhere provided symbols of resistance to incarceration (e.g., Camp 2016; Clark 2017; Tamura 2004).

Kooskia Work Camp

The Kooskia facility differed significantly from Minidoka and other WRA camps, holding only 256 Japanese who were considered "enemy aliens" (Burton et al. 2000). Created within a former CCC camp and Federal Prison, incarcerated Japanese came to Kooskia between May 1943 and May 1945 to work as laborers on U.S. Highway 12 along the Clearwater River (Clark 2016; Hosken and Tiede 2018). The site was so remote that fences were not required as it was unlikely escapees would survive long in the Idaho mountains. In an act reminiscent of the Morrisey Internment Camp, imprisoned Japanese petitioned in July 1943 for better treatment, including the provision of health care under the Geneva Convention (Camp 2018; Hosken and Tiede 2018).

The University of Idaho conducted surface survey and testing of the site in 2010 and 2013, finding incinerated refuse deposits and over 10,000 artifacts from the Federal Prison and the Japanese American work camp. Belongings included a Japanese medicine bottle, Japanese ceramics, prison uniform buttons, candy bar wrappers, cold cream jars, and other items, some of which were likely from the camp's Canteen (Camp 2016; Fitz-Gerald 2015; Hosken and Tiede 2018; Ng and Camp 2015: 169–173). Artifacts related to dental hygiene were highlighted by Hosken and Tiede (2018), including mouthwash bottles, toothpaste tubes and caps (Japanese-manufactured Lion brand), a toothbrush handle, two false teeth, a denture, a human tooth, and an impression tray. The petition for better health care and the oral hygiene practices of the incarcerated represented a means to navigate imprisonment (Hosken and Tiede 2018). Ocular health items include fragments of safety goggles, sun glasses, and a Murine eye serum bottle, possibly tied to issues with pterygium, a condition associated with high-elevation ultraviolet radiation (Camp 2018). Employing gender theory and body conceptions of the Japanese, Fitz-Gerald (2015) argues that the twenty-four cold cream jars in the sample from Kooskia could have served as cosmetics for traditional Japanese theater performances, a recreation also documented in the historical records.

Kumasaka's Garden

Before World War II, the Kumasaka family's Green Lake Gardens Company in Seattle, Washington, grew flowers and vegetables for sale at Pike Place Market, or to wholesale grocers, and they were the first farm to grow chrysanthemums in a greenhouse (Valentino 2017). A community center on their property hosted a Japanese language school for Nisei children. While many Japanese farms disappear from the historical record in 1942 (e.g., Campbell 2021), the Kumasaka farm was watched over by their lawyer and family friend during the family's incarceration at Minidoka, and they returned there after the war (Valentino 2017). The farm then provided a refuge for returning Japanese to get reestablished in the Seattle area. By 1967, however, the family was forced to sell their farm to make room for the North Seattle College campus. Remnants of the farm structures and landscaping include concrete and utilities, and rows of ornamental pine trees, holly, bamboo, cherry, plum, and other trees. It is currently in an area that has been left in a "natural" condition but is recognized as significant in the history of the college and the region.

9

The Past in the Present in the Pacific Northwest

Many historic sites in the Pacific Northwest are embedded in places of great and awesome natural beauty, surrounded by windswept, empty plains, or by densely wooded evergreen forests, regularly in view of massive volcanic peaks. They often front great rivers, estuaries, and ocean beaches. Visitors to these sites can feel transformed in time, feeling as if they have been placed in a timeless landscape. Many of the sites studied in this book, like the lands of the Pacific Northwest, are remote from urban areas. As Burley et al. (1996: 35) suggest, these places push the modern times away and convey a "sense of time transcended." That there is an "intangible communion" between environment and historic place is certainly an important aesthetic. Archaeologists who work at such places uncover long-buried belongings of peoples of the past and come into intimate contact with the places where ancestors worked and lived, struggled, and raised families. This experience of landscape and the intimate contact with past things influences the perspectives of historical archaeologists in unique ways (e.g., Burley et al. 1996: 46, 135). And yet, the historical archaeology of these places also engages with modern people involved in modern issues and controversies, such as unsustainable resource extraction, damming of rivers for hydropower, urban sprawl, and climate change. What was once seen as boundless resources driving settlement and development are now limited and contested. Archaeology in urban areas undergoing redevelopment—where parking lots and ruined buildings are the mantle under which past neighborhoods once thrived, or in the massive work camps and factories of twentieth-century industrial sites—represents the contrapose to timelessness, where the full measure of human impact and change on the Pacific Northwest is evident.

This chapter examines the role of historical archaeology in exploring human continuity and change in the Pacific Northwest, while engaging directly with the modern world. I first examine a few cases associated with the archaeology of modernity, and provide a few examples of public archaeology and engagement through a variety of outreach programs. I then take up historical archaeology's enduring role in framing and exploring the American experience in the Pacific Northwest.

Archaeology and Modernity

In contrast to other regions of the United States, Europe, and elsewhere, the study of modern material culture and the period of late twentieth-century to early twenty-first century modernity (e.g., González-Ruibal 2019; Rathje and Murphy 1992; Rathje et al. 1992) is largely absent in the Pacific Northwest. Exceptions include the few World War II landfills explored in chapter 8, which are controversial as sources of environmental contamination. There are a few good material descriptions of cold-war era historic properties, such as bomb shelters (e.g., Holstine 2011), and also a few university projects that explore waste streams, recycling, and the materiality of campus traditions (Camp 2010; Camp et al. 2011; Campbell et al. 2018; Molander and Lenihan 2007; Stapp and Longenecker 1986).

A study of university life prior to the 1990 Centennial of Washington State University was the goal of a field school that explored male and female dorms, an administrative building, and a barn associated with the Pullman, Washington, campus (Stapp and Longenecker 1986). Partly designed as public archaeology to expose students and faculty to the history of student practices, the 1985 field school found variations in primary refuse tied to gender and the function of sites, and explored the nature of shifting campus life after World War II, where greater institutionalized services were present in housing and food amenities. Notably, a 1940s era cache of liquor bottles found in a basement of Stimson Hall contrasted with the ban on alcoholic beverages on campus (Stapp and Longenecker 1986:41).

Twenty years after the Pullman study, a similar project called the Campus Trash Project studied the refuse of the University of Idaho's campus in Moscow, Idaho (Camp 2010; Camp et al. 2011). Part of a method and theory class in archaeology, students explored modern surface litter across four areas of campus, including a football tailgating parking lot, a student recreation center, the library quad, and an alley behind sorority and fraternity houses. The project identified disconnects between the orthodoxy of refuse disposal and its actual practice, including disregard of cigarette butt receptacles. A sample of the tailgating parking lot unsurprisingly found numerous bottle caps, aluminum can tabs, and cigarette butts, and an assemblage dominated by items associated with alcohol consumption. A small student project at the

University of British Columbia Okanagan documented food wastes tied to the cafeteria (Molander and Lenihan 2007), examining issues of food waste, as well as the relationship between portion size and waste. Both the University of Idaho and University of British Columbia Okanagan studies explored sustainability and commented on ways to increase recycling, decreasing food and solid wastes.

Another novel study by anthropology students at the University of Idaho explored the documentary, oral history, and physical remains of the "Bolvile Run," a 70-mile (113 km) route between Moscow and Bolvile, Idaho, where hundreds of students would visit taverns (Campbell et al. 2018). Besides the landscapes of the alcohol-fueled college tradition, including past and present bars and taverns, the students documented photographs, signatures of participants, and other souvenirs of the practice. The development of the college tradition coincides roughly with the repeal of the twenty-first amendment in 1933, the advent of paved roads between northern Idaho communities in 1940, and the increased availability of automobiles in the late twentieth century, and was partially powered by lower drinking ages in Idaho between 1972 and 1988.

Public and Community Archaeology

Besides the public outreach associated with the campus refuse projects, historical archaeologists have continuously, albeit sporadically, conducted public and community archaeology in the Pacific Northwest. Public archaeology is a series of practices on a continuum between those where most of the power is in the hands of the practicing archaeologist to those where it is given over in whole or in part to the community. These include the educational (also gateway or deficit) model, where archaeologists strive to fill educational deficits within the public about archaeological values, finds, and knowledge, as well as public relations approaches that attempt to improve the perceptions of archaeology (e.g., Grima 2016; Little 2012; Matsuda 2016; Richardson and Amansa-Sánchez 2015). More critical approaches address the power differential between archaeologists and their publics, including multiple perspectives and democratic and multivocal approaches that speak to greater collaboration and participation with communities, sometimes to directly support communities' agendas and desires to explore their own archaeological values.

While published literature is sparse (e.g., Butler et al. 2021; Longenecker 1988; Parks and Merrifield 2021; Ross and Hogg 1976; Warner et al. 2014; Wilson 2015, 2021; Wilson et al. 2022), historical archaeology has connected museums, stakeholders, and the public, primarily through educational models. One of the most important regional museums of anthropology, the Oregon State Museum of Anthropology (now the Museum of Natural and Cultural History) in Eugene, was founded through the Smithsonian Institution's involvement in Bonneville Dam salvage archaeology, leading to the first archaeology permit law in Oregon (Griffin 2009: 92). Many local and regional museums, particularly those tied to heritage sites associated with colonial forts and historic houses, have at one time or another exhibited belongings excavated from their collections, drawing public attention to particular sites and time periods. More recently, co-creation in archaeology and museums provide opportunities to share power with descendant and local communities to create projects that address community needs and interests (Bollwerk et al. 2015; Wilson 2015: 229–231).

Since the early 1990s, Forest Service Passport-in-Time (PIT) projects in Washington, Oregon, and Idaho have conducted volunteer archaeology (Osborn 2023), and other agencies and universities across the region have directed other public archaeology programs. Many of the projects cited in this book had some public archaeology component. The Sandpoint project discussed in chapter 8, for example, included numerous talks, presentations, tours, archaeology teaching kits, and other outreach activities to provide information to communities regarding this historical archaeology project (Petrich-Guy 2016; Weaver 2014: appendix A, 131–139). Likewise, much of the work at the Rogue War battlefields in southwestern Oregon, discussed in chapter 5, included public and community archaeology components to build dialogue around connections to sites, and to question settler narratives (Tveskov et al. 2019). Engagement of descendant communities at Miners' Fort and other sites of the Rogue Battlefield sought to respect the "sovereignty, cultural perspectives, and protocols" of Indigenous partners, leading to participation and blessing of the project by tribal leaders and community members. This continues a multi-decade relationship between Indigenous people and archaeologists that interweaves academic interests with community needs. The desire to seek nuance in how people navigated the stressful times of settler colonialism is a primary goal of Tveskov et al.'s (2019) work, placing historical archaeology in a place not only to preserve important sites but to provide access and engagement with multiple groups, including descendant Indigenous and settler communities. A multiple perspectives model engages descendant community needs while allowing local communities access to a more nuanced history. Likewise, the Chinese Diaspora Project intentionally seeks to use historical archaeology to rewrite the narratives of Chinese American history (e.g., Fang

2021). While there are many more examples of historical archaeology's engagement with the public, the following provides a brief window into the varieties of outreach and public- and community-based historical archaeology in the region.

Public Archaeology in Boise

Warner et al. (2014: 214) rue the lack of reporting on public archaeology in Idaho, suggesting that much of the public side of archaeology work has been unreported or is difficult to find in governmental reports. Substantial public outreach was tied to the 1986 excavations at the Foote House near Boise, associated with the use of volunteers, tours of the site, considerable media attention, site and history brochures, and a traveling exhibit (Longenecker 1986, 1988). Excavations at the Cyrus Jacobs–Uberuaga House in downtown Boise, Idaho, discussed in chapter 8, was primarily conceived as a public archaeology program (Warner, Schwartz, et al. 2014). Following essentially an educational model, a cultural anthropologist joined the team to conduct before-and-after surveys to address who was visiting the dig site, how they learned about it, and what they learned from the program. The project also developed an online presence including website and Facebook pages. Media releases generated newspaper, television, and radio stories. A "tour plan" helped cycle the over 1,000 visitors to the site over the two-week dig, allowing them to explore the excavation site, artifact screening location, and outdoor laboratory. Designated student "talkers" helped explain the site's history and archaeologists' findings. The survey demonstrated the benefits of multiple sources of public outreach, the public's engagement with the project, and the increase in public knowledge about archaeology.

The River Street project, also noted in chapter 8, employed a somewhat different approach, attempting to directly confront race and racism associated with the public and descendant communities of the diverse River Street community (White 2016: 72). The project created a space where visitors and volunteers could generate dialogue about redlining and racism in Boise, while confronting the continuing legacy of racism today. The project explicitly used the NHPA process to "demonstrate how preserving the history of the River Street Neighborhood may be deployed as a peaceful but powerful weapon to dismantle structural racism in the American West" (White 2016: 11–12). As public heritage, the River Street Project included community members, providing a non-confrontational space to address the difficult issues of structural racism. With inclusiveness as a goal, "descendants were given an opportunity to contribute, participate and interact with the project however they liked. Research questions and goals were created in collaboration with local residents" (White 2017: 19). Descendants provided oral histories of the neighborhood to build the historical narrative. The artifacts and sites provided contrasts to both reinforce community heritage and to humanize the neighborhood's occupants. This built connections between the former and present inhabitants of the neighborhood and the larger Boise community.

The Archaeology Roadshow

While not specific to historical archaeology, Portland State University's "Archaeology Roadshow" has since 2012 integrated archaeological practitioners, including agencies, Tribes, museums, private-sector cultural resources management firms, archaeology volunteers, and students to provide exhibits, hands-on activities, and an opportunity for collectors to interact with experts in artifact identification (Butler et al. 2021; Parks and Merrifield 2021). Derived from similar "archaeology day" types of programs, the Roadshow provides booths and activities that explore aspects of archaeology, usually tied to a particular theme. Many of the agencies, firms, and Tribes explore historical archaeology topics, and visitors can learn about the role of archaeology and its importance in history and preservation. An "artifact identification" component creates a safe space for visitors to learn about family heirlooms and items they have found, and also to learn how collecting results in losses in scientific value and heritage tied to descendant communities (Butler et al. 2021). Perhaps one of the most important aspects of the Roadshow is its ability to build a community of practice around archaeology that transcends agency, Tribe, and avocational boundaries (Wilson 2021). The multiple perspectives of the participants and the presence of numerous agencies, Tribes, and professional and avocational groups permits a more democratic and dialogic approach to public archaeology.

Long-Term Public and Community Engagement at Fort Vancouver

Fort Vancouver's long history of public archaeology includes many instances of community engagement with professional archaeologists (Wilson 2021). Louis Caywood's excavation to relocate and study the fort was widely reported in local newspapers, providing an educational approach to a place of importance to the regional community (Wilson 2015: 225). Excavations in the 1970s included participatory approaches, using volunteers as laborers, including students from the Multnomah School of the Bible and the Oregon Archaeological Society. Later, based on the extensive excavations at Fort Vancouver, Lester Ross (1975b) developed a "hypothetical narrative" of gentleman's dining customs for the sesquicentennial edition of Clark County History. Avocational archaeologists continued to serve at Fort Vancouver, epitomized by the "citizen archaeology" conducted by the Oregon Archaeological Society between 1970 and the present (Wilson 2015).

Since 2001, the National Park Service, with partners Portland State and Washington State Universities, has conducted research that contributes to the public understanding of Oregon and Washington's colonial period, while expanding the education of students in historical archaeology and heritage management (Wilson 2015: 231). The program integrates National Park Service interpreters with archaeologists to train students on how to create dialogue with visitors, using National Park Service guidance, and following Grima's (2016: 55) conception of placing archaeologists within the wider and intersecting communities that are connected to archaeological sites (Marks 2011; Wilson 2015; Wilson et al. 2022). As part of this program, National Park Service staff developed a "Kids Dig!" program that introduces children to archaeological fieldwork and interpretation, using a mock dig site (figure 9.1). Field school students and National Park Service staff build on children's extant knowledge about the past and archaeology to connect past belongings and the current world (Wilson 2015; Wilson et al. 2022: 244–247). Students at the field school also engage with the visiting public to share research goals, field methods, and educational values of the work, seeking personal connections to the site, and enlarging and sometimes countering traditional narratives (Marks 2011; Wilson 2015; Wilson et al. 2022). In particular, the exploration of the Fort Vancouver Village has sought an enlarged story with new perspectives and relevance to descendant communities (Wilson 2015, 2018; Wilson et al. 2022).

The recent public archaeology search for the first Fort Vancouver incorporated interviews and surveys to assess the public's views on heritage, archaeology, and place attachment (Clearman 2020; Wilson et al. 2022). Interviews sought information on the landscape history of the neighborhood in which the first Fort Vancouver was situated to expand traditional historical and ethnohistoric/ethnographic knowledge. Clearman's (2020) results suggest that neighborhoods associated with well-known historical sites already have long and intimate connections with the place and its history, but that public archaeology significantly strengthens those connections, binding the identity of the resident to heritage connected to place. Community members exposed to past belongings discovered during the project identified with their past owners, and included history beyond the usual scope. Further, archaeology broadens the timeline to people and exposes places that are not as readily observable, such as the presence and belongings of Indigenous peoples, en-

Figure 9.1. Kids Dig! at Fort Vancouver, July 3, 2010.

hancing the interconnectedness of the neighborhood residents to community heritage (Clearman 2020; Wilson et al. 2022). Increased connections to the national park unit resulted in improved conceptions of stewardship and why the neighborhood matters.

Indigenous Archaeology Field Schools

An outgrowth of archaeologist's desire to engage and collaborate with the public is increasing partnerships with Indigenous communities to conduct archaeological field schools (e.g., Gonzalez et al. 2018; Gonzalez and Edwards 2020; Rahemtulla 2020). Within the multiple perspectives and community-based side of public archaeology, these schools engage directly with Tribal governments and community members, providing access to archaeological knowledge and, in many cases, privileging traditional knowledge. Community-based participatory research shares power with the community, even deferring to the group's needs, addressing questions that directly benefit them, and with the information controlled by them (e.g., Colwell 2016). Some of these projects focus on historical archaeological sites, exploring topics of importance to tribal understanding of the colonial era (e.g., Kretzler 2019), and most directly engage with or are directed by Indigenous communities, decolonizing the field through active collaboration and participation. This includes research questions and fieldwork locations, putting traditional and scientific information on the same plane of teaching, mixing academics, elders, and traditional practitioners as instructors, and engaging students to become immersed in the host community by living within or near it (Gonzalez and Edwards 2020; Kretzler and Gonzalez 2021; Rahemtulla 2020). Unlike projects led by archaeologists, these projects allow the community to guide research questions and increase the important collaborations and relationships between community and researchers.

One of the sites the Grand Ronde community selected for work is the Bureau of Indian Affairs (BIA) Agency School, which operated as a day and boarding school between the late nineteenth century and the 1950s. In contrast to the trauma experienced at other Indian schools (see chapter 6), the Grande Ronde school is reported as a place of community pride, as many tribal members served as teachers and administrators (Gonzalez et al. 2018; Kretzler and Gonzalez 2021). Excavation of the ca. 1900–1945 schoolhouse privy found belongings associated with the teacher's and students' practices at the school, including chalk, scissors, and heavily used pencils (worn down to the erasers), and food uses, including the consumption of strawberries, blackberries, and huckleberries. The documentary record suggests an economy of resources, evidenced by the intensive use of the pencils. Not reflected in the official school records, culturally important plants including plantain and St. John's Wort were found in the privy deposits, and elders' oral histories collected as part of the project suggest that teachers led tours of native plants and foods at times, conflicting with the official function of the school to assimilate the students to agriculture, trades, and homemaking (Gonzalez et al. 2018). Comic books and chewing gum wrappers provide evidence of contraband that students brought to school and that wound up in the privy. Such resistance to orthodoxy in schools is perhaps typical in the American experience, but discovery of these actions in the government school provides a contrast with the victimization narratives attached to residential schools and other colonial-period Indigenous places. Trauma associated with other schools should not be discounted, but rather the nuance associated with these schools is evident from the work at the Grand Ronde reservation.

Public archaeology in the Pacific Northwest is helping to build communities that are aware of the scientific and spiritual benefits of archaeological sites, building opportunities for dialogue with diverse local heritage interest groups, and providing educational opportunities to learn about important archaeological sites and how they are studied and protected. Many projects are finding ways to better collaborate, integrate, and serve Indigenous and other descendant communities using archaeological, oral history, and Indigenous methods.

The Other "Public Archaeology" and Critiques of Cultural Resources Management

After documenting the long and contentious fight over the future of Fort Nisqually and its archaeological resources, Creighton (2004) concluded her case study by questioning the balance between the "positive effects" in saving heritage in Washington State against the "traditional and constitutional issue" of private property rights, in her case, the rights of a timber corporation. She asks whether the costs to owners of historic sites, such as Fort Nisqually, is in balance with the public good (Creighton 2004: 174). In contrast, Rich Hutchings and Marina La Salle have critiqued the practice of archaeology as "disaster capitalism," and archaeology and its education as part of a "heritage industrial complex," essentially holding that archaeology is embedded with developers and government agencies that are degrading important Indigenous places (Hutchings and La Salle 2014, 2015; La Salle and Hutchings 2016; cf., Martindale et al. 2016). While instances of historical archaeology working with Tribes and other marginalized groups in the Pacific Northwest are relatively recent, there is a long history of archaeologist-tribal relations that transcends more recent debates. For example, Sprague (1974) commented on the need for better coordination with Tribes as part of a general soul-searching of the Society for American Archaeology regarding "human rights and dignity" that began in the 1970s. His experience in the Pacific Northwest foreshadowed many of the concepts and models of Indigenous Archaeology today, such as engaging with and reporting to Tribes, negotiating competing tribal interests, tribal employment, and even cooperation and collaboration regarding human burials. Sprague (1993) summarized the history of anthropological work and tribal burials, describing tribal government agreements with the University of Idaho for gathering, study, and return to tribal people of human remains, accompanied by anthropological reporting. More recently, Stark's (2016) review and survey suggest that Tribal member's perspectives often recognize the value of scientific inquiry in knowing about the past, and yield a general desire to partner with the academy growing out of issues of repatriation. These shifts in perspective and increased community engaged projects, like that at the Grand Ronde (noted above), are indicative of the future of much of the field toward a better understanding of the American experience. This is underscored by increasing work to explore the history of Native, Chinese, Japanese, and other American groups and to address legacies of racism in the Pacific Northwest (e.g., Fang 2021; Johnson 2017; Wegars 1996).

The Gap

As noted in the dearth of post–World War II work, historical archaeology's explorations of the Pacific Northwest largely end at World War II. While researchers are beginning to document Cold War sites, with a few exceptions the latter half of the twentieth century, and all of the twenty-first century, is largely ignored by historical archaeologists. The growing interest in the materiality of modernity elsewhere is largely absent. Many western communities exploded in population after World War II, and major changes in settlement and technology took place. Plastics became much more available and diverse. The transportation revolution, including the interstate highway system, led to readily available (and inexpensive) foods, and major transitions moved toward informality in household design in the mid- to late twentieth century, including the introduction of the ranch-style house and mid-century modern architecture. Revolutions in medicine, economics, and information technology are hallmarks of the period. This creates a gap in our material understanding of the American experience in the Pacific Northwest through historical archaeology. The reasons for this gap have to do with (1) current legal conceptions of site significance based on age, (2) interest in exploration of the unique without understanding the full character of the mundane, and (3) legislative and policy directions associated with cultural resources management.

Most of the archaeological work conducted since the 1970s has been done under the cultural resources management framework guided by governmental laws and regulations. The U.S. National Register of Historic Places limits what should be considered significant to fifty years of age. In Oregon, the age for recording sites is seventy-five years for private and public (non-Federal) lands, and in British Columbia, it is set at a fixed date, 1846, beyond which sites generally are not protected. Until recently, many academics have focused emphasis on sites that tie to contact-period colonial studies, or well-known (and funded) park sites, or sites that are related to marginalized groups whose histories are limited or absent, often related to processes of settler colonialism.

Many of the sites selected for more extensive historical archaeological studies in the Pacific Northwest contain unusual or unique historical attributes, including the locations of famous people with a deep historical record, and locations of underrepresented minorities. While not countenancing a trend away from the restorative justice functions of an engaged historical archeology, I suggest that we need to document the materiality of people who formed dominant majorities of settler communities to sufficiently contrast with Indigenous and other minorities, a point noted by Montgomery (2022: 477; also see Praetzellis and Praetzellis 1988). For example, Riordan's (1985) novel study of the experience of African American soldiers was relevant only through contrast with White soldiers from the same time period. It also directly engages citizens who are not minorities, by humanizing the "other" while providing knowledge on the full spectrum of representation. These contrasts help decolonize the field, providing a means to conduct comparisons while engaging with the nuance associated with other settler groups. In addition, attention should be paid to the historical archaeology of antiracist allies and enemies, including those central characters and groups instrumental in altering the narratives.

There is considerably more capacity for gendered examination of historical archaeological sites. While some important contributions have been made in terms of Victorian gentility (e.g., Warner 2017), settler colonial contexts like Champoeg or Fort Vancouver (McAleer 2004; Manion 2014; Stone 2010; Sukau 2022), or World War II workplace settings (e.g., Roulette et al. 2010), more attention is warranted to incorporate feminist-centered perspectives in the historical archaeology of the Pacific Northwest.

Bias is also present against the study of more recent (and mass-produced) things. As noted in chapter 8, in the early twentieth century, many small farmsteads spread across the West, but by the mid–twentieth century, the shift to cities and new suburban areas resulted in mass-produced bungalows and ranch-style houses, with people working in urban environments. Shifts in how refuse is treated have impacted the ability of historical archaeologists to explore individual households and individuals, with refuse deposited as sheet trash around dwellings giving way to city dumps and landfills. Refuse is sometimes deposited far from its point of origin, making it harder to study.

The nature of cultural resources management archaeology in the Pacific Northwest is also a problem. Besides Klimko's (2004: 168) admonition that cultural resources management restricted the ability of Canadian historical archaeologists to address larger problems, in the United States it has restricted where American historical archaeologists study and the character of their investigations. Many of the projects and sites explored in this book are tied to federal property, federal money, or federal permits, associated with the Section 106 process of the NHPA. With some exceptions, these tend to be non-urban, remote areas, often associated with national forests, reservoirs, and other public lands. As a consequence, we know more about these areas than we do about areas of concentrated populations, giving shorter shrift to the examination of urban archaeological resources. Historical archaeologists have long observed the obvious need for cultural resources management to balance sampling with the limitations of funding and scheduling. This includes determining what archaeological resources and values remain after the undertaking is completed, the likelihood of resources being destroyed permanently by the project that initiated the work, and limitations on reporting and publication (e.g., Chance and Chance 1979: 4). Clearly, there is a need for researchers to collect scientifically valid information that allows for comparison across time periods and to compare more recent material culture with that of the past in an anthropological framework. The synthesis and academic comparison of related historical archaeology data are limited in the Pacific Northwest, confined to sites like the excellent clearinghouses of the Asian American Comparative Collection and its online presence (University of Idaho 2022), online collections of material culture including tin cans and Chinese ceramics hosted by Southern Oregon University (Southern Oregon University 2018a, 2018b), and online articles and guides to material culture at protected historical archaeology sites, such as Fort Vancouver (e.g., NPS 2023).

Conclusion

As illustrated in the chapters of this book, historical archaeology has engaged with the tremendous material, environmental, and social change in the Pacific Northwest over the last 250 years. The most obvious material changes are those associated with technology, including innovations in ceramics, glass bottles, armaments, architectural fasteners, and window glass related to national and global changes in industrial production, transportation innovations, and the marketing of manufactured goods. Technological change is also reflected in shifting industrial production tied to national and global markets, with innovations in agriculture, fishing, logging, mining, and transportation, which influenced the types of crops grown, and the ways in which resources were extracted and moved to market. Profound impacts are also associated with technological change that affected both Indigenous and settler communities, leading to increased displacement of peoples, shifting focus on resource extraction, and industries that affected the environment—and ultimately the relationships between nations and people.

The age of explorers introduced new species of animals to the Pacific Northwest, the most important of which was the horse, and also diseases that had distressing costs to many Indigenous populations. Historical archaeology demonstrates how the earliest direct explorer contacts yielded only isolated cultural ripples across the region and bore no real direct effects on Indigenous peoples. In contrast, the fur trade altered the demand for certain animal species, such as the sea otter and beaver, which affected communities in different ways, in some cases creating dependency on trade goods and significant stress when populations of animals plummeted, which led to violence in the upper

Peace River region (e.g., Burley and Hamilton 1991: 16; Burley et al. 1996:93, 124–134), but also provided opportunities, such as deer hunting among the *St'át'imc* at Bridge River (Prentiss 2017; Smith 2017: 240–243), that elevated the prestige value and significance of certain species. Responses by Indigenous people to the fur traders were highly variable, with some finding that desired products fit into existing social and cultural structures, like for the *Ktunaxa* (Kootenai), while others emphasized other elements of the fur trade that were more appropriate to their culture, like the *Niitsitapi* (Blackfeet) (Moore 2012). Ultimately, the fur trade lasted a long time in Canada, and had lasting impacts, creating both settler and Native American/First Nations communities that are closely connected to fur trade posts and their heritage. Historical archaeology reveals the daily lives of fur trade people and how disparate peoples formed new and powerful legacies that are intrinsic to the American experience in the Pacific Northwest. More recently, Indigenous communities have begun to advocate, sponsor, or direct these studies, such as at the Tsek'ehne village site/McLeod's Lake Post in British Columbia (Quackenbush 1990; Yellowhorn 2002) and at the Grand Ronde Reservation in Oregon (Gonzalez et al. 2018; Kretzler and Gonzalez 2021). In some cases, archaeologists have joined with Indigenous communities to recover lost grave sites of children from Residential/Boarding schools (e.g., Harris et al. 2017; Simons et al. 2021).

American settlement led to more direct conflicts and contested spaces, also echoed in British Columbia. Settlers arriving over the Oregon Trail and via ships imposed new order and new conceptions of land, industry, and religion, but also brought a variety of new people with very different practices and material belongings. Historical archaeologists have explored the deluge of manufactured goods into the Pacific Northwest, and the ways in which the industrial revolution impacted consumer habits, with some variations throughout the region over time. For minority populations, like African, Chinese, Japanese American, and Indigenous communities, racialization by the majority White populations led to adaption, survival, and for Indigenous people, survivance, in the face of devastating laws and policies, and overt and structural violence. Rejecting tropes that forced minority populations into essentialized categories that could be minimized or ignored, historical archaeologists have begun to counter terminal, victimization, acculturation, and defeatist approaches to these populations, and toward explanations that embrace the agency of people and populations. Minority populations, such as the Chinese and Japanese, brought new practices, ideas, religion, business organizations, and associations into the region. Both Western and Eastern manufactured goods tied to global and transnational systems linked peoples of the Pacific Northwest to European and Asian worlds. Historical archaeology has explored the novel ways in which individuals and groups adjusted and adapted to changing economic opportunities, but also the increasingly racialized views imposed on minority populations, which in some cases, combined with violence, led to shifting populations, with depopulation of many places in rural settings and concentration in urban environments, including the Vancouver, British Columbia, and Portland, Oregon, Chinatowns. In spite of dislocations associated with government policies, Indigenous people found a way to connect with ancient landscapes through mixed-race communities like Kanaka Flat near Jacksonville, Oregon, and engagement in wage labor at salmon canneries or hops picking camps (e.g., Newell 1987, 1991; Oliver 2013; Rose 2009, 2013). This does not discount the years of dislocation and trauma caused by colonialism and settler colonialism, but highlights resistance, survival, and Indigenous survivance of communities over time. Historical archaeology has explored how Chinese, Japanese, and African American people carved out unique spaces that straddled national laws and policies, creating communities and organizations that are commemorated at some heritage places and in many cases continue in some form today.

The impacts of increasing development and modernity is reflected in damage to ecosystems and the natural environment. It is ironic that much of the work of historical archaeology in the Pacific Northwest is tied to dams and reservoirs that have impacted native fisheries, or timber sales that have in some cases deforested regions and affected streams, plants, and animals. Modern-day fights over the environment are sometimes uncomfortably connected to a colonial past, and battles over landscapes and resources continue. For example, challenges to the supremacy of natural over heritage resources began with logging in the 1980s and 1990s. This speaks to the economic and capitalist values of natural resources trumping the values of heritage resources within cultural landscapes in which they are situated. For example, conflicting approaches to documentation and assessment of heritage resources in the Stein River Valley in British Columbia, near Lytton, exposed issues associated with landscape, humanistic, and ethnographic approaches, and processual archaeology that myopically focused on distributions of material things (Wickwire 1992). Conflicting recommendations partly reflected theoretical approaches but also aligned with who was paying the bills. Likewise, conflicts over logging at Meares Island examine some of the earliest colonial history and modern battles over resources (Gough 1998). Ongoing conflicts over Indigenous heritage and landscapes, resources, and the shortcomings of cultural resources management as an effective tool to address it are explored and reinterpreted at numerous places on both sides of the border (e.g., Capuder 2013 vs. Creighton 2004; Acheson 2022 vs. Sauer 1995).

Controversies over the exploration of twentieth-century landfills are another related aspect of how settler damage to the environment has led to conflict over the heritage values of properties, versus the desire to "clean up" waste. The results of human endeavor, particularly associated with the rapid ramp-up of industrial production during and post–World War II, has resulted in considerable environmental damage, including hazardous waste "superfund" sites that require significant remediation. As discussed in chapter 8, World War II landfills at the Hanford Workers Camp and Kaiser Shipyards provide unique challenges to study, but also provide valuable information on workers under extraordinary circumstances. After the pioneering work by William Rathje (Rathje 1979, Rathje and Murphy 1992; Rathje et al. 1992), the question on whether modern or even twentieth-century refuse is an appropriate target of study should no longer be debated. The significance of refuse disposal sites as heritage sites, however, remains hotly contested (e.g., Stapp and Longenecker 2009: 103–105).

Historical archaeology in the Pacific Northwest has explored the relationships among people, including Indigenous and settler, workers and operators, soldiers, officers, and combatants. Material items augment, explore, confirm, and contradict the historical record, and create a fuller, less racist, and more nuanced vision of what happened in the past. It is clear that some immigrants wielded the trappings of Victorianism and religion to try to rework past cultural landscapes, matching their desires to develop and forever change the region. The Northwest was too big, though, and the confluence of people who flooded the areas persevered in spite of racist ideologies, often creating spaces within the region to exist and thrive, and leaving material memories of the past. Indigenous communities persisted, and using capitalism's need for labor, reconnected with traditional landscapes, while integrating commercial products into traditional practices.

While the historical archaeology of the Pacific Northwest is incomplete, it should be clear that historical archaeology contributes uniquely to exploring the Pacific Northwest and has revealed in many ways the American experience. Understanding the intertwined relationships of people with each other amid Pacific Northwest landscapes should guide our mediations to address climate and social problems, recognizing this long history of confluence, conflict, and persistence.

WORKS CITED

Abraham, Terry, and Priscilla Wegars
  2003   Urns, Bones and Burners: Overseas Chinese Cemeteries. *Australasian Historical Archaeology* 21:58–69.
  2005   Respecting the Dead: Cemeteries and Burial Practices in the Interior Pacific Northwest. In *Chinese American Death Rituals: Respecting the Ancestors,* Sue Fawn Chung and Priscilla Wegars, editors, pp. 157–183. Alta Mira Press, Lanham, MD.

Acheson, Cassidy
  2022   Reawakening Memory and Refusing Erasure: Sqilxw Legacies of Resistance through Familial Stories of Mary Ann and Mary Teresa. Master's thesis, University of British Columbia Okanagan.

Acheson, Steven R.
  1995   In the Wake of the Iron People: A Case for Changing Settlement Strategies among the Kunghit Haida. *The Journal of the Royal Anthropological Institute* 1(2):273–299.

Acheson, Steven, and James P. Delgado
  2004   Ships for the Taking: Culture Contact and the Maritime Fur Trade on the Northwest Coast of North America. In *The Archaeology of Contact in Settler Societies,* Tim Murray, editor, pp. 48–77. Cambridge University Press, Cambridge, UK.

Adams, William Hampton
  1973   An Ethnoarchaeological Study of a Rural American Community: Silcott, Washington, 1900–1930. *Ethnohistory* 20(4):335–346.
  1975   Archaeology of the Recent Past: Silcott, Washington, 1900–1930. *Northwest Anthropological Research Notes* 8(1):156–165.
  1977   History, Historicity, and Archaeology. *Northwest Anthropological Research Notes* 11(2):135–142.
  2002   Machine Cut Nails and Wire Nails: American Production and Use for Dating 19th-Century and Early-20th-Century Sites. *Historical Archaeology* 36(4):66–88.

Adams, William H., and Linda P. Gaw
  1977   A Model for Determining Time Lag of Ceramic Artifacts. *Northwest Anthropological Research Notes* 11(2):218–231.

Addis, Cameron
  2005   The Whitman Massacre: Religion and Manifest Destiny on the Columbia Plateau, 1809–1858. *Journal of the Early Republic* 25:221–258.

Aikens, C. Melvin, Thomas J. Connolly, and Dennis L. Jenkins
    2011   *Oregon Archaeology.* Oregon State University Press, Corvallis.

Akin, Marjorie, James C. Bard, and Gary J. Weisz
    2015   Asian Coins Recovered from Chinese Railroad Labor Camps: Evidence of Cultural Practices and Transnational Exchange. *Historical Archaeology* 49(1):110–121.

Ames, Kenneth M.
    2017   Postscript to The Fur-Trade Archaeology of the Cathlapotle and Meier Sites, Lower Columbia River. In *The Fur-Trade Archaeology of the Cathlapotle and Meier Sites, Lower Columbia River,* Kenneth M. Ames and Katie Henry, editors, pp. 363–418, U.S. Fish and Wildlife Service Region 1, Cultural Resource Series 18, Portland, OR.

Ames, Kenneth M., and Thomas J. Brown
    2019   Radiocarbon Dating the Fur Trade: Bayesian Analyses of Fur-Trade Era Radiocarbon Dates from the Lower Columbia River. *International Journal of Historical Archaeology* 23(2):283–312.

Ames, Kenneth M., and Herbert D. G. Maschner
    1999   *Peoples of the Northwest Coast: Their Archaeology and Prehistory.* Thames and Hudson, New York.

Ames, Kenneth M., and Emily E. Shepard
    2019   Building Wooden Houses: The Political Economy of Plankhouse Construction on the Southern Northwest Coast of North America. *Journal of Anthropological Archaeology* 53:202–221.

Applen, Jeffery A.
    1997   Battle of Big Bend. Master's thesis, Oregon State University, Corvallis.

Aranyosi, E. F.
    2017a   National Register of Historic Places Registration Form: Yama & Nagaya Village (山&長屋邑). Bremerton, WA.
    2017b   The Yama Project: A Multidisciplinary Analysis of a Historic Transnational Japanese Village on Bainbridge Island. *Archaeology in Washington* 17:1–15.

Arnold, Jeanne E., David M. Schaepe, and Naxaxalhts'i (McHalsie, Albert "Sonny")
    2017   Excavations in Captain Charlie's Pithouse at Ts'qó:Ls Village (DiRi 1), Hope, B.C. In *Archaeology of the Lower Fraser River Region,* Mike P. Rousseau, editor, pp. 51–60. Archaeology Press, Simon Fraser University, Vancouver, BC.

Atherton, John H.
    1975a   Archaeological and Historical Investigations at Champoeg, Oregon, 1975. Portland State University. Manuscript, Oregon State Parks, State Historic Preservation Office, Report No. 1299, Salem, OR.
    1975b   Archaeological Investigations at Champoeg, Oregon, 1973. *Northwest Anthropological Research Notes* 9(1):103–120.

Atwood, Kay, and Dennis J. Gray
    2003   Gold! Oregon Encyclopedia. www.oregonhistoryproject.org/articles/gold. Accessed 15 October 2022.

Avey, Michael G.
    1986   The Americans Are Coming! An Attempt to Locate Hudson Bay Company/

Puget Sound Agricultural Company Archaeological Features in the Fort Steilacoom Historic District (45PI105H). Department of Anthropology, Pierce College at Fort Steilacoom, Lakewood, WA.

Banach, Patricia K.
2017 Meier and Cathlapotle Copper Artifacts. In *The Fur-Trade Archaeology of the Cathlapotle and Meier Sites, Lower Columbia River*, Kenneth M. Ames and Katie Henry, editors, pp. 171–235, U.S. Fish and Wildlife Service Region 1, Cultural Resource Series Number 18, Portland, OR.

Barman, Jean
2007 *The West Beyond the West: A History of British Columbia*, 3rd edition. University of Toronto Press, Toronto, ON.

Barman, Jean, and Bruce M. Watson
1999 Fort Colvile's Fur Trade Families and the Dynamics of Race in the Pacific Northwest. *Pacific Northwest Quarterly* 90(3):140–153.

Barnes, John
2008 The Struggle to Control the Past: Commemoration, Memory, and the Bear River Massacre of 1863. *The Public Historian* 30(1):81–104.

Barry, J. Neilson
1941 Site of Wallace House, 1812–1814 One Mile from Salem. *Oregon Historical Quarterly* 42(3):205–207.

Barth, Gunther
1964 Chinese Sojourners in the West: The Coming. *Southern California Quarterly* 46(1):55–67.

Bass, Kayley Marie
2017 The Hidden History of Western Washington Logging Camps: St. Paul and Tacoma Lumber Company's Camp #5 ca. 1934–1947. Master's thesis, Central Washington University, Ellensburg.

Bastier, Andrew, and Chelsea Rose
2016 Archaeological Analysis of Hanley Farm (35JA339) Spring House and Bunk House Artifact Collection, Jackson County, Oregon. Southern Oregon University Laboratory of Anthropology Report No. 2016.06, Ashland.

Baugher, Sherene, and Richard F. Veit
2014 *The Archaeology of American Cemeteries and Gravemarkers*. University Press of Florida, Gainesville.

Beals, Herbert K.
1980 Chinese Coins in Six Northwestern Aboriginal Sites. *Historical Archaeology* 14:58–72.

Beals, Herbert K., and Harvey Steele
1981 Chinese Porcelains from Site 35-TI-1, Netarts Sand Spit, Tillamook County, Oregon. In *University of Oregon Anthropological Papers No. 23*, Don E. Dumond, editor, Department of Anthropology, University of Oregon, Eugene.

Bearss, Edwin C., and Merle Wells
1990 National Register of Historic Places Registration Form, Bear River Massacre National Historic Landmark. Washington, DC.

Beaule, Christine D.
  2017   Challenging the Frontiers of Colonialism. In *Frontiers of Colonialism,* Christine D. Beaule, editor, pp. 1–25. University Press of Florida, Gainesville.

Beaulieu, Sarah E.
  2019   Morrissey Internment Camp. *The Midden* 49(2):4–10.
  2020   The Prisoner of War Diet: A Material and Faunal Analysis of the Morrisey WWI Internment Camp. *Journal of Conflict Archaeology* 15(2):118–145.
  2022   The Materiality of Mental Health at the Morrissey World War I Internment Camp. *Historical Archaeology* 56(3):482–503.

Beckham, Stephen Dow
  1971   *Requiem for a People: The Rogue Indians and the Frontiersmen.* University of Oklahoma Press, Norman.
  1984   "This Place Is Romantic and Wild:" An Historical Overview of the Cascades Area, Fort Cascades, and the Cascades Townsite, Washington Territory. Report to Portland District, U.S. Army Corps of Engineers, Heritage Research Associates Report No. 27, Eugene, OR.
  1990   Cultural Resource Reconnaissance of the Umpqua River North Spit, Oregon Dunes National Recreation Area, Siuslaw National Forest. Report to USDA Forest Service, Siuslaw National Forest, Corvallis, OR. Heritage Research Associates Report No. 98, Eugene, OR.
  2006   Historical Setting. In *In the Shadow of Fort Vancouver: Historical Archaeology of Blocks 24 and 25, City of Vancouver, Clark County, Washington,* Rick Minor, editor, pp. 8–15. Heritage Research Associates Report No. 229, Eugene, OR.
  2012   National Register of Historic Places Multiple Property Documentation Form: The Oregon Trail, Oregon, 1840 to 1880. Salem, Oregon.

Bedard, Elisabet Louise
  1990   The Historic and Ethnographic Background of Fort D'Epinette (HaRc 27): Considerations for the Archaeological Determination of Ethnicity. Master's thesis, Simon Fraser University, Vancouver, BC.

Beliso-DeJesús, Aisha M., Jemima Pierre, and Junald Rana
  2023   White Supremacy and the Making of Anthropology. *Annual Review of Anthropology* 52:417–435.

Bell, James W.
  1990   Report of the Geophysical Survey of Fort Clatsop National Monument, Astoria, Oregon. Manuscript, Lewis and Clark National Historical Park. Astoria, OR.
  1991   Report of the Remote Sensing Survey at Fort Vancouver National Historic Site. Manuscript, Fort Vancouver National Historic Site, Vancouver, WA.
  1996   Report of the Ground Penetrating Radar Survey at Fort Clatsop, 1996. Manuscript, Lewis and Clark National Historical Park. Astoria, OR.

Benson, James R., Jacqueline Cook, and Guy F. Moura
  1987   Excavations at Site 45OK92: A Prehistoric Site Underlying Astor's Fort Okanogan. Wells Reservoir Archaeological Project, Volume 3, Central Washington Archaeological Survey, Archaeological Report 87-3, Ellensburg, WA.

Bewall, Douglas A.
  1982   Archeological Testing at the Willamette Mission Hospital Site. Master's thesis, Oregon State University, Corvallis.

Binder, Andrea Mary
  2011   Deep Is the Grave. Master's thesis, University of Wyoming, Laramie.

Binford, Lewis R.
  1962   Archaeology as Anthropology. *American Antiquity* 28(2):217–225.
  1965   Archaeological Systematics and the Study of Cultural Process. *American Antiquity* 31(2):203–210.

Bischof, Fred
  1983   Analysis of Bellvue Farm Nails. In *San Juan Archaeology, Volume I*. Roderick Sprague, editor, pp. 437–439. Laboratory of Anthropology, University of Idaho, Moscow.

Blackman, Margaret B
  1973   Totems to Tombstones: Culture Change as Viewed through the Haida Mortuary Complex, 1877–1971. *Ethnology* 12(1):47–56.

Blatt, Samantha H., Kenneth C. Reid, Cameron E. Quade, Emily Moes, and Katie Taylor
  2017   Boots Made for Walking: Two Late Nineteenth Century Burials from Walters Ferry, Idaho. *Idaho Archaeologist* 40(1):1–20.

Boag, Peter G.
  1993   Overlanders and the Snake River Region: A Case Study of Popular Landscape Perception in the Early West. *The Pacific Northwest Quarterly*. Vol. 84.
  2014   Death and Oregon's Settler Generation: Connecting Parricide, Agricultural Decline, and Dying Pioneers at the Turn of the Twentieth Century. *Oregon Historical Quarterly* 115(3):344–379.

Bollwerk, Elizabeth, Robert Connolly, and Carol McDavid
  2015   Co-creation and Public Archaeology. *Advances in Archaeological Practice* 3(3):178–187.

Boulware [Drew], Brooke L.
  2008   The Deathscape of St. Paul: Historic Cemeteries as Cultural Landscapes. Master's thesis, Oregon State University, Corvallis.

Bown, Tom
  2016   The Historic Songhees Village, Victoria, British Columbia: 50 Years of Historic Archeology at DcRu-25 and DcRu-123. *The Midden* 46(3):18–27.

Bowyer, Gary C.
  1992   Archaeological Symbols of Status and Authority: Fort Hoskins, Oregon, 1856–1865. Master's thesis, Oregon State University, Corvallis.
  2002   Twentieth Century Material Culture Variability: Valve Marks, Milk Cans, and Tobacco Tins. In *Contributions to the Archaeology of Oregon 2002*, Lou Ann Speulda and Gary C. Bowyer, editors, pp. 109–119, Association of Oregon Archaeologists Occasional Papers No. 7, Eugene.

Boyd, Robert T.
  1975   Another Look at the "Fever and Ague" of Western Oregon. *Ethnohistory* 22(2):135–154.
  1990   Demographic History, 1774–1874. In *Handbook of North American Indians,*

Volume 7, Northwest Coast, Wayne Suttles, editor, pp. 135–148. Smithsonian Institution, Washington, DC.
    1994   Smallpox in the Pacific Northwest: The First Epidemics. *BC Studies* 101:5–40.
    1996   Commentary on Early Contact-Era Smallpox in the Pacific Northwest. *Ethnohistory* 43(2):307–328.
    1999   *The Coming of the Spirit of Pestilence: Introduced Infectious Diseases and Population Decline among Northwest Coast Indians, 1774–1874.* University of Washington Press, Seattle.

Boyd, Robert T., Kenneth M. Ames, and Tony A. Johnson (editors)
    2015   *Chinookan Peoples of the Lower Columbia.* University of Washington Press, Seattle.

Boyle, Ramona, and Richard Mackie
    2015   The Hudson's Bay Company in Barkerville. *BC Studies* 185:79–107.

Brauner, David R.
    1989   The French-Canadian Archaeological Project, Willamette Valley, Oregon: Site Inventory and Settlement Pattern Analysis. Report to the Oregon State Historic Preservation Office from Department of Anthropology, Oregon State University, Corvallis.

Brauner, David, Catherine Dickson, Steven Littlefield, and Mary White
    1998   Archaeological Evaluation of the 1875–1919 Barlow Road Tollgate Site, Clackamas County, Oregon. Report to the Oregon Department of Transportation from Oregon State University, Corvallis.

Brauner, David, Rebecca McClelland Poet, and James Bell
    1993   Eden's Gate: Champoeg State Park Historic Sites Archaeological Project 1990–1992. Department of Anthropology, Oregon State University, Corvallis. Manuscript, Oregon State Parks, State Historic Preservation Office, Salem.

Brooks, Saffron
    2021   Goian Bego: Basque Gravestone Symbol Analysis in the Intermountain West. Master's thesis, University of Idaho, Moscow.

Brown, Jamelon Emmick
    2014   If There Is Anything Left to Work On: Dental Health in Historic Sandpoint, Idaho. In *The Other Side of Sandpoint: Early History and Archaeology Beside the Track, the Sandpoint Archaeology Project 2006–2013, Volume 2: Material Culture,* Mark S. Warner, editor, pp. 201–213. SWCA Report No. 14-48, Portland, OR.

Brown, James A.
    1971   The Dimensions of Status in the Burials at Spiro. *Memoirs of the Society for American Archaeology* 25:92–112.

Brown, Jennie Broughton
    1932   *Fort Hall on the Oregon Trail: A Historical Study.* Caxton Printers, Caldwell, ID.

Bunting, Robert
    1995   The Environment and Settler Society in Western Oregon. *Pacific Historical Review* 64(3):413–432.

Burley, David V.
  1989 Function, Meaning and Context: Ambiguities in Ceramic Use by the Hivernant Metis of the Northwestern Plains. *Historical Archaeology* 23(1):95–106.
Burley, David V., and Scott Hamilton
  1991 Rocky Mountain Fort: Archaeological Research and the Late Eighteenth-Century North West Company Expansion into British Columbia. *BC Studies* 88:3–20.
Burley, David V., and Philip M. Hobler
  1997 Archaeology and the British Columbia Fur Trade. *The Midden* 29(1):2–5.
Burley, David V., J. Scott Hamilton, and Knut R. Fladmark
  1996 *Prophecy of the Swan: The Upper Peace River Fur Trade of 1794–1823*. UBC Press, Vancouver, BC.
Burton, Jeffery F., and Mary M. Farrell
  2001 *This Is Minidoka: An Archeological Survey of Minidoka Internment National Monument, Idaho*. Western Archeological and Conservation Center Publications in Anthropology 80, National Park Service, Tucson, AZ.
Burton, Jeffery F., Mary M. Farrell, Florence B. Lord, and Richard W. Lord
  2000 *Confinement and Ethnicity: An Overview of World War II Japanese American Relocation Sites*. Western Archeological and Conservation Center Publications in Anthropology 74, National Park Service, Tucson, AZ.
Bush, Amanda Joy
  2006 The Victorian Individual as Displayed Through Fashion: An Investigation of Urban Privies in Vancouver, Washington. Paper presented at the 59th Annual Northwest Anthropological Conference, Seattle, WA.
Butler, Virginia L.
  2007 Relic Hunting, Archaeology, and Loss of Native American Heritage at the Dalles. *Oregon Historical Quarterly* 108(4):624–643.
Butler, Virginia L., Lyssia Merrifield, Virginia Parks, and Shelby Anderson
  2021 Ten Years On: Engaging the Public Through the Archaeology Roadshow. In *Journal of Northwest Anthropology* Special Publication 4, pp. 6–25.
Butler, William B.
  2009 Some Observations on the Smithsonian Institution River Basin Surveys Excavation and Reporting Standards and Conventions. *Plains Anthropologist* 54:211–215.
Byram, R. Scott
  2002 Brush Fences and Basket Traps: The Archaeology and Ethnohistory of Tidewater Weir Fishing on the Oregon Coast. Doctoral dissertation, University of Oregon, Eugene.
  2005 The Work of a Nation: Richard D. Cutts and the Coast Survey Map of Fort Clatsop. *Oregon Historical Quarterly* 106(2):254–271.
Cameron, Darby James
  2009 An Agent of Change: William Drewry and Land Surveying in British Columbia, 1887–1929. Master's thesis, University of Victoria, Victoria, BC.

Camp, Stacey L.
- 2010 Teaching with Trash: Archaeological Insights on University Waste Management. *World Archaeology* 42(3):430–442.
- 2014 Class and Social Standing Within the Sandpoint Chinatown: An Analysis of Ceramic and Glass Tablewares and Gaming Artifacts. In *The Other Side of Sandpoint: Early History and Archaeology Beside the Track, The Sandpoint Archaeology Project 2006-2013, Volume 1: Sandpoint Stories*, Robert M. Weaver, editor, pp. 73–87. SWCA Report No. 14–48, Portland, OR.
- 2016 Landscapes of Japanese American Internment. *Historical Archaeology* 50(1):169–186.
- 2018 Vision and Ocular Health at a World War II Internment Camp. *World Archaeology* 50(3): 530–546.
- 2021 The Future of Japanese Diaspora Archaeology in the United States. *International Journal of Historical Archaeology* 25(3):877–894.

Camp, Stacey Lynn, Josh Allen, Elaine Bayly, Jamie Capawana, Sara Galbraith, Shea Henry, Meaghan Jones, Kyle Parker-McGlynn, Mary Petrich-Guy, Heather Sargent, and Rachel Stokeld
- 2011 Cultivating Sustainability through Anthropology University of Idaho's Campus Trash. *Anthropology News* (4):11.

Campbell, Renae J.
- 2017a Connections and Distinctions: Historical Archaeological Analysis of Japanese Ceramics Recovered from Three Issei Communities in the American West, 1903–1942. Master's thesis, University of Idaho, Moscow.
- 2017b Reanalysis of Japanese-Manufactured Ceramics Recovered from Japanese Gulch Village (1903–1930), Mukilteo, Washington. *Archaeology in Washington* 17:62–89.
- 2021 Japanese Ceramics and the Complexities of Consumption in "This Knife-Fork Land." *International Journal of Historical Archaeology* 25(3):718–739.

Campbell, Renae J., Caroline E. Herritt, and Daniel J. Polito
- 2018 The Bovill Run: History and Practice of North Central Idaho's Bar Hopping Tradition. *Idaho Archaeologist* 41(1):31–53.

Campbell, Sarah Kathleen
- 1989 Postcolumbian Culture History in the Northern Columbia Plateau: A.D. 1500–1900. Doctoral dissertation, University of Washington, Seattle.

Cannon, Kenneth P., Molly Boeka Cannon, Kenneth Reid, Joel Pederson, Sara Shults, and Jonathan Peart
- 2014 Preliminary Results of Archaeological Investigations at the Bear River Massacre Site, Franklin County, Idaho. Paper presented at the 34th Great Basin Anthropological Conference, Boise, Idaho.

Capuder, Karen Marie
- 2013 Forked Tongues at Sequalitchew: A Critical Indigenist Anthropology of Place in Nisqually Territory. Doctoral dissertation, University of Washington, Seattle.

Carley, Caroline D.
- 1981 Historical and Archaeological Evidence of 19th Century Fever Epidemics and

            Medicine at Hudson's Bay Company's Fort Vancouver. *Historical Archaeology* 15(1):19–35.
1982   HBC Kanaka Village/Vancouver Barracks 1977. Office of Public Archaeology, Institute for Environmental Studies, University of Washington, Reports in Highway Archaeology No. 8. Seattle.

Carley, Caroline D., and Robert Lee Sappington
1984   *Archaeological Test Excavations of the Historic Component of 45-WT-1, Texas City/Riparia, Whitman County, Washington, 1983.* University of Idaho Anthropological Research Manuscript Series, No. 77, Moscow.

Carlson, Catherine C.
2000   Archaeology of a Contact-Period Plateau Salishan Village at Thompson's River Post, Kamloops, British Columbia. In *Interpretations of Native North American Life: Material Contributions to Ethnohistory*, Michael S. Nassaney and Eric S. Johnson, editors, pp. 272–295. University Press of Florida, Gainesville.
2006   Indigenous Historic Archaeology of the 19th-Century Seewepemc Village at Thompson's River Post, Kamloops, British Columbia. *Canadian Journal of Archaeology* 30(2):193–250.

Carlson, David R.
2017   The Issei at Barneston Project: An Investigation into Issues of Race and Labor at an Early Twentieth-Century Japanese-American Sawmill Community. *Archaeology in Washington* 17:30–61.
2021   The Materiality of Anti-Japanese Racism: "Foreignness" and Racialization at Barneston, Washington (1898–1924). *International Journal of Historical Archaeology* 25(3):686–717.

Cavanagh, Ted
1997   Balloon Houses: The Original Aspects of Conventional Wood-Frame Construction Re-Examined. *Journal of Architectural Education* 51(1):5–15.

Cavender, Baily M.
2018   The Little Town That Could: The Railroad in Sandpoint, Idaho 1880–1935. *Idaho Archaeologist* 41(1):20–30.

Caywood, Louis R.
1948a   The Archaeological Excavation of Fort Vancouver. *Oregon Historical Quarterly* 49(2):99–116.
1948b   The Exploratory Excavation of Fort Clatsop. *Oregon Historical Quarterly* 49(3):205–210.
1951   Exploratory Excavations at Fort Spokane 1950. Manuscript, Fort Vancouver National Monument, United States National Park Service, Vancouver, WA.
1954a   Archeological Excavations at Fort Spokane 1951, 1952 and 1953. Manuscript, National Park Service, Region Four, San Francisco, CA.
1954b   Excavations at Two Fort Okanogan Sites, 1952. Manuscript, National Park Service, Region Four, San Francisco, CA.
1955   Final Report Fort Vancouver Excavations. Manuscript, Fort Vancouver National Historic Site, National Park Service, Vancouver, WA.

Cenarrusa, Pete T.
  1984   Chapter 73: An Act Relating to Antiquities. In *General Laws of the State of Idaho*, pp. 135–138. Caxton Printers, Caldwell, ID.

Chance, David H.
  1972   *Fort Colvile: The Structure of a Hudson's Bay Company Post, 1825–1871 and after*. University of Idaho Anthropological Research Manuscript Series, No. 4, Laboratory of Anthropology, University of Idaho, Moscow.
  1973   Influences of the Hudson's Bay Company on the Native Cultures of the Colvile District. *Northwest Anthropological Research Notes*, Memoir No. 2. Northwest, Moscow, ID.
  1981   *Sentinel of Silence: A Brief History of Fort Spokane*. Pacific Northwest National Parks Association.
  1986   *People of the Falls*. Kettle Falls Historical Center, Kettle Falls, WA.
  1990   Brief History of Fort Nisqually. Report to the National Park Service, Pacific West Region, San Francisco, CA. Manuscript, Department of Archaeology and Historic Preservation. Olympia, WA.

Chance, David H., and Jennifer V. Chance
  1976   Kanaka Village/Vancouver Barracks, 1974. Office of Public Archaeology, Institute for Environmental Studies Reports in Highway Archaeology No. 3, University of Washington, Seattle.
  1977   *Kettle Falls: 1976 Salvage Archaeology in Lake Roosevelt*. Laboratory of Anthropology, University of Idaho Anthropological Research Manuscript Series No. 39. Moscow.
  1979   *Kettle Falls: 1977 Salvage Archaeology in and beside Lake Roosevelt*. Laboratory of Anthropology, University of Idaho Anthropological Research Manuscript Series No. 53. Moscow.
  1985a   The Excavation of the "Root Cellar" at Fort Spokane. Alfred W. Bowers Laboratory of Anthropology Letter Report 85–16, University of Idaho.
  1985b   Kettle Falls 1978: Further Archaeological Excavations in Lake Roosevelt. Alfred W. Bowers Laboratory of Anthropology, University of Idaho Anthropological Reports No. 84. Moscow.

Chance, David, Jennifer Chance, Caroline Carley, Karl Gurcke, Timothy Jones, George Ling, Michael Pfeiffer, Karl Roenke, Jacqueline Storm, Robert Thomas, and Charles Troup
  1982   Kanaka Village/Vancouver Barracks 1975. Office of Public Archaeology, Institute for Environmental Studies Reports in Highway Archaeology No. 7, University of Washington Seattle.

Chaplin, Joyce E.
  2003   Expansion and Exceptionalism in Early American History. *The Journal of American History* 29(4):1431–1455.

Chapman, Judith A. [Sanders]
  1983   Willamette Mission Archeological Project: Phase III Assessment. Master's thesis, Oregon State University, Corvallis.
  1993   *French Prairie Ceramics: The Harriet D. Munnick Archaeological Collection: Circa 1820–1860, A Catalog and Northwest Comparative Guide*. Anthropology Northwest No. 8, Department of Anthropology, Oregon State University, Corvallis.

2014   William Earl: A Gentleman Farmer and His Wife: 1846–1865. In *Alis Volat Propriis: Tales from the Oregon Territory, 1848–1859*, Chelsea Rose and Mark Tveskov, editors, pp. 67–96. Association of Oregon Archaeologists Occasional Papers 9, Eugene.

Chapman, Judith, and Terry Ozbun
2002   The Archaeology of Ragged Creek Cabin. In *Contributions to the Archaeology of Oregon, 2002*, Lou Ann Speulda and Gary Bowyer, editors, pp. 49–69. Association of Oregon Archaeologists Occasional Papers No. 7, Eugene.

Chen, Chia-lin
1972   A Gold Dream in the Blue Mountains: A Study of the Chinese Immigrants in the John Day Area, Oregon, 1870–1910. Master's thesis; Dissertations and Theses. Paper 962, Portland State University, Portland, OR.

Chen, Ying-ying
2001   In the Colonies of Tang: Historical Archaeology of Chinese Communities in the North Cariboo District, British Columbia (1860s–1940s). Doctoral dissertation, Simon Fraser University, Vancouver, BC.

Chénier, Ani
2009   Negotiations of Individual and Community Identity: A Study of Chinese-Canadian Mortuary Material Culture in Vancouver and Victoria, 1900–1960. Master's thesis, McMaster University, Hamilton, ON.

Chittenden, Hiram Martin
1901   *American Fur Trade of the Far West*. Francis P. Harper, New York.

Christian, Terrance, Chelsea Rose, Lisa A. Rice, Aaron Ennis, and Duane Ericson
2021   The Buck Rock Tunnel Archaeological Site: Documenting Chinese Laborers and the Construction of the Oregon & California Railroad. *Oregon Historical Quarterly* 122(4):388–411.

Chung, Sue Fawn, and Priscilla Wegars
2005   Introduction. In *Chinese American Death Rituals: Respecting the Ancestors*, Sue Fawn Chung and Priscilla Wegars, editors, pp. 11–28. Altamira Press, Lanham, NY.

Cipolla, Craig N.
2021   Theorizing Indigenous-Colonial Interactions in the Americas. In *The Routledge Handbook of the Archaeology of Indigenous-Colonial Interaction in the Americas*, Lee M. Panich and Sara L. Gonzalez, editors, pp. 109–125. Routledge, London.

Clark, Bonnie J.
2017   Digging Yesterday: The Archaeology of Living Memory at Amache. In *Historical Archaeology Through a Western Lens*, Mark Warner and Margaret Purser, editors, pp. 210–232. University of Nebraska Press, Lincoln.

Clark, Jorie
2002   The Archaeology of Railroad Logging in Central Oregon: The Lumberman's Last Frontier. In *Contributions to the Archaeology of Oregon 2002*, Lou Ann Speulda and Gary C. Bowyer, editors, pp. 89–107, Association of Oregon Archaeologists Occasional Papers No. 7, Eugene.

Clearman, Amy Carolyn
  2020 Engaging Communities in Archaeology on Private Property in an Urban Neighborhood: The Search for the First (1825–1829) Fort Vancouver, Vancouver, Washington. Master's thesis, Portland State University, Portland, OR.

Coates, Colin Macmillan
  1984 Death in British Columbia 1850–1950. Master's thesis, University of British Columbia, Vancouver.
  1987 Monuments and Memories. *Material History Bulletin* 25:111–19.

Cobb, John N.
  1921 Pacific Salmon Fisheries. Appendix to the Report of the U.S. Commissioner of Fisheries for 1921. B.F. Doc. No. 902.

Cochran, Matthew D., and Mary C. Beaudry
  2006 Material culture studies and historical archaeology In *The Cambridge Companion to Historical Archaeology,* Dan Hicks and Mary C. Beaudry, editors, pp. 191–204. Cambridge University Press, Cambridge, UK.

Cohen, Amie, and Mark Tveskov
  2008 The Tseriadun Site: Prehistoric and Historic Period Archaeology on the Southern Oregon Coast. SOULA Research Report 2008-3, Southern Oregon University Laboratory of Anthropology, Ashland.

Cole, Douglas, and David Darling
  1990 History of the Early Period. In *Handbook of North American Indians Volume 7,* William C. Sturtevant, general editor; Wayne Suttles, volume editor, pp. 119–134. Smithsonian Institution Washington, DC.

Collier, Donald, Alfred E. Hudson, and Arlo Ford
  1942 Archaeology of the Upper Columbia Region. *University of Washington Publications in Anthropology* 9(1): 1–178, Seattle.

Colwell, Chip
  2016 Collaborative Archaeologies and Descendant Communities. *Annual Review of Anthropology* 45:113–127. DOI: 10.1146/annurev-anthro-102215-095937

Combes, John D.
  1962 *Excavations at Fort Spokane, Summer of 1962.* Washington State University Laboratory of Archaeology and Geochronology No. 20 Pullman.
  1964 Excavations at Spokane House—Fort Spokane Historic Site: 1962–1963. Washington State University, Pullman.
  1965 A Preliminary Investigation at Old Military Fort Spokane, Washington. Washington State University Laboratory of Anthropology Report of Investigations No. 30, Pullman.

Conlin, Joseph R.
  1979 Old Boy, Did You Get Enough of Pie? A Social History of Food in Logging Camps. *Journal of Forest History* October:164–185.

Connolly, Thomas J., Richard L. Bland, and Ward Tonsfeldt
  2011 Tracking the Kerry Line: Evidence from a Logging Railroad Camp in the Nehalem Valley, Oregon. *Journal of Northwest Anthropology* 45(2):199–208.

Connolly, Thomas J., Christopher L. Ruiz, Douglas Deur, Perry Chocktoot, Jaime L. Kennedy, Dennis L. Jenkins, and Julia A. Knowles
   2022   Looking Back, Looking Forward: Resilience and Persistence in a Klamath Tribal Community. *Journal of Anthropological Archaeology* 65:1–17.

Connolly, Thomas J., Christopher L. Ruiz, Jeanne McLaughlin, Guy L. Tasa, and Elizabeth Kallenbach
   2010   The Archaeology of a Pioneer Family Cemetery in Western Oregon, 1854–1879. *Historical Archaeology* 44(4):28–45.

Connolly, Thomas J., Mark E. Swisher, Christopher L. Ruiz, and Elizabeth A. Kallenbach
   2009   A Window on the Past: Pane Glass at the Beatty Curve Archaeological Site, South-Central Oregon. *Journal of Northwest Anthropology* 43(2):141–151.

Converse, Kristin O.
   2011   "Like Nuggets from a Gold Mine": Searching for Bricks and Their Makers in "The Oregon Country." Master's thesis, Sonoma State University, Sonoma, CA.

Cooper, H Kory, Kenneth M Ames, and Loren G Davis
   2015   Copper and Prestige in the Greater Lower Columbia River Region, Northwestern North America. *Journal of Northwest Anthropology* 42(2):143–166.

Cotter, John L., and Edward B. Jelks
   1957   Historic Site Archaeology at Jamestown. *American Antiquity* 22(4):387–389.

Couch, Samuel L.
   1996   Topophilia and Chinese Miners: Place Attachment in North Central Idaho. Doctoral dissertation, University of Idaho, Moscow.

Courchane, Chalk
   n.d.   Jacques Raphael Finlay: In the Pacific Northwest before 1808. www.oregonpioneers.com/bios/JacquesRafaelFinlay.pdf. Accessed 8 December 2021.

Crabtree, Don E.
   1968   Archaeological Evidence of Acculturation along the Oregon Trail. *Tebiwa* 11(2):38–42.

Creighton, Janet
   2004   Cultural Resources in Conflict: Historic Preservation and Private Property at Northwest Landing, DuPont, Washington. Doctoral dissertation, Washington State University, Pullman.

Cressman, L. S.
   1933   Aboriginal Burials in Southwestern Oregon. *American Anthropologist* 35(1):116–130.

Croes, Dale R., and Steven Hackenberger
   2022   1980s WARC (Washington Archaeological Research Center): An Experiment in Communitarianism for Pacific Northwest Archaeology-And It Did WARC (Work). *Journal of Northwest Anthropology* 56(1):70–91.

Croney, Cohen E.
   2008   An Iron Trade Point from Caribou County, Idaho. *Idaho Archaeologist* 31(1):17–18.

Cromwell, Robert J.
   2002   A Synthesis of Archaeological Data and Recommendations for Future Archae-

ological Research at Fort Clatsop National Memorial, Astoria, Oregon. Manuscript, Lewis and Clark National Historical Park. Astoria, OR.

2006a   The Ceramic Wares of the ca. 1810–1826 North West Company/Hudson's Bay Company Fort Spokane, 45SP5. Northwest Cultural Resources Institute Short Report No. 6(1), Fort Vancouver National Historic Site, National Park Service, Vancouver, WA.

2006b   Results of a Cartographic and Archaeological Surface Survey of the Fort Hall National Historic Landmark Site (10BK29), and an Associated Early 20th Century Homestead Site, May 2001. Northwest Cultural Resources Institute Short Report No. 6(2), National Park Service, Fort Vancouver National Historic Site, Vancouver, WA.

2006c   "Where Ornament and Function Are so Agreeably Combined": Consumer Choice Studies of English Ceramic Wares at Hudson's Bay Company Fort Vancouver. Doctoral dissertation, Syracuse University, Syracuse, NY.

2017a   Comparing the Fur Trade Ceramics of Chinookan and 19th Century Fur Trade Sites along the Columbia River. In *The Fur-Trade Archaeology of the Cathlapotle and Meier Sites, Lower Columbia River,* Kenneth M. Ames and Katie Henry, editors, pp. 235–303, U.S. Fish & Wildlife Service Region 1. Cultural Resource Series 18, Portland, Oregon.

2017b   "Where Ornament and Function are so Agreeably Combined": A New Look at Consumer Choice Studies Using English Ceramic Wares at Hudson's Bay Company, Fort Vancouver. In *Historical Archaeology Through a Western Lens,* Mark Warner and Margaret Purser, editors, pp. 51–84. University of Nebraska Press, Lincoln.

2018   Tracing the Fur Trade: British Fort Sites along the Columbia River. In *British Forts and Their Communities,* Christopher R. DeCorse and Zachary J.M. Beier, editors, pp. 126–150. University Press of Florida, Gainesville.

Cromwell, Robert J., Elaine C. Dorset, Eric Gleason, Jacqueline Cheung, and Leslie O'Rourke

2014   Results of Archaeological Testing of the East and South Vancouver Barracks, Vancouver National Historic Reserve National Historic District (DT191). Northwest Cultural Resources Institute Report No. 17, Fort Vancouver National Historic Site, National Park Service, Vancouver, WA.

Cromwell, Robert J., Gregory P. Shine, Jacqueline Y. Cheung, Stephen L. DeVore, Eric B. Gleason, Elizabeth Horton, and Kendall A. MacDonald

2009   Cultural Resources Survey and Archaeological Testing of the Historical U.S. Army Vancouver Arsenal for the Vancouver National Historic Reserve Visitor Center Expansion Project. Northwest Cultural Resources Institute Report No. 5, Fort Vancouver National Historic Site, National Park Service, Vancouver, WA.

Cromwell, Robert J., Helen Delight Stone, and David R. Brauner

2000   Archaeological Testing of the Newell Historic Farmstead Site (ORMA-41), Champoeg State Park, Oregon. Department of Anthropology, Oregon State University. Manuscript, Oregon State Parks, State Historic Preservation Office, Report No. 17339, Salem.

Crosman, Kathleen
2011 The Army in the Woods: Spruce Production Division Records at the National Archives. *Oregon Historical Quarterly* 112(1):100–106.

Cross, Osborne
1940 The Journal of Major Osborne Cross. In *The March of the Mounted Riflemen: First United States Military Expedition to Travel the Full Length of the Oregon Trail from Fort Leavenworth to Fort Vancouver, May to October, 1849*, Raymond W. Settle, editor, pp. 31–272. The Arthur H. Clark Company, Glendale, CA.

Curl, James Stevens
1975 The Architecture and Planning of the Nineteenth-Century Cemetery. *Garden History* 3(3):13–41.

Czehatowski, Michel
1983 The Analysis of Bottles from American Camp. In *San Juan Archaeology, Volume II*, Roderick Sprague, editor, pp. 613–621. Laboratory of Anthropology, University of Idaho, Moscow.

Daehnke, Jon
2013 "We honor the house": lived heritage, memory, and ambiguity at the Cathlapotle Plankhouse. *Wicazo Sa Review* 28(1):38–64.

Darby, Melissa C.
2019 *Thunder Go North: The Hunt for Sir Francis Drake's Fair and Good Bay*. University of Utah Press, Salt Lake City.

Daugherty, Richard A.
1992 State of Washington Archaeological Site Inventory Form: Yama/Nagaya Village (45KP105). Western Heritage, Lacey, WA, Manuscript, Department of Archaeology and Historic Preservation, Olympia, WA.

Davis, David
1997 Log Chutes on Chuckanut Mountain: Results of a Case Study in Whatcom County. *Archaeology in Washington* 6:55–62.

Deagan, Kathleen
1982 Avenues of Inquiry in Historical Archaeology. *Advances in Archaeological Method and Theory* 5:151–177.

Deetz, James
1988 American Historical Archaeology: Methods and Results. *Science* 239(4838):362–366.
1996 *In Small Things Forgotten: An Archaeology of Early American Life*. 2nd edition. Anchor, New York.

Dennis, John Stoughton, younger
1892 A Short History of the Surveys Performed Under the Dominion Lands System, 1869 to 1889. *Sessional Papers* 13:1.

Dethlefsen, Edwin, and James Deetz
1966 Death's Heads, Cherubs, and Willow Trees: Experimental Archaeology in Colonial Cemeteries. *American Antiquity* 31(4):502–510.

Deur, Douglas
2012 An Ethnohistorical Overview of Groups with Ties to Fort Vancouver National

Historic Site. Pacific West Region: Social Science Series Publication Number 2011-12, 2011, Northwest Cultural Resources Institute Report No. 15, Fort Vancouver National Historic Site, National Park Service, Vancouver, WA.

Dixon, Kelly J.
2014 Historical Archaeologies of the American West. *Journal of Archaeological Research* 22(3):177–228.
2020 Repercussions of Rapid Colonization: Archaeological Insights from the North American West. In *The Routledge Handbook of Global Historical Archaeology*, Charles E. Orser, Jr., Andrés Zarankin, Pedro Paulo A. Funari, Susan Lawrence, and James Symonds, editors, pp. 886–931. Routledge, Abingdon, Oxon.

Dobyns, Henry
1993 Disease Transfer at Contact. *Annual Review of Anthropology* 22:273–291.

Donovan, Sally
2005 National Register of Historic Places Registration Form: Kam Wah Chung Company Building. National Historic Landmarks Survey, National Park Service.

Dorset, Elaine C.
2012 A Historical and Archaeological Study of the Nineteenth Century Hudson's Bay Company Garden at Fort Vancouver: Focusing on Archaeological Field Methods and Microbotanical Analysis. Master's thesis, Portland State University, Portland, OR.

Drew, Brooke
2010 Ideology in Historic Cemeteries: A Case Study from St. Paul, OR. *Field Notes: A Journal of Collegiate Anthropology* 2(1):1–14.

Eichelberger, Justin E.
2011 Foodways at Fort Yamhill, 1856–1866: An Archaeological and Archival Perspective. *Journal of Northwest Anthropology* 45(1):37–56.
2014 An Introduction to U. S. Army Material Culture and Garrison Life in Western Oregon: Archaeological Investigations at Fort Yamhill and Fort Hoskins, 1856–1866. In *Alis Volat Propriis: Tales from the Oregon Territory, 1848–1859*, Chelsea Rose and Mark Tveskov, editors, pp. 135–156. Association of Oregon Archaeologists Occasional Papers 9, Eugene.
2019a Colonial Identities of United States Army Commissioned Officers: The Negotiation of Class and Rank at Fort Yamhill and Fort Hoskins, Oregon, 1856–1866. *Historical Archaeology* 53(1):103–125.
2019b Material Expressions of Class, Status and Authority amongst Commissioned Officers at Fort Yamhill and Fort Hoskins, Oregon, 1856–1866. Doctoral dissertation, Oregon State University, Corvallis.

Ericson, Duane A.
2012 Archaeological Survey of the Abandoned Hardrock Mines in the Jacksonville Area, Jackson County, Oregon. AML Archaeology Reports No. 6, U.S. DOI Bureau of Land Management, Medford District, Medford, OR.

Erigero, Patricia C.
1992 Cultural Landscape Report: Fort Vancouver National Historic Site, Vol. 2. Cul-

tural Resources Division, Pacific Northwest Region, National Park Service, Seattle, WA.

Erlandson, Jon, Robert J. Losey, and Neil Peterson
2001 Early Maritime Contact on the Northern Oregon Coast: Some Notes on the 17th Century Nehalem Beeswax Ship. In *Changing Landscapes: "Telling Our Stories" Proceedings of the Fourth Annual Coquille Cultural Preservation Conference, 2000,* Jason Younker, Mark A. Tveskov, and David G. Lewis, editors, pp. 45–53. Coquille Indian Tribe, North Bend, Oregon.

Erlandson, Jon M., Mark A. Tveskov, and Madonna L. Moss
1997 Return to Chetlessenten: The Antiquity and Architecture of an Athapaskan Village on the Southern Northwest Coast. *Journal of California and Great Basin Anthropology* 19(2):226–240.

Evans-Janke, Leah K.
2007 Silver City Material Culture: The Archaeology of Daily Life. Doctoral dissertation, University of Idaho, Moscow.

Evenson, Lindsey M.
2016 Pre-1900s Chinese Placer Mining in Northeastern Washington State: An Archaeological Investigation. Master's thesis, Eastern Washington University, Cheney.

Ewers, John C.
1955 *The Horse in Blackfoot Indian Culture with Comparative Material from Other Western Tribes.* Smithsonian Institution Bureau of Ethnology Bulletin 159, Washington DC.

Ewonus, Paul, and George Ewonus
2019 The Wild Horse Canyon: Shifting Strategies of Colonial Settlement in the Okanagan. *The Midden* 49(2):11–20.

Fagan, John L.
1993 The Chinese Cannery Workers of Warrendale, Oregon, 1876–1930. In *Hidden Heritage: Historical Archaeology of the Overseas Chinese,* Priscilla Wegars, editor, pp. 215–218. Baywood, Amityville, NY.

Fang, Jennifer
2021 Erasure and Reclamation: Centering Diasporic Chinese Populations in Oregon History. *Oregon Historical Quarterly* 122(4):324–341.

Fee, Jeffrey M.
1993 Idaho's Chinese Mountain Gardens. In *Hidden Heritage: Historical Archaeology of the Overseas Chinese,* Priscilla Wegars, editor, pp. 65–96. Baywood, Amityville, NY.

Ferguson, Linda L.
1983a American Camp Ceramics. In *San Juan Archaeology Volume II,* Roderick Sprague, editor, pp. 587–612. Laboratory of Anthropology, University of Idaho, Moscow.
1983b Bellevue Farm Ceramics. In *San Juan Archaeology Volume I,* Roderick Sprague, editor, pp. 393–416. Laboratory of Anthropology, University of Idaho, Moscow.
1983c Ceramic Conclusions. In *San Juan Archaeology Volume II,* Roderick Sprague,

editor, pp. 769–784. Laboratory of Anthropology, University of Idaho, Moscow.

1983d   English Camp Ceramics. In *San Juan Archaeology Volume I,* Roderick Sprague, editor, pp. 157–186. Laboratory of Anthropology, University of Idaho, Moscow.

1983e   Old San Juan Town Ceramics. In *San Juan Archaeology Volume I,* Roderick Sprague, editor, pp. 285–312. Laboratory of Anthropology, University of Idaho, Moscow.

Fielder, George, and Roderick Sprague
1974   *Test Excavations at the Coeur d'Alene Mission of the Sacred Heart, Cataldo, Idaho, 1973.* University of Idaho Anthropological Research Manuscript Series No. 13. Laboratory of Anthropology, University of Idaho, Moscow.

Finegan, Chance Nicholas
2019   Protected Areas, Indigenous Peoples, and Reconciliation in the United States of America. Doctoral dissertation, York University, Toronto, ON.

Finger, John R.
1972   A Study of Frontier Enterprise: Seattle's First Sawmill 1853–1869. *Journal of Forest History* 15(4):24–31.

Fiset, Louis, and Gail M. Nomura
2005   Introduction: Nikkei in the Pacific Northwest. In *Nikkei in the Pacific Northwest: Japanese Americans and Japanese Canadians in the Twentieth Century,* Louis Fiset and Gail M. Nomura, editors, pp. 3–19. University of Washington Press, Seattle.

Fitzgerald, Kimberli
2018   Uncovering and Interpreting the Chinese Shrine at Salem's Pioneer Cemetery. Master's thesis, Adams State College, Alamosa, CO.

Fitzgerald, Kimberli, Kirsten Straus, and Kylie Pine
2021   Searching for Salem's Early Chinese Community. *Oregon Historical Quarterly* 122(4):456–485.

Fitz-Gerald, Kyla
2015   Cold Cream, Masculinity, and Imprisonment: The Archaeology of Japanese American Internees at Idaho's Kooskia Internment Camp, 1943–1945. Master's thesis, University of Idaho, Moscow.

Fladmark, Knut R.
1973   The Richardson Ranch Site: A 19th Century Haida House. In *Historical Archaeology in Northwestern North America,* Ronald M. Getty and Knut R. Fladmark, editors, pp. 53–95. University of Calgary Archaeological Association, Calgary, AB.

1985   Early Fur-Trade Forts of the Peace River Area of British Columbia. *BC Studies* 65:48–65.

Folan, William J.
1969   Yuquot, British Columbia: The Prehistory and History of a Nootkan Village. *Northwest Anthropological Research Notes* 3(2):217–239.

Folan, William J., and John Dewhirst (editors)
1980a   *The Yuquot Project: The Indigenous Archaeology of Yuquot, a Nootkan Outside*

Village. Vol. 1. History and Archeology Number 39. National Historic Parks and Sites Branch, Parks Canada, Environment Canada.

1980b   *The Yuquot Project, Volume 2.* History and Archeology Number 43. National Historic Parks and Sites Branch, Parks Canada, Environment Canada.

1981   *The Yuquot Project, Volume 3.* History and Archeology Number 44. National Historic Parks and Sites Branch, Parks Canada, Environment Canada.

Folan, William J., and John T. Dewhirst
1970   Yuquot: Where the Wind Blows from All Directions. *Archaeology* 23(4):276–286.

La Follette, Cameron
2022   Discovery of Timbers of Oregon's Manila Galleon and New Light on the Early Beeswax Controversy. *Oregon Historical Quarterly* 123(3):296–303.

La Follette, Cameron, and Douglas Deur
2018   Views across the Pacific: The Galleon Trade and Its Traces in Oregon. *Oregon Historical Quarterly* 119(2):160–191.

La Follette, Cameron, Douglas Deur, Dennis Griffin, and Scott S. Williams
2018   Oregon's Manila Galleon. *Oregon Historical Quarterly* 119(2):150–159.

La Follette, Cameron, Dennis Griffin, and Douglas Deur
2018   The Mountain of a Thousand Holes: Shipwreck Traditions and Treasure Hunting on Oregon's North Coast. *Oregon Historical Quarterly* 119(2):282–313.

Fong, Kelly N., Laura W. Ng, Jocelyn Lee, Veronica L. Peterson, and Barbara L. Voss
2022   Race and Racism in Archaeologies of Chinese American Communities. *Annual Review of Anthropology* 51:233–250.

Foucault, Michel
1995   *Discipline and Punish: The Birth of the Prison.* Alan Sheridan, editor. 2nd edition. Vintage Books, New York.

Francaviglia, Richard V
1971   The Cemetery as an Evolving Cultural Landscape. *Annals of the Association of American Geographers* 61(3):501–509.

Francis, Peter D., and John E. P. Porter
2010   A Possible Simon Fraser Signature Site, Stuart Lake, British Columbia. *Canadian Journal of Archaeology* 34(1):89–105.

Freeman, Alicia, Mark Warner, Margaret Clark, and Ray von Wandruszka
2012   Chemical Analysis of Gunpowder Recovered in an Archaeological Excavation at Sandpoint, Idaho. *Idaho Archaeologist* 35(1):1–6.

Freeman, Otis W.
1954   Early Wagon Roads in the Inland Empire. *The Pacific Northwest Quarterly* 45(4):125–130.

French, Diana E.
1995   Ideology, Politics, and Power: The Socio-Historical Implications of the Archaeology of the D'Arcy Island Leper Colony, 1891–1924. Doctoral dissertation, University of British Columbia, Vancouver.

1996   Historical and Archaeological Investigations of the D'Arcy Island Leper Colony, 1891–1924. *The Midden* 28(1):10–12.

French, Jamie
    2016   Just Beneath the Surface: Analysis of Excavations at 35WS453, The Dalles Chinatown. Master's thesis, Oregon State University, Corvallis.

Frescoln, Carol A.
    1975   A Comparison of the Bottle Glass from English Camp and San Juan Town, San Juan Island, Washington. In *Miscellaneous San Juan Island Reports 1971–1973*, pp. 1–80. University of Idaho Anthropological Manuscript Series No. 16, Moscow.

Gaines, John P., Alonzo A. Skinner, and Beverly S. Allen
    1851   Letter No. 67. Oregon City, O.T., May 14, 1851. In Report of the Commissioner of the General Land Office, 32nd Congress, 1st Session. S. Ex. Doc. No. 1, Volume III, Part 1, pp. 468–472. A. Boyd Hamilton, Washington, D.C.

Gambell, Kevin
    2009   Cemetery Spaces of shxwõwhámel stó:lō and the île-à-la-crosse Métis. Master's thesis, University of Saskatchewan, Saskatoon.

Garth, Thomas R.
    1947   Early Architecture in the Northwest. *The Pacific Northwest Quarterly* 38(3):215–232.
    1948   The Archeological Excavation of Waiilatpu Mission. *Oregon Historical Quarterly* 49(2):117–136.
    1949   A Report on the Second Season's Excavations at Waiilatpu. *The Pacific Northwest Quarterly* 40(4):295–315.
    1951   Archeological Excavations at Fort Walla Walla. Manuscript, National Park Service, Region 4, San Francisco, CA.
    1952a   Archeological Excavations at Fort Walla Walla. *The Pacific Northwest Quarterly* 43(1):27–50.
    1952b   The Mansion House, Grist Mill, and Blacksmith Shop at the Whitman Mission: A Final Report. Manuscript, National Park Service, Region Four Vancouver, WA.

Gaw, Linda P.
    1975   The Availability and Selection of Ceramics in Silcott, Washington, 1900–1930. *Northwest Anthropological Research Notes* 9(1):166–179.

Gehr, Keith D.
    1975   The Bay View Cannery—Skamokawa Village Site. *Northwest Anthropological Research Notes* 9(1):121–138.

Gibson, James R.
    1985   *Farming the Frontier: The Agricultural Opening of the Oregon Country 1786–1846*. University of Washington Press, Seattle.

Giedion, Sigfried
    1941   *Space, Time and Architecture: The Growth of a New Tradition*. Harvard University Press, Cambridge, MA.

Gile, Albion
    1955   Notes on Columbia River Salmon. *Oregon Historical Quarterly* 56(2):140–154.

Goebel, Ted
    1995   Bear Creek Archaeology: Archaeological Excavations at Fort Lane, Hanley

Farm, Beekman House, Jacksonville Courthouse, and Cove Creek Rockshelter. Manuscript, Department of Sociology/Anthropology, Southern Oregon State College, Ashland.

Gonzalez, Sara L., and Briece Edwards

2020   The Intersection of Indigenous Thought and Archaeological Practice: The Field Methods in Indigenous Archaeology Field School. *Journal of Community Archaeology and Heritage* 7(4):239–254.

Gonzalez, Sara L., Ian Kretzler, and Briece Edwards

2018   Imagining Indigenous and Archaeological Futures: Building Capacity with the Confederated Tribes of Grand Ronde. *Archaeologies* 14(1):85–114.

González-Ruibal, Alfredo

2019   *An Archaeology of the Contemporary Era*. Routledge, New York.

Goodwin, Jessica

2014   Drawing from the Well: The Material Life of the Jacobs Family, Boise, Idaho, 1864–1907. Master's thesis, University of Idaho, Moscow.

2018   The Cyrus Jacobs-Uberuaga House Archaeology Project: A Study in Class, Gender, and Place in Nineteenth Century Boise, Idaho. *Idaho Archaeologist* 41(1):54–68.

Gosling, F. G.

1999   *The Manhattan Project: Making the Atomic Bomb*. U.S. Department of Energy DOE/MA-0001 -01/99, Washington, DC.

Gough, Barry M.

1998   Possessing Meares Island. *Journal of Canadian Studies* 33(2):177–185.

Grabert, G. F.

1965   Archaeological Excavations at Fort Okanogan, (45OK64) 1964. Interim Report, Part I to the National Park Service, Region Four by Department of Anthropology, University of Washington, Seattle.

1968   The Astor Fort Okanogan. University of Washington Department of Anthropology Reports in Archaeology No. 2, Seattle.

1973   Early Fort Okanogan: Euro-American Impact on the Historic Okanogan Tribes. In *Historical Archaeology in Northwestern North America*, Ronald M. Getty and Knut R. Fladmark, editors, pp. 109–125. University of Calgary Archaeological Association, Calgary, AB.

Grant, Louis S.

1940   Fort Hall under the Hudson's Bay Company, 1837–1856. *Oregon Historical Quarterly* 41(1):34–39.

Gregory, Ronald L.

2001   *Life in Railroad Logging Camps of the Shevlin-Hixon Company, 1916–1950*. Oregon State University Department of Anthropology: Anthropology Northwest No. 12, Corvallis.

Griffin, Dennis

2009   The Evolution of Oregon's Cultural Resource Laws and Regulations. *Journal of Northwest Anthropology* 43(1):87–116.

Griffin, Dennis, and Thomas E. Churchill
- 2003   Cultural Resource Management in the Pacific Northwest: Working Within the Process. *Journal of Northwest Anthropology* 36(2):27–42.

Grima, Reuben
- 2016   But Isn't All Archaeology "Public" Archaeology? *Public Archaeology* 15(1):50–58.

Gurcke, Karl
- 1983   A Preliminary Study of San Juan Island Bricks. In *San Juan Archaeology, Volume II*, Roderick Sprague, editor, pp. 815–828. Laboratory of Anthropology, University of Idaho, Moscow.
- 1987   *Bricks and Brick Making for Historic Archaeologists*. University of Idaho Press, Moscow.

Hajda, Yvonne
- 2005   Slavery in the Greater Lower Columbia Region. *Ethnohistory* 52(3):563–588.
- 2013   Social and Political Organization. In *Chinookan Peoples of the Lower Columbia*, Robert T. Boyd, Kenneth M. Ames, and Tony A. Johnson, editors, pp 146–162. University of Washington Press, Seattle.

Haines, Francis
- 1938   The Northward Spread of Horses Among the Plains Indians. *American Anthropologist* 40(3):429–437.

Hamilton, Scott
- 2000   Dynamics of Social Complexity in Early Nineteenth-Century British Fur-Trade Posts. *International Journal of Historical Archaeology* 4(3):217–273.
- 2021   Where Are the Children Buried? National Centre for Truth and Reconciliation, University of Manitoba, Edmonton. https://nctr.ca/records/reports/#highlighted-reports

Hann, Don
- 2021   Chinese Mining Kongsi in Eastern Oregon: A Case Study of Cultural Amnesia. *Oregon Historical Quarterly* 122(4):344–367.

Hardesty, Donald L.
- 1981   Historic Sites Archaeology on the Western American Frontier: Theoretical Perspectives and Research Problems. *North American Archaeologist* 2(1):67–82.
- 2010   *Mining Archaeology in the American West: A View from the Silver State*. University of Nebraska Press, Lincoln.

Harrington, J. C.
- 1955   Archeology as an Auxiliary Science to American History. *American Anthropologist* 57(6):1121–1130.

Harris, Donald A.
- 1972   A Preliminary Report on the 1971 Archaeological Excavations of Fort St. James, British Columbia. National Historic Sites Service Manuscript Report Number 77, National and Historic Parks Branch, Department of Indian Affairs and Northern Development.
- 1974   The Archaeological Excavations at the Site of Fort St. James, British Columbia, 1972. Manuscript Report Number 228, Department of Indian and Northern Affairs, Parks Canada.

Harris, Jillian, Alex Maass, and Andrew Martindale
  2017 Practising Reconciliation. In *Reflections of Canada: Illuminating Our Opportunities and Challenges at 150+ Years,* Philippe Tortell, Margot Young, and Peter Nemetz, editors. Peter Wall Institute for Advanced Studies, University of British Columbia, Vancouver.

Harrison, Brian Faris
  1979 Fort Stevens Archaeological Project Preliminary Report 1979. Clatsop Community College, Astoria, OR.
  1988 Historical Archaeology at the Officer's Quarters, Old Fort Stevens, 1980. Clatsop Community College, Astoria, OR.
  1990 Old Post Archaeology: Excavations at Fort Stevens 1979–1980. Clatsop Community College, Astoria, OR.

Harrison, Glenn
  1993 Abner Hackleman's 1845 Trip to Oregon. www.columbiagorge.org/wp-content/uploads/docs/Hackleman's,_Abner,_1845_Trip_to_Oregon.pdf

Harrison, John
  2008 Canneries. Northwest Power and Conservation Council. www.nwcouncil.org/reports/columbia-river-history/canneries. Accessed 14 September 2022.

Hartse, Caroline M.
  2017 Yama and Beyond: Construction and Negotiation of Identity at a Late Nineteenth- to Early Twentieth-Century Japanese-American Community. *Archaeology in Washington* 17:16–29.

Hartse, Caroline, and Jean Hannah
  2021 Introduction of Lifecycle of Community Framework: Grappling with Multiple, Complex Datasets in Interpreting Yama/Nagaya, a Late Nineteenth- to Early Twentieth-Century Pacific Northwest Japanese Immigrant Village. *International Journal of Historical Archaeology* 25(3):663–685.

Haskin, Leslie L.
  1942 Three Early Oregon Potteries of Barnet Ramsay. *Oregon Historical Quarterly* 43(3):175–193.

Haught-Bielmann, Amanda
  2018 Home Swede Home: An Archaeological Analysis of Swedish Cultural Identity in Idaho. *Idaho Archaeologist* 41(1):7–19.

Hawker, Ronald William
  1987 *Monuments in the Nineteenth-Century Public Cemeteries of Victoria, British Columbia.* Material History Bulletin 26.
  1991 A Faith of Stone: Gravestones, Missionaries, and Culture Change and Continuity Among British Columbia's Tsimshian Indians. *Journal of Canadian Studies* 26(3):80–100.

Heffner, Sarah Christine
  2015 Exploring Health-Care Practices of Chinese Railroad Workers in North America. *Historical Archaeology* 49(1):134–147.

Heitzmann, Roderick J.
  2004 Ground Probing Radar Survey: Kootenae House National Historic Site of Canada, Near Invermere, B.C. Calgary, Alberta, Canada. Report to Lake Louise,

Yoho and Kootenay National Parks Field Unit, Radium Hot Springs, B.C., from Western Canada Service Centre, Parks Canada.

2006   Kootenae House National Historic Site of Canada Archaeological Inventory. Calgary, Alberta, Canada. Report to Lake Louise, Yoho and Kootenay National Parks Field Unit, Parks Canada from Western and Northern Service Centre, Parks Canada

Henning, G. R., and Mary Henning

1990   Technological Change from Sail to Steam: Export Lumber Shipments from the Pacific Northwest, 1898–1913. *International Journal of Maritime History* II(2):133–145.

Hill, Cayla L.

2014   The Expansion of Catholicism: An Exploration of St. Joseph's College, the First Catholic Boarding School for Boys within the Oregon Territory. Master's thesis, Oregon State University, Corvallis.

2019   Caution! High Water: A Historical Archaeological Investigation of the Champoeg Townsite (ORMA26) after the 1861 Flood. Doctoral dissertation, Oregon State University, Corvallis.

Hills, Timothy J., Judith S. Chapman, and Douglas C. Wilson

1996   Weyerhaeuser Camp 2 (OR-KL-46): The Archaeology and Socioeconomic History of a Depression-Era Railroad Logging Camp in Southern Oregon. Report to Pacific Gas Transmission Co., Archaeological Investigations Northwest, Inc. Report No. 114. PGT Project Report No. 19. Portland, OR.

Hobler, Philip M.

2000   Old Bella Bella, Genesis and Exodus. *Urban History Review* 28(2):6–18.

Holschuh, Dana Lynn

2013   An Archaeology of Capitalism: Exploring Ideology through Ceramics from Fort Vancouver and Village Sites. Master's thesis, Portland State University, Portland, OR.

Holstine, Craig

2011   Waiting for the End of the World: A Prototype Fallout Shelter under Interstate 5 in North Seattle. *Journal of Northwest Anthropology* 45(2):209–220.

Horrocks, Brenda M

2019   More Than Hatchetmen: Chinese Exclusion and Tong Wars in Portland, Oregon. Master's thesis, Utah State University, Logan.

Horton, Elizabeth A.

2010   Results of Archaeological Testing of Officers' Quarters (HH-10), American Camp, San Juan Island National Historical Park, San Juan County, Washington. Northwest Cultural Resources Institute Report No. 9, Fort Vancouver National Historic Site, National Park Service, Vancouver, WA.

2011a   Results of Archaeological Investigations for Replacement of Visitor Dinghy Dock and Repair of Formal Garden Fence at English Camp, San Juan Island National Historical Park, San Juan County, Washington. Northwest Cultural Resources Institute Short Report No. 35, Fort Vancouver National Historic Site, National Park Service, Vancouver, WA.

2011b Results of Supplemental Archaeological Testing of An Officers' Quarters (HS-10) American Camp (45SJ300), San Juan Island National Historical Park, San Juan County, Washington. Northwest Cultural Resources Institute Short Report No. 52, Fort Vancouver National Historic Site, National Park Service, Vancouver, WA.

2014 Space, Status, and Interaction: Multiscalar Analyses of Officers, Soldiers, and Laundresses at Nineteenth Century Fort Vancouver, Washington. Doctoral dissertation, Washington State University, Pullman.

Horton, Elizabeth A., and Douglas C. Wilson
2015 Results of Archaeological Testing Conducted for Reconstruction of the U.S. Army Fort Vancouver Flagstaff on the Main Parade Ground, Fort Vancouver National Historic Reserve Historic District (DT191), Vancouver, Clark County, Washington. Northwest Cultural Resources Institute Short Report No. 85, Fort Vancouver National Historic Site, National Park Service, Vancouver, WA.

Hosken, Kaitlyn Nicole
2023 "Suited to the Wants of the Country": Historical Ceramics from the Fort Vancouver Sutler's Store, Vancouver, Washington. Master's thesis, Portland State University, Portland, OR.

Hosken, Kaitlyn, and Kristen Tiede
2018 "Caring for Their Prisoner Compatriots": Health and Dental Hygiene at the Kooskia Internment Camp. *Historical Archaeology* 52(3):585–599.

Houston, C. Stuart, Mary I. Houston, and John C. Jackson
1997 Pierre St. Germain: A Metis Hero of the First Franklin Expedition. *Manitoba History* 34:2–9.

Huntting, Marshall T.
1955 *Gold in Washington.* State of Washington Department of Conservation and Development, Division of Mines and Geology Bulletin No. 42, Olympia, WA.

Hussey, John A.
1957 *The History of Fort Vancouver and Its Physical Structure.* Abbott, Kerns, and Bell, Portland, OR.

1958 Suggested Historical Area Report Fort Clatsop Site, Oregon. National Park Service, Region Four, San Francisco, CA.

1976 Historic Structure Report, Historical Data, Volume II. Denver Service Center, Historic Preservation Team, National Park Service, Denver, CO.

Hussey, Larry
1975 Preliminary Report Excavations at Fort Walla Walla (45-WW-33), Walla Walla, Washington. Walla Walla Community College, Walla Walla, WA.

1984 *Fort Walla Walla Archaeological Council Bulletin* 1(1). Walla Walla, WA.

Hutchings, Richard M
2021 Whistlin' Dixie? Comments on the Association for Washington Archaeology's Statement on Racism, Anti-Racism, Diversity, and Inclusion. *Journal of Northwest Anthropology* 55(1):189–201.

Hutchings, Rich, and Marina La Salle
2014 Teaching Anti-Colonial Archaeology. *Archaeologies* 10(1):27–69.

224 · Works Cited

    2015   Archaeology as Disaster Capitalism. *International Journal of Historical Archaeology* 19(4):699–720.

Hutchinson, Ian, and Mark E. Hall
    2020   Chinook Salmon, Late Holocene Climate Change, and the Occupational History of Kettle Falls, a Columbia River Fishing Station. *Environmental Archaeology* 25(4):397–410.

Hutchison, Daniel J., and Larry R. Jones
    1993   *Emigrant Trails of Southern Idaho: Adventures in the Past.* Idaho Cultural Resource Series, Number 1. Bureau of Land Management and Idaho State Historical Society, Boise.

Innis, Harold A.
    1930   *The Fur Trade in Canada: An Introduction to Canadian Economic History.* Yale University Press, New Haven, CT.

Ivy, Don, and R. Scott Byram
    2002   *Changing Landscapes: Sustaining Traditions, Proceedings of the 5th and 6th Annual Coquille Cultural Preservation Conferences.* Coquille Indian Tribe, North Bend, OR.

Jackson, John C.
    1984   Red River Settlers vs. Puget Sound Agricultural Company, 1854–55. *Oregon Historical Quarterly* 85(3):278–289.

Jaehnig, Manfred E. W.
    1997   Evaluation of Archaeological Deposits at the Gimlet Placer Chinese Site, OR-BA-11, Baker County, Oregon. Report to Unity District, Wallowa-Whitman National Forest by Mount Emily Archaeological Services, Baker City, OR.

James, Ronald L.
    1995   *Ruins of a World: Chinese Gold Mining at the Mon-Tung Site in the Snake River Canyon.* Bureau of Land Management, Idaho Cultural Resource Series No. IV, Boise.

Jepsen, David J., and David J. Norberg
    2017   *Contested Boundaries: A New Pacific Northwest History.* John Wiley & Sons, Malden, MA.

Jetté, Melinda Marie
    2007   "Beaver Are Numerous, but the Natives . . . Will Not Hunt Them": Native-Fur Trader Relations in the Willamette Valley, 1812–1814. *The Pacific Northwest Quarterly* 98(1):3–17.

Johnson, Paula
    2017   Weedy Shrubs Shroud Stone: Uncovering the Role of Senryu Poetry and Immigration in Japanese Communities of Washington. *Archaeology in Washington* 17:90–101.

Jones, Terry L., Al W. Schwitalla, Marin A. Pilloud, John R. Johnson, Richard R. Paine, and Brian F. Codding
    2021   Historic and Bioarchaeological Evidence Supports Late Onset of Post-Columbian Epidemics in Native California. *Proceedings of the National Academy of Sciences* 118(28).

Jones, Timothy W.
- 1980   *Archaeological Test Excavations in the Boise Redevelopment Project Area, Boise, Idaho.* University of Idaho Anthropological Research Manuscript Series No. 59, Moscow.
- 1982   *Excavation of the Foote Site Dump (10-AA-96).* University of Idaho Anthropological Research Manuscript Series, No. 68, Laboratory of Idaho, University of Idaho, Moscow.
- 1983   San Juan Trade Market Participation. In *San Juan Archaeology, Volume II,* Roderick Sprague, editor, pp. 829–867. Laboratory of Anthropology, University of Idaho, Moscow.

Jones, Timothy W., Mary Anne Davis, and George Ling
- 1979   Idaho City: An Overview and Report on Excavation. University of Idaho Anthropological Research Manuscript Series No. 50, Moscow.

Jorgenson, Mica
- 2015   "Into That Country to Work": Aboriginal Economic Activities during Barkerville's Gold Rush. *BC Studies* 185:109–136.

Kaehler, Gretchen Anne
- 2017   Patterns in Glass: The Interpretation of European Glass Trade Beads from Two Protohistoric Sites in the Greater Lower Columbia Region. In *The Fur-Trade Archaeology of the Cathlapotle and Meier Sites, Lower Columbia River,* Kenneth M. Ames and Katie Henry, editors, pp. 45–170, U.S. Fish and Wildlife Service Region 1, Cultural Resource Series 18, Portland, OR.

Kardas, Susan
- 1971   "The People Bought This and the Clatsop Became Rich." A View of Nineteenth-Century Fur Trade Relationships on the Lower Columbia between Chinookan Speakers, Whites, and Kanakas. Doctoral dissertation, Bryn Mawr College, Bryn Mawr, PA. ProQuest Dissertations Publishing, Ann Arbor, MI.

Keddie, Grant
- 1990   The Question of Asiatic Objects on the North Pacific Coast of America: Historic or Prehistoric. *Contributions to Human History* 3:1–26. http://staff.royalbcmuseum.bc.ca/wp-content/uploads/2014/12/Asiatic-Objects.pdf
- 2004   Japanese Shipwrecks in British Columbia—Myths and Facts: The Question of Cultural Exchanges with the Northwest Coast of America. Victoria, BC. http://staff.royalbcmuseum.bc.ca/wp-content/uploads/2013/08/Japanese Shipwrecks-Grant-Keddie.pdf
- 2019   The Importation of Old Chinese Coins for the Playing of Fan Tan Gambling Games in British Columbia. *The Midden* 49(3):4–7.

Kenady, Stephen M.
- 1973   Environmental and Functional Change in Garrison Bay. In *Miscellaneous San Juan Island Reports 1970–1972,* pp. 40–83. University of Idaho Anthropological Manuscript Series No. 7, Moscow.

Kiers, Roger A.
- 1998   Searching for Chemical Traces of Lewis and Clark at Fort Clatsop National Memorial. Report to the National Park Service, from University of Washington, Department of Anthropology, Seattle.

Kirk, Ruth
1991   Fort Nisqually. *Columbia* 5(2):22–27.

Kirk, Ruth, and Richard D. Daugherty
2007   *Archaeology in Washington.* University of Washington Press, Seattle.

Klimko, Olga
2004   Fur Trade Archaeology in Western Canada: Who Is Digging up the Forts? In *The Archaeology of Contact in Settler Societies,* Tim Murray, editor, pp. 157–175. Cambridge University Press, Cambridge, UK.

Klippenstein, Frieda Esau
1992   The Role of the Carrier Indians in the Fur Trade at Fort St. James, 1806–1915. Microfiche Report Series, Canadian Heritage, Parks Canada.

Knudson, Ruthann, Timothy W. Jones, and Robert Lee Sappington
1982   *The Foote House (10-AA-96), an Historic Archaeological Complex in the Boise River Canyon, Idaho.* University of Idaho Anthropological Research Manuscript Series, No. 72, Laboratory of Anthropology, University of Idaho, Moscow.

Kopp, Peter A.
2011   "Hop Fever" in the Willamette Valley: The Local and Global Roots of a Regional Specialty Crop. *Oregon Historical Quarterly* 112(4):406–433.

2016   *Hoptopia: A World of Agriculture and Beer in Oregon's Willamette Valley.* California Studies in Food and Culture. University of California Press, Oakland.

Kopperl, Robert
2022   Response to Hutchings' "Whistlin' Dixie? Comments on the Association for Washington Archaeology's Statement on Racism, Anti-Racism, Diversity, and Inclusion" by Richard Hutchings. *Journal of Northwest Anthropology* 56(1):127–131.

Kretzler, Ian Edward
2019   An Archaeology of Survivance on the Grand Ronde Reservation: Telling Stories of Enduring Native Presence. Doctoral dissertation, University of Washington, Seattle.

Kretzler, Ian, and Sara L. Gonzalez
2021   Unsettling the Archaeology of Reservations: A View from Grand Ronde, Oregon. In *The Routledge Handbook of the Archaeology of Indigenous-Colonial Interaction in the Americas,* Lee M. Panich and Sara L. Gonzalez, editors, pp. 449–467. Routledge, London.

Kroeber, A.L.
1927   Disposal of the Dead. *American Anthropologist* 29(3):308–315.

Krotscheck, Ulrike, and Krista Aurora Sonenshine
2018   The Evergreen State College 2018 Archaeological Excavation at Bush Homestead, Tumwater, Washington. Report to the Department of Archaeology and Historic Preservation from The Evergreen State College Archaeology Lab, Olympia, WA.

Kuo, Susanna C., and Rick Minor
2016   The Oswego Furnace. *The Journal of the Society for Industrial Archeology* 42(1):37–54.

Kvamme, Kenneth L., and Matthew D. Reynolds
- 2003 Electrical Resistance Survey at the Fort Clatsop National Memorial, Oregon. Report to Fort Clatsop National Memorial, National Park Service, Astoria, Oregon, from Archeo-Imaging Lab, University of Arkansas, Fayetteville.

de Laguna, Frederica
- 1960 *The Story of a Tlingit Community: A Problem in the Relationship Between Archeological, Ethnological, and Historical Methods.* Smithsonian Institution Bureau of American Ethnology Bulletin No. 172.

Lai, David Chuen-Yan
- 1974 A Feng Shui Model as a Location Index. *Annals of the Association of American Geographers* 64(4):506–513.
- 1987 The Chinese Cemetery in Victoria. *BC Studies* 75:24–42.

LaLande, Jeffrey Max
- 1981 Sojourners in the Oregon Siskiyous: Adaptation and Acculturation of the Chinese Miners in the Applegate Valley, ca. 1855–1900. Master's thesis, Oregon State University, Corvallis.
- 1982 "Celestials" in the Oregon Siskiyous: Diet, Dress, and Drug Use of the Chinese Miners in Jackson County, ca. 1860–1900. *Northwest Anthropological Research Notes* 16(1):1–61.
- 1985 Sojourners in Search of Gold: Hydraulic Mining Techniques of the Chinese on the Oregon Frontier. *Journal of the Society for Industrial Archeology* 11(1):29–52.
- 2005 Report on an Archaeological Survey of the Wheeler Ridge 1942 Japanese Aerial-Bombing Site. Rogue River-Siskiyou National Forest, Medford, OR.
- 2017 "The State of Jefferson": A Disaffected Region's 160-Year Search for Identity. *Oregon Historical Quarterly* 118(1):14–41.

Lally, Jessica
- 2008 Analysis of Chinese Porcelain Associated with the Beeswax Wreck, Nehalem, Oregon. Master's thesis, Central Washington University, Ellensburg.
- 2016 Analysis of the Beeswax Shipwreck Porcelain Collection, Oregon, USA. In *Early Navigation in the Asia-Pacific Region,* Chunming Wu, editor, pp. 169–194. Springer Singapore.

Lange, Erwin F.
- 1937 The Oregon City Public School. *Oregon Historical Quarterly* 38(1):92–108.

Langford, Theresa, and Douglas C. Wilson
- 2002 Archaeology of the U.S. Parade Ground: Fort Vancouver National Historic Site. Manuscript, Fort Vancouver National Historic Site, National Park Service, Vancouver, WA.

Larson, Lynn L., and Guy F. Moura
- 1984 *An Archaeological Investigation of Western State Hospital and the Fort Steilacoom Historic District (45PI105H).* Report to the Department of Social and Health Services. Office of Public Archaeology, from the Institute for Environmental Studies, University of Washington Reconnaissance Reports No. 44, Seattle.

Losey, R. J. (editor)
    2000   *Changing landscapes: Proceedings of the 3rd Annual Coquille Cultural Preservation Conference, 1999.* Coquille Indian Tribe, North Bend, Oregon.

Laughlin, William S
    1941   Excavations in the Calapuya Mounds of the Willamette Valley; Oregon. *American Antiquity* 7(2):147–155.

Lee, Jocelyn
    2020   Small Towns and Mining Camps: An Analysis of Chinese Diasporic Communities in 19th-Century Oregon. Master's thesis, University of Massachusetts, Boston.

Leonard, Frank
    2016   "Eighth Wonder of the World:" The Cariboo Wagon Road as British Columbia's First Megaproject. *Journal of the Canadian Historical Association* 27(1):169–200.

Lewis, David G.
    2014   Four Deaths. *Oregon Historical Quarterly* 115(3):424–447.
    2017   Mounds of the Tualatin-Yamhill Kalapuyan Area. Quartux: *Journal of Indigenous Anthropology.* https://ndnhistoryresearch.com/2017/08/01/mounds-of-the-tualatin-yamhill-kalapuyan-area/

Lightfoot, Kent G.
    1995   Culture Contact Studies: Redefining the Relationship between Prehistoric and Historical Archaeology. *American Antiquity* 60(2):199–217.
    2005   *Indians, Missionaries, and Merchants: The Legacy of Colonial Encounters on the California Frontiers.* University of California Press, Berkeley.

Lightfoot, Kent G., and Sara L. Gonzalez
    2018   The Study of Sustained Colonialism: An Example from the Kashaya Pomo Homeland in Northern California. *American Antiquity* 83(3):427–443.

Lightfoot, Kent G., Antoinette Martinez, and Ann M. Schiff
    1998   Daily Practice and Material Culture in Pluralistic Social Settings: An archaeological Study of Culture Change and Persistence from Fort Ross, California. *American Antiquity* 63(2):199–222.

Lightfoot, Kent G., Lee M. Panich, Tsim D. Schneider, Sara L. Gonzalez, Matthew A. Russell, Darren Modzelewski, Theresa Molino, and Elliot H. Blair
    2013   The Study of Indigenous Political Economies and Colonialism in Native California: Implications for Contemporary Tribal Groups and Federal Recognition. *American Antiquity* 78(1):89–103.

Lim, Imogene L.
    2002   Pacific Entry, Pacific Century: Chinatowns and Chinese Canadian History. In *Re/Collecting Early Asian America: Essays in Cultural History,* Josephine Lee, Imogene L. Lim, and Yuko Matsukawa, editors, pp. 15–29. Temple University Press, Philadelphia, PA.

Lindgren, Waldemar
    1901   The Gold Belt of the Blue Mountains of Oregon. US Geological Survey Annual Reports, No. 22:561–776. Washington, DC.

Ling, George
- 1982 The Oriental Ceramics. In *Kanaka Village/Vancouver Barracks 1975*, David Chance, editor, pp. 250–257. Office of Public Archaeology, Institute for Environmental Studies Reports in Highway Archaeology No. 7, University of Washington, Seattle.
- 1983 English Camp Chinese Ceramic Analysis. In *San Juan Archaeology Volume I*, Roderick Sprague, editor, pp. 187–188. Laboratory of Anthropology, University of Idaho, Moscow.

Little, Barbara J.
- 1992 *Text-Aided Archaeology*. CRC Press, Boca Raton, FL.
- 1994 People with History: An Update on Historical Archaeology in the United States. *Journal of Archaeological Method and Theory* 1(1):5–40.
- 2012 Public Benefits of Public Archaeology. In *Oxford Handbook of Public Archaeology*, R. Skeates, C. McDavid, and J. Carman, editors, pp. 395–413. Oxford University Press, Oxford, UK.

Litzenberg, Vanessa Renee
- 2022 Stoneware and Earthenware from the Beeswax Wreck: Classification of the Dubé Collection and Discussion of the Interpretation of the Materials in Protohistoric Sites. Master's thesis, Portland State University, Portland, OR.

Litzkow, Jamie M.
- 2018 Early Gold Discoveries in Washington Territory (ca. 1853–ca. 1868). Poster Presented at the 71st Annual Northwest Anthropology Conference, Boise, ID.

Lynch, Michelle R.
- 2015 Heiltsuk Adoption of Euro-American Material Culture at Old Bella Bella, British Columbia, 1833–1899. Master's thesis, Simon Fraser University, Vancouver, BC.

Lomax, Alfred L.
- 1931 Oregon City Woolen Mill. *Oregon Historical Quarterly* 32(3):240–261.

Longenecker, Julia G.
- 1986 Mary Hallock Foote Stone House in the Canyon Archaeological Excavation. University of Idaho, Moscow.
- 1988 The Archaeological Investigation of a Victorian Gentlewoman in Idaho Territory: Project Director's Narrative Evaluation. Report to the Idaho Humanities Council, from the Alfred W. Bower Laboratory of Anthropology, University of Idaho, Moscow.
- 1992 Mary Hallock Foote: Stone House in the Canyon Archaeological Excavation. Letter report to the John Calhoun Smith Memorial Fund, from the Alfred W. Bower Laboratory of Anthropology, University of Idaho, Moscow.

Longenecker, Julia G., and Darby C. Stapp
- 1993 The Study of Faunal Remains from an Overseas Chinese Mining Camp in Northern Idaho. In *Hidden Heritage: Historical Archaeology of the Overseas Chinese*, Priscilla Wegars, editor, pp. 97–122. Baywood, Amityville, NY.

Loring, William Wing
- 1940 Report of Colonel Loring. In *The March of the Mounted Riflemen: First United States Military Expedition to Travel the Full Length of the Oregon Trail from Fort*

Leavenworth to Fort Vancouver, May to October, 1849, Raymond W. Settle, editor, pp. 329–344. The Arthur H. Clark Company, Glendale, CA.

Lowie, Robert H.
 1908 Catch-words for Mythological Motives. *The Journal of American Folklore* 21(80):24–27.

Lueger, Richard
 1981 Ceramics from Yuquot, British Columbia. In *Yuquot Project, Volume 3*, William J. Folan and John Dewhirst, editors, pp. 103–170. History and Archaeology Number 44, National Historic Parks and Sites Branch, Parks Canada, Environment Canada.

Mack, Cheryl A.
 1997 Washington Archaeological Site Inventory Form: Kalama't, Indian Race Track, 45SA291. United States Forest Service, Mt. Adams Ranger District, Gifford Pinchot National Forest, Trout Lake, WA.
 2005 Hook Tenders and Rigging Rustlers: Data Recovery Excavations at Camp 3, Trout Creek Archaeological Site (45SA222). Heritage Program, Gifford Pinchot National Forest, USDA Forest Service, Trout Lake, WA.

Mackie, Richard S.
 1997 *Trading Beyond the Mountains: The British Fur Trade on the Pacific, 1793–1843*. University of British Columbia Press, Vancouver.

Maddoux, Maryanne
 2015 A Game of Silent Irreverence: Passive Resistance in The Dalles, Oregon. Master's thesis, Oregon State University, Corvallis.
 2019 At River's Edge: An Examination of Overseas Chinese Settlements in Northern Oregon during the Exclusion Act Era. Doctoral dissertation, Oregon State University, Corvallis.

Manion, Mollie Jo
 2006 A Settlement Model at the Robert Newell Farmstead (35MA41), French Prairie, Oregon. Master's thesis, Oregon State University, Corvallis.
 2014 Where Have All the Women and Children Gone? An Examination of Domestic Life at the Newell Farmstead (35MA41) in the Early Oregon Country. Doctoral dissertation, Oregon State University, Corvallis.

Marks, Jeffrey
 2011 Defining a Unique Model of Public Engagement and Evaluating its Implementation at the 2011 NPS Fort Vancouver Public Archaeology Field School. Master's thesis, Institute of Archaeology, University College London, UK.

Marshall, Daniel Patrick
 2018 *Claiming the Land: British Columbia and the Making of a New El Dorado*. Ronsdale Press, Vancouver, BC.

Marshall, Yvonne, and Alexandra Maas
 1997 Dashing Dishes. *World Archaeology* 28(3):275–290.

Martindale, Andrew
 2006 Methodological Issues in the Use of Tsimshian Oral Traditions (Adawx) in Archaeology. *Canadian Journal of Archaeology* 30(2):158–192.

Martindale, Andrew, and Irena Jurakic
  2006   Identifying Expedient Glass Tools from a Post-Contact Tsimshian Village Using Low Power (10–100X) Magnification. *Journal of Archaeological Science* 33(3):414–427.
Martindale, Andrew, Natasha Lyons, George Nicholas, Bill Angelbeck, Sean P. Connaughton, Colin Grier, James Herbert, Mike Leon, Yvonne Marshall, Angela Piccini, David M. Schaepe, Kisha Supernant, and Gary Warrick
  2016   Archaeology as Partnerships in Practice: A Reply to La Salle and Hutchings. *Canadian Journal of Archaeology* 40(1):181–204.
Masich, Andrew E.
  1983a   American Camp Military Artifacts. In *San Juan Archaeology Volume II*, Roderick Sprague, editor, pp. 623–669. Laboratory of Anthropology, University of Idaho, Moscow.
  1983b   Military Life at American Camp, 1859–1874. In *San Juan Archaeology Volume II*, Roderick Sprague, editor, pp. 459–475. Laboratory of Anthropology, University of Idaho, Moscow.
Matsuda, Akira
  2016   A Consideration of Public Archaeology Theories. *Public Archaeology* 15(1):40–49. DOI: 10.1080/14655187.2016.1209377
Matthews, Christopher N.
  2012   Gilded Ages and Gilded Archaeologies of American Exceptionalism. *International Journal of Historical Archaeology* 16(4):717–744.
Mawhirter, Matthew
  2013   The Civilian Conservation Corps Variation and Flexibility on the Columbia National Forest. Master's thesis, Washington State University, Pullman.
May, Bridget A.
  1991   Progressivism and the Colonial Revival. *Winterthur Portfolio* 26(2/3):107–122.
May, Nathan J.
  2018a   Companions of Our Exile: An Archaeology of Domestic Life on Fort Boise, Idaho. Master's thesis, University of Idaho, Moscow.
  2018b   Top Shot: Recreational and Military Firearms of Fort Boise, Idaho. *Idaho Archaeologist* 41(1):69–84.
  2020   Historical Archaeology of Fort Boise's Surgeon's Quarters Porch Evidences the Behavior of Children. *Journal of Northwest Anthropology* 54(2):240–263.
McAleer, Carolyn Patricia
  2003   Patterns from the Past: Exploring Gender and Ethnicity through Historical Archaeology among Fur Trade Families in the Willamette Valley of Oregon. Master's thesis, Oregon State University, Corvallis.
McDonald, Kendal Lyle
  2002   Archaeological Applications of Magnetometry and Ground Penetrating Radar on Flood Plains of the Pacific Northwest. Master's thesis, Portland State University, Portland, OR.
McIlrath, Laura
  2002   Bridal Veil Historical Archaeological Site Archaeological Survey and Testing 1999 and 2001. Report to the Trust for Public Lands from Archaeological Services of Clark County, Brush Prairie, WA.

McKithan, Cecil
- 1977   National Register of Historic Places Inventory Nomination Form: Jacksonville Historic District. Washington DC.

McManamon, Francis P.
- 2018   Fifty Years of the National Historic Preservation Act. *Annual Review of Anthropology* 47:553–574.

Mead, George R.
- 1996   Two Dragon Camp: A Chinese Settlement in the Camp Carson Mining Area, Union County, Oregon. Heritage Program, La Grande Ranger District, Wallowa-Whitman National Forest, Union County, OR.

Mead, George R., and Bruce Womack
- 1975   An 1880/1890 Northeast Oregon Homestead Site (35 UN 71) near Telocaset, Oregon: Historical Archaeology sans History. *Northwest Anthropological Research Notes* 9(1):139–147.

Merrell, Carolynne, and Robyn Johnson
- 2011   An Idaho Shield-Bearing Warrior Site with Great Plains Affiliation. *Idaho Archaeologist* 34(1):7–12.

Meyer, Richard E.
- 1990   Image and Identity in Oregon's Pioneer Cemeteries. In *Sense of Place: American Regional Cultures,* Barbara Allen and Thomas J. Schelereth, editors, Folklore 9, pp. 88–102. University Press of Kentucky, Lexington.
- 1992   Images of Logging on Contemporary Pacific Northwest Gravemarkers. In *Cemeteries and Gravemarkers: Voices of American Culture,* Richard E. Meyer, editor, pp. 61–85. University Press of Colorado, Utah State University Press, Logan.

Minor, Rick
- 2006   In the Shadow of Fort Vancouver: Historical Archaeology of Blocks 24 and 25, City of Vancouver, Clark County, Washington. Heritage Research Associates Report No. 229, Eugene, OR.

Minor, Rick, and Stephen Dow Beckham
- 1984   Archeological Testing at Fort Cascades and the Cascades Townsite (45SA9). Report to the Portland District, U.S. Army Corps of Engineers; Heritage Research Associates Report No. 28. Eugene, OR.
- 1988   Archaeological Testing at Fort Lugenbeel, Skamania County, Washington. Report to Portland District, U.S. Army Corps of Engineers, Heritage Research Associates Report No. 74, Eugene, OR.

Minor, Rick, Linda P. Hart, Kendra R. Carlisle, and Curt D. Peterson
- 2010   Interstate 5 Columbia River Crossing Section 106 Archaeology Technical Report: Appendix 1C Archaeological Discovery and Evaluation: WSDOT Parcels. Heritage Research Associates Report No. 345, Eugene, OR.

Minor, Rick, Linda K. Jacobs, and Theresa M. Tilton
- 1981   *The Stauffer-Will Farmstead: Historical Archaeology at an Aurora Colony Farm.* University of Oregon Anthropological Papers No. 24. Eugene.

Miss, Christian J., Lorelea Hudson, and Sharon A. Boswell
- 2000   Data Recovery Excavations and Documentation of Manley-Moore Lumber

Company Logging Sites, Pierce County, Washington. Report to U.S. Forest Service and Plum Creek Timber Company, L.P. from Northwest Archaeological Associates, Inc., Seattle, WA.

Mitchell, Donald H
1970   The Investigation of Fort Defiance: Verifications of the Site. *BC Studies* 4:3–20.

Mitchell, Donald H., and J. Robert Knox
1972   The Investigation of Fort Defiance: A Report on Preliminary Excavations. *BC Studies* 16:32–56.

Molander, Stephanie, and Jessica Lenihan
2007   Ways to Waste: The Garbology of Post-Consumer Refuse in the UBC Okanagan Cafeteria. Okanagan, BC. https://open.library.ubc.ca/handle/2429/22870/garbology

Montgomery, Lindsay M.
2022   The Archaeology of Settler Colonialism in North America. *Annual Review of Anthropology* 51:475–491.

Montgomery, Lindsay M., and Kisha Supernant
2022   Archaeology in 2021: Repatriation, Reclamation, and Reckoning with Historical Trauma. *American Anthropologist* 124(4):800–812.

Montón-Subías, Sandra, and Almudena Hernando
2018   Modern Colonialism, Eurocentrism and Historical Archaeology: Some Engendered Thoughts. *European Journal of Archaeology* 21(3):455–471.

Montón-Subías, Sandra, Natalia Moragas Segura, and James M. Bayman
2020   The First Missions in Oceania: Excavations at the Colonial Church and Cemetery of San Dionisio at Humåtak (Guam, Mariana Islands). *Journal of Pacific Archaeology* 11(2):62–73.

Moore, Kaitlyn Ann
2012   Negotiating the Middle Ground in a World-System: The Niitsitapi (Blackfoot) and Ktunaxa (Kootenai) in the Northern Rocky Mountain Fur Trade. Master's thesis, University of Arizona, Tucson.

Morris, Grace P.
1937   Development of Astoria, 1811–1850. *Oregon Historical Quarterly* 38(4): 413–424.

Moss, Madonna L., and George B. Wasson
2009   Intimate Relations with the Past: The Story of an Athapaskan Village on the Southern Coast of North America. *World Archaeology* 29(3):317–332.

Moura, Guy F.
1990a   A Testing and Evaluation of the 1833 Fort Nisqually, 45-PI-55 at Northwest Landing, Pierce County, Washington, Volume 1. Report to Weyerhaeuser Real Estate Company, from Western Heritage Inc., Olympia, WA.
1990b   Faunal Remains from 45-PI-55, 1833 Fort Nisqually. In Data Resulting from Analysis of Beads and Floral Remains from 45-PI-401, 45-PI-405, and 45-PI-55 Together with Analyses of Faunal Remains, Wood, Metal, Bricks, Ceramics, Clay Pipes, Vessel Glass, Flat Glass, Leather and Miscellaneous Items from 45-PI-55, Janet Creighton, editor. Report to Weyerhaeuser Real Estate Company from Western Heritage Inc., Olympia, WA.

1990c   Flat Glass from 45-PI-55, 1833 Fort Nisqually. In Data Resulting from Analyses of Beads and Floral Remains from 45-PI-401, 45-PI-405, and 45-PI-55 Together with Analyses of Faunal Remains, Wood, Metal, Bricks, Ceramics, Clay Pipes, Vessel Glass, Flat Glass, Leather and Miscellaneous Items from 45-PI-55, Volume II. Janet Creighton, editor, Western Heritage, Inc., Olympia, WA.

1991   Washington Glass Bead Chronology. *Archaeology in Washington* 3:17–25.

1992   Food, Folks and the Fur Trade: Journal Entries & Faunal Remains from Fort Nisqually. *Archaeology in Washington* 4:71–75.

Muckle, Robert

2001   The Seymour Valley Archaeology Project. *The Midden* 33(2):2–6.

2008   Capitano Archaeology in the Seymour Valley. *The Midden* 40(3):10.

2012   Reconstructing an Early 20th Century Japanese Camp in the Seymour Valley: The 2012 Capilano University Archaeology Field School. *The Midden* 44(3/4):9–11.

2017   Archaeology of an Early Twentieth-Century Nikkei Camp in the Seymour Valley: A Photo Essay. *BC Studies* 192:125–148.

2021   Archaeology of Early Twentieth-Century Japanese Canadian Logging Camps in British Columbia. *International Journal of Historical Archaeology* 25(3): 740–761.

Mullaley, Meredith J.

2011   Rebuilding the Architectural History of the Fort Vancouver Village. Master's thesis, Portland State University, Portland, OR.

Mullins, Paul R, and Robert Paynter

2000   Representing Colonizers: An Archaeology of Creolization, Ethnogenesis, and Indigenous Material Culture among the Haida. *Historical Archaeology* 34(3):73–84.

Myers, Danielle D.

1999   On Gold Mountain: Chinese Vernacular Architecture and Two Dragon Camp. *Archaeology in Washington* 7:71–80.

Nagaoka, Lisa (editor)

1990   Fort Simcoe Excavation Report. Report to Washington State Parks and Recreation Commission in 1977 from Thomas Lorenz, Robert Thomas, and Lynn Larson, Department of Anthropology, University of Washington. Seattle.

Nassaney, Michael S.

2015   *The Archaeology of the North American Fur Trade.* University Press of Florida, Gainesville.

National Park Service (NPS)

1981   *Oregon National Historic Trail Comprehensive Management and Use Plan.* National Park Service, Washington, DC.

2023   Transfer Print Ceramics at Fort Vancouver. www.nps.gov/articles/000/transferprintfova.htm. Accessed 10 October 2022.

Nelson, Herbert B.

1963   The Vanishing Hop-Driers of the Willamette Valley. *Oregon Historical Quarterly* 64(3):267–271.

Nelson, Peter
2007 Power and Place: The Dynamics of Non-Verbal Communication in the Interrelationship at Fort Vancouver. Undergraduate honors thesis, University of Washington, Seattle.

Nesbitt, Paul E.
1969 The Cofchin Ranch Site: A Preliminary Report on an Historic Indian Habitation Unit. *The Washington Archaeologist* 13(1):2–14.
1970 Further Data on the Cofchin Ranch Site. *The Washington Archaeologist* 14(2):12–14.
1972 Champoeg State Park Archaeological Project: Preliminary Investigations 1972. Manuscript, Oregon State Parks, State Historic Preservation Office, Report No. 1296, Salem.

New, Alexander J. S.
2013 Cooperation in the Wilds of the Idaho Territory: Interaction between the Jesuits and Coeur d'Alene Indians at the Cataldo Mission, 1848–1878. Master's thesis, University of Idaho, Moscow.

Newell, Dianne
1987 Surveying Historic Industrial Tidewater Sites: The Case of the B.C. Salmon Canning Industry. *Journal of the Society for Industrial Archeology* 13(1):1–16.
1991 The Industrial Archaeology of the Organization of Work: A Half Century of Women and Racial Minorities in British Columbia Fish Plants. *Material History Review* 33(1):25–36.

Newman, Thomas M.
1959 Tillamook Prehistory and Its Relation to the Northwest Coast Culture Area. Master's thesis, University of Oregon, Eugene.

Nicandri, David L.
2010 *River of Promise: Lewis and Clark on the Columbia*. University of Oklahoma Press, Norman.

Ng, Laura, and Stacey Lynn Camp
2015 Consumption in World War II Japanese American Incarceration Camps. In *Historical Archaeologies of Capitalism*, M.P. Leone and J.E. Knauf, editors, pp. 149–180. Contributions to Global Historical Archaeology, Springer International Publishing, Switzerland.

Nicholas, George P.
2006 Decolonizing the Archaeological Landscape: The Practice and Politics of Archaeology in British Columbia. *American Indian Quarterly* 30(3/4):350–380.

Nicholas, George P., John R. Welch, and Eldon C. Yellowhorn
2008 Collaborative Encounters. In *Collaboration in Archaeological Practice: Engaging Descendant Communities*, Chip Colwell-Chanthaphonh and T.J. Ferguson, editors, pp. 273–298. Altamira Press, Danville, CA.

Nicholls, Lou Ann Speulda
1986 Champoeg: A Perspective of a Frontier Community in Oregon, 1830–1861. Master's thesis, Oregon State University, Corvallis.

Noël-Hume, I.
1969 *A Guide to Artifacts of Colonial America*. University of Pennsylvania Press: Philadelphia.

Nokes, R. Gregory
2006 "A Most Daring Outrage": Murders at Chinese Massacre Cove, 1887. *Oregon Historical Quarterly* 107(3):326–353.
2022 Chinese Massacre at Deep Creek. *The Oregon Encyclopedia.* www.oregonencyclopedia.org/articles/chinese_massacre_at_deep_creek. Accessed 11 March 2023.

O'Bannon, Patrick William
1983 Technological Change in the Pacific Coast Canned Salmon Industry: 1864–1924. Doctoral dissertation, University of California, San Diego, San Diego.

O'Gorman, J. Tim
1983 The History of the Pig War. In *San Juan Archaeology Volume I,* Roderick Sprague, editor, pp. 33–62. Laboratory of Anthropology, University of Idaho, Moscow.

Oland, Maxine, Siobhan M. Hart, and Liam Frink (editors)
2012 *Decolonizing Indigenous Histories: Exploring Prehistoric/Colonial Transitions in Archaeology.* The University of Arizona Press, Tucson.

Oliver, Jeff
2013 Reflections on Resistance: Agency, Identity and Being Indigenous in Colonial British Columbia. In *Historical Archaeologies of Cognition: Exploration of Faith, Hope, and Charity,* J. Symonds, A. Badcock, and J. Oliver, editors, pp. 98–114. Equinox Publishing., Sheffield, UK.

Oliver, Kali Dene-Varen
2014 Adopting an Orphaned Archaeological Collection: Walla Walla, Washington's Hussey Collection. Master's thesis, University of Idaho, Moscow.

O'Brien, Melanie
2015 Notice of Intent to Repatriate Cultural Items: Washington State Parks and Recreation Commission, Olympia, WA. *Federal Register* 80(150):46598–46599.

O'Grady, Patrick, David L. Minick, and Daniel O. Steuber
2022 Making Up for the Past: How the Oregon Archaeological Society Addresses Its "Collector" Origins. *Advances in Archaeological Practice* 10(1):101–113.

O'Neill, Brian L., and Mark A. Tveskov
2008 *A Contact Period Fishing Camp on the Rogue River, Southwest Oregon.* University of Oregon Anthropological Papers 67, The Museum of Natural and Cultural History and the Department of Anthropology, University of Oregon, Eugene.

O'Rourke, Leslie M.
2009 Archaeological Survey at The Site of The Rosler Homestead, American Camp, San Juan Island National Historical Park, San Juan County, Washington. Northwest Cultural Resources Institute Short Report Number 17. Fort Vancouver National Historic Site, National Park Service, Vancouver, WA.

O'Rourke, Leslie M., Todd A. Miles, and Douglas C. Wilson
2010 Results of National Park Service Archaeological Evaluation and Testing on the Vancouver National Historic Reserve for the Columbia River Crossing Project. Northwest Cultural Resources Institute Report No. 8, Fort Vancouver National Historic Site, National Park Service. Vancouver, WA.

Orser, Charles E.
- 2001 The Anthropology in American Historical Archaeology. *American Anthropologist* 103(3):621–632.
- 2010 Twenty-First-Century Historical Archaeology. *Journal of Archaeological Research* 18(2):111–150.

Osborn, Jill
- 2023 PIT's History. Passport in Time. www.passportintime.com/pit-s-history.html. Accessed 2 March 2023.

Ostrogorsky, Michael
- 1977 Fort Boise Test Excavation Military Dump (10 AA 112) Preliminary Report. *Idaho Archaeologist* 1(3):3–8.
- 1982 An Idaho Model of Frontier Settlement. *North American Archaeologist* 3(1):79–83.

Palmié, Stephan
- 2006 Creolization and its Discontents. *Annual Review of Anthropology* 35:433–456.

Panich, Lee M.
- 2013 Archaeologies of Persistence: Reconsidering the Legacies of Colonialism in Native North America. *American Antiquity* 78(1):105–122.

Parks Canada
- 2005 *Parks Canada Archaeological Recording Manual: Excavations and Surveys*. Parks Canada.

Parks, Virginia, and Lyssia Merrifield
- 2021 An Idea That Took Root: Archaeology Roadshow in Oregon. *Journal of Northwest Anthropology* 55(2):46–53.

Parsley, Colleen
- 2011 Preliminary Findings of the 2011 Archaeological Investigation of Nanaimo's Third Chinatown: Phase I. *The Midden* 43(4):15–19.

Pasacreta, Laura J
- 2005 White Tigers and Azure Dragons: Overseas Burial Practices in the Canadian and American West (1850s to 1910s). Master's thesis, Simon Fraser University, Vancouver, BC.

Paullin, Pamela K.
- 2007 Boring to the Core: The Archaeology, History, and Dendrochronology of a Railroad Logging Camp, Ladee Flat, Clackamas County, Oregon. Master's thesis, Oregon State University, Corvallis.

Paynter, Robert
- 2000a Historical and Anthropological Archaeology: Forging Alliances. *Journal of Archaeological Research* 8(1):1–37.
- 2000b Historical Archaeology and the Post-Columbian World of North America. *Journal of Archaeological Research* 8(3):169–216.

Peeps, J. Calder
- 1958 Fort Langley in Re-Creation. *The Beaver* 289:30–39.

Pegg, Brian
- 2018 The Archaeology of 1858 in the Fraser Canyon. *BC Studies* 196:67–87.

Pegg, Brian, Amy Besla, Grant Coffey, Andie Froese, and Andrew Haugo
   2011   When the World Washed Away: Colonial History in the Fraser Canyon. *The Midden* 43(4):10–14.

Pegg, Brian, Colin Cromarty, Jillian Elcock, and Nadine Martin
   2013   Just over the Mountain: The Archaeology of Gold Rush History in the Fraser Canyon. *The Midden* 45(3):1–10.

Penner, Liisa
   1993   Cemeteries and Gravesites in Astoria. *Cumtux* 13(3):38–43.

Petersen, Fred W.
   2000   Anglo-American Wooden Frame Farmhouses in the Midwest, 1830–1900: Origins of Balloon Frame Construction. *Perspectives in Vernacular Architecture* 8:3–16.

Peterson, Curt D., Scott S. Williams, Kenneth M. Cruikshank, and John R. Dubè
   2011   Geoarchaeology of the Nehalem Spit: Redistribution of Beeswax Galleon Wreck Debris by Cascadia Earthquake and Tsunami (~A.D. 1700), Oregon, USA. *Geoarchaeology* 26(2):219–244.

Peterson, Ella M.
   2008   Recognizing Individual Potters in Historic Oregon Sites: A Visual and Chemical Analysis of Early Oregon Redware. Master's thesis, Oregon State University, Corvallis.

Peterson, Joan Teresa
   1989   Brickmaking on Southeastern Vancouver Island: An Historical Archaeological Investigation. Master's thesis, University of Victoria, Victoria, BC.

Petrich-Guy, Mary C.
   2016   Assessment and Participant Feedback of Sandpoint Archaeology Project Teaching Kits in Idaho Elementary Classrooms. Master's thesis, University of Idaho, Moscow.

Pfeiffer, Michael A.
   1981   Clay Tobacco Pipes from Spokane House and Fort Colvile. *Northwest Anthropological Research Notes* 15(2):221–235.
   1982   The Clay Pipes. In *Kanaka Village/Vancouver Barracks 1975,* David Chance, editor, pp. 113–127. Office of Public Archaeology, Institute for Environmental Studies Reports in Highway Archaeology No. 7, University of Washington, Seattle.
   1983   Clay Tobacco Pipes from Bellevue Farm. In *San Juan Archaeology Volume I,* Roderick Sprague, editor, pp. 417–436. Laboratory of Anthropology, University of Idaho, Moscow.

Philpot, Mary
   1976   *In This Neglected Spot: The Rural Cemetery Landscape in Southern British Columbia.* Thesis, University of British Columbia, Vancouver.

Poet, Rebecca McClelland
   1996   Women of Valor: The Sisters of Notre Dame de Namur, St. Paul, Oregon 1844–1852. Master's thesis, Oregon State University, Corvallis.

Popper, Virginia S.
   2020   Flexible Plant Food Practices among the Nineteenth-Century Chinese Mi-

grants to Western North America. In *Chinese Diaspora Archaeology in North America,* Chelsea Rose and J. Ryan Kennedy, editors, pp. 306–333. University Press of Florida, Gainesville.

Porter, John, and Don Steer
   1987   Archaeological Investigations at Fort Langley National Historic Park. *The Midden* 19(2):3–4.

Porter, John E. P., Malcolm James, Karlis Karklins, Charles Bradley, Lynne Sussman, Stephen Davis, and Alison Landals
   1995   Archaeological Investigations at Fort Langley National Historic Site, British Columbia 1986–1989. Microfiche Report Series No. 532, Parks Canada.

Praetzellis, Adrian, and Mary Praetzellis
   1992   Faces and Facades: Victorian Ideology in Early Sacramento. In *The Art and Mystery of Historical Archaeology: Essays in Honor of James Deetz,* Anne Elizabeth Yentsch and Mary C. Beaudry, editors, pp. 75–99. CRC Press, Boca Raton, LA.
   2001   Mangling Symbols of Gentility in the Wild West: Case Studies in Interpretive Archaeology. *American Anthropologist* 103(3):645–654.

Praetzellis, Mary, Adrian Praetzellis, and Marley R. Brown, III
   1988   What Happened to the Silent Majority? Research Strategies for Studying Dominant Group Material Culture in Late Nineteenth Century California. In *Documentary Archaeology in the New World,* Mary Beaudry, editor, pp. 192–202. Cambridge University Press, Cambridge, England.

Prentiss, Anna Marie (editor)
   2017   *The Last House at Bridge River: The Archaeology of an Aboriginal Household in British Columbia During the Fur Trade Period.* University of Utah Press, Salt Lake City.

Prince, Paul
   2002a   Culture Contact at Kimsquit in Long-term Regional Context. In *Archaeology of Coastal British Columbia: Essays in Honour of Professor Philip M. Hobler,* Roy L. Carlson, editor, pp. 217–232. Archaeology Press, Simon Fraser University, Burnaby, BC.
   2002b   Cultural Coherency and Resistance in Historic-Period Northwest-Coast Mortuary Practices at Kimsquit. *Historical Archaeology* 36(4):50–65.
   2016   Colonial Housing Reform and Transitions in Architecture in the Bella Coola Area of British Columbia. *Historical Archaeology* 50(2):47–68.

Purser, Margaret
   1992   Oral History and Historical Archaeology. In *Text-Aided Archaeology,* Barbara Little, editor, pp. 25–35. CRC Press, Boca Raton, FL.

Quackenbush, William George
   1990   Tastes of Canadians and Dogs: The History and Archaeology of McLeods Lake Post, British Columbia, GfRs-2. Master's thesis, Simon Fraser University, Vancouver, BC.

Quimby, George I.
   1948   Culture Contact on the Northwest Coast, 1785–1795. *American Anthropologist* 50(2):247–255.

1978 Trade Beads and Sunken Ships. In *Archaeological Essays in Honor of Irving B. Rouse,* Robert C. Dunnell and Edwin S., Jr. Hall, editors, pp. 231–246. Mouton, New York.

1985 Japanese Wrecks, Iron Tools, and Prehistoric Indians of the Northwest Coast. *Arctic Anthropology* 22(2):7–15.

Quimby, George I., and Alexander Spoehr
1951 Acculturation and Material Culture–I. *Fieldiana Anthropology* 36(6):107–147.

Rahemtulla, Farid
2020 Unsettling the Archaeology Field School: Development of a Community Engaged Model at the University of Northern British Columbia. *Canadian Journal of Archaeology* 44(1):105–132.

Rajala, Richard A.
1989 Bill and the Boss: Labor Protest, Technological Change, and the Transformation of the West Coast Logging Camp, 1890–1930. *Journal of Forest History* 33(4):168–179.

1996 A Dandy Bunch of Wobblies: Pacific Northwest Loggers and the Industrial Workers of the World, 1900–1930. *Labor History* 37(2):205–234.

Rathje, William L.
1979 Modern Material Culture Studies. *Advances in Archaeological Method and Theory* 2:1–37.

Rathje, W. L., W. W. Hughes, D. C. Wilson, M. K. Tani, G. H. Archer, R. G. Hunt, and T. W. Jones
1992 The Archaeology of Contemporary Landfills. *American Antiquity* 57(3):437–447.

Rathje, William L., and Cullen Murphy
1992 *Rubbish!: The Archaeology of Garbage.* HarperCollins, New York.

Ray, Verne F.
1936 Native Villages and Groupings of the Columbia Basin. *The Pacific Northwest Quarterly* 27(2):99–152.

Reese, Jo
1989 Microarchaeological Analysis of the Chinese Workers' Area at the Warrendale Cannery Site, Oregon. In *Contributions to the Archaeology of Oregon 1987–1988,* Rick Minor, editor, pp. 197–221. Association of Oregon Archaeologists Occasional Paper No. 4, Eugene.

Rhoads, William B.
1976 The Colonial Revival and American Nationalism. *Journal of the Society of Architectural Historians* 35(4):239–254.

Richardson, Lorna-Jane, and Jaime Almansa-Sánchez
2015 Do you even know what public archaeology is? Trends, theory, practice, ethics. *World Archaeology* 47(2):194–211.

Rickey, Don, Jr.
1963 *Forty Miles a Day on Beans and Hay: The Enlisted Soldier Fighting the Indian Wars.* University of Oklahoma Press, Norman.

Riordan, Timothy Benedict, III
  1977   Silcott Harvest 1931: A Study of the Individual Through Archaeology. *Northwest Anthropological Research Notes* 11(2):232–239.
  1985   The Relative Economic Status of Black and White Regiments in the Pre-World War I Army: An Example from Fort Walla Walla, Washington. Doctoral dissertation, Washington State University, Pullman.

Riordan, Timothy B., and William Hampton Adams
  1985   Commodity Flows and National Market Access. *Historical Archaeology* 19(2):5–18.

Rippee, Kassandra, and Stacy Scott
  2023   Changing Tides: Tribal Engagement in Oregon's Coastal Archaeology. *Archaeological Papers of the American Anthropological Association* 34:145–154.

Robbins, William G.
  2022   Oregon Donation Land Law. The Oregon Encyclopedia. Oregon Historical Society, Portland, OR. www.oregonencyclopedia.org/articles/oregon_donation_land_act. Accessed 26 September 2022.

Rock, James T.
  1984   Cans in the Countryside. *Historical Archaeology* 18(2):97–111.
  1989   Tin Canisters: Their Identification. Yreka, CA. https://cdm16085.contentdm.oclc.org/digital/collection/p16085coll5/id/2210/rec/5. Accessed 13 February 2023.

Roddy, Charles A.
  1983   Buttons Excavated on San Juan Island. In *San Juan Archaeology Volume II*, Roderick Sprague, editor, pp. 785–794. Laboratory of Anthropology, University of Idaho, Moscow.

Roenke, Karl G.
  1978   Flat Glass: Its Use as a Dating Tool for Nineteenth Century Archaeological Sites in the Pacific Northwest and Elsewhere. *Northwest Anthropological Research Notes*, Memoir Number 4, Moscow, ID.
  1982   Window Glass Thickness at Vancouver. In *Kanaka Village/Vancouver Barracks 1975*, David Chance, editor, pp. 128–140. Office of Public Archaeology, Institute for Environmental Studies Reports in Highway Archaeology No. 7, University of Washington, Seattle.
  1983   Flat Glass from San Juan Sites. In *San Juan Archaeology Volume II*, Roderick Sprague, editor, pp. 795–812. Laboratory of Anthropology, University of Idaho, Moscow.

Rogers, Michael
  2001   Detection of Burials at the Confederated Tribes of Siletz Indians Historic Period Cemetery, Oregon: A Comparison of Ground-Based Remote Sensing Methods. Anthropology, Anthropology, and Physics. Master's thesis, Oregon State University, Corvallis.

Ronda, James P.
  1984   *Lewis and Clark among the Indians*. University of Nebraska Press, Lincoln.

Rose, Chelsea
  2009   "A Sound of Revelry By Night:" Archaeology, History, and the Myth of The

Mining Camp Kanaka Flat, Oregon. Master's thesis, Sonoma State University, Rohnert Park, CA.

2013   Lonely Men, Loose Women: Rethinking the Demographics of a Multiethnic Mining Camp, Kanaka Flat, Oregon. *Historical Archaeology* 47(3):23–35.

2020   Burned: The Archaeology of House and Home in Jacksonville, Oregon's, Chinese Quarter. In *Chinese Diaspora Archaeology in North America*, Chelsea Rose and J. Ryan Kennedy, editors, pp. 163–187. University Press of Florida, Gainesville.

Rose, Chelsea, Andrew Bastier, and Katie Johnson

2014   Results of Archaeological Testing and Monitoring for the Britt Festival Renovations in the Britt Gardens Site, 35JA789, Jacksonville, Oregon. Southern Oregon University Laboratory of Anthropology Report No. 2013.16, Ashland.

Rose, Chelsea, Jacqueline Y. Cheung, and Eric Gleason

2021   "Bona Fide" Merchants: Negotiating Life, Labor, and Transnational Mobility in the Time of Chinese Exclusion. *Oregon Historical Quarterly* 122(4):412–441.

Rose, Chelsea, and Katie Johnson

2015   59 Bottles of Booze in the Road: First and Main Streets Sidewalk Project Monitoring and Inadvertent Discoveries, Jacksonville, Jackson County, Oregon. Southern Oregon University Laboratory of Anthropology Report No. 2014.05, Ashland.

2016   Rising from the Ashes: Jacksonville Chinese Quarter Site (35JA737) Data Recovery Excavations. Report to Oregon Department of Transportation from Southern Oregon University, Laboratory of Anthropology, Southern Oregon University Laboratory of Anthropology Research Report 2013.09, Ashland.

2018   Champoeg Archaeological Investigations. Report to Oregon Parks and Recreation Department from Southern Oregon University Laboratory of Anthropology Ashland.

2020   Results of Archaeological Testing at the Kam Wah Chung State Heritage Site, John Day Chinatown Site 35GR2086. Southern Oregon University Laboratory of Anthropology Report 2019.08, Ashland.

2022   "Ein Pheif Und Ein Lager Beer!": Archaeological Investigations at the Eagle Brewery and Saloon, Jacksonville, Oregon. Southern Oregon University Laboratory of Anthropology Report No. 2021.10, Ashland.

Rose, Chelsea, and Chris Ruiz

2014   Strangers in a Strange Land: Nation Building, Ethnicity, and Identity in the Oregon Territory. In *Alis Volat Propriis: Tales from the Oregon Territory, 1848–1859*, Chelsea Rose and Mark Tveskov, editors, pp. 181–208. Association of Oregon Archaeologists Occasional Papers 9, Eugene.

Ross, R. E., and T. C. Hogg

1976   Stones in the Pit: Scientific Archaeology in Elementary Schools. *Northwest Anthropological Research Notes* 10(2):227–233.

Ross, Alexander

1849   *Adventures of the First Settlers on the Oregon or Columbia River.* Smith, Elder and Co., London, UK.

Ross, Douglas Edward
 2009 Material Life and Socio-Cultural Transformation Among Asian Transmigrants at a Fraser River Salmon Cannery. Doctoral dissertation, Simon Fraser University, Vancouver, BC.
 2010 Comparing the Material Lives of Asian Transmigrants through the Lens of Alcohol Consumption. *Journal of Social Archaeology* 10(2):230–254.
 2011 Factors Influencing the Dining Habits of Japanese and Chinese Migrants at a British Columbia Salmon Cannery. *Historical Archaeology* 45(2):68–96.
 2012 Artifacts: Grappling with Fluid Material Origins and Identities in Archaeological Interpretations of Culture Change. *Journal of Anthropological Archaeology* 31(1):38–48.
 2013 *An Archaeology of Asian Transnationalism.* University Press of Florida, Gainesville.
 2015 Barkerville in Context: Archaeology of the Chinese in British Columbia. *BC Studies* 185:161–192.
 2017a Archaeology of Asian Labour Migration at a Fraser River Salmon Cannery. In *Archaeology of the Lower Fraser River Region,* Mike K. Rousseau, editor, pp. 201–208. Archaeology Press, Simon Fraser University, Vancouver, BC.
 2017b Archaeology of the Chinese and Japanese Diasporas in North America and a Framework for Comparing the Material Lives of Transnational Migrant Communities. In *Historical Archaeology Through a Western Lens,* Mark Warner and Margaret Purser, editors, pp. 174–209. University of Nebraska Press, Lincoln.
 2021 A History of Japanese Diaspora Archaeology. *International Journal of Historical Archaeology* 25(3):592–624.
Ross, Lester A.
 1975a Early Nineteenth Century EuroAmerican Technology within the Columbia River Drainage System. *Northwest Anthropological Research Notes* 9(1):32–50.
 1975b Luxury in the Wilderness. *Clark County History* 16:39–47.
 1976 Fort Vancouver, 1829–1860, A Historical Archeological Investigation of the Goods Imported and Manufactured by the Hudson's Bay Company. Manuscript, Fort Vancouver National Historic Site, Vancouver, WA.
 1977 Transfer Printed Spodeware Imported by the Hudson's Bay Company: Temporal Markers for the Northwestern United States, ca. 1836–1853. *Northwest Anthropological Research Notes* 11(2):192–217.
 1990 Trade Beads from Hudson's Bay Company Fort Vancouver (1829–1860), Vancouver, Washington. *Beads: Journal of the Society of Bead Researchers* 2:29–67.
Ross, Lester A., Gary C. Bowyer, and Lou Ann Speulda
 1995 Historical Demographic Patterns. In *Archaeological Investigations PGT-PG&E Pipeline Expansion Project, Idaho, Washington, Oregon, and California, Volume IV,* Randall F. Schalk, editor, pp. 11.1–11,108. Infotec Research, Inc. and Far Western Anthropological Research Group, Inc., Fresno, CA.
Ross, Marion D., and Christopher Owens
 1979 *Historic Area Study of Jacksonville: An Early Oregon Mining and Agricultural Settlement.* Historic American Buildings Survey, National Park Service, Washington DC.

Rossillon, Mary P.
    1983   Bellevue Farm Feature Descriptions, Artifact Analysis, and Possible Structure Functions. In *San Juan Archaeology Volume I*, Roderick Sprague, editor, pp. 315–355. Laboratory of Anthropology, University of Idaho, Moscow.

Roulette, Bill R., and Judy S. Chapman
    1996   Data Recovery for the William Earl Site, OR-LIN-14. Archaeological Investigations Northwest, Inc. Report No. 50, Portland, OR.

Roulette, Bill R., David V. Ellis, and Maureen Newman
    1994   Data Recovery at OR-MU-57, the U.S. Courthouse Site, Portland, Oregon. Report to CRSS Constructors, Inc. and the General Services Administration, Region 10 from Archaeological Investigations Northwest, Inc. AINW Report No. 42, Portland, OR.

Roulette, Bill R., Jessica A. Hale, and Melissa Lehman
    2010   Life in War Time: Archaeological Investigations at the Part of Site 45CL927 Located on the Iron Partners, LLC Property, Vancouver, Clark County, Washington. Report to Brady Environmental, Inc., Applied Archaeological Research, Inc., Report No. 906, Portland, OR.

Roulette, Bill R., Michelle R. Lynch, and Laura K. Sechrist
    2018   The Wrong Side of the Tracks: Results of Archaeological Investigations in the Vancouver Waterfront Development Area, Vancouver, Washington. Applied Archaeological Research, Inc., Report No. 1661, Portland, OR.

Roulette, Bill R., and William G. White
    2005   Results of Inventory Phase Archaeological Investigations on Historic Vancouver Blocks 61 and 65 at the Proposed Site of the Columbian Newspaper's Downtown Campus. Report to Douglas Ness and the Columbian Newspaper by Applied Archaeological Research, Applied Archaeological Research Report No. 474, Portland, OR.
    2011   Historical Archaeological Research on Block 55, Vancouver, WA. Report to the Vancouver Housing Authority, Applied Archaeological Research, Inc., Report No. 382, Portland, OR.

Ruiz, Christopher L.
    2010   The Archaeology of a 19th Century Post-Treaty Homestead on the Former Klamath Indian Reservation, Oregon. Master's thesis, University of Oregon, Eugene.

Ruiz, Christopher L., Marlene Jampolsky, and Jon C. Krier
    2021   Longevity: The Archaeology of a Chinese Gift Store and Restaurant in Eugene, Oregon's, Market District. *Oregon Historical Quarterly* 122(4):512–531.

Ruiz, Christopher, and Patrick O'Grady
    2008   Jacksonville Site A: Archaeological Test Excavations at the Main Street Warehouse and Chinese Quarter (35JA737). Report to City of Jacksonville from the Museum of Natural and Cultural History and State Museum of Anthropology, Museum Report 2008-052, University of Oregon, Eugene.

Saastamo, Susan Ann
    1971   The Application of a Functional Typology in the Analysis of Artifacts from the Excavation of Old Fort Colvile, 1970. Master's thesis, University of Idaho, Moscow.

La Salle, Marina, and Rich Hutchings
   2016   What Makes Us Squirm—A Critical Assessment of Community-Oriented Archaeology. *Canadian Journal of Archaeology* 40(1):164–180.

Sachs, Aaron
   2013   *Arcadian America: The Death and Life of an Environmental Tradition.* Yale University Press, New Haven, CT.

Sands, Hope, and Brian Buchanan
   2020   Exploring the Archaeological and Geographical Past of Fort Spokane: A Proposal. In EWU Digital Commons 2020 Symposium Papers, 2018. Eastern Washington University Digital Commons, Cheney. https://dc.ewu.edu/srcw_2020_posters/49.

Sauer, Sandra R.
   1995   The O'Keefe Ranch: An Archaeological Perspective. Master's thesis, Simon Fraser University, Vancouver, BC.

Schablitsky, Julie M.
   1996   Duty and Vice: The Daily Life of a Fort Hoskins Soldier. Master's thesis, Oregon State University, Corvallis.
   2007   A Redware Jar on Every Table: The Archaeology of the Simmons House and Boston Town, Thompson Mills State Heritage Site, Linn County, Oregon. University of Oregon Museum of Natural and Cultural History Report 2007–003, Eugene.

Schablitsky, Julie M., and Tom Connolly
   2005   Kam Wah Chung State Heritage Site, Archaeological Inventory, Preliminary Report. Museum of Natural and Cultural History, Museum Report 2005–248, The State Museum of Anthropology, University of Oregon, Eugene.

Schablitsky, Julie M., and Christopher Ruiz
   2009   Archaeological Monitoring and Investigations Along Oregon State Highway 238, Jacksonville, Oregon. Museum of Natural and Cultural History, Museum Report 2005–248, The State Museum of Anthropology, University of Oregon, Eugene.

Schablitsky, Julie, Tom Connolly, and Chris Ruiz
   2006   Exploratory Archaeological Study of the Kam Wah Chung State Heritage Site in the City of John Day, Grant County, Oregon. State Museum of Anthropology Museum Report 2006–31, University of Oregon Museum of Natural & Cultural History, Eugene.
   2007   Archaeological Testing (2006) at the Kam Wah Chung Site, Oregon. State Museum of Anthropology Museum Report 2007–047, University of Oregon Museum of Natural & Cultural History, Eugene.

Schaepe, David M., Bill Angelbeck, David Snook, and John R. Welch
   2017   Archaeology as Therapy: Connecting Belongings, Knowledge, Time, Place, and Well-Being. *Current Anthropology* 58(4):502–533.

Schaepe, David M, George Nicholas, and Kierstin Dolata
   2020   Recommendations for Decolonizing British Columbia's Heritage-Related Processes and Legislation. Report to the First Peoples' Heritage, Language and Culture Council, Brentwood Bay, BC.

Scheans, Daniel J.
 1984 Buena Vista Stonewares: A Nineteenth Century Oregon Pottery. *Northwest Anthropological Research Notes* 18(1):34–53.

Schindler, Harold
 1999 The Bear River Massacre: New Historical Evidence. *Utah Historical Quarterly* 67(4):300–308.

Schlesser, Norman D.
 1975 Hudson's Bay Company Fort Umpqua, 1836–1852. *Northwest Anthropological Research Notes*:70–86.

Schmeer, Blaine A.
 1987 *Pottery on the Willamette: A History of the Oregon Pottery Company, 1866–1896.* Halcyon Publications, Canby, OR.

Schroer, Blanche Higgins, W. C. Everhart, and Charles W. Snell
 1976 National Register of Historic Places Inventory Nomination Form (National Historic Landmarks), Cataldo Mission. Washington DC.

Schumacher, Paul J. F.
 1957 Archaeological Field Notes Fort Clatsop, Astoria, Oregon. Manuscript, Lewis and Clark National Historical Park, National Park Service, Astoria, Oregon.
 1961 Field Notes—Archeological Excavations at Fort Clatsop. Manuscript, Lewis and Clark National Historical Park, National Park Service, Astoria, OR.

Schwantes, Carlos Arnaldo
 1996 *The Pacific Northwest: An Interpretive History,* 2nd edition. University of Nebraska Press, Lincoln.

Scott, Harvey W.
 1906 Jason Lee's Place in History. *Washington Historical Quarterly* 1(1):21–33.

Scott, Leslie M
 1931 Modern Fallacies of Champoeg. *Oregon Historical Quarterly* 32(3):213–216.

Sekora, Lynda J., and Lester A. Ross
 1995 Historic Land-Use Systems. In *Archaeological Investigations PGT-PG&E Pipeline Expansion Project, Idaho, Washington, Oregon, and California Volume IV,* Randall F. Schalk, editor, pp. 10.1–10.85. Infotec Research, Inc. and Far Western Anthropological Research Group, Inc., Fresno, CA.

Shaw, Derek Gretchen, Gretchen Kaehler, Jennifer Olander, and Bradley Bowden
 2009 National Register Evaluations of the Hop Farms at Fort Lewis. Historical Research Associates, Inc. and ENSR/AECOM, Redmond, WA.

Shepherd, Nick, and S. Lawrence
 2006 Historical Archaeology and Colonialism. In *Cambridge Companion to Historical Archaeology,* Dan Hicks and Mary C. Beaudry, editors, pp. 69–86. Cambridge University Press, Cambridge, UK.

Shields, Norman
 2008 Chee Kung Tong Building, Barkerville, British Columbia. *Journal for the Study of Architecture in Canada* 33(2):53–72.

Silliman, Stephen W.
 2012 Between the Longue Durée and the Short Purée: Postcolonial Archaeologies of Indigenous History in Colonial North America. In *Decolonizing Indigenous Histories: Exploring Prehistoric/Colonial Transitions in Archaeology,* Maxine

Oland, Siobhan M. Hart, and Liam Frink, editors, pp. 113–131. University of Arizona Press, Tucson.

2015   A Requiem for Hybridity? The Problem with Frankensteins, Purées, and Mules. *Journal of Social Archaeology* 15(3):277–298.

2020   Colonialism in Historical Archaeology. In *The Routledge Handbook of Global Historical Archaeology,* Charles E. Orser, Andrés Zarankin, Pedro Paulo A. Funari, Susan Lawrence, James Symonds, editors, pp. 41–60. Routledge, New York.

Silverstein, Michael

1990   Chinookans of the Lower Columbia. In *Handbook of North American Indians Volume 7,* William C. Sturtevant, general editor; Wayne Suttles, volume editor, pp. 533–546. Smithsonian Institution Washington, DC.

Simmons [Simmons-Rogers], Alexandra L.

1982   Red Light Ladies: A Perspective on the Frontier Community. *Northwest Anthropological Research Notes* 16(1):107–114.

1989   Red Light Ladies in the American West: Entrepreneurs and Companions. *Australian Journal of Historical Archaeology* 7:63–69.

Simmons, Stephanie Catherine

2014   Exploring Colonization and Ethnogenesis through an Analysis of the Flaked Glass Tools of the Lower Columbia Chinookans and Fur Traders. Master's thesis, Department of Anthropology, Portland State University, Portland, OR.

2017   Exploring Colonization and Ethnogenesis through an Analysis of the Flaked Glass Tools of the Lower Columbia Chinookans and Fur Traders. In *The Fur-Trade Archaeology of the Cathlapotle and Meier Sites, Lower Columbia River,* Kenneth M. Ames and Katie Henry, editors, pp. 285–362, U.S. Fish and Wildlife Service Region 1, Cultural Resource Series 18, Portland, OR.

Simons, Eric, Andrew Martindale, and Alison Wylie

2021   Bearing Witness: What Can Archaeology Contribute in an Indian Residential School Context? In *Working with and for Ancestors: Collaboration in the Care and Study of Ancestral Remains,* C. Meloche, K. Nichols, and L. Spake, editors, pp. 21–31. Routledge.

Simonsen, Bjorn, and Carol Judd

2020   Archaeological Investigations and Associated Archival Research Relating to Fort Rupert on Northern Vancouver Island. *The Midden* 50(1):14–28.

Sims, Cort

1982   Test Excavations at the Fort Sherman Site (10-KA-48). Manuscript, Panhandle Chapter of the Idaho Archaeological Society.

Sinclair, Donna L.

2004   Part I, "Our Manifest Destiny Bids Fair for Fulfillment": An Historical Overview of Vancouver Barracks, 1846–1898, with Suggestions for Further Research. Report to Fort Vancouver National Historic Site, National Park Service from Center for Columbia River History, Vancouver, WA.

2005   Part III, Riptide on the Columbia: A Military Community Between the Wars, Vancouver, Washington and the Vancouver National Historic Reserve, 1920–1942, with Suggestions for Further Research. Report to Fort Vancouver National Historic Site, National Park Service from Center for Columbia River History, Vancouver, WA.

Sinclair, Donna, and Richard McClure
2003   "No Goldbricking Here": Oral Histories of the CCC in the Columbia National Forest, 1933–1942. History Department, Portland State University and Heritage Program, Gifford Pinchot National Forest, Portland, OR.

Sisson, David A.
1993   Archaeological Evidence of Chinese Use along the Lower Salmon River, Idaho. In *Hidden Heritage: Historical Archaeology of the Overseas Chinese*, Priscilla Wegars, editor, pp. 33–63. Baywood, Amityville, NY.

Skibo, James M., and Michael Brian Schiffer
2008   *People and Things: A Behavioral Approach to Material Culture*. Springer, New York.

Smith, Angèle
2004   Fitting into a New Place: Irish Immigrant Experiences in Shaping a Canadian Landscape. *International Journal of Historical Archaeology* 8(3):217–230.

Smith, Brian F., Sara Clowery, Larry J. Pierson, and Linda Dudik
2012   Atomic Archaeology: The Manhattan Project's Hanford Engineer Works Construction Camp Historical Landfill Study: An Archaeological Trenching and Data Recovery Program at Waste Sites 600-109 (45BN1536) and 600-202 (45BN1437) Benton County, Washington. Report to Washington Closure Hanford, LLC., Federal Engineers & Constructors, Inc. and the U.S. Department of Energy from Brian F. Smith and Associates, Inc. Poway, CA.

Smith, Harlan I, and Gerard Fowke
1901   Cairns of British Columbia and Washington. In *Memoirs of the American Museum of Natural History, Publications of the Jesup North Pacific Expedition, Anthropology III*, pp. 55–75. Knickerbocker Press, New York.

Smith, Lisa Michelle
2017   Cultural Change and Continuity across the Late Pre-Colonial and Early Colonial Periods in the Bridge River Valley: Archaeology of the S7istken Site. In *The Last House at Bridge River: The Archaeology of an Aboriginal Household in British Columbia during the Fur Trade Period*, Anna Marie Prentiss, editor, pp. 226–246. University of Utah Press, Salt Lake City.

Smits, Nicholas J
2008   Roots Entwined: Archaeology of an Urban Chinese American Cemetery. *Historical Archaeology* 42(3):111–122.

Sobel, Elizabeth A.
2012   An Archaeological Test of the "Exchange Expansion Model" of Contact Era Change on the Northwest Coast. *Journal of Anthropological Archaeology* 31(1):1–21.

South, Stanley
1977   *Method and Theory in Historical Archeology*. Academic Press, New York.
1978   Pattern Recognition in Historical Archaeology. *American Antiquity* 43(2):223–230.

Southern Oregon University
- 2018a Chinese Material Culture Collection. Hannon Library, Southern Oregon Digital Archives, Southern Oregon University. https://soda.sou.edu/chinese
- 2018b Jim Rock Historic Can Collection. Hannon Library, Southern Oregon Digital Archives, Southern Oregon University. https://soda.sou.edu/cans/index.html

Speulda, Lou Ann
- 1988 *Champoeg: A Perspective of a Frontier Community in Oregon, 1830–1861*. Anthropology Northwest 3, Department of Anthropology, Oregon State University, Corvallis.

Speulda, Lou Ann, Clayton G. Lebow, and Richard M. Pettigrew
- 1987 Archeological Investigations at the Ewing Young/Sidney Smith Cabin Site (OR-YA-1) Yamhill County, Oregon. Report to Yamhill County, Oregon, from Infotech Research Incorporated, IRI Report No. PNW87-9.

Speulda, Lou Ann, and Gary C. Bowyer
- 2002 Homesteading in Central Oregon: Archaeological Expressions of a National Phenomenon. In *Contributions to the Archaeology of Oregon 2002*, Lou Ann Speulda and Gary C. Bowyer, editors, pp. 71–88. Association of Oregon Archaeologists Occasional Papers No. 7, Eugene.

Spores, Ronald
- 1993 Too Small a Place: The Removal of the Willamette Valley Indians, 1850–1856. *American Indian Quarterly* 17(2):171–191.

Sprague, Paul E.
- 1981 The Origin of Balloon Framing. *Journal of the Society of Architectural Historians* 40(4):311–319.

Sprague, Roderick (editor)
- 1983 *San Juan Archaeology, Volumes I and II*. Moscow, ID.

Sprague, Roderick
- 1967 Aboriginal Burial Practices in the Plateau Region of North America. Doctoral dissertation, University of Arizona, Tucson.
- 1968 A Suggested Terminology and Classification for Burial Description. *American Antiquity* 33(4):479–485.
- 1973 Location of the Pig Incident, San Juan Island. In Miscellaneous San Juan Island Reports 1970–1972, pp. 18–38. University of Idaho Anthropological Manuscript Series No. 7, Moscow.
- 1974 American Indians and American Archaeology. *American Antiquity* 39(1):1–2.
- 1975 The Development of Historical Archaeology in the Pacific Northwest. *Northwest Anthropological Research Notes* 9(1):6–19.
- 1981 A Functional Classification for Artifacts from 19th and 20th Century Historical Sites. *North American Archaeologist* 2(3):251–261.
- 1993 American Indian Burial and Repatriation in the Southern Plateau with Special Reference to Northern Idaho. *Idaho Archaeologist* 16(2):3–14.
- 1998 The Literature and Locations of The Phoenix Button. *Historical Archaeology* 32(2):56–77.
- 2002 China or Prosser Button Identification and Dating. *Historical Archaeology* 36(2):111–127.

Stapp, Darby Campbell
- 1984 Late Protohistoric Burials with Copper Artifacts in the Pacific Northwest. Master's thesis, University of Idaho, Moscow.
- 1990 The Historic Ethnography of a Chinese Mining Community in Idaho. Doctoral dissertation, University of Pennsylvania, Philadelphia.
- 1993 The Documentary Record of an Overseas Chinese Mining Camp. In *Hidden Heritage: Historical Archaeology of the Overseas Chinese,* Priscilla Wegars, editor, pp. 3–31. Baywood, Amityville, NY.

Stapp, Darby, and Julia Longnecker
- 1986 Washington State University Centennial Digs: Report of 1984–86 Investigations. Washington Archaeological Research Center, Washington State University, Pullman.
- 2009 *Avoiding Archaeological Disasters: A Risk Management Approach.* Techniques and Issues in Cultural Resource Management No. 2. Left Coast Press, Walnut Creek, CA.

Stark, Vicki Hall
- 2016 Repatriation: Progressive Negotiation and Partnership. *Idaho Archaeologist* 39(1):35–46.

Steele, Harvey W.
- 1975 U.S. Customs and the Hudson's Bay Company, 1849–1853. *Northwest Anthropological Research Notes* 9(1):87–102.
- 1989 Non-Ferrous Artifacts from 35TI1: Metallurgical and Metallographic Comparisons. In *Contributions to the Archaeology of Oregon 1987–1988,* Rick Minor, editor, pp. 179–196. Association of Oregon Archaeologists Occasional Papers No. 4, Eugene.

Steele, Harvey W., Lester A. Ross, and Charles H. Hibbs
- 1975 Fort Vancouver Excavations–XII, OAS Sale Shop Excavation. Manuscript, Fort Vancouver National Historic Site, Vancouver, WA.

Steer, Donald N., Helen Lemon, Linda Southwood, and John Porter
- 1980 Archaeological Investigation at Fort Langley National Historic Park, 1979. Parks Canada Microfiche Report Series No. 114.

Steeves, Laban Richard
- 1984 Chinese Gold Miners of Northeastern Oregon, 1862–1900. Master's thesis, University of Oregon, Eugene.

Stein, Julie K. (editor)
- 1992 *Deciphering a Shell Midden.* Academic Press, Cambridge, MA.

Stein, Julie K.
- 2000 *Exploring Coast Salish Prehistory: The Archaeology of San Juan Island.* University of Washington Press, Seattle.

Stein, Julie K., Roger Kiers, Jennie Deo, Kate Gallagher, Chris Lockwood, and Scotty Moore
- 2006 A Geoarchaeological Analysis of Fort Clatsop, Lewis and Clark National Historical Park. University of Washington, Department of Anthropology, Seattle.

Stenger, Alison
- 1993 Sourcing and Dating of Asian Porcelains by Elemental Analysis. In *Hidden*

Heritage: Historical Archaeology of the Overseas Chinese, Priscilla Wegars, editor, pp. 315–331. Baywood, Amityville, NY.

Stern, Theodore
1993   *Chiefs and Chief Traders: Indian Relations at Fort Nez Perce's, 1818–1855.* Oregon State University Press, Corvallis.
1996   *Chiefs and Change in the Oregon County: Indian Relations at Fort Nez Perce's, 1818–1855.* Oregon State University Press, Corvallis.

Stilson, Leland M.
1990a   1988 Test Excavations at the 1843 Fort Nisqually (45-PI-56), DuPont, Washington: A Preliminary Report. Manuscript, Department of Archaeology and Historic Preservation, No. 1333419, Olympia, WA.
1990b   Archaeological Test Excavation Summary: A Preliminary Report on the 1988 Fort Nisqually Archaeological Investigations. *Occurrences* 10(1):20–32.
1990c   A Data Recovery Study of 45-PI-401, Hudson's Bay Dwellings at Northwest Landing, Pierce County, Washington. Report to Weyerhaeuser Real Estate Company, from Western Heritage, Inc., Olympia, WA.
1991a   A Data Recovery Study of 45-PI-405, the 1843 Fort Nisqually Village at Northwest Landing, Pierce County, Washington, Volume I. Report to Weyerhaeuser Real Estate Company from Western Heritage, Olympia, WA.
1991b   A Data Recovery Study of 45-PI-405, the 1843 Fort Nisqually Village at Northwest Landing, Pierce County, Washington, Volume II. Report to Weyerhaeuser Real Estate Company, from Western Heritage, Olympia, WA.

Stokeld, Rachel K.
2016   A Comparative Analysis of Two Early Fur Trade Period Sites on the Lower Columbia River of Oregon and Washington. Master's thesis, University of Idaho: Moscow.

Stone, Helen Delight
2010   Culture Contact and Gender in the Hudson's Bay Company of the Lower Columbia River, 1824–1860. Doctoral dissertation, University of Leicester, UK.

Stout, Harriet M.
1973   *Excavations at Fort Colvile, 1971.* University of Idaho Anthropological Research Manuscript Series, No. 10, Moscow.

Straus, Kirsten
2018   "Beneath This Sod": Intersections of Colonialism, Urbanization, and Memory in the Cemeteries of Salem and Portland, Oregon. Master's thesis, Portland State University, Portland, OR.

Striker, Michael, and Roderick Sprague.
1993   Excavations at the Warren Chinese Mining Camp Site, 1989–1992. University of Idaho Anthropological Reports, No. 94, Alfred W. Bowers Laboratory of Anthropology, University of Idaho, Moscow.

Strong, Emory
1960   Phoenix Buttons. *American Antiquity* 25(3):418–419.
1975   The Enigma of the Phoenix Button. *Historical Archaeology* 9(1):74–80.

Strong, W. Duncan, W. Egbert Schenck, and Julian H. Steward
1930   *Archaeology of the Dalles-Deschutes Region.* University of California Publica-

Suckling, Mark D.
1983 The Comparison of Hinges from American Camp and English Camp. In *San Juan Archaeology Volume II*, Roderick Sprague, editor, pp. 735–757. Laboratory of Anthropology, University of Idaho, Moscow.

[Preceding entry continuation:] tions in American Archaeology and Ethnology, 29(1):1–154. University of California Press, Berkeley.

Sukau, Dana Marie
2022 Dress and Identity: Using Sartorial Artifacts to Explore Identity at Fort Vancouver. Master's thesis, Portland State University, Portland, OR.

Sullivan, Daniel D.
1986 Neutron Activation Analysis and Chemical Inference for the Identification of Buena Vista Ceramics. Master's thesis, Portland State University, Portland, OR.

Sussman, Lynne
1979 *Spode/Copeland Transfer-Printed Patterns*. Canadian Historic Sites Occasional Papers in Archaeology and History No. 22, Parks Canada.

Suttles, Wayne P., and Barbara Savadkin Lane
1990 Southern Coast Salish. In *Handbook of North American Indians. Northwest Coast, Volume 7*, William C. Sturtevant, general editor; Wayne Suttles, volume editor, pp. 485–502. Smithsonian Institution, Washington, DC.

Swanson, Earl H.
1961 Historic Archaeology at Fort Okanogan, Washington, 1957. *Tebiwa* 5(1):1–10.

Taber, Emily Celene
2018 Using Archival and Archaeofaunal Records to Examine Victorian-Era Fish Use in the Pacific Northwest. Master's thesis, Portland State University, Portland, OR.

Taber, Emily C., Douglas C. Wilson, Robert Cromwell, Katie A. Wynia, and Alice Knowles
2019 Transfer-Printed Gastroliths and Identity at Fort Vancouver's Village. *Historical Archaeology* 53(1):86–102.

Tamura, Anna Hosticka
2004 Gardens Below the Watchtower: Gardens and Meaning in World War II Japanese American Incarceration Camps. *Landscape Journal* 23(1):1–21.

Tasa, Guy L., Brian L. O'Neill, Robert H. Winthrop, and Thomas J. Connolly
1993 A Cultural Resource Evaluation of the Mary Furlong and Crispen Ranch Localities, in the Canyonville to Tiller Section of the Tiller-Trail Highway (OR FH 16), Douglas County, Oregon. State Museum of Anthropology, University of Oregon, OSMA Report 93-3.

Taylor, Amanda, and Julie K. Stein
2011 *Is it a House? Archaeological Excavations at English Camp, San Juan Island, Washington*. Burke Museum, University of Washington, Seattle.

Taylor, Breanne
2020 Material Culture and the Social Dynamics of Residential Life at a Company Town: Archaeological Investigations at the Fairfax Townsite (45PI918), Pierce County, Washington, USA. Master's thesis, Simon Fraser University, Vancouver, BC.

Taylor, Breanne, Michael Daniels, and Todd Ogle
2017 Archaeological Survey of Champoeg State Heritage Area, Marion County, Or-

egon. Report to the State of Oregon Parks and Recreation Department from Willamette Cultural Resources Associates, Ltd. WillametteCRA Report No. 17–20, Portland, OR.

Thomas, Bryn
- 1988 An Archaeological Assessment of the Officers' Row Development, Clark County, Washington. Eastern Washington University, Archaeological and Historical Services Short Report No. 167. Cheney.
- 2008 Results of 1993 Test Excavations at Fort Hall Bannock County, Idaho. Archaeological and Historical Services Short Report 412, Eastern Washington University, Cheney. [1994] draft edited by Robert J. Cromwell, Manuscript, Fort Vancouver National Historic Site, Vancouver, WA.

Thomas, Bryn, and Charles Hibbs Jr.
- 1984 Report of Investigations of Excavations at Kanaka Village Vancouver Barracks Washington 1980 / 1981 Volumes 1 and 2. Report to the Washington State Department of Transportation, from Archaeological and Historical Services, Eastern Washington University, Cheney.

Thomas, Bryn, Lynn L. Larson, and Marilyn G. Hawkes
- 1984 Archaeological Investigations at 30 Historic Sites, Chief Joseph Dam Project, Washington. Report to the U.S. Army Corps of Engineers, Seattle District by the Office of Public Archaeology, Institute for Environmental Studies, University of Washington, Seattle.

Tinker, George E.
- 1993 *Missionary Conquest: The Gospel and Native American Cultural Genocide.* Fortress Press, Minneapolis, MN.

Tonsfeldt, Ward
- 2013 The U.S. Army Spruce Production Division at Vancouver Barracks, Washington, 1917–1919. Report to Fort Vancouver National Historic Site, National Park Service, from East Slope Cultural Services, Inc. Bend, OR.

Tonsfeldt, Ward, and Katherine C. Atwood
- 2003 Historic Structures Report for Vancouver Barracks, West Barracks, Vancouver National Historic Reserve Historical Background and Context. Report to National Park Service, Columbia Cascades Support Office from Ward Tonsfeldt Consulting, Bend, OR.

Townsend, Kristopher K., Robert H. Dunsmore, and Richard S. Buswell
- 2017 Mullan Road Center Line. https://trailresearch.org/mullan-road/mullan-road-centerline.php, accessed 8 April 2023.

Trigger, Bruce G.
- 2006 *A History of Archaeological Thought.* Cambridge University Press, New York.

Truth and Reconciliation Commission of Canada (TRC)
- 2015a *Canada's Residential Schools, The History, Part 1, Origins to 1939.* McGill-Queen's University Press, Montreal, QC.
- 2015b *Missing Children and Unmarked Burials.* McGill-Queen's University Press, Montreal, QC.

Tuck, Janna Beth
- 2010 A Beer Party and Watermelon: The Archaeology of Community and Resis-

tance at CCC Camp Zigzag, Company 928, Zigzag, Oregon, 1933–1942. Master's thesis, Portland State University, Portland, OR.

Tuohy, Donald R.
1958 Horseshoes and Handstones, the Meeting of History and Prehistory at the Old Mission of the Sacred Heart. *Idaho Yesterdays* II(2):20–27.

Turner, Frederick Jackson
1920 *The Frontier in American History.* Henry Holt and Company, New York.

Turnipseed, Donna, Michael Striker, and Roderick Sprague
1994 Florence Tells Her Secrets. University of Idaho Anthropological Reports, No. 96, Alfred W. Bowers Laboratory of Anthropology, University of Idaho, Moscow.

Tveskov, Mark Axel
2000 The Coos and Coquille: A Northwest Coast Historical Anthropology. Doctoral dissertation, University of Oregon, Eugene.
2007 Social Identity and Culture Change on the Southern Northwest Coast. *American Anthropologist* 109(3):431–441.
2015 Archaeological Investigations at the Battle of Hungry Hill Site, Josephine County, Oregon. Report to Medford District, Bureau of Land Management from Southern Oregon University Laboratory of Anthropology, SOULA Research Report 2015-1, Ashland.
2017 A "Most Disastrous" Affair: The Battle of Hungry Hill, Historical Memory, and the Rogue River War. *Oregon Historical Quarterly* 118(1):42–73.
2018 Landscapes of War: Indigenous Resistance to Settler Colonialism in the Oregon Territory, 1855–56. In *Conference Proceedings, Fields of Conflict Conference*, Nikita Moreira, Michael Derderian, and Ashley Bissonnette, editors, pp. 4–18. Mashantucket Pequot Museum & Research Center, Mashantucket, CT.
2020a Battlefield Site Identification and Documentation: The Battle of Big Bend, 27 & 28 May 1856, Curry County, Oregon. Report to the National Park Service American Battlefield Protection Program, Report MT.2020.03, Southern Oregon University, Ashland.
2020b Battlefield Site Identification and Documentation: The Affair at the Harris Homestead, 9 & 10 October 1855, Josephine County, Oregon. Report to the National Park Service American Battlefield Protection Program, Report MT.2020.02, Southern Oregon University, Ashland.
2021a Archaeological Investigations at Miners' Fort, 35CU241, Curry County, Oregon. Manuscript, SHPO Permit #AP 2147. Medford, OR.
2021b Archaeological Investigations at the Enlisted Men's Barracks and Officers' Quarters at Fort Lane (35JA569). Report to Oregon Parks and Recreation Department from the Sociology and Anthropology Program Southern Oregon University, Ashland.

Tveskov, Mark Axel, and Chelsea Rose
2019 Disrupted Identities and Frontier Forts: Enlisted Men and Officers at Fort Lane, Oregon Territory, 1853–1856. *Historical Archaeology* 53(1):41–55.

Tveskov, Mark Axel, Chelsea Rose, Geoffrey Jones, and David Maki
2019 Every Rusty Nail Is Sacred, Every Rusty Nail Is Good: Conflict Archaeology,

Remote Sensing, and Community Engagement at a Northwest Coast Settler Fort. *American Antiquity* 84(1):48–67.

Tveskov, Mark, and Amy Cohen
2008   The Fort Lane Archaeology Project. SOULA Research Report 2008-1, Southern Oregon University, Laboratory of Anthropology, Ashland.
2014   Frontier Forts, Ambiguity, and Manifest Destiny: The Changing Role of Fort Lane in the Cultural Landscape of the Oregon Territory, 1853–1929. In *Rethinking Colonial Pasts through Archaeology*, Neal Ferris, Rodney Harrison, and Michael V. Wilcox, editors, pp. 191–211. Oxford University Press, Oxford, UK.

Tveskov, Mark, and Katie Johnson
2014   The Spatial Layout and Development of Fort Lane, Oregon Territory 1853–1856. In *Alis Volat Propriis, Tales from the Oregon Territory, 1848–1859*, Chelsea Rose and Mark Tveskov, editors, pp. 115–134, Association of Oregon Archaeologists Occasional Papers, No. 9, Eugene.

Tveskov, Mark, Chelsea Rose, Katie Johnson, and Ben Truwe
2017   Archaeological Investigations within Geisel Monument State Heritage Site, Curry County, Oregon. SOULA Research Report 2016.17, Southern Oregon University Laboratory of Anthropology, Ashland.

Tyler, Norman
2000   *Historic Preservation: An Introduction to its History, Principles, and Practice.* 2nd edition. W. W. Norton & Company, New York.

Tyler, Thomas R.
1976   Excavation of San Juan Town, Washington, Site 45SJ290. In *Miscellaneous San Juan Island Reports 1972–1974*, pp. 1–56. University of Idaho Anthropological Research Manuscript Series No. 22, Moscow.
1983   Structural Analysis of San Juan Town. In *San Juan Archaeology Volume 1*, Roderick Sprague, editor, pp. 205–248. Laboratory of Anthropology, University of Idaho, Moscow.

Uldall, Tamara, and Lara C. Rooke
2016   Archaeological Assessment for the Fort Steilacoom Park Projects, Pierce County, Washington. Report to City of Lakewood by Northwest Cultural Resource Services, Project Number 2016-5, Seattle, WA.

U.S. Census Bureau
1910   1910 Abstract–Supplement for Washington. https://www2.census.gov/library/publications/decennial/1910/abstract/supplement-wa.pdf. Accessed 15 January 2003.

U.S. Forest Service
1991   National Register of Historic Places Registration Form for the Barlow Road. National Park Service.

University of Idaho
2021   Archaeology Field Studies Class Excavates Coeur d'Alene's Fort Sherman. www.uidaho.edu/class/csj/students-and-alumni/johnson. Accessed 7 May 2023.
2022   Asian American Comparative Collection. www.uidaho.edu/class/anthrolab/collections/aacc. Accessed 7 May 2023.

Unruh, John D., Jr.
   1979   *The Plains Across: The Overland Emigrants and the Trans-Mississippi West, 1840–60*. University of Illinois Press, Urbana.

Utley, Robert M.
   2003   *The Indian Frontier: 1846–1890*. Revised Edition. University of New Mexico Press, Albuquerque.

Valentino, Alicia
   2017   The Story of the Green Lake Gardens Company and the Kumasaka Family. *Archaeology in Washington* 17:102–120.

Veracini, Lorenzo
   2011   Introducing: Settler Colonial Studies. *Settler Colonial Studies* 1(1):1–12.
   2014   Understanding Colonialism and Settler Colonialism as Distinct Formations. *Interventions* 16(5):615–633.

Vizenor, G. (editor)
   2008   *Survivance: Narratives of Native Presence*. University of Nebraska Press, Lincoln.

Wadsworth, William Thomas Dowler
   2020   Above, Beneath, and Within: Collaborative and Community-Driven Archaeological Remote Sensing Research in Canada. Master's thesis, University of Alberta, Edmonton.

Wadsworth, William T. D., Kisha Supernant, and Ave Dersch
   2021   Integrating Remote Sensing and Indigenous Archaeology to Locate Unmarked Graves. *Advances in Archaeological Practice* 9(3):202–214.

Walker, Deward E., Jr.
   1965   Some Limitations of the Renascence Concept in Acculturation: The Nez Perce Case. *Midcontinent American Studies Journal* 6(2):135–148.

Walker, Deward E, Jr., and Roderick Sprague
   1998   History Until 1846. In *Handbook of North American Indians Volume 12: Plateau*, Deward E., Jr. Walker, editor, pp. 138–148. Smithsonian Institution, Washington, DC.

Walker, Henry P.
   1978   The Enlisted Soldier on the Frontier. In *The American Military on the Frontier: Proceedings of the 7th Military Symposium*, James P. Tate, editor, pp. 119–133. Office of Air Force History, Headquarters U.S.A.F and United States Air Force Academy, Washington, DC.

Wallace, Kelsey
   2021   Work to Begin on Lone Fir Cemetery's Cultural Heritage Garden at Block 14. Metro News. www.Oregonmetro.Gov/News/Work-Begin-Lone-Fir-Cemeterys-Cultural-Heritage-Garden-Block-14. Accessed 18 September 2021.

Walters, L. V. W.
   1938   Social Structure. In *The Sinkaietk or Southern Okanagon of Washington*, Leslie Spier, editor, pp. 73–99. General Series in Anthropology Number 6, Contributions from the Laboratory of Anthropology, 2, George Banta, Menasha, WI.

Warner, Mark S. (editor)
   2014   The Other Side of Sandpoint: Early History and Archaeology Beside the Track,

The Sandpoint Archaeology Project 2006–2013, Volume 2: Material Culture of Everyday Life. Report to the Idaho Transportation Department, District 1 from SWCA Environmental Consultants, SWCA Report No. 14–48, Portland, OR.

Warner, Mark S.
2017   The Mild Wild West: Settling Communities and Settling Households in Turn-of-the-Century Idaho. In *Historical Archaeology Through a Western Lens*, Mark Warner and Margaret Purser, editors, pp. 304–322. University of Nebraska Press, Lincoln.

Warner, Mark S., and James C. Bard
2014   Remembering Trixie Colton: The World of Sandpoint's Prostitutes. In *The Other Side of Sandpoint: Early History and Archaeology Beside the Track, The Sandpoint Archaeology Project 2006–2013, Volume 1: Sandpoint Stories*, Robert M. Weaver, editor, pp. 89–101. Report to the Idaho Transportation Department, District 1 from SWCA Environmental Consultants, SWCA Repot No. 14–48, Portland, OR.

Warner, Mark S., Breanne Kisling, and Molly Swords
2014   A "Community" on the Margins: Chinese Life in Turn of the Century Sandpoint. In *The Other Side of Sandpoint: Early History and Archaeology Beside the Track, The Sandpoint Archaeology Project 2006–2013, Volume 1: Sandpoint Stories*, Robert M. Weaver, editor, pp. 55–71. Report to the Idaho Transportation Department, District 1 from SWCA Environmental Consultants, SWCA Report No. 14–48, Portland, OR.

Warner, Mark S., Dan Martin, and Jamelon Brown
2014   The Archaeology of Sex. In *The Other Side of Sandpoint: Early History and Archaeology Beside the Track, The Sandpoint Archaeology Project 2006–2013, Volume 2: Material Culture of Everyday Life*, Mark S. Warner, editor, pp. 31–51. Report to the Idaho Transportation Department, District 1 from SWCA Environmental Consultants, SWCA Report No. 14–48, Portland, OR.

Warner, Mark S., Molly Swords, and Amanda Haught-Bielmann
2014   "Prospects Appear to Be Brightening Each Day": The Economies of Sandpoint. In *The Other Side of Sandpoint: Early History and Archaeology Beside the Track, The Sandpoint Archaeology Project 2006–2013, Volume 1: Sandpoint Stories*, Robert M. Weaver, editor, pp. 103–117. Report to the Idaho Transportation Department, District 1 from SWCA Environmental Consultants, SWCA Report No. 14–48, Portland, OR.

Warner, Mark, Tracy Schwartz, Stacey Camp, Jessica Goodwin, and Amanda Bielmann
2014   Public Archaeology in the West: A Case Study from Boise, Idaho. *Journal of Northwest Anthropology* 48(2):213–234.

Warner, Mark, and Alleah Schweitzer
2018   Epilogue: What Historical Archaeology in Idaho Has Done—And What We Still Need to Do. *Idaho Archaeologist* 41(1):85–86.

Watson, Bruce McIntyre
2010   *Lives Lived West of the Divide: A Biographical Dictionary of Fur Traders Work-*

ing West of the Rockies, 1793–1858. Centre for Social, Spatial, and Economic Justice, University of British Columbia Okanagan, Kelowna.

Weaver, Robert M. (editor)
2014 The Other Side of Sandpoint: Early History and Archaeology Beside the Track, The Sandpoint Archaeology Project 2006–2013, Volume 1: Sandpoint Stories. Report to the Idaho Transportation Department, District 1 from SWCA Environmental Consultants, SWCA Report No. 14-48, Portland, OR.

Weaver, Robert M.
1976 A Preliminary Study of Archaeological Relationships at the Mission of the Sacred Heart of Jesus to the Coeur d'Alene Indians. Master's thesis, University of Idaho, Moscow.
1977 The Jesuit Reduction System Concept: Its Implications for Northwest Archaeology. *Northwest Anthropological Research Notes* 11(2):163–173.

Webb, Garrett
2013 Environmental Impact of the Euro-American Emigration through Southwestern Idaho (1840–1862): Effect on Native Lifeways. *Idaho Archaeologist* 36(1):1–14.

Weeks, Kent R.
1962 Fort Simcoe Archaeological Survey. Washington Archaeological Research Center, Washington State University, Pullman.

Wegars, Priscilla Spires
1989 Floral Remains from the Pierce Chinese Mining Site, 10-CW-436. *Northwest Anthropological Research Notes* 23(1):103–107.
1991 The History and Archaeology of the Chinese in Northern Idaho, 1880 through 1910. Doctoral dissertation, University of Idaho, Moscow.
1996 Rice Bowls in the Diggings: Chinese Miners Near Granite, Oregon. In *Proceedings of the Society for California Archaeology,* pp. 161–169. Society for California Archaeology Volume 9.
2002 The Ah Hee Diggings near Granite, Oregon. In *Contributions to the Archaeology of Oregon 2002,* Lou Ann Speulda and Gary C. Bowyer, editors, pp. 31–48. Association of Oregon Archaeologists Occasional Papers No. 7, Eugene.

Wegars, Priscilla, and Roderick Sprague
1981 Archaeological Salvage of the Joso Trestle Construction Camp, 45-FR-51, Lower Monumental Project. University of Idaho Anthropological Research Manuscript Series No. 65, Moscow.

Weigand, Phil, Sue Ward, and Garman Harbottle
1981 Mexican Sherds Recovered from the Archaeological Excavations at Yuquot, British Columbia. In *The Yuquot Project, Volume 3,* William J. Folan and John Dewhirst, editors, 44:171–178. History and Archaeology Number 44, National Historic Parks and Sites Branch, Parks Canada, Environment Canada.

Wernz, Maralee L.
2001 A Study of Acculturation: ORMU57, Portland's Old Chinatown, ca. 1870–1920. Master's thesis, Oregon State University, Corvallis.

Wessen, Gary C.
2022 A Few Comments on "Whistlin' Dixie? Comments on the Association for

Washington Archaeology's Statement on Racism, Anti-Racism, Diversity, and Inclusion" by Richard Hutchings. *Journal of Northwest Anthropology* 56(1):132–135.

Weymouth, John W.
2001   The Integration of Four Seasons Magnetic Surveys at Fort Clatsop National Memorial. Report to Fort Clatsop National Memorial from the University of Nebraska, Lincoln.

Whaley, Gray H.
2006   "Trophies" for God: Native Mortality, Racial Ideology, and the Methodist Mission of Lower Oregon, 1834–1844. *Oregon Historical Quarterly* 107:6–35.

2010   *Oregon and the Collapse of Illahee: U.S. Empire and the Transformation of an Indigenous World, 1792–1859*. The University of North Carolina Press, Chapel Hill, NC.

White, Richard O.
1975   Chapter 134: Conservation and Protection of Archaeological Resources. 1975 Session Laws of the State of Washington.

White, Stephen W.
1975   Gunflints: Their Possible Significance for the Northwest. *Northwest Anthropological Research Notes* 9(1):51–69.

White, William Anderson, III
2016   Creating Space for a Place: The River Street Archaeology Project. *Arizona Anthropologist* 27:69–82.

2017a   The Archaeology of the River Street Neighborhood: A Multi-Racial Urban Region of Refuge in Boise, Idaho. Doctoral dissertation, University of Arizona, Tucson.

2017b   Writ on the Landscape: Racialization, Whiteness, and River Street. *Historical Archaeology* 51(1):131–148.

White, William A., III, and Eileen M. Heideman
2008   Cultural Resources Assessment for the Blakely Harbor Park Improvements, Kitsap County, Washington. Report to Bainbridge Island Metropolitan Park and Recreation District, from Northwest Archaeological Associates, Inc., NWAA Report No. WA07-129, Seattle, WA.

Whitman, Narcissa Prentiss
2002   *The Letters of Narcissa Whitman*, 3rd edition. Glen Adams. editor. Ye Galleon Press, Fairfield, WA.

Wickwire, Wendy C.
1992   Ethnography and Archaeology as Ideology: The Case of the Stein River Valley 1. *BC Studies* 91–92:51–78.

Wike, Joyce
1958   Problems in Fur Trade Analysis: The Northwest Coast. *American Anthropologist* 60(6):1086–1101.

Williams, Gerald W.
2018   The Spruce Production Division. *Forest History Today* Spring/Fall:39–46. Reprinted from 1999.

Williams, Scott S.
2007   A Research Design to Conduct Archaeological Investigations at the Site of the

"Beeswax Wreck" of Nehalem Bay, Tillamook County, Oregon. Beeswax Shipwreck Project, Olympia, WA.

2016   The Beeswax Wreck, A Manila Galleon in Oregon, USA. In *Early Navigation in the Asia-Pacific Region,* Chunming Wu, editor, pp. 147–167. Springer Singapore.

2020   The Cape Falcon Cove Site, Smugglers Cove/Oswald West State Park, Tillamook County, Oregon. Beeswax Wreck Project, Olympia, WA.

2023   Maritime Archaeology in the Pacific Northwest: Recent Work and Thoughts for Future Research. In *What Are We Searching For? Anthropological and Archaeological Research in the Pacific Northwest—2023,* Darby C. Stapp and Julia G. Longenecker, editors, pp. 127–135. Journal of Northwest Anthropology Special Publication No. 7, Richland, WA.

Williams, Scott S., Mitch Marken, and Curt D. Peterson

2017   Tsunami and Salvage: The Archaeological Landscape of the Beeswax Wreck, Oregon, USA. In *Formation Processes of Maritime Archaeological Landscapes,* Alicia Caporaso, editor, pp. 141–161. Springer International.

Williams, Scott S., Curt D. Peterson, Mitch Marken, and Richard Rogers

2018   The Beeswax Wreck of Nehalem: A Lost Manila Galleon. *Oregon Historical Quarterly* 119(2):192–209.

Willson, Christopher A.

2008   A Hafted, Metal Projectile Point from the Payette River, Idaho. *Idaho Archaeologist* 31(1):13–16.

Wilson, Douglas C.

1998   Refuse Concentrations and Disposal at Military Fort Spokane (45LI2H/45LI10H): A Survey and Preliminary Evaluation. Report to National Park Service, Lake Roosevelt National Recreation Area, from Archaeology Consulting, Archaeology Consulting Report No. 9.

1999   Results of Archaeological Testing Around 16 Standing Structures of the Bridal Veil Historical Archaeological Site. Letter report to the Trust for Public Land by Archaeology Consulting, Portland, OR.

2004   Data Recovery Investigations of The Officer's Trail, English Camp, San Juan Island National Historical Park, San Juan County, Washington. Manuscript, Fort Vancouver National Historic Site, National Park Service, Vancouver, WA.

2005   Research Design: Archaeological Investigation of the Fort Clatsop Site, Clatsop County, Oregon. Report to Lewis and Clark National Historical Park from the Pacific West Region, National Park Service. Vancouver, WA.

2006   Searching for Lewis & Clark at Fort Clatsop. Paper presented at the 59th Annual Northwest Anthropological Conference, Seattle, WA.

2008   *Research Design and Treatment Plan for 45BN1437, Solid Waste Site 600-202:* Historical Archaeology of an "Atomic Boomtown," the World War II Hanford Construction Camp, Benton County, Washington. Report to the U.S. Department of Energy, Richland Operations Office, from Northwest Cultural Resources Institute, Fort Vancouver National Historic Site, National Park Service, Northwest Cultural Resources Institute Report No. 2, Vancouver, WA.

2012   Middle Village. *Columbia: The Magazine of Northwest History* 26(2):4–9.

2014   The Decline and Fall of the Hudson's Bay Company Village at Fort Vancouver.

2015   In *Alis Volat Propriis: Tales from the Oregon Territory, 1848–1859*, Chelsea Rose and Mark Tveskov, editors, pp. 21–42. Association of Oregon Archaeologists Occasional Paper Series No. 9. Association of Oregon Archaeologists, Eugene.

2015   A Mongrel Crowd of Canadians, Kanakas and Indians: The United States National Park Service Public Archaeology Programme and Fort Vancouver's Village. *Journal of Community Archaeology & Heritage* 2(3):221–237.

2018   The Fort and the Village: Landscape and Identity in the Colonial Period of Fort Vancouver. In *British Forts and Their Communities: Archaeological and Historical Perspectives*, Christopher R. DeCorse and Zachary J. M. Beier, editors, pp. 91–125. University Press of Florida, Gainesville.

2020   Emporium of The West: Archaeological Testing of Fort Astoria/ Fort George, Astoria, Clatsop County, Oregon. Northwest Cultural Resources Institute Report No. 22, Fort Vancouver National Historical Site and Regional Office, Interior Region 8, 9, 10, and 12, National Park Service, Vancouver, WA.

2021   Public and Community Archaeology in the Pacific Northwest. *Journal of Northwest Anthropology* 55(2):40–45.

Wilson, Douglas C., Kenneth M. Ames, and Cameron M. Smith

2017   Contextualizing the Chinook at Contact. In *Frontiers of Colonialism*, Christine D. Beaule, editor, pp. 110–144. University Press of Florida, Gainesville.

Wilson, Douglas C., Kristine M. Bovy, Virginia Butler, Robert Cromwell, Loren G. Davis, Christopher R. DeCorse, Brian F. Harrison, R. Lee Lyman, Michele L. Punke, Cameron Smith, Nancy A. Stenholm, and Kenneth Ames

2009   Historical Archaeology at the Middle Village: Station Camp/McGowan Site (45PC106), Station Camp Unit, Lewis & Clark National Park, Pacific County, Washington. Report to the Washington State Historical Society and Washington State Department of Transportation from the Northwest Cultural Resources Institute, Fort Vancouver National Historic Site, National Park Service, Northwest Cultural Resources Institute Report No. 1, Vancouver, WA.

Wilson, Douglas C., Amy Clearman, and Kaitlyn Hosken

2022   Decolonizing Fort Vancouver Through Archaeological Interpretation. In *Creating Participatory Dialogue in Archaeological and Cultural Heritage Interpretation: Multinational Perspectives*, John H. Jameson and Sherene Baugher, editors, pp. 237–253. Springer International Publishing.

Wilson, Douglas C., Robert J. Cromwell, and Janna B. Tuck

2016   The Fields of Fort Vancouver: Archaeological Survey, Testing, and Monitoring Projects 2000–2014, Fort Vancouver National Historic Site (45CL163), Vancouver National Historic Reserve Historic District (DT191), Clark County, Washington. Fort Vancouver National Historic Site, Northwest Cultural Resources Institute Report No. 18. Vancouver, WA.

Wilson, Douglas C., and Theresa E. Langford (editors)

2011   *Exploring Fort Vancouver*. University of Washington Press, Seattle.

Wilson, Douglas C. Katie A. Wynia, Amy Clearman, Cheryl Paddock

2020   Archaeological Overview and Assessment, Fort Vancouver National Historic Site and the Vancouver National Historic Reserve, Clark County, Washington, and Clackamas County, Oregon. Northwest Cultural Resources Institute Report No. 21, Fort Vancouver National Historic Site, Vancouver, WA.

Winthrop & Winthrop
- 1983 Hanley Farm Archaeological Study, Jacksonville, Oregon. Report to the Southern Oregon Historical Society from Winthrop & Winthrop, Consulting Anthropologists. Ashland, OR.

Withee, Katee
- 2021 Stacked Rock Features: Archaeological Evidence of Chinese Miners on the Malheur National Forest. *Oregon Historical Quarterly* 122(4):368–387.

Wolf, Eric R.
- 1982 *Europe and the People without History.* University of California Press, Berkeley.

Wolfe, Patrick
- 2006 Settler Colonialism and the Elimination of the Native. *Journal of Genocide Research* 8(4):387–409.

Woodward, John A.
- 1975 Oxen, Axes and China Teacups: Six Papers on the Pioneer Lumbering of Larch Mountain, Multnomah County, Oregon. Mt. Hood Community College, Gresham, OR.
- 1977 A Report on the Metal Artifacts from the Mostul Cemetery, An Historic Clackamas River Indian Site. *Northwest Anthropological Research Notes* 11(2):155–162.
- 1986 Prehistoric Shipwrecks on the Oregon Coast? Archaeological Evidence. In *Contributions to the Archaeology of Oregon 1983–1986,* Kenneth M. Ames, editor, pp. 219–264. Association of Oregon Archaeologists Occasional Papers No. 3, Eugene.

Woodworth-Ney, Laura
- 1996 Tribal Sovereignty Betrayed: The Conquest of the Coer D'Alene Indian Reservation, 1840–1905. Doctoral dissertation, Washington State University, Pullman.

Wynia, Katie Ann
- 2013 The Spatial Distribution of Tobacco Pipe Fragments at the Hudson's Bay Company Fort Vancouver Village Site: Smoking as a Shared and Social Practice. Master's thesis, Portland State University Dissertations and Theses, Paper 1085.
- 2022 Archaeological Investigations at the Shane and Smith House Sites at Fort Clatsop Unit of Lewis and Clark National Historical Park, Clatsop County, Oregon. Draft Report to Lewis and Clark National Historical Park, from Department of Anthropology, Portland State University, Portland, OR.

Yellowhorn, Eldon Carlyle
- 2002 Awakening Internalist Archaeology in the Aboriginal World. Doctoral dissertation, McGill University, Montreal, QC.

Young, F. G.
- 1920 Ewing Young and His Estate: A Chapter in the Economic and Community Development of Oregon. *Oregon Historical Quarterly* 21(3):171–315.

Younker, Jason, Mark A. Tveskov, and David G. Lewis (editors)
- 2001 *Changing Landscapes: "Telling Our Stories," Proceedings of the Fourth Annual Coquille Cultural Preservation Conference, 2000.* Coquille Indian Tribe, North Bend, Oregon.

INDEX

Page numbers in *italics* indicate illustrations.

Abraham, Terry, 122
Acapulco, Mexico, 38
Acculturation, 23, 51, 195
Acheson, Cassidy, 137
Adventure (ship), 41
Africans and African Americans: and community creation, 196; and education, 169; enslaved, 85; and home ownership, 168; as immigrants, 4; legislation pertaining to, 195; and mining, 140; organizations of, 196; and racialization and racism, 158, 195; and resistance, 177; as settlers, 90–91, 96; as soldiers, 173, 193; and violence, 195; and World War II shipyards, 177
Agriculture: African Americans and, 90–91; American settlers and, 103; Chinese and Chinese descendants and, 172; French Canadians and, 70, 88; fur traders and, 66, 72, 83, 85, 88, 89–90; grain cultivation, 66, 84, 131, 158, 160; hops cultivation, *134*, 135, 196; Hudson's Bay Company and, 64, 65, 66, 68, 83, 99, 100, 135; and impact on natural environment, 132; Indigenous peoples and, 72, 74, 79, 83, 105, 190, 196; Japanese and Japanese descendants and, 132, 135, 179, 181; missions and missionaries and, 72, 74, 78, 79; and orchards, 66, 68, 133, 158; soldiers and, 104; and technological change, 194; and Turnerian hypothesis, 19; vegetable cultivation, 66, 169
Akin, Marjorie, 161
Alapetsa/Rosie (Sqilxw woman), 136
Alaska, 3, 6, 18, 52
Albany, OR, 131
Albert, Prince, 9
Alpowa Creek, 158
American Board of Commissioners for Foreign Missions, 74
Ames, Kenneth M., 3

Animals: antelope, 157; bears, 65; beavers, 34, 40, 46, 54, 55, 65, 79, 82, 157, 194; bison, 45, 46, 54; buffalo, 49; cattle, 66, 67, 68, 75, 83, 88, 105, 131, 136, 139, 157, 170; deer, 34, 42, 55, 67, 75, 82, 157, 195; dogs, 71, 89; domesticated, 62, 67, 71, 75, 78, 90, 157; elk, 34, 42, 56, 67, 68, 157; and environmental damage, 196; game, 88; goats, 157; horses, 34, 44, 50, 51, 52, 68, 83, 84, 88, 90, 113, 131, 143, 149, 157, 194; impact of fur trade on, 194; impact of human migration on, 88; Indigenous peoples and, 51–52, 107, 113, 135; mules, 44, 84, 88, 143, 149; muskrats, 55; non-native, 194; oxen, 88, 115, 149; pigs, 68, 99, 131, 141, 157; rabbits/hare, 50; sea otters, 39, 53, 65, 194; sheep, 66, 67, 68, 75, 99, 157; unspecified types of, 96, 161, 164, 172, 174; wild, 67, 157. *See also* Birds; Fish and shellfish
Anthropologists and anthropology: and acculturation models, 23, 51; and adaptation models, 23; archaeology and, 15, 19; and burials and cemeteries, 110, 191; and cultural anthropology, 186; and historical archaeology, 8, 23, 51, 63, 184, 185, 194; and material culture, 7, 8, 19; museums of, 185; and nation-state expansion, 22; and oral traditions, 6; on Pacific Northwest, 3; and public archaeology, 186; and Rogue River War, 95
Applegate River, 139
Applegate Trail, *86*
Archaeological features: ash deposits, 161, 165; cellars, 16, 47, 63, 64, 66, 73, 74, 76–77, 160, 161, 165, 167, 171, 179; chimneys, 90; cistern, 155; corrals, 69, 74; deciduous tree stands, 160; depressions, 47, 101, 124; dumps, 101, 104, 136, 153, 158, 161, 167, 173, 175, 176, 177, 179; fencing, 69, 71, 160, 165, 179; fields, 160; footings, 133, 165, 179; forges, 41; foundations, 78, 165, 167, 179; gardens, 155, 179; hearths and fireplaces,

41, 47, 49, 52, 66, 70, 73, 74, 81, 90, 96, 107; landfills, 197; orchards, 160; palisades, 19, 45, 46, 47, 66, 67; paths, roads, and pavements, 73, 160, 179; pickets, 49, 63; pits, 42, 46, 52, 66, 124, 153, 165; post holes, 73; posts, 52; privies, 44, 64, 67, 102, 104, 136, 153, 161, 190; refuse deposits, 165, 180; rock alignments, 179; sandstone fireplaces, 45; saw pits, 47; shell middens, 98, 101; tent pads and platforms, 147, 162; walls, 44, 49, 74, 153, 160, 171, 179; wells, 101, 165; wok ovens, 147, 162; yards, 155, 168, 170. *See also* Buildings and structures

Archaeological methodologies and tools: acculturation framework, 51; aerial photography, 49, 106; artifact analysis, 22–23; auger surveys and testing, 43, 106; backhoes, 42; block excavations, 42; consumer product distribution analysis, 158; data recovery excavations, 50; electrical resistivity, 42, 129; electromagnetic conductivity, 28; excavation units, 168; geoarchaeological analyses, 38; geographical information systems (GIS), 28; global positioning system (GPS), 29; grids, 29; ground-penetrating radar (GPR), 28, 42, 46, 93, 106, 129, 148; landscape-level analysis, 97; magnetometry/magnetic gradiometer surveys, 28, 42, 87, 90, 93, 124, 129; mapping of surface features, 62, 89; metal detectors, 28, 87, 106, 124, 175; micro analysis, 139; morphology, 113; multiscalar analysis, 24–25, 69; near-surface geophysical remote sensing, 28, 129; outdoor laboratories, 186; pedestrian survey, 28; phenomenology, 97; phosphorus and mercury testing, 43; probes, 28, 170; remote sensing, 42, 96; sampling, 96; screening, 28, 186; shovel testing, 93, 168; subsurface survey, 50; surface collection, 89, 106, 144, 161; surface surveys, 89, 180; surveys, 78; SYMAP program, 28; test excavations, 43, 46, 48, 50, 65, 89, 95, 136, 148, 170; testing, unspecified types of, 62, 90, 170, 180; test units, 106, 175; trace element chemical analysis, 113; trenching, 42, 43, 52; use of human remains detection dogs, 89; vegetation clearance, 129

Archaeological Society of British Columbia, 170

Archaeologists and archaeology: and anthropological theory, 19; and artifacts, 7–8; and behavioral archaeology, 21, 26; and bias, 22; and burials and cemeteries, 17; and community archaeology, 14, 26, 184, 189–90; and community collaboration, 184, 186–87, 188, 191; and cultural resources management, 25; as decolonizing tool, 129; educational/gateway/deficit model of, 184; education for, 25; and environmental remediation, 176; evolution of, 15–16; impact of, 191; Indigenous, 24, 191; and outreach, 183; on Pacific Northwest, 3; processual, 21; and public archaeology, 14, 25, 26, 127, 182, 183, 184, 185, 186, 187, 188–90; salvage, 11, 49, 67, 79, 93, 113, 160, 162, 165, 166, 167, 170, 185; and volunteer archaeology, 185, 187. *See also* Indigenous peoples, and archaeological collaboration

Archaeology Roadshow, 187

Architecture: adobe, 61, 63, 74; bermed-earth, 147; brick, 30, 76, 77, 91, 101; British, 50; clapboard-clad, 69; dovetail notched, 70; frame, 80, 140, 150; French Canadian, 67, 70, 73, 90; gabled, 147; log, 76, 147, 150; Midwestern, 31; 19th-century style, 107; notched-log, 92; post/pile-in-the-ground, 46, 70, 90; on pilings or stilts, 137, 152; post-on-sill, 70, 78; post-World War II, 192, 193; rammed-earth, 147; ranch-style, 192, 193; saddle-notched, 46, 73; sod-roofed, 61; and technology, 22, 30, 194; terraced gardens, 147; 20th-century style, 107; two-saddle, side-notch, 147; and Victorianism, 9; wattle-and-daub, 90; Western style, 81. *See also* Artifacts, associated with architecture and structures; Buildings and structures; Dwellings

Arthur DeWint and Mary Haviland Hallock (Molly) Foote House, 167

Artifact (term), 7

Artifacts: accoutrements, 106; American, 44, 73, 82, 136, 144, 150; argillite, 79; Asian, 138, 161, 164, 167, 172; baking ovens, 90; beeswax, 38; blacksmithing-related, 82, 151; bone, 75, 79, 114, 151; bric-a-brac, 163, 168; British and English, 36, 44, 73, 136, 144; and Brunswick pattern of refuse disposal, 21; Canadian, 79, 81, 136, 150; for card playing, 161; carpet bags, 143–44; charcoal, 42; Chinese, 136, 144, 163; and class, 8, 9; classifications of, 7–8, 21–22, 89, 93; cloth, 75; combs, 114, 151, 155, 171; commercial items, 64; cosmetics, 154; crystals, 75; cups, 114; curios, 74; dental, hygiene, and health items, 74, 106, 151, 161, 163, 167, 168, 171, 175; dishware, 151, 175; domestic items, 104; eating utensils and flatware, 150; and economic data, 23; eggshells, 168; erasers, 169; European, 66, 75, 79, 81, 82, 112; European American, 90; European Canadian, 40, 81; as evidence of resistance, 71; fishhooks, 50, 157; fishing gear, 175; for food storage, preparation, and use, 73; furnishings, 168; fur trade-related, 47, 49; for gambling, 79, 161, 163, 172; gastroliths, 71, 90; and gender, 90, 151; German, 136; grooming items, 73, 105, 106; hair grower, 167; handball court remains, 169; hard rubber, 151; harmonica fragments, 175; and hierarchy, 104; historical archaeology and, 6, 8, 20, 21, 22–23, 29–32, 35, 50, 102; housewares and household maintenance items, 16, 154; for hunting, 73; industrial items, 64; inkwell, 56; inlaid boxes, 171; knives, 81; lamps, 151; laundry items, 154; leather, 117, 155; liquor flasks, 151; made from beaver teeth, 79; mapping of densities of, 28; marbles, 151; military insignia, 106; mining pans, 140; music-related, 161; needles, 50, 75; nesting turtles, 164; for opium smoking, 163, 171; pencils and pencil parts, 73, 90, 151, 169; personal adornment items, 106; photography equipment, 175; pollen, 70; pro-Irish items, 174; railroad ties, 153; repatriation of, 114–15; rocks, 42; Scottish, 136; shaving cream, 167; slate, 73, 90, 134, 151; smoking pipes and pipe parts, 30, 48, 49, 66, 70, 79, 98, 99, 104, 114, 143, 144, 171; souvenirs, 168; spectacles fragments, 114; stakes, 81; and status, 67, 71, 151; stemware, 163; sticks, 42; stone, 46, 81; surgical knife handle, 74; tablewares, 138, 154; talc shakers, 155; teak timbers, 38; teawares, 154, 171; thermometer tubes, 74; thimbles, 50; for tobacco chewing, 161; toiletries, 154; toys, 90, 106, 155, 160, 163, 168; tumblers, 163; and Victorianism, 9, 151, 167; wagon parts, 75; and wealth, 157; weaving shuttle, 75; wooden, 42, 75, 153; writing slates and tablets, 73, 90, 114, 134. *See also* Beads; Buttons; Ceramics; Ceramics, forms of; Chinese and Chinese descendants, artifacts associated with; Foods and beverages; Foods and beverages, alcoholic; Indigenous peoples, artifacts associated with; Jewelry; Weapons and ammunition

Artifacts, associated with architecture and structures: and dating of archaeological sites, 30, 31, 70; fasteners, 30, 31, 32, 95; hardware, 32, 95; hinges, 101; manufactured in US, 32; nails, 30, 31, 46, 48, 49–50, 61, 64, 70, 73, 75, 89, 107, 143; ovens, 162; sawed steatite, 61; transportation of, 31. *See also* Architecture; Buildings and structures; Dwellings

Artifacts, clothing and clothing-related: boot polish cans, 155; boots, 117, 155; buckles, 50; children's, 156, 160, 163; and gender, 160, 168–69; Indigenous peoples and, 156; Japanese and Japanese descendants and, 155; related to clothing, 71, 73, 90; ribbon, 117; shoe polish, 167; shoes, 156; socks, 117; and status, 168–69; workmen's clothing, 151

Artifacts, glass: amethyst glass fragment, 106; bird feeder, 164; black, 98; canning jars, 150, 154, 166, 167; Chinese-style, 171; colored press-molded, 168; crown glass, 30–31; debitage, 56; dishes, 95, 150; for drinking, 30, 140, 163; flat glass, 30, 31, 32, 101; fragments, 153; gaming pieces, 164, 172; gastroliths, 71; Indigenous peoples and, 53, 55, 56, 106, 107, 144, 157; knives, 56; marbles, 134, 167; mirror glass, 61, 151; plate glasses, 30; pressed, 95, 133, 150; projectile points, 56; saws, 56; scrapers, 56; tableware, 138; and technological change, 194; for unspecified containers, 61; unspecified items, 81; vessels, 23, 163; Western-style, 171; window glass, 30–31, 61, 64, 70, 77, 89, 194. *See also* Beads: glass; Bottles

Artifacts, metal: boot polish cans, 155; brass, 50, 53, 64, 164, 171, 172; bridle rings, 87; bronze, 74; buckles, 50; call bell top, 172; cans, 143, 155; cast-iron, 53, 156; chain links, 151; cleavers, 142; coffee pots, 151, 156; coffin hardware, 126; coins, 15, 36, 142, 147, 161, 164, 172; copper, 50, 57, 64, 112, 113; ferrous, 55, 171; fishhooks, 157; graniteware, 151, 156; hardware, 32, 95, 126; hinges, 101; hooks (iron dogs), 151; horseshoes, 82, 143; Indigenous peoples and, 45, 53, 54, 82, 88,

157; iron, 37, 46, 50, 55, 64, 112, 114, 117, 151; kettles, 50; knives, 88; lead, 53, 55, 98; logging tools, 151; loops, 117; mule shoes, 143; nails, 30, 31, 46, 48, 49–50, 61, 64, 70, 73, 75, 89, 107, 143; ornaments, 88; pewter, 75; pins and pin parts, 28, 45, 50, 156, 171; projectile points, 88; razors, 151; rivets, 117; saw teeth, 151; scales, 74, 95; scissors, 50; sheep shears, 75; silver, 36, 75, 150; spikes, 153; spoons, 75; spring traps, 157; substitutes for stone, 54; tacks, 171; tea tins, 171; tin cans, 30, 143, 151, 153, 154, 157, 161, 166; tinned enamelware, 151; tobacco tins and tabs, 151, 153, 154, 157; unspecified metal, 81; watches, watch chains, and watch parts, 150, 171; wire, 112
Ashland, OR, 162
Asia, 48, 102
Asian American Comparative Collection, 30, 194
Asians and Asian descendants: archaeological sites related to, 25; and canneries, 138; and ceramics, 30; as consumers, 139; and early contacts with Indigenous peoples, 37; and immigration, 4–5, 25; increased population of, 5; and shipwrecks, 27, 37. *See also* Chinese and Chinese descendants; Japanese and Japanese descendants
Astor, John Jacob, 44, 49
Astoria, OR, 42
Athapaskan language, 98
Auburn, OR, 139
Aurora, OR, 133
Australia, 122
Austro-Hungarian Empire, 174

Bailey, William J., 89
Baker City, OR, 139
Ball, John, 90
Banff, Canada, 85
Barclay, Forbes, 108, 109
Barclay, Maria Pambrun, 108–10
Barclay House, 108
Barkerville, British Columbia, *134*, 144–45
Barkley, James, 156
Barlow Road, *87*, 115
Barman, Jean, 3, 83
Barneston, WA, *134*, 154, 155
Basques, 26, 127, 168, 169

Battles: Big Bend, *86*, 95, 97; Evan's Creek, 94; Gettysburg, 100; Hungry Hill, *86*, 95, 96, 97; Little Bighorn, 172; White Bird Canyon, 172
Baugher, Sherene, 110
Bay View cannery, 139
Beads: for abacuses, 144; Chinese and Chinese descendants and, 144, 171; clam-shell, 75; copper, 57, 112, 113; drawn, 46, 82; for gambling, 144; glass, 45, 48, 50, 52, 55, 57, 61, 66, 75, 81, 82, 90, 95, 98, 106, 107, 112, 144, 157; Indigenous peoples and, 45, 52, 54, 55, 57, 61, 75, 81, 82, 90, 98, 106, 107, 112, 113, 144, 157; Native Hawaiians and, 66; plastic, 107; steatite, 82; technique for finding, 28; trade, 30; tube, 113; unspecified types of, 54, 171; wound, 46
Bear River Massacre, 86–87, 88
Beatty Curve, OR, 31, *134*, 156–57
Beaver Indians (Dunne-za/Dane-zaa people), 45, 46
Bedard, Elisabet Louise, 46
Beeswax Wreck sites, *36*, 37, *38*, 55
Belgians, 76
Bella Bella site, 24, *60*, 80–81
Bella Coola River and Valley, 40, 81
Bellevue Farm, 99, 100, 102
Bennett Hills, 51
Benson, James R., 50
Berry, W. J., 75
Binder, Andrea Mary, 115
Binford, Lewis R., 7–8
Birds: chickens, 83, 93, 105, 168, 169; ducks, 141; geese, 141; poultry, 157; swallows, 117; turkeys, 141; unspecified species, 42, 61, 68, 71, 90; waterfowl, 157. *See also* Animals; Fish and shellfish
Bishop of Quebec, 76
Blackfeet/Niitsitapi people, 54
Blackman, Margaret B., 127
Black Rock Tunnel, *159*
Blanchet, Francis Norbert, 76
Blue Mountains, 139, 146, 147
Bodega y Quadra, Juan Francisco de la, 40
Boise, ID, *2*, *5*, *159*, 166–69, 186–87
Boise Basin, 140, 146
Boise Basin Gold Rush, 166
Boise River Valley, 166
Boise-San Francisco stage route, 117
Bolon, Andrew, 1

Bolvile Run, 184
Bonneville Dam, 185
Boston, MA, 111
Bottles: for alcohol or liquor, 56, 79, 93, 101, 104, *125*, 126, 140, 142, 143, 155, 163, 167, 172, 173, 175; for bitters, 167; dark olive glass, 79; for iodine, 74; for medicines, patent medicines, or remedies, 74, 155, 163, 167, 171; for perfume, 102, 167; pharmaceutical or prescription, 167; for unspecified use, 57, 81
Bowyer, Gary C., 105
Brauner, David, 24
Breitenstein, Lee, *18*
Bridge River, 195
Bridge River Band/Xwísten people, 82
Bridge River Site/St'át'imc ancestral site, *60,* 82
British and English: and architecture, 50; artifacts manufactured by, 30, 36, 44, 48, *57,* 73, 79, 102, 126, 136, 142, 144, 161, 167; and clothing, 8, 71; and Fort Vancouver, 68; and fur trade, 4, 12, 48, 109; and hierarchy, 71; and hygiene, 71; and logging and lumbering, 149; military of, *86,* 92, 100, 101–2, 144; and Pacific Northwest, 40, 41; as U.S. soldiers, 92
British Columbia: agriculture in, 66; archaeological methodologies in, 29; archaeological sites in, 23, 24, 36, 44, 46–47, 52–54, 62–63, 65–66, 80–82, 136, 137–39, 143–45, 154, 169–70, 174, 195; burials and cemeteries in, 119–20, 123–25, 127–30; Canadian Cordillera in, 3; canneries in, *134,* 137–38; Cariboo Wagon Road in, 144, 161; Chilkoot Trail in, 6; Chinese and Chinese descendants in, 123, 124–25, 126, 136, 137, 138–39, 143, 144–45, 169–70, 196; commercial fishing in, 80, 137; current-day research in, 184; early contact in, 40; education in, 80, 128–29; environmental diversity in, 3; Fraser Canyon War in, 92; and Fraser River War, 144; fur trade in, 46, 62, 66, 81–82, 195; gold mining in, 99, 119, 123, 136, 139, 143, 145, 161, 170; grave markers in, 20; historic preservation in, 23, 27–28, 192, 196; Hudson's Bay Company in, 136, 142, 144; identity in, 3; Indian reservations in, 136; Indigenous archaeological collaboration in, 27, 62, 128–30, 195; Indigenous peoples in, 24, 52–54, 62–63, 80–82, 100, 126–30, 136–37, 138–39, 143–44, 145; industry in, *134;* Irish in, 145; Japanese and Japanese descendants in, 137, 138–39, 154; land rights in, 132; logging and lumbering in, 144, 154; maps of, *2, 36, 60, 134, 159;* Native Hawaiians in, 66; as part of Pacific Northwest, 1, 5; as political unit, 3; population in, 1; prisoners of war in, 174; proclamation of, as colony, 65, 143; racism and social inequality in, 170; ranching in, 136; river drainage in, 2; roads in, 161; salmon processing in, 66; Scandinavians in, 137; settlement patterns in, 1, 196; violence and competition in, 143, 195
British Northwest Company, 40
Brookings, OR, 176
Brooks, Saffron, 127
Brumback, A. M., 113
Buck Rock Tunnel, 162
Buddhists and Buddhism, 127, 155
Buena Vista, OR, 135
Buena Vista pottery company, 24
Buildings and structures: additions to, 67; administrative buildings, 183; "bachelor's" quarters, "men's house," or men's quarters, 45, 46, 63, 64, *70,* 154; bakeries, *70,* 105; barns, 72, 78, 160, 183; barracks, 92, 93, 97, 101, 104, 105, 173, 179; bastions, *44,* 49, 61, 63, 67, *70;* bathhouses, 155; and bay windows, 105; blacksmith shops, *44,* 49, 64, 68, *70,* 74, 78, 89, 105; boarding houses, 161; boat sheds and boat-works, 47, 69; bomb shelters, 183; bunkhouses, 137, 138, 143, 150, 175; cabins, 73, 137, 146, 147, 152, *153,* 156; at canneries, 137; carpenter shops, 68, *70,* 89; chapels and churches, *70,* 72, 76–77, 78; Chinese and Chinese descendants and, 147; "Chinese Shanty," 141–42; commissaries, 101; community halls, *153;* cooper shop, *70;* covered outdoor areas, 73; dairy or kitchen, 61; dating of, *70;* dining halls and cars, *44,* 45, *153,* 154, 175, 179; dorms, 183; drug stores, 101; dugouts, 147; educational, 175; fire stations, 179; flag pole, 101; fur stores, *70;* fur trade officers' quarters, 45, 64; fur trade structure, 54; galleries, *44,* 49, 63, 66; and gender, 90; grist mills, 74; harness shops, 68, *70,* 78; health clinics, hospitals, and infirmaries, 70, 72, 101, 175, 179; hotels, 89, 101, 161; huts, 137; "Indian Hall," 46, 64; Indigenous people's trade shops, *70;* interior structures of, 67, 69;

jails, *70;* at Japanese incarceration camps, 179; kitchens, 63, *70,* 72, 76, 93, 97, 101, 105, 175; laborers' quarters, 42; laundresses' quarters, 101; laundries, 165, 170, 179; lavatories, 179; magazines, 46; mat lodge or wickiup, 156; meat houses, 64; mercantile businesses, 170; military officers' quarters, *26,* 92, 93, 97, 101, 102, 104, 105, 173, 175; offices, 68, 69, *70;* opera houses, 170; outbuildings, 69, 97, 105, 133; outhouses, 155; parsonages, 73, 78; post offices, 161; powder magazines, 63, *70;* preservation of, 21; quartermaster's depots, 91; quarters, *44,* 78; ramadas, 156, 157; rebuilt, 67; recreation halls, 175, 179; remodeled, 67; restaurants, 161; for retail trade, 69; rock shelters, 147; salmon-salting facilities, 70; saloons, 101, 161, 164, 165, 167; schools, *70,* 72, 76, 77, 161, 179, 190; servants' quarters, 64; sewage disposal plant, 179; shacks, 137; shops, 21, 46, 72, *153,* 154, 161, 165, 175; skid cabins, 152, *153;* stables, 105; stage stops, 89; and status, 68, 105; stockades, *44,* 47, 48, 61, 66, 69, *70,* 101; storehouses and storerooms, *44,* 61, 63, *70,* 72, 101; stores, *44,* 45, 49, 64, *70,* 89, 93, 148, 152, 158, 165; surgeon's quarters, 167; sutler's buildings, 101; temples, 148; tents, 152; theaters, 167; trading posts/rooms, 61, 63; truck shed, 175; warehouses, 46, 49, 68, 69, *70,* 89, 179; wash houses, *70,* 171; wharves, 69. *See also* Architecture; Dwellings; Indigenous peoples, dwellings of

Burials and cemeteries: and age, 122–23; along major routes of travel, 111, 115–16; anthropology and, 110; associated with fur trade, 91, 111, 114, 115; associated with missionaries, 72–73, 78, 111; of Basque persons, 127; and bone houses, 124; and burial goods, 111, 112, 113, 114–15, 116, 117–18, 123, 124, 125–26; and burners for paper offerings, 124; Chinese and Chinese descendants and, 6, 111, 120, 122–27, 130, 146; and class, 119, 121; and coffins, 113, 114, 117, 126; and commercial park cemeteries, 111; dog graves in, 71; and exhumation, 47, 114, 115, 117–18, 122–23, 124, 126; and family graveyards, 111, 116; and gender, 121, 122–23, 126; and grave markers, 20, 24, 26, 108–10, 118–21, 123, 124, 126, 127; historical archaeology and, 13, 15, 16, 17, 20, 24, 26, 110, 122, 127, 130; at Japanese incarceration camps, 179; legislation on, 20–21, 47, 111, 114; of marginalized groups, 26, 110, 120, 122; and memorialization of the dead, 117; of mental health patients, 125, 126; and race and ethnicity, 114, 118, 121; and reburial of pioneers, 111, 121; and religion, 118, 120, 121; rural, 111, 121, 122, 123. *See also* Indigenous peoples: burials and cemeteries associated with

Burley, David V., 45, 182

Burlington Northern and Santa Fe Railroad/Great Northern Railroad, 162

Bushby, William, 112

Bush Homestead, *86,* 90–91

Buttons: African-American troops and, 174; bone, 82; Chinese, 164; collar, 150, 171; colored, 157; decorative, 156, 157; four-hole, 157; and gender, 156; gold-plated, 150; machine-made, 82; metal, 112, 114; from military uniforms, 101; mourning, 157; nonregulation, 106; pearl, 157; phoenix, 112–13; pie-cut style, 157; plain, 157; plastic, 117; printed, 157; prison uniform, 180; prosser, 53, 157, 171; sew-through, 171; shell, 81, 157, 171; and status, 8, 106; two-hole, 157; unspecified type of, 46, 50, 66, 95, 172; uses of, 7–8; Victorian, 157; of Western origin, 164; William Astons, 144

Byram, R. Scott, 42, 137

California: Alien Land legislation in, 178; archaeological site in, 24; and Bear River Massacre, 86–87; Chinese and Chinese descendants in, 143; and Franciscan missionaries, 78; Francis Drake in, 35; fur traders in, 61; gold in, 76, 83, 131, 139, 142; Hudson's Bay Company and, 68; Indigenous peoples and, 51; lumbering in, 149; and migration, 85; nuns in, 76; and Oregon, 3; railroads in, 162; Russians in, 24; volunteer troops from, 104

California Trail, 115

Camp 3 (WA), *134,* 151

Camp and Mill News, 152

Campbell, Renae J., 30, 155

Campbell, Sarah Kathleen, 52

Camp Hemlock, *159,* 175

Campment du Sable, 88, 89

Camp Reehers, 175
Camp Sumner, 84
Campus Trash Project, 183
Camp Vancouver. *See* Fort Vancouver/Camp Vancouver/Vancouver Barracks
Camp Zig Zag, *159,* 175
Canada: and boundary with U.S., 32; Chinese and Chinese descendants in, 169; and colonization, 92; and cultural resources management, 193; economy of, 136; fur trade in, 15, 195; and Great Depression, 174; Hudson's Bay Company in, 62, 63; immigration restrictions in, 178; Japanese and Japanese descendants in, 178; Métis in, 72; and migration, 71, 85; missionaries in, 79; population of, 63; racism in, 155; residential Indigenous schools in, 128; settler colonialism in, 63; townships in, 132; and trade protectionism, 136. *See also* British Columbia; European Canadians
Canadian Confederation, 63
Canadian Cordillera, 2, 3
Canadian National Topographic Series, 29
Canadian Truth and Reconciliation Commission (TRC), 128–29
Canneries. *See under* Economic activities and trades
Canyon City, OR, 139
Capitalism, 11, 23, 24, 25, 59
Capuder, Karen Marie, 67
Cariboo region, British Columbia, 139, 144, 145
Cariboo Wagon Road, 144, 161
Carrier First Nations peoples, 63
Cascade Range, *2,* 3, 51, 84
Cataldo Mission, *60,* 78–79
Cathlapotle site, 39, 55–56, 57, 58
Catholics: biases against, in historical interpretation, 74, 88; and burials and cemeteries, 79, 121, 128; and chapels and churches, 69, 76–77, 78; and education, 76; Franciscans, 78; and identity, 121, 128; and Indigenous peoples, 76, 78, 79, 128; Jesuits, 76, 78; and material culture, 77–78, 79; and missions, 69, 76, 77–79, 128; nuns, 76; priests, 76, 77–78
Cayouse, Pierre, 76
Cayuse people, 73, 75
Cayuse War, 74, 92
Caywood, Louis: and Fort Clatsop, 42; and Fort Okanogan, 49, 61; and Fort Spokane, 19, 47,
48, 114; and Fort Vancouver, 15, *18,* 47, 69, 187; and National Park Service, *18,* 42; and race, 19; and Society for Historical Archaeology, 20; and study of fur traders' lives, 19
Cemeteries. *See* Burials and cemeteries
Central Oregon Homesteads, *159*
Ceramics: American, 102, 126, 142, 148, 161, 167, 171; and American nationalism, 94; Asian, 30, 138, 163; availability of, 77; British, 126, 142, 161; Chinese, 18, 30, 37, *38,* 39, 48, 49, 50, 55, 57, 77, 79, 102, 124–26, 147, 162, 163, 167, 171, 194; costs of, 30, 133; dating of, 23, 37, 102; and dating of archaeological sites and artifacts, 49, 64; domestic, 176; early regional scholarship on, 30; English, 30, 48, *57,* 79, 102, 167; from English and American military sites, 101; European, 48, 50, 75, 81, 148, 171; European-American, 172; French, 94, 167; and gender, 90; German, 167; Indigenous peoples and, 24, 37, 53, 55, *57;* Japanese, 30, *31,* 102, 154, 155, 156, 163, 167, 180; maker's marks on, 173; manufacture of, 17, 30, 39; Mexican, 40; Neutron Activation analysis (NAA) of, 24; sherds, 30, 37, 39, 55, 75; social context of, 80; Spanish, 40; and status, 71, 134–35, 151, 165; and technological change, 194; and Victorianism, 9; and wealth, 134–35, 160
Ceramics, decoration and glazes on: Bamboo pattern, 79, 125, 147, 163, 172; bright bands and colors, 80; brown glaze, 124, *125,* 126, 167, 171–72; carved lines, *31;* cobalt lines, *31;* as commentary, 155; Copeland pattern transferprint, 61, 75; decals, 126; Double Happiness pattern, 147, 163; fine decoration, 79; flow blue, 77; Four Seasons Flowers pattern, *125,* 126, 147, 163, 172; Garrett style, 75; Geisha Girl motifs, 163; gilt, 102, 106; hand-decorated, *31;* 48, 49, 53, *57,* 102; landscape style, 155; matching, 165, 167; minimal, 79; paint, 168; shell edge, 102; Tiger Lily floral scroll motif, *38;* transferprinted, 48, 50, 53, 71, 75, 79, 95, 102, 106, 150, 167; unspecified glaze, 102; Winter Green pattern, 124, 124n4, *125,* 126, 142, 147, 163, 172
Ceramics, forms of: bowls, 30, *31,* 39, 79, 80, 102, 124, 125, 147, 154, 167; buttons (prosser), 53, 157, 171; communal serving dishes, 80; containers, 124, 172; cream pitch-

ers, 167; crocks, 151, 172; cups, 71, 80, 95, 102, 125, 142, 147, 150, 154, 167; dishes, *125,* 138, 154; dolls, doll parts, and doll's dishes, 134, 151, 155, 167; doorknobs, 150; individualized place settings, 80; jars, 16, 39, 148, 172; kiln wasters, 24; liquor bottles, *125,* 126, 172; marbles, 134, 167; medicine vials, 126; plates and platters, 95, 151, 154, 167; saucers, 80, 95, 147, 150; sherds, 37, 153; smoking pipes, 106, 140; spoons, 172; tablewares, 126, 133, 138; tea caddy, *57;* teapots, 71, 154, 155; tea sets, miniature, 155, 167; teaware, 90, 133, 134, 151, 154, 155, 167; tureens, 167; vessels, 30, 40, 71, 125, 126, 168, 171, 172

Ceramics, types of: China (prosser), 53, 117, 157, 171; creamware, 48, 49, 50, 53, 57; earthenware, 39, 40, 79, 102, 150, 174; lusterware, 102; Majolica, 40; mochaware, 102; pearlware, 48, 53; plainware, 40, 80; redware, 17, 140; sponge wares, 80; stoneware, 16, 37, 39, 48, 50, 102, 124, *125,* 126, 150–51, 167, 172; unspecified, 46; utilitarian ware, 30; whiteware, 50, 53, 63, 71, 79, 80, 95, 126, 161, 167. *See also* Porcelain

Chamorro people, 78

Champoeg, OR, 24, 88, 89–90, *91,* 193

Chance, David H., 83

Chapman, Judith A. [Sanders], 30

Chemeketa Plain, 73

Chen, Ying-ying, 145

Chih Kung T'ang/Hong-men society building, 144

Chilkoot Trail, 6

China, 126, 136, 144, 145

China Bend, 143

Chinese and Chinese descendants: and age, 122–23; and agriculture, 172; and ancestral ties, 145; and burials and cemeteries, 6, 26, 120, 122–27, 130, 146; as business owners, 141, 163, 170; and canneries, 137, 138, 139, 169, 170, 172; and celebrations, 147; and clothing and footwear, 147; and community creation, 196; as consumers, 138; as cooks, 136, 163, 170; diet of, 138, 141, 142, 147, 164, 172; and education, 142; and fishing, 24; and gaming, 142, 144, 147, 164, 171, 172; as gardeners, 136, 170; and gender, 122–23; and general stores, 148; and Hansen's disease, 170; historical resources on, 6, 145; home province of, 122; and identity, 126, 139, 142, 145, 169, 172; increased study of, 191; Japanese as replacements for, 154; as labor, 132, 135, 136, 138, 154, 161–62, 170; as labor brokers, 145, 148; and laundries, 141, 163, 165, 170–71; legislation pertaining to, 8, 141, 142, 148, 169, 170, 172, 195; and living arrangements, 145; and logging, 170; and medicine, 148; as merchants, 145, 148, 170–71; and mining, 23, 24, 139, 140, 141, 143, 144, 145–46, 147–48, 169, 170, 172; and naturalization, 169; and opium consumption, 138, 144; organizations of, 144, 145, 172, 196; and post offices, 148; and prostitution, 144; and racism, 6, 8, 122, 124, 141, 142, 146, 148, 158, 169, 170–71, 172, 195; and railroad construction, 161–62; and recreational games, 138; and residences, 148; and resistance, 122, 148, 170, 172; as restaurant workers, 164; in rural settings, 172; as servants, 163, 170; and settlement patterns, 145, 146, 169; and skilled trades, 142; and social ties, 124, 145, 146, 148, 172; and status, 170–71; and taxes, 141, 148, 169; and temples, 148; and ties to homeland communities, 126, 139, 145, 169, 172; and urban-rural connections, 169; in urban settings, 24, 172; values of, 145; and violence, 141, 142, 148, 169, 172, 195; and wealth, 123, 147. *See also* Asians and Asian Americans; Japanese and Japanese descendants

Chinese and Chinese descendants, artifacts associated with: abacus beads, 144; animal remains, 141, 142, 144; buttons, 8, 148; canning jars, 148; ceramics, 124, 125–26, 142, 147, 148; children's belongings, 142; cleavers, 142; coffin hardware, 126; coin purse, 142; coins, 15, 142, 147; and cultural continuity, 141; dominos, 144; fencing, 123; foods and beverages, 144, 147; gaming pieces, 8, 144, 147; hazelnut shells, 142; liquor bottles, 142; opium smoking paraphernalia, 144, 147; pans, 142; picture frame, 142; seeds, 142; from shrines, 126; slate pencils, 142; tools, 141; woks, 142; women's items, 141–42; wooden altars, 123; wooden burial markers, 123; writing items, 141

Chinese company/*gūng sī*, 145–46
Chinese Consolidated Benevolent Association, 123, 125
Chinese Diaspora Project, 185
Chinook (location), 57
Chinook people, 48, 56, 57–58
Chippewa people, 114
Christianity, 117, 127–28, 155
Christophe, King, 112
Chung, Sue Fawn, 122
Church of St. Paul, 76, *77*
Civilian Conservation Corps (CCC), 160, 174–76, 180
Civil War, 94, 97, 166
Clahclellah site, 56
Clallam people, 103
Clark, William, 42
Clark County History, 188
Clatsop-Nehalem people, 37
Clatsop people, 38, 43
Clayoquot Sound, 41
Clearman, Amy Carolyn, 188
Clearwater River, 41, 139, 180
Cluggage, James, 140
Coast Range, 2, 40, 176
Coast Reservation, 24, 97, 98, 103, 104, 106
Coast Salish people, 7, 129, 135, 145
Coates, Colin Macmillan, 120
Coeur d'Alene, ID, 103
Coeur d'Alene Encampment, 78, 79
Coeur d'Alene Mission of the Sacred Heart, 78
Coeur d'Alene people, 78, 79
Coeur d'Alene Wars, 92
Cold War, 124, 192
Colonial (term), 33
Colonialism: definitions of, 9, 33; explorer narratives of, 43; fur traders and, 9; healing from, 13; Indigenous peoples and, 9, 10, 13, 23, 24, 25, 35, 51, 59, 65, 196; and oral traditions, 6; scholarship on, 10, 23, 24, 35, 51, 69. *See also* Settler colonialism
Colonial revival (term), 33
Colonial Williamsburg, 17
Columbia City. *See* Vancouver, WA
Columbia Detachment of the Royal Engineers, 92
Columbia District, 54, 92
Columbian Quincentennial, 23

Columbia Plateau, 2
Columbia Rediviva (ship), 41
Columbia River: agriculture along, 84; archaeological sites along, 3, 39, 41, 46, 48, 49, 50, 55, 112; canneries along, 137, 139; depth of, 61; European "discovery" of, 41; and fishing, 166; fur trade posts and forts along, 40, 46, 49, 50, 61, 64; Indigenous peoples along, 48, 52, 55, 57, 58, 83; industrialization along, 166; Lewis and Clark Expedition and, 41, 56; map of, *38*; migration along, 85; mining along, 143; and pollution, 166; present-day population along, 1; salmon fishery on, 64
Columbia River Gorge, 99, 151
Colvile, Andrew Wedderburn, 49n2, 64
Colville Tribes, 49, 49n2, 83
Colville Valley, 65, 83
Combes, John D., 48
Concomly (Chinook headman), 57, 58
Confederated Tribes of the Colville Reservation, 50
Confederated Tribes of the Grand Ronde Community of Oregon, 105
Confederation of Canada, 79
Connolly, Thomas J., 31, 117, 156
Consumers and consumerism: Asians and Asian descendants and, 139; and ceramic prices, 30; Chinese and Chinese descendants and, 138; and gender, 139; and industrial revolution, 195; Japanese and Japanese descendants and, 138; military officers and, 106; modern ideas of, 165; soldiers and, 94, 106; and Victorianism, 133, 167; and wealth, 168
Converse, Kristin O., 30
Cook, James, 40
Cosper Creek, 105, 106
Cotter, John L., 17
Cove Creek Civilian Conservation Corps camp, 175
Cowlitz River, 85
Cox, Ross, 49
Crabtree, Don E., 87–88
Crazy Horse, 97
Cree people, 108
Creighton, Janet, 67, 191
Crook, George, 97
Cross, Osborne, 84

Index

Cultural resources management: artifacts recovered from, 79; conflict about, 25, 196; at Fort Vancouver, 69; at Fort Walla Walla, 173; funding for, 193; "gray literature" produced by, 67; laws and regulations associated with, 192, 193–94; private sector and, 187; in San Juan Islands, 103; at Vancouver Barracks, 93
Cutler, Lyman, 99
Cutts, Richard, 42
Cyrus and Mary Ellen Jacob house/Cyrus Jacobs-Uberuaga House, 167, 168, 186
Czehatowski, Michel, 102

Daisy Creek, 140
Dakelh people, 145
Dalles, The, 113, 170
Darby, Melissa C., 35
D'Arcy Leper colony, *159*, 170
Daughters of the American Revolution (DAR), 115, 116
Dean Channel, 40, 81
Deetz, James, 20, 119
De Laguna, Frederica, 18, 19, 23
Demers, Modeste, 76
Denny Island, 80
Depoe Bay, 35
Deschutes River, 112
DeSmet, Pierre-Jean, 76, 78
Dethlefsen, Edwin, 20
DeWint, Arthur, 167
Diseases and medical conditions: and age, 120; bone spurs, 118; Chinese and Chinese descendants and, 148; chronic infections, 118; colds, 167; consumption, 167; coughs, 167; crushing injuries, 118; degenerative illnesses, 118; dental, 118; digestive disorders, 167; diphtheria, 120; dysentery, 52, 74; European Americans and, 117–18; fractured ribs, 118; and germ theory, 120; Hansen's disease, 170; Indigenous peoples and, 52, 53, 58, 72, 73, 74, 79, 80, 82, 85, 88, 128, 194; and infant mortality, 116–17; and life expectancy, 120; malaria, 52, 58, 70, 73; measles, 52, 74; miasmic theory of, 120; missionaries and, 72; pterygium, 180; scarlet fever, 120; small pox, 52, 120; syphilis, 163; treatments for, 70, 79, 138, 148, 161, 162, 163, 192; typhoid, 120; urinary disorders, 163, 167; venereal, 163

Don Island, 138–39
Douglas, James, 99, 100
Drake, Francis, 35, 36
Drake's Bay, 35
Dunne-za/Dane-zaa people (Beaver Indians), 45, 46
DuPont, 66
Dupuis, Edward, 89
Dwellings: African Americans and, 168–69; at American Camp, 101; and bathtubs, 167; British Americans and, 21; cabins, 90, 95, 131, 133; at Champoeg, 89, 90, *91;* for chaplains and priests, 76; Chinese and Chinese descendants and, 141, *142,* 148, 167; communal, 80; at fur trade forts and posts, 1, 42, 43, *44,* 45, 49, 61, 63, 64, 66, 67, 68, 69, *70,* 135; and gendered spaces, 90; and glass windows, 150; on homesteads, 133, 160; locating of, 90; at logging and lumbering sites, 150; mid-19th century, 89; at military installations, 92–93, 104, 105; at missions, 72, 73, 74, 75, 76; 19th-century artifacts from, 42; parsonages, 73; post-World War II, 192; preservation of, 33, 185; public archaeology and, 186; and status, 165–66, 168; telephones in, 150; tents as, 152; two-story, 133; and Victorianism, 167, 168. *See also* Buildings and structures; Indigenous peoples, dwellings of

Eagle Cliff, WA, 137
Earl, Louisa, 133
Earl, Robert, 131, 135
Earl, William, 131, 133, 139
East India Company, 48
East Indian persons, 120
East Kootenay, British Columbia, 123–24
Ecology. *See* Environment
Economic activities and trades: animal husbandry, 131; blacksmithing, *44,* 49, 61, 64, 68, *70,* 74, 78, 89, 105; boatbuilding, 61, 164, 176; canneries, 24, 132, *134,* 137–39, 169, 170, 172, 179, 196; cattle supply, 139; ceramics manufacture, 17, 24, 30, 132; fishing, 24, 64, 65, 80, 132, 137; grain supply, 139; hops cultivation and processing, 135; and impact on natural environment, 132, 139; Indigenous peoples and, 144, 196; iron production, 132; laundry services, 145, 165, 170; logging

and lumbering, 130; miso production, 138; orcharding, 133; peddling, 131; and profit sharing, 146; prostitution, 145; ranching, 131, 132, 136, 139, 160; restaurants, 144, 161, 164; sake brewing, 138; selling fresh vegetables, 138, 147; soy sauce production, 138; and technological change, 194; trade item manufacturing, 61; tradesmen and, 144; wheat cultivation, 160; woodworking, 61. *See also* Agriculture; Logging and lumbering; Mining

Egyptian Theater, 167

Elizabethtown, OR, 95, 117

Elk City, ID, 139

Elkton, OR, 61

Emmett, ID, 127

England. *See* Great Britain and England

English Camp, San Juan Island, 86, *100,* 101–2

Enslaved persons, 9, 58, 85

Environment: and agriculture, 132; and alteration of water sources, 11, 88, 132, 182, 196; Civilian Conservation Corps and, 174; and cleanup projects, 160, 176, 197; and climate change, 182; diversity of, 3; features of, *2;* and fisheries and fish canning, 132, 196; and fur trade, 4, 34, 40, 46, 53, 194; and historic preservation, 197; human adaption to, 8; importance of, 3, 5, 11–12, 27; and industry, 132, 166, 176, 194, 197; and introduction of new species, 34, 71, 88, 132, 194; and landfills, 160, 176, 183, 197; and modern issues, 12, 194; and Oregon Trail migration, 88; and overexploitation of natural resources, 34, 40, 46, 53, 88, 132, 182, 194, 196; and pollution, 166; and ranching, 132; and sustainability, 11–12; and technology, 11, 194; and urbanization, 182; U.S. military and, 92

Esther Short Park, 165, 166

Ethnography, 18, 23, 36, 52, 57, 65

Ethnohistory, 23, 37, 57, 65

Eugene, OR, 135, 185

European Americans: and agriculture, 74; burials of, 117–18, 123; clothing styles of, 90; and commercial fishing and canneries, 137; and education, 74; and frontiers, 19; and gold mining, 145; and historic preservation, 33; and Indigenous peoples, 9–10, 17–18, 54, 57, 58; and law, 74; as majority of population, 5; and medicine, 74; and race and ethnicity, 106; and religion, 74; as soldiers, 106

European Canadians, 40, 41, 53, 81, 128, 144. *See also* French Canadians

Europe and the People without History (Wolf), 23

Europeans: British, 121; Belgians, 76; and burials, 126; and colonization, 9, 20; and conflict, 41, 53; and demand for furs, 65; and disease, 52; Germans, 92; and gold rushes, 143; Greeks, 168; as immigrants, 4; and Indigenous peoples, 33, 35, 37, 40, 53, 57, 58; Irish, 92; and land, 41, 43; and logging and lumbering, 151; Portuguese, 140; Russians, 24; Scandinavians, 137; Scots, 121; Serbians, 168; and shipwrecks, 35, 37; Spanish, 40, 43; values of, 81, 83; Welsh, 68, 121

Ewen Cannery, *134,* 138–39

Ewing Young-Sidney Smith Cabin, *86,* 90

Explorers: British, 35–36, 40; and Chinook territory, 51; historical archaeology and, 5; and Hudson's Bay Company, 51; and impact on Indigenous peoples, 194; on implements possessed by Indigenous peoples, 37; on Indigenous horse herds, 51; map of sites associated with, *36;* maritime, 35–36, 40; preservation of sites related to, 33; Russian, 40; Spanish, 40, 43. *See also* Lewis and Clark expedition

Fairfax, WA, *134,* 154

Fee, Jeffrey M., 147

Fellows, William, 164

Ferguson, Linda L., 30

Fergusson, Pete, 164

Finlay, Jacques Raphael (Jaco), 47, 61, 114

Fish and shellfish: bass, 166; catfish, 166; chub, 157; clams, 75; early abundance of, 10; and environmental damage, 196; eulachon, 145; Indigenous peoples and, 62; mussels, 61; non-native, 166; reduced dietary reliance on, 68; salmon, 34, 50, 54, 64, 66, 68, 81, 137, 145, 157, 166, 196; shad, 166; steelhead, 47, 157, 166; sturgeon, 166; suckers, 157; as supplement to military rations, 105; trout, 166. *See also* Animals; Birds

Fisherville, British Columbia, 123

Fishery site, 64

Fishing: American immigrants and, 137; and canneries, 24, 132, *134*, 137–39, 169, 170, 172, 179, 196; Chinese and Chinese descendants and, 24; commercial, 24, 64, 65, 80, 132, 137; environmental impact of, 132; and fish preservation, 137; gear for, 56, 175; Hudson's Bay Company and, 64; impact of dams and reservoirs on, 196; Indigenous peoples and, 47, 56, 65, 80, 137, 145, 157; Japanese and Japanese descendants and, 138, 155; soldiers and, 175; and technological change, 137, 194; and water pollution, 166

Fitzgerald, Kimberli, 130

Fitz-Gerald, Kyla, 180

Fladmark, Knut R., 23, 40, 44, 52

Flathead people, 78

Fletcher, Francis, 36

Flood of 1894, 99

Florence, ID, *134*, 139, 146

Foods and beverages: antelope, 157; apples, 66; Asian, 138, 147; baking powder, 160; barley, 66, 84; bass, 166; beans, 63, 75; beaver, 157; beef, 67, 68, 75, 105, 106, 147, 157, 163, 164, 170; beets, 179; berries, 145; blackberries, 190; canned and preserved, 137, 138, 151, 155, 167, 169, 172, 138; catfish, 166; catsup, 134, 163; cherries, 181; chicken, 63, 93, 105, 141, 168, 169; Chinese olive, 142, 147; chubs, 157; coffee, 63, 105; condiments, 138, 163; cooking oil, 155; corn, 63, 66, 75; costs of, 192; cranberries, 66; dairy, 66; deer, 67, 75, 82, 157; domestic, 138, 142; dried fruit, 105; duck, 141; eggs, 63, 93, 168; elk, 67, 68, 157; extracts and flavorings, 163; fish, 68, 105, 157; fowl, 68; fruit, 151, 153, 157, 172; geese, 141; and gender, 160; goats, 157; grains, 84; grape juice, 163; ground pepper, 134; ham, 105; hazel nuts, 63, 142; horses, 157; huckleberries, 52, 190; imported, 142; Indigenous peoples and, 156, 157; Japanese, 155; lard, 160; Lea & Perrins Worcestershire Sauce, 101–2; legumes, 150; marrow, 61, 68, 75; meats, 105, 151, 153; milk, 105, 153, 163; miso, 138; molasses, 105; mussels, 61; oats, 66, 84; olive oil, 134; peaches, 63, 75; peas, 63, 66, 75; pemmican, 34, 45, 55; pepper sauce, 134; pickled vegetables, 138; pickles, 134; plantain, 190; plums, 181; pond lily wocus, 157; pork, 68, 106, 138, 141, 147, 157; potatoes, 53, 63, 66, 83, 179; poultry, 157; prepared, 160; prisoners of war and, 174; produce, 105; quality of, 174; rice, 138; roots, 157; salmon, 66, 68, 81, 137, 145, 157, 166; salted pork, 63; sauces, 163; seeds, 157; shad, 166; sheep, 67, 68, 157; soups and stews, 67, 138; soy sauce, 138, 172; spices, 160, 163; squash, 75; and status and wealth, 134, 166; steelhead, 157, 166; storage of, 73, 150–51; strawberries, 190; sturgeon, 166; suckers, 157; sugar, 105; Szechuan peppers, 142; tea, 147; trout, 166; turkey, 141; unspecified, 170; U.S. military and, 105; vegetables, 84, 138, 153, 169, 179; venison, 106; waste of, 184; waterfowl, 157; wheat, 66, 75, 83, 84, 89, 131; wild, 142; wild game, 147; wild plants, 138; Worcestershire sauce, 163

Foods and beverages, alcoholic: ale, 167; beer, 155, 161, 163, 175, 176; champagne, 106, 163, 167; gin, 151, 161, 175; liquors, 101, 142, 143, 147; sake, 138, 155, 172; unspecified types of, 101, 138, 140, 151, 155, 163, 166, 167, 175, 177, 183, 184; whiskey, 105, 147, 151, 155, 161, 167, 172, 176; wine, 147, 161, 163, 167, 175, 176

Foote, Mary Haviland Hallock (Molly), 167

Foote House, 186

Fort Astoria/Fort George, *36*, 48–49, 50, 61, 63, 115

Fort Boise, 166, 167

Fort Bridger, WY, 85

Fort Cascades, *86*, 99

Fort Clatsop, 17, *36*, 41–43

Fort Colvile: archaeology at, 21, 64, 102; buildings and archaeological features at, 64; Hudson's Bay Company and, 60, 61, 114, 143; as larger, significant post, 60, 64; layout of, 64–65; location of, *60*, 61, 64; and move from Fort Spokane, 114; and move to Fort Sheppard, 143; naming of, 49n2, 64; purposes of, 64; racial diversity at, 65

Fort Defiance, *36*, 41, 43

Fort D'Epinette/Fort St. John's, *36*, 44, 45–46, 61

Fort George/Fort Astoria, *36*, 48–49, 50, 61, 63, 115

Fort Hall, 16, *60*, 61–62, 85, *86*, 90

Fort Hope, *60*, 81, 143

Fort Hoskins, *86*, 104–5
Fort Kamloops/Thompson's River Post/*Secwepemc* Kamloops Village, 36, 54
Fort Lane, *86*, 94, 97, *98*, 103
Fort Langley: activities at, 66, 137; archaeology at, 65–66; first location of, 65–66; and founding of British Columbia as a colony, 143; historic reconstruction at, 17, 19; Hudson's Bay Company and, 59, 60, 65, 66, 137; map of, *60*; second location of, 65, 66; size of, 60, 66
Fort Langley National Historic Site, 65, 66
Fort Lugenbeel, *86*, 99
Fort McLoughlin, 80
Fort Nez Percé/Fort Walla Walla: activities at, 63; African Americans at, 173–74; archaeology at, 63–64, 92, *159*, 173–74; burnings of, 63; characteristics of, 63; Hudson's Bay Company and, 59; Indigenous peoples and, 63–64; location of, *36*, *50*, *60*; Northwest Company and, 63; as part of Walula City, 63; U.S. military and, 63, 173
Fort Nisqually, 60, 66–68, 191
Fort Okanogan, *36*, *44*, 49–50, *60*, 61, 82
Fort Okanogan Interpretative Center, 50
Fort Orford, *86*, 94, 97
Fort Ross, 24
Fort Rupert, 61
Fort San Miguel, 40
Fort Sherman, 103
Fort Simcoe, 103
Fort Spokane/Spokan House: abandonment of, 47, 61, 63, 114; activities at, 47; archaeology at, 19, 47–48, 50, 173; description of, 47; historical interpretation of, 19; Hudson's Bay Company and, 47, 48, 61, 114; Indigenous peoples and, 47, 48, 114; maps of, *36*, *44*, *159*; Northwest Company and, 47, 48, 114; Pacific Fur Company and, 47, 48; and technological change, 173; U.S. military and, 173
Fort Steilacoom, *86*, 94
Fort Stevens, *86*, 94
Fort St. James, 43, *60*, 62–63
Fort St. John's/Fort D'Epinette, *36*, *44*, 45–46, 61
Fort St. John's massacre, 45, 61
Fort Umpqua, *60*, 61, 103, 104
Fort Vancouver: activities at, 135, 137; archaeology at, 50, 59, 102; artifacts from, 8, 17, *18*, 30, 48, 90, *112;* buildings at, 8, 135; as collection point for pelts, 49, 61; communication with, 64; establishment of, 48, 61; first Catholic mass at, 76; first location of, *36*, *47*, *50*, 188; function of, 49; goods available at, 77; and historic preservation, 74, 194; as Hudson's Bay Company headquarters, 58; maps of, *36*, *86*; Marcus and Narcissa Whitman at, 59; and National Historic Preservation Act of 1966, 20; officers at, 105–6; and proximity to Camp Vancouver, 91; public archaeology at, 187, 188–89; second location of, 47, 50, 68–72; settler colonial contexts at, 193; size of, *60;* and status and wealth, 135; surgeon at, 108; wheat shipments to, 89
Fort Vancouver/Camp Vancouver/Vancouver Barracks: archaeology and archaeological features at, 93, 94, 165, 173, 174; buildings and spaces at, 92–93, 94; and City of Vancouver, 164; and Civilian Conservation Corps (CCC), 175; as Columbia District headquarters, 92, 173; construction at, 92, 173; establishment of, 91; ethnicity at, 92; hierarchy at, 93; historical documentation on, 94; lumber milling at, 152, 174; Regiment of Mounted Riflemen at, 84; renaming of, 91; renovation at, 173; size of, 92; U.S. Army and, 91; Vancouver Arsenal at, 92; Victorianism at, 93; wharf at, 92
Fort Vancouver National Monument/National Historic Site, 1, *4*, 17
Fort Vancouver Village, 1, 5, 19, 90, *112*, 188
Fort Victoria, 60
Fort Walla Walla. *See* Fort Nez Percé/Fort Walla Walla
Fort Waters, 74
Fort William, 112–13
Fort Yale, 143
Fort Yamhill, *26*, *86*, 104, 105–6
Fowke, Gerard, 113
Francaviglia, Richard, 118–19
Fraser, Simon, 43, 44
Fraser Canyon War, 92
Fraser River: canneries along, 137, 138; Fort Langley at, 65; gold mining along, 65, 103, 139, 143; Indigenous settlements along, 81; tributaries of, 54
Fraser River Canyon, 81, 143
Fraser River Valley, 119, 128, 135

Fraser River War, 144
French, Jamie, 171
French-Canadian Archaeological Project, 76
French Canadians: and agriculture, 70, 88; building styles of, 67, 70, 73, 90; in Colville Valley, 65; and education, 72, 76; at Fort Nisqually, 67; at Fort Vancouver, 68; and fur trade, 70, 72, 76, 88; graves of, 121; and intermarriage, 67, 76, 88; and religion, 72, 76, 88, 121; and White settlers, 65, 121; in Willamette Valley, 72, 73, 76, 88, 121. *See also* European Canadians
French Prairie, 72, 76, 88, 121, 131
Frescoln, Carol A., 101
Friday Harbor, 101
Fur trade: and agriculture, 66, 67; Americans and, 4, 48; British and, 4, 12, 48; in Canada, 15, 62, 63, 195; and colonialism, 9; and copper, 113; ecological impact of, 4, 34, 40, 46, 53, 194; and hierarchy, 45, 46, 54; and industry, 60–61; maritime, 24, 40, 57, 113; mature state of, 39–40; processes of, 44, 54, 61, 64, 65, 68; scholarship on, 3, 15, 16, 17, 19, 20, 24, 29, 34, 51, 59, 63–64, 69, 79; sites associated with, 17, 19, 23, 28, *36*, 44–51, 60–71, 88; social impact of, 4; and status, 45, 55; terrestrial, 40, 41, 43–50. *See also* Hudson's Bay Company; Indigenous peoples, and fur trade; Northwest Company; Pacific Fur Company
Fur traders: and agriculture, 66, 72, 83, 85, 88, 89–90; and alternate employment, 62; British, 109; children of, 10, 69, 72; and Christian missions, 88; and colonialism, 13; and education, 69, 72; independent, 114; and intermarriage, 67, 76, 88, 114; and manufacturing, 61; marginalization of, 83; and religion, 76; scholarship on, 19, 24, 51, 59, 69; seasonal activities of, 43–44; and trade goods, 44; and violence, 45, 46, 53. *See also* Indigenous peoples, and fur trade: and interactions with fur traders and companies

Gardin/Home Guard Indians, 63
Garth, Thomas R., 63, 74, 76
Gatke, Robert Moulton, 16, 73
Gaw, Linda P., 165
Geisel, Andrew, 117
Geisel, Henry, 117

Geisel, John (father), 95, 117
Geisel, John (son), 117
Geisel Homestead and Monument, *86*, 95, 96, 117, 120
Geisel Massacre, 96, 117
Gender: and burials and cemeteries, 113, 121, 122–23, 126; and buttons, 156; and ceramics, 77, 90; Chinese and Chinese descendants and, 122–23; and Civilian Conservation Corps, 174; and consumer behavior, 139; and diet, 160; and dwelling spaces, 90; and homesteading, 160; and logging camps, 151, 152; and mining, 140; and railroad construction and operations, 161; and resistance, 176; and studies of colonial homes, 25; and studies of male incarceration camps, 25; and topics for future study, 193; and Victorianism, 9, 93, 133, 141, 151, 168, 193; and wealth, 168; during World War II, 176, 193
Geneva Convention, 180
George Bush Homestead, *86*, 90–91
German Americans, 133
Germany, 92, 100, 174
Geronimo, 97
Gifford Pinchot National Forest, 51, 175
Ginakangeek village, *60*, 81
Gleason, Eric, *171*
Goebel, Ted, 97
Gold Beach, OR, 95, 96
Golden Hind (ship), 35
Gold mining. *See* Mining: of gold
Grabert, G. F., 50
Graham Island, 52
Grand Coulee Dam, 64
Grand Ronde Indian Agency, 105
Grand Ronde Reservation, 95, 107, 113, 190, 191, 195
Grand Ronde Tribe, 106
Grant, Ulysses S., 97
Grant House, 92
Graves. *See* Burials and cemeteries
Gray, Robert, 41, 57
Great Basin, 2, 3, 22
Great Britain and England: brick manufacturing in, 30; clothing standards in, 8; colonies of, 17; and colonization, 72; commerce centers in, 22; and glass tariffs, 30–31; nail industry in, 31, 32; and Queen Victoria, 9; and Royal Engineers, 92; and Royal Marines, 100, 101,

102, 144; and San Juan Islands, 99–100; and Spain, 40; and U.S./Canada boundary, 32, 99–100, 103; U.S. soldiers from, 92
Great Depression, 152, 158, 159, 160, 165, 174
Great Migration of 1843, 85, 89
Great Northern/Burlington Northern and Santa Fe Railroad, 162
Great Plains, 51
Great Salt Lake, 85
Greeks, 168
Greenhow, Thomas, 136
Green Lake Gardens Company, 181
Griffin Bay, 101
Griffin Gulch, OR, 139
Grima, Reuben, 188
Guangdong Province, China, 122
Guangzhou, China, 145
Gulf Islands, 129
Gŭng sī/Chinese company, 145–46
Gurcke, Karl, 30

Hague Convention, 174
Haida Gwaii/Queen Charlotte Islands, 40, 52, 53
Haida people, 40, 53–54, 103, 127, 145
Haiti, 112
Hajda, Yvonne, 9
Hamilton, Basil G., 16, 46
Hamilton, Scott, 45
Hanford, WA, *159*, 176, 177
Hanford Workers Camp, 177, 197
Hannah, Jean, 155
Hapgood, Hume and Company cannery, 137
Hardesty, Donald L., 19
Harney, William S., 100
Harrington, J. C., 17, 29
Harris, Jillian, 129
Harris Homestead, *86*, 95
Harrison, Benjamin, 150
Hartse, Caroline, 155
Hatheway, John S., 91
Hawaii, 68, 123. *See also* Native Hawaiians
Hayman, Erma, 168
Health. *See* Diseases and medical conditions
Heiltsuk people, 80–81
Hells Canyon, 148
Henderson's Brothel, 163
Hermann's Bordello, 163
Hezeta, Bruno de, 40
Hill, Cayla L., 77

Historical archaeology: African Americans and, 196; and anthropology, 8, 15, 19, 23, 51, 63, 185, 194; and artifacts, 6, 8, 20, 21, 22–23, 29–32, 35, 50, 102; benefits of, 8, 197; biases in, 6, 10; and collaboration with descendants, 24, 26–27, 126, 130, 185, 187, 189–90, 191, 195; and community archaeology, 14, 184, 185, 186; and cultural resources management, 11, 25, 93, 193–94; and dates of sites, 27–28; documentation of change by, 194; and educational models, 184–85; education in, 188; and ethnography and ethnohistory, 18, 23; evolution of, 5–6, 10, 15, 16–27; formal status for, 20; goals of, 1, 17; and history, 8, 18; influences on, 182; and marginalized populations, 8, 11, 195–96; methodologies of, 1, 6, 8, 17, 18–19, 20, 21, 22–26, 27, 28–32, 97; and National Historic Preservation Act of 1966, 20; and oral histories, 1, 6, 8, 24; and Pacific Northwest, 176; and post-World War II sites, 192; and public archaeology, 14, 25, 26, 184, 185, 186, 187; and relationship to current issues, 182; and salvage projects, 17, 19, 20, 165, 196; and selection of sites to investigate, 192–93; and settler colonialism, 13, 185; and topics for future research, 192–93; and understanding of Pacific Northwest, 5–6; and urban sites, 193; and Victorianism, 9, 19, 20, 107; and volunteer archaeology, 185; and written records, 1, 6, 8, 17, 20, 24, 28. *See also* Indigenous peoples, historical archaeology and
Historical Archaeology, 20
Historical archaeology, focuses of: African Americans, 160, 173, 195; American exceptionalism, 19; Asians and Asian descendants, 25, 138; Basques, 26; burials and cemeteries, 13, 15, 16, 17, 20, 24, 26, 110, 122, 127, 130; canneries, 24, 138; capitalism, 11, 24, 25; ceramics, 30; Chinese and Chinese descendants, 6, 23, 24, 26, 122, 147, 148, 160, 169, 170, 185, 191, 195, 196; Civilian Conservation Corps camps, 160; climate, 159; colonialism, 24; competition, 20; conflict, 99, 103, 197; consumerism, 23, 24, 25, 26, 30, 195; domestic developments, 5; early exploration and settlement, 5, 8, 10–11, 20, 25, 28, 33, 35, 107, 194; economy, 159, 195–96; entrepreneurs' role in settlement,

99; environmental change, 12; extractive industry creators, 5; farming, 130; fishing, 24, 130; frontier forts, 25, 34, 92; frontiers, 19–20, 22; fur trade, 16, 19, 20, 24, 33, 35, 50–51, 59, 69, 82, 99, 194–95; gender, 193; global contexts, 23; homesteads, 25, 158, 160; households, 20; Hudson's Bay Company sites, 102; identity, 11, 20, 25, 169; industrial developments, 5, 28; inequality, 20, 25; Japanese and Japanese descendants, 25, *31*, 154, 160, 178–80, 191, 195, 196; Lewis and Clark overwintering site, 42; logging and lumbering, 130, 149, 150; Manhattan Project, 176; marginalized peoples, 11, 25, 26, 191, 195; military posts and troops, 24, 99, 102, 104, 107, 160, 197; mining, 24, 130, 145, 147; missions and missionaries, 52, 72, 74; modernity, 182; 19th-century manufacturing, 130; material culture, 102; Oregon Trail, 16; "pioneer industries," 16–17; and race and ethnicity, 10, 17–18, 19, 24, 25, 96, 160, 165, 173, 191, 193, 195; ranching, 130; refuse disposal behavior, 26; Rogue River War, 94, 95, 96; settlement creators, 5; settler colonialism, 10, 24; settlers, 197; site formation processes, 26; technology, 11, 159; 20th-century work and incarceration camps, 25, 160, 176; urban areas, 28, 160; workers, 197; World War II shipyards, 176. *See also* Indigenous peoples, historical archaeology and

Historic preservation: and ages of sites, 27; and establishment of sites, 33; and Fort Vancouver, 74; and Indigenous peoples, 49, 67; motives for, 33; and private property, 67; and types of sites protected, 33; and Waiilatpu Mission, 74

Historic reconstruction: at Colonial Williamsburg, 17; at Fort Clatsop, 17; at Fort Langley, 19, 65, 66; at Fort Vancouver, 17, 69; motives for, 59; negative impacts of, 19; role of historical archaeology in, 17; on San Juan Island, 101

Historic Sites Service Operations Method, 29

Hobler, Philip M., 80

Home Guard Indians/*Gardin*, 63

Homesteads: activities at, 131, 160; African Americans and, 90–91; archaeological sites associated with, 86, 89, 95, *159*, 160; definition of, 133; dwellings on, 133, 160; failure and abandonment of, 159, 161, 174; and gender, 160; and gold rushes, 139; and government policies, 160; and landscape level analysis, 25; and railroads, 160; U.S. legislation on, 133; variety in, 160–61; William Earl Homestead, 131, 133–35

Hong-men society/*Chih Kung T'ang* building, 144, 172

Hosken, Kaitlyn Nicole, 94, 180

Hub Camp, 152

Hudson Bay, 64

Hudson's Bay Company: and agriculture, 64, 65, 66, 68, 83, 99, 100, 135; and boat building, 66; and British/English goods, 31, 102; and Canadian immigrants, 85; and cemeteries, 91; in Champoeg area, 88, 89; clay tobacco pipe styles related to, 48; and company stores, 66, 68, 144; and consumer items, 113; and cranberry packing, 66; and dairying, 66, 67, 68; and education, 69; and employee racial diversity, 65, 67, 71; expansion of activities of, 60, 61, 64, 70; and fishing, 64; and Fort Colvile, 64–65, 114; and Fort Hall, 62; and Fort Hope, 81, 143; and Fort Langley, 59, 65–66, 137; and Fort Nez Percé/Fort Walla Walla, 50, 63; and Fort Okanogan, 49; and Fort Spokane, 47, 63, 114; and Fort St. James, 62–63; and Fort Vancouver, 5, 8, 47, 58, 59, 68–72, 91, 108, 113, 137; and Fort Yale, 143; and gold mining, 142; headquarters of, 48, 58, 71; and Indigenous peoples, 63, 64, 65, 73, 79, 83, 99, 103; and iron production, 66; leaders of, 49n2, 60, 64, 99; and livestock, 66, 68, 99; and lumbering, 64, 68; and Northwest Company, 44, 45, 49, 54, 114; piers of, 101; and profit, 65; and Puget Sound Agricultural Company, 66, 67; ransoming of enslaved colonists by, 74; and retail sales, 133; and Rocky Mountain Fort, 45; and salmon curing and canning, 66, 68, 137; and status, 68; and Thompson's River Post, 54; trails of, 136

Hudspeth's Cutoff, 85

Humbird Lumber/Sand Point Lumber Company, 162

Hunting: along Oregon Trail, 88; Asians and, 138; children and, 167; equipment for, 73, 114, 156, 157; as "frontier" activity, 19; In-

digenous peoples and, 43, 51, 54, 73, 81, 82, 145, 156, 157, 195; soldiers and, 105; during Victorian era, 167–68
Hussey, John A., 42
Hutchings, Rich, 191

Idaho: African Americans in, 168–69; archaeological sites in, 16, 20, *31*, 88, 103, 117–18, 146, 158, 162–63, 166–69, 178–80, 186–87; Basque in, 127, 168, 169; Bear River Massacre in, 87–88; Bolvile Run in, 184; burials and cemeteries in, 20, 117–18, 122, 123, 127; Campus Trash Project in, 183, 184; capital of, 166; Chinese and Chinese descendants in, 122, 123, 145, 146, 161, 162, 163–64, 167, 191; Civilian Conservation Corps camps in, 175, 180; collaboration with descendants in, 186–87, 191; drinking age in, 184; elites in, 167–68; Forest Service Passport-in-Time projects in, 185; fur trade in, 46; gold mining in, 63, 139–40, 145, 166, 170; Greeks in, 168; historic preservation in, 20; Indigenous peoples in, 20, 51, 87–88, 191; Japanese and Japanese descendants in, 168, 178–80, 191; Japanese internment camps in, *31,* 178–80; land rights in, 132; maps of, *2, 36, 60, 86, 134, 159;* military posts in, 103, 166; Oregon Trail in, 85, *87;* as part of Inland Empire, 19; as part of Pacific Northwest, 1; public archaeology in, 186; railroads in, 161, 162, 166; roads in, 161, 184; Serbians in, 168; townships in, 132
Idaho City, ID, *134,* 140
Idaho State Historic Preservation Office, 87
Independence, MO, 85
Indian Camp, Bellevue Farm, 102
Indian Race Track/Kalama't site, *36,* 51–52
Indian Wars, 83, 174
Indigenous peoples: and agency, 12, 25, 34, 81, 96, 128, 187, 195; and alienation, 92; and ancestral and sacred things and places, 7, 67, 110; and art, *4,* 51, 127; and assimilation, 51, 62, 72, 73, 83, 84, 129, 137, 159, 190; Canadian restrictions on, 144; ceremonies of, 80; and Christianity, 59, 72, 74, 78, 127–28; and colonialism, 9, 10, 13, 23, 24, 25, 33–34, 35, 51, 59, 65, 196; and communication, 3; and credit, 46; diet of, 50, 54, 61, 62, 67, 81; and disease, 52, 53, 58, 72, 73, 74, 79, 80, 82, 85, 88, 128, 194; displacement of, 194; and early contact, 33–35, 37, 40; and environment, 46, 92; and equality, 82; Euro-Indigenous offspring as, 10, 37, 39; heritage and landscapes of, 196; and hierarchy, 53; historical maps showing, 28; and horses, 51–52, 113, 135; and Hudson's Bay Company, 64, 65, 79, 83, 103; and identity, 135, 157; impact of, on Euro-American settlements, 35; and Indian reservations, 97, 98, 103, 104, 107, 113, 135, 156, 190, 195; and intermarriage, 65, 67, 76, 88, 90, 96, 114, 136; and kin ties, 10; lands of, 9, 99, 135, 136; legislation pertaining to, 74, 80, 195; and Lewis and Clark expedition, 41–42; marginalization of, 85; and medicine, 74, 81, 127; and meeting places, 47; and missionaries, 41, 59, 72, 73, 74, 76, 84, 127, 128; and Oregon Trail migration, 71, 88; orphaned, 69, 76; and perceptions of Pacific Northwest, 3; and political and social organization, 9–10, 54; and post-World War II public projects, 19; pre-contact, 41, 50, 101; protection of sites related to, 23; and racism, 65, 92, 158, 195; and resistance, 59, 71, 81, 103, 113, 128, 137, 144, 157, 190, 196; and seasonality, 49, 50, 51, 52, 58, 80, 86, 135, 145; and secret societies, 127; settlement patterns of, 53, 80, 84; settlements and communities of, 37, 48, 49, 50, 54, 55; and settler colonialism, 9, 10, 13, 156, 196; and shipwrecks, 35, 37–38, 55; and sites of cultural and historical significance, 67; and slavery, 58, 74; and social inequality, 92; social networks of, 135; and status, 51, 53, 55, 58, 71, 81, 82, 127; and subsistence, 82; suppression of, 85; and technological change, 194; and tools, 71, 107; and trade, 3, 37, 38, 39, 42, 45, 46, 47, 51, 53–54, 55–56, 58, 62, 63, 113; and transportation routes, 170; treaties with, 71, 132–33; and U.S. military, 24, 92, 103; and wealth, 51, 58, 113, 157. *See also* Artifacts, associated with Indigenous peoples
Indigenous peoples, activities of: agriculture, 72, 74, 79, 83, 105, 190, 196; animal husbandry, 107; argillite carving, 53; at canneries, 137, 196; as couriers, 145; as cowboys, 136; dancing, 135; feasting, 54; fishing, 47, 56, 65, 80, 137, 145, 157; food gathering, preparation,

and storage, 47, 52, 54, 137; fur trapping, 144; gambling, 47, 135; gathering, 51, 52, 107, 136, 145, 157; gift giving/potlaches, 80, 127, 128, 135; horse racing, 51–52, 135; hunting, 43, 51, 54, 82, 145, 156, 157, 195; as laborers, 9, 10, 63, 132, 135, 136, 197; laundry services, 145; mining, 139, 140, 143–44, 145; as packers, 145; prostitution, 145; providing food to immigrants and settlers, 53, 54, 63; as ranch hands, 136; selling items to tourists, 135; unspecified "folk industries," 46; using sweat lodges, 135; wage work, 80, 145, 196; woodworking, 149

Indigenous peoples, and archaeological collaboration: and Archaeology Roadshow, 187; at Bridge River site, 82; at burial and cemetery sites, 113, 128, 129–30, 191, 195; with early archaeologists, 114; increases in, 26–27, 184, 189–90, 191; at Indian reservation sites, 104, 105, 106, 107, 195; issues addressed by, 72; with museums, 185; and Native American Graves Protection and Repatriation Act of 1990, 114; Native protests leading to, 114; at residential schools, 128, 129–30, 190, 195; at Rogue River War sites, 185; at *Secwepemc* Village site, 54; at Tsek'ehne village site, 62, 195

Indigenous peoples, artifacts associated with: abraders, 52, 56, 79; adzes, 55; alcohol bottles, 56; of American origin, 144; animal remains, 50, 61, 62, 82; argillite, 53, 57, 79; arrowheads, 46; arrow points, 56; associated with fur trade, 49, 57; awls, 61; basalt spear point, 75; basket items, 54; beads, 45, 52, 54, 55, 57, 61, 75, 81, 82, 90, 98, 106, 107, 112, 113, 144, 157; beeswax, 37, 38, 39; bone objects, 50, 52, 56, 61, 62; bottle glass, 57; brass materials, 53; of British origin, 144; buttons, 53, 144, 156; canoes, 37; cast-iron, 53, 156; ceramics, 24, 37, 53, 55, 57, 106, 107; child's shoe, 156; clothing, 37; cobble tool, 43; coffee pots, 156; commercial manufactured products, 41; copper items and materials, 50, 53, 54; crystal, 54; cupreous, 55; debitage, 56; dentalia, 75; dishware, 156; eating utensils, 156; European-manufactured, 17; as evidence of resistance, 71; ferrous, 55; figurines, 82; fishing net weights, 56; flaked stone, 62, 73, 81, 90; flute, 61; food remains, 52, 107; foreign, 9, 41; glass, 52, 53, 55, 56, 106, 107, 144, 157; graniteware, 156; hair combs, 156; hammerstones, 52; hand mauls, 81; hat pins, 156; of Indigenous manufacture, 41, 52, 53; iron, 37, 46, 55; jewelry, 82, 107, 156; jingle/tinkler cones, 82; knives, 56, 81, 88, 156; lead, 53, 55; lithic debitage, 28, 43, 50, 52, 56, 106; marbles, 156; medicines, 37; metal, 45, 53, 54, 82, 88, 157; mussel shells, 61; nails, 107; of non-Indigenous origin, 52–53; obsidian, 73, 157; ornaments, 88; painted pebbles, 52; pencils, 156; pigment stones, 52; plankhouse remains, 56; plastic, 107; points, 79; pot fragments, 53; projectile points, 37, 39, 47, 48, 50, 56, 61, 73; refashioned from non-Indigenous items, 81, 88; sandstone, 79; saws, 56; scholarship on, 35; scrapers, 50, 56, 73, 81, 82; shell, 47; slate, 81, 156; smoking pipes and pipe parts, 50, 53, 57, 75, 82, 144; steatite, 50, 82; stone, 47, 50, 56, 57, 62, 73, 75, 81, 82; stove, 156; tablets, 156; tent stakes, 107; tin can fragments, 106; tinklers, 50, 157; tools, 56, 57, 62, 75, 81, 156; toys, 62, 156; tubular pipes, 82; weapons and ammunition, 53, 57, 156; wooden boxes, 52

Indigenous peoples, burials and cemeteries associated with: and age, 121, 129; artifacts from, 48; and burial goods, 112, 128; changes in, 127; and coffins, 128; and exhumation, 13, 15, 16, 17, 47, 48, 110, 111, 114; and grave markers, 127–28; Indigenous descendants and, 113, 129, 130; legislation on, 47, 111; locations of, 47, 48, 52, 67, 112, 117, 121, 128, 129, 130, 195; and religion, 128; and resistance, 128; as sacred spaces, 67; and status, 128; unmarked, 117

Indigenous peoples, dwellings of: communal houses, 80; houses, 37, 52–53, 61; longhouses, 101; mat lodges, 82, 156; pit houses, 49, 54, 81–82, 143, 144; plankhouses, 55, 56, 57, 98, 149; pre-contact, 82; sizes of, 80, 149; Western-style houses, 80; wickiups, 156

Indigenous peoples, and education: at Hudson's Bay Company schools, 69; on Indian reservations, 156, 190; at missions, 72, 73, 74, 76, 78; at residential schools, 27, 76, 77, 80, 127, 128–29, 190, 195

Indigenous peoples, and fur trade: and adaptation, 53, 56–58, 62–63, 71, 113; and establishment and locations of fur trade posts, 33, 34, 35, 49, 54, 55, 58, 63–64; importance to, 34, 35, 64; and interactions with fur traders and companies, 10, 15, 33, 34, 35, 45, 46, 48, 53, 54–56, 57–58, 62, 64, 65, 67, 68, 71, 76, 83, 88, 113, 114; and intermarriage, 65, 67, 76, 88, 114; and offspring with fur traders, 10; opportunities created by, 195; and persistence and survivance, 34, 35, 53–55, 56–58, 62, 71, 195; scholarship on, 15, 34, 35, 50–51, 53, 56, 79, 82; and seasonality, 34, 50, 57; and settlement patterns, 53, 54, 56, 57, 82; and status and wealth, 53, 55, 58; and supplies, 144; and violence, 45, 46, 53, 194–95

Indigenous peoples, historical archaeology and: and burials and cemeteries, 15, 16, 17, 113, 127, 130; and collaboration with descendants, 130, 185, 189–90, 191, 195; and conflict, 99, 103, 194–95; and disease, 52; and early contact, 33, 35, 194; and focus on Indigenous peoples, 10, 52; and fur trade, 16, 50–51, 82, 99, 102–3, 194–95; and horses, 51–52; impact of colonialism on, 18, 24, 25; impact of missions on, 72; and Indigenous agency, 24, 25; and Indigenous collaboration, 26–27; methodologies and interpretations of, 23, 24–25, 28, 35; and persistence and survivance, 197; and pre-contact sites, 8–9, 17, 18, 102; and race and ethnicity, 17–18, 24, 25, 107, 195, 197; and residential schools, 195; and settler colonialism, 185; and settler communities, 103; and settlers, 197; and technology, 194; and U.S. military, 103; and Victorianism, 107

Indigenous peoples, persistence and survivance of: and capitalism, 197; Chinook and, 55, 56; Coeur d'Alene and, 79; Haida and, 53–54; Heiltsuk and, 80–81; Kimsquit and, 128; Klamath and, 156–57; *Ktunaxa* (Kootenai) and, 195; in mixed-race communities, 196; Modoc and, 156–57; Molalla and, 106–7; Mowachaht/Muchalaht and, 41, 80–81; *Niitsitapi* and, 195; Okanogan and, 61; and race and ethnicity, 195; St'át'imc and, 82; *Stó:lō* and, 128; Tsimshian and, 127–28; Umpqua and, 106–7

Indigenous peoples, scholarship on: and acculturation theory, 25, 51, 195; and enrichment thesis, 34–35, 53, 56; and exploitation/deprivation thesis, 34–35, 53; and focus on Indigenous peoples, 10; lack of Indigenous voices in, 95–96; and narratives of Native disappearance, 10; and race and ethnicity, 10, 17–18; terminal narratives on, 51, 195

Indigenous peoples, and settlers: and beeswax, 37; and class, 96; and conflict, 84–85, 92, 95, 96, 100, 103, 135; different narratives of, 130; and hops harvesting, 135; and identity, 97; and intermarriage, 10, 96, 103; and land, 9, 103, 132–33, 135; and manifest destiny, 97; nuances of relationship between, 107; and Oregon Trail, 84–85; and race and ethnicity, 96; scholarship on, 197; and settler industries, 13; and settlers as Indigenous allies, 10

Indigenous peoples, tribes and confederations of: Bridge River Band/Xwísten, 82; Canadian, 68; Carrier First Nations, 63; Cayuse, 73, 75; Chamorro, 78; Chinook, 48, 56, 57–58; Chippewa, 114; Clallam, 103; Clatsop, 38, 43; Clatsop-Nehalem, 37; Coast Salish, 7, 129, 135, 145; Coeur d'Alene, 78, 79; Colville, 49, 83; Confederated Tribes of the Colville Reservation, 50; Confederated Tribes of the Grand Ronde Community of Oregon, 105; Coquille, 24; Cree, 108; Dakelh, 145; Dunne-za/Dane-zaa (Beaver Indians), 45, 46; East Coast, 68; Flathead, 78; *Gardin*/Home Guard Indians, 63; Grand Ronde Tribe, 106; Haida, 40, 53–54, 103, 127, 145; Heiltsuk, 80–81; Kalapuyan, 88; Kamloops Indian Band, 54; Klamath, 156; Ktunaxa/Kootenai, 54, 195; Kunghit Haida, 53; Lummi, 103; Modoc, 156; Molalla, 106; Mowachaht/Muchalaht, 41, 80; Native Hawaiians, 65, 66, 68; Nehalem-Tillamook, 37, 38, 39; Nez Percé, 113; Niitsitapi/Blackfeet, 54, 195; Nisqually, 66, 67; Nlaka'pamux, 144; Nuu-chah-nulth, 79; Okanogan, 49, 61, 83; Palus, 113; Pend d'Oreille, 83; Penelakut, 129; Qua-to-mah, 98; Rogue Indians, 90; Rogue River, 140; Saanich, 103; Sanpoil/Nespelem, 83; Santiam, 135; Sekani, 62; Shasta, 95, 97, 140; Shoshone, 51, 86; Shoshone-Bannock, 16, 51; Shwayip/sxoie'łp^u, 64; Snxwemi'ne/Upper Spokane people, 47; Southern Plateau, 51; Spokane, 48, 83, 114; Sqilxw, 136–37; St'át'imc, 82, 145, 195; *Stó:lō*, 81, 128, 135; Takelma, 94, 95, 96; Tillamook, 18, 37;

Tlingit, 18; Tsilhquot'in, 145; Tsimshian, 81; Umpqua, 106, 140; Upper Chinook, 55; Walula, 63; Yakama, 1, *4*, 51–52, 103

Indigenous peoples, and violence: Bear River Massacre, 86–87, 88; and claiming of Indigenous lands, 135; Coeur d'Alene Wars, 92; Fort St. John's Massacre, 45, 46; and fur trade and fur traders, 45, 46, 53, 84–85; against gold miners, 143; against immigrants and settlers, 100, 117, 120, 195; against missionaries and missions, 74, 75, 76, 84–85, 88; Pig War, 103; Puget Sound War, 92, 94; Rogue River War, 92, 94–96, 103; and status, 53; structural, 67; unspecified warfare, 51; Yakima War, 63, 92, 99

Interior Mountains, 2

Interior Plateau, 2

International Boundary, 23

Invermere, British Columbia, 46

Iowa, 131

Ireland, 92

Irish and Irish descendants, 68, 121, 136, 145

Isthmus of Panama, 91

Jackson Creek, 139, 140

Jacksonville, OR: archaeology in, 5, *134*, 140–41, 148, 196

Jacob, Cyrus, 167, 168

Jacob, Mary Ellen, 167, 168

Jamestown, VA, 17, 29

Japan, 154, 155, 176

Japanese and Japanese descendants: and agriculture, 132, 135, 179, 181; artifacts of, 154, 155; and assimilation, 155; and burials and cemeteries, 120; as business owners, 181; and canneries, 132, 137, 138, 179; and communal meals, 138; and community creation, 196; and construction, 179; as consumers, 138; and cultural persistence, 155; diet of, 138, 155; and education, 155, 179, 181; entrepreneurial activities of, 138; and fishing, 138, 155; and identity, 139; increased study of, 191; and industrial jobs, 178; and interactions with White community members, 155; as labor, 154, 163, 180; legislation pertaining to, 195; and livestock, 132; and logging and lumbering, 132, 151, 154, 163, 179; and mining, 132; organizations of, 196; popular depictions of, 178; population of, 154; and property ownership, 178; and racism, 132, 154, 155, 158, 178, 179, 195; and ranching, 132; and religion, 155; as replacements for Chinese and Chinese descendants, 154; and resistance, 155–56, 179–80; and status, 155; and ties to host countries, 139; and ties to Japan, 139; and unions, 178, 179; and U.S. Army, 179; and violence, 195; as working class, 168; World War II incarceration of, 25, 160, 176, 178–80

Japanese-China conflict, 124

Japanese internment camps, 25, *31*, 160, 178–80

Japanese Navy, 178

Japan Gulch, Mukilteo, WA, *134*, 154

Jason Lee cemetery, 121

Jefferson, Thomas, 4, 41

Jelks, Edward B., 17

Jesuits, 76, 78

Jewelry: bracelets, 107, 112, 113, 164; brooches, 50; jade, 164; pendants, 45, 82, 112, 113; rings, 50, 82, 112; unspecified types of, 64, 105, 155, 156, 171; wedding bands, 163

Joe, Patrick, 81

John Day, OR, *134*, 148

Johnson, Robyn, 51

Johnson, William, 90

Jordan Valley, OR, 127

Josephine County, OR, 131

Josephine Creek, 139

Joset, Joseph, 78

Jurakic, Irena, 81

Kaiser Shipyards, 176–77, 197

Kalama't/Indian Race Track site, *36*, 51–52

Kalapuyan people, 88

Kamloops, British Columbia, 136

Kamloops Indian Band, 54

Kam Wah Chung Company building, 148

Kanaka (term), 66n3

Kanaka Flat, OR, 140, 196

Kardas, Susan, 19

Kelton, Utah, 168

Kettle Falls, 61, 64, 65, 113

Kimsquit cemetery, 128

Kimsquit community, 81

Klamath Falls, OR, 152, 156

Klamath Indian Reservation, 156

Klamath people, 156

Klimko, Olga, 193

Klippenstein, Frieda Esau, 63
Kooskia Work Camp, *159*, 178, 180
Kootenai House site, 16, *36*, 46–47, 54
Kopchitchin, British Columbia, 143, 144
Kretzler, Ian Edward, 106
Ktunaxa/Kootenai people, 54, 55, 195
Kumasaka's Garden, *159*, 181
Kunghit Haida people, 53
Kuper Island Indian Residential School, 129
Kwantlen Polytechnic University, 143

Lake House, British Columbia, *134*, 143–44
Lake Mountain, 143, 144
Lake Okanagan, 136
Lake Oswego, 132
Lake Roosevelt, 20, 64
Lake Sacajawea, 113
Lane, Joseph (Tyee Joe), 96
La Salle, Marina, 191
Latino Americans, 5
Latschar, John, 85
Laumeister and Gowen brewery, 102
Leavenworth, KS, 84
Lee, Anna Maria Pittman, 121
Lee, Francis, 72
Lee, Jason: exhumation and reburial of, 121; mission of, 16, 72, 73, 76; and Nathaniel Wyeth, 72, 85; veneration of, 73, 122
Lee Yuen Hong, 171, 172
Legislation: Chinese Exclusion Act of 1882 (U.S.), 141, 169; Dawes Act (U.S.), 107; Donation Land Claim Act (U.S.), 132, 133; Federal Indian Act (Canada), 80; Geary Act of 1892 (U.S.), 141, 148; Heritage Conservation Act (Canada), 23; homestead acts (U.S.), 133; National Historic Preservation Act of 1966 (NHPA; U.S.), 20, 193; Native American Graves Protection and Repatriation Act of 1990 (NAGPRA; U.S.), 47, 111, 114
Lewis, David G., 113
Lewis and Clark expedition: archaeological remains of, 42, 43, 56; on beeswax at Nehalem Bay, 37; bicentennial of, 42; and Cathlapotle site, 55; commemoration of, as national historical trail, 20; and Fort Clatsop/"station camp," 42, 56; impact of, 4, 41, 43; Indigenous peoples and, 37, 41–42, 55; public and scholarly perceptions of, 41; route of, 41, 43, 56

Lewis and Clark River, 42
Lewiston, ID, 158
Lightfoot, Kent, 24
Lim, Imogene L., 169
Ling, George, 30
Linn County, OR, 131
Lion Island, 138–39
Little Luckiamute River, 104
Logging (term), 148
Logging and lumbering: British and, 149; Chinese and Chinese descendants and, 170; and consumerism, 150, 163; and creation of communities, 148; decrease in, 144; dwellings at sites associated with, 150; environmental impact of, 132; equipment and tools for, 149–50, 151; at Fort Clatsop site, 43; and gender, 131, 151, 152, 153–54; and gold rushes, 139; Hudson's Bay Company and, 64, 68; Japanese and Japanese descendants and, 151, 154–55, 163, 179; measurements for, 151n5; modern conflicts over, 196; and population growth, 150, 162, 166; processes for, 149–50, 152; and railroads, 150, 152, 153; reduction in, 144; represented on grave markers, 131; and sawmills, 131; scholarship on, 132; soldiers and, 152; and standard of living, 150, 152–53; and status, 151, 152–53; and technology, 22, 149–50, 194; and transportation, 149; U.S. Army and, 151–52
Lone Fir cemetery, 122, 125–26
Longtain, Andre, 89
Loring, William Wing, 84
Lower Columbia River, 113
Lower Fraser River, 143
Lower Granite Lake, 158
Lower Monumental Dam, 113
Lower Salmon River, 146
Lumbering (term), 148. *See also* Logging and lumbering
Lummi people, 103
Lupton, James A., 94
Lupton Massacre, 94
Lynch, Michelle R., 81
Lytton, British Columbia, 196

Maas, Alexandra, 24
Mackenzie, Alexander, 40, 43, 44
Maddoux, Maryanne, 171
Malheur National Forest, 148

Manhattan Project, 176, 177
Manifest destiny, 83, 85, 92, 97
Manila, Philippines, 38
Manion, Mollie Jo, 90
Maritime Archaeological Society, 38
Marshall, Yvonne, 24
Martindale, Andrew, 81
Marysville, CA, 126
Maschner, Herbert D. G., 3
Material culture (term), 7. *See also* Artifacts; Artifacts, associated with architecture and structures; Artifacts, clothing and clothing-related; Artifacts, glass; Artifacts, metal; Beads; Buttons; Ceramics; Ceramics, forms of; Chinese and Chinese descendants, artifacts associated with; Foods and beverages; Foods and beverages, alcoholic; Indigenous peoples, artifacts associated with; Weapons and ammunition
Mawhirter, Matthew, 175
McLeod's Lake, 24, 62
McLeod's Lake Post, *60*, 62, 63, 195
McLoughlin, John, 60, 71, 72
McMinnville College, 113
Meares, John, 40
Meares Factory, 40–41
Meares Island, 41, 196
Meeker, Ezra, 16, 135
Meeker, Jacob, 135
Meier Site, *36*, 55–56, 57
Merrell, Carolynne, 51
Methodist Episcopal Church, 72
Methodists, 76, 79
Métis: and burials and cemeteries, 121, 128; in Canada, 72; at Fort Colvile, 65; at Fort Nisqually, 67; at Fort St. John's/Fort D'Epinette, 46; at Fort Vancouver, 68; and Haida people, 53; and intermarriage, 67; marginalization of, 121; as stone carvers, 53
Mexican Americans, 139
Mexican War, 91
Mexico, 40
Middle Village, 34, *36*, 48, 56–58
Mill Creek, 73, 131
Miller's CC Index, 30, 134
Miller's Island, 112
Miners' Fort, *86*, 95, 96, 97, 185
Minidoka National Historic Site, *31*, 179
Minidoka Relocation Center, *159*, 178–80, 181

Mining: African Americans and, 140; Americans and, 99, 103; and boom and bust cycles, 119; and burials and cemeteries, 119; Chinese and Chinese descendants and, 23, 24, 123, 140, 141, 143, 144, 145–46, 147–48, 161, 169, 170, 172; of coal, 61; environmental impact of, 132; and gender, 140; of gold, 63, 65, 76, 83, 94, 119, 131, 139–40, 143, 145, 161, 166, 170; Hudson's Bay Company and, 61, 142; as impetus for creating settlements, 160; Indigenous peoples and, 139, 140, 143–44, 145; Irish and, 145; Japanese and Japanese descendants and, 132; Native Hawaiians and, 139, 140, 146; opportunities provided by, 131, 136, 145; and population growth, 119, 140; Portuguese and, 140; processes for, 140; and race and ethnicity, 140–41, 146; and transportation, 144; and violence, 143
Minnesota, 118
Mission Bottom cemetery, 121
Missions and missionaries: activities of, 80; and agriculture, 72, 74, 78, 79; artifacts of, 73, 74–78, 79; and burials and cemeteries, 127, 128; Catholic, 69, 76–79, 128; and colonization, 59, 72; and education, 78; fur traders and, 88; goals of, 72, 73, 84; impact of, 41, 72; impetus for, 61; and livestock, 78; Pierre-Jean DeSmet and, 78; preservation of, 33; Protestant, 59, 72–76, 79; purchases by, 68, 73
Missouri River, 41
Miyagi prefecture, Japan, 138
Modernity: at Fort Lane, 97; historical archaeology on, 14; impact of, 196; scholarship on, 183, 192; and transportation, 161, 164; and urbanization, 33, 164
Modoc people, 156
Molalla Encampment, 106–7
Molalla people, 106
Montana, 46, 161
Montana State University, 43
Mormons, 85
Morrissey Internment Camp, *159*, 174
Moscow, ID, 183, 184
Mountain Home, ID, 51
Mountain View Cemetery, 108, *109*, 124
Mount Auburn cemetery, 111
Mount Hood, 87, 115, *116*, 127
Mount Hood National Forest, 175
Mowachaht/Muchalaht people, 41, 80

Mukilteo, WA, *134*, 154
Mullan Road, *159*, 161
Multnomah County, OR, 125
Multnomah Masonic Lodge 84, 108
Multnomah School of the Bible, 187
Myers, Danielle D., 147

Nagasaki, Japan, 177
Nampa, Idaho, 117
Namu, British Columbia, 80
Nanaimo, British Columbia, *159*, 170
Native Hawaiians: in Colville Valley, 65; dwellings of, 66; at Fort Vancouver, 68; and fur trade, 65; and Hudson's Bay Company, 66, 108; and intermarriage, 140; and mining, 139, 140, 146; need for collaboration with, 130; and term for "human being," 66n3; and White settlers, 65
Neahkahnie Mountain, 39
Nehalem, OR, 37
Nehalem Bay, 36, 37
Nehalem-Tillamook people, 38, 39
Nesham, Aubrey, *18*
Nespelem/Sanpoil people, 83
Nestacanna (Indigenous leader), 52
Netarts Sand Spit, 24, 37
Netherlands, 30
New Caledonia District, 54, 62
Newell, Robert, 89–90
Newell House, *91*
Newman, Thomas M., 18, 37
New Spain, 38
New Western History, 12, 25
New York State, 118, 135
New Zealand, 123
Nez Perce Tribe, 113
Niitsitapi/Blackfeet people, 54, 195
1942 Bomb Site, *159*
Nisei. *See* Japanese and Japanese descendants
Nisqually Tribe, 66, 67
Nk'maplqs, 136
Nlaka'pamux people, 144
Noël Hume, Ivor, 7
Nootka Conventions, 40
Nootka Sound site, 24, 80
North American Cordillera, 2, 3
Northern Pacific Railroad, 161, 162
North Seattle College, 181
North Thompson River, 54

Northwest Coast, 52
Northwest Company: clay tobacco pipe styles related to, 48; founder of, 114; headquarters of, 48; and Hudson's Bay Company, 44, 45, 47, 49, 54, 114; and Pacific Fur Company, 44; posts and forts of, 45, 46–47, 48, 49, 54, 60, 63–64, 88; Simon Fraser and, 43
Northwest Landing, 67
Nuu-chah-nulth people, 79

Oblate doctrine, 128
Oddfellow's Rural Cemetery, 122, 126–27, 130
Officers, military: artifacts of, 8, 93, 94, 101–2, 104–5; as consumers, 106; diet of, 45, 105; housing for, 8, *26*, 45, 92–93, 94, 97, 101, 104, 105–6, 172, 175; and identity, 97; and military authority, 8; and race and ethnicity, 92; and status, 45, 93, 106. *See also* Soldiers
O'Gorman, J. Tim, 103
Okanagan City, British Columbia, 143
Okanagan Lake, 136
Okanagan Valley, 136
Okanogan people, 49, 61, 83
Okanogan River, 49
O'Keefe, Cornelius, 136
O'Keefe Ranch, *134*, 136–37
Old Songhees Village, 79
Oliver, Jeff, 135
Olson, Eric, *18*
Olympia, WA, 90
Oregon: African Americans in, 140; agriculture in, 135; archaeological permitting in, 39, 185; archaeological sites in, *26*, 29, 48–49, 61, 72–73, 76–78, 88–90, *91*, 94, 95, 96, 97, 98–99, 103, 104–7, 116–17, 125–26, 140–42, 146, 153–54, 156–57, 162, 170–72; Basques in, 127; burials and cemeteries in, 108–10, 111, 115–17, 118–19, 120–22, 125–27, 130; and California, 3; Cascade Range in, 3; Chinese and Chinese descendants in, 122, 125–27, 141–42, 145, 146, 148, 169, 170–72; Civilian Conservation Corps in, 175; climate in, 135, 160; fishing in, 137; Forest Service Passport-in-Time projects in, 185; Francis Drake in, 35; French Canadians in, 88, 121; fur trade in, 48–49, 61, 88; gaming laws in, 171; gold in, 94, 131, 139, 140, 145, 170; Great Depression in, 152, 160; historic preservation in, 20–21, 192; homesteading in, 131, 160;

Indian reservations in, 94, 95, 98, 103, 104, 105, 195; Indigenous peoples in, 9, 27, 36, 48, 72, 73, 76, 88, 90, 94–95, 96, 97–99, 103, 104, 105, 106–7, 108, 109, 117, 120, 121, 137, 140, 156–57, 185, 195, 196; industrialization in, 160; Irish and Irish descendants in, 121; Japanese and Japanese descendants in, 154, 178; Japanese incarceration in, 178; land rights in, 132, 178; logging and lumbering in, 131, 148, *149*, 152–54; maps of, *2, 36, 60, 86, 134, 159*; masonic lodges in, 108; Métis in, 121; mining in, 145, 148, 170; missions and missionaries in, 72–73, 76; mountains in, 139, 140, 146; National Park Service program in, 188; Native Hawaiians in, 140; as part of Pacific Northwest, 1; and poll tax on ethnic minorities, 141; population and settlement patterns in, 1, 140; Portuguese in, 140; railroads in, 153, 162; ranching in, 131, 136; Rogue River War in, 92, 94–95, 185; territorial government in, 90; and trade, 97; urbanization in, 160; U.S. military in, 94, 95, 96, 97, 104–6; volunteer troops from, 104; and World War I, 160; and World War II, 176
Oregon and California Railroad (O&C), 162
Oregon Archaeological Society, 187, 188
Oregon City, OR, 73, 76, 84, 85, 108
Oregon City Woolen Mills, 108
Oregon Coast, 35, 98, 137
Oregon College of Education/Western Oregon University, 89
Oregon Historical Society, 42
Oregonian, 108
Oregon Parks and Recreation, 73, 98, 105
Oregon Pioneer Association, 108
Oregon Provisional Government, 132
Oregon Short Line Railroad, 166
Oregon State Museum of Anthropology/Museum of Natural and Cultural History, 185
Oregon State University: and Champoeg excavations, 89, 90; and Fort Hoskins excavations, 104; and Fort Yamhill excavations, *26*, 105; and St. Paul excavations, 76; and Willamette Mission excavation, 73
Oregon Trail: artifacts related to, 76; Barlow Road route of, *87*; burials along, 115–16; and disease, 74; impact of, 4, 9, 71, 83; map of, *86*; memorialization of, 115–16; migration along, 4, 9, 61, 71, 74, 76, 83, 88; as national historic trail, 20; physical remainders of, 86; and race, 74; Regiment of Mounted Riflemen on, 84, 91; routes and segments of, 85, 131, 170; sites along, 16, 85, 87–88; supply centers for, 166; trade along, 62
Oregon Tribes, 10
Orkney Islanders, 65, 68
Oro Fino City, British Columbia, 139
Otter Point State Park, 96
Ottoman Empire, 174
Owyhee Mountains, 140

Pacific coast, 35
Pacific Fur Company, 44, 47, 48, 49, 88
Pacific House Restaurant, 164
Pacific International Livestock Exposition Pavilion, 178
Pacific Islanders, 4–5. *See also* Native Hawaiians
Pacific Lutheran University, 67
Pacific Northwest: agricultural lands in, 10; British and, 40, 41; civil unrest in, 5; climate in, 2, 7, 159; coordination of researchers in, 25; cultural diversity in, 3, 4–5; economy of, 3; environment in, 1, 2, 3, 5, 196; evolution of historical archaeology in, 16; as frontier, 5, 21–22; geographic extent of, 1; and global and transnational systems, 195; and Great Depression, 174; and immigration, 4–6; Indigenous peoples and, 3, 10; labor in, 10; landscape of, 182; maps of, *2, 36, 60, 86, 134, 159*; natural resources in, 10; near surface geophysical remote sensing in, 28; politics in, 3, 5; popular perceptions of, 5, 84; population in, 1, 5, 150; post–World War II public projects in, 11, 17, 19; race and ethnicity in, 5; river drainage in, 2; Russians and, 40; scholarship on, 3, 5–6, 9, 10–11; settlement patterns in, 1, *2*, 5, 160; ship construction in, 41; size of, 1, 6; social activism in, 5; soil in, 2; Spanish and, 40, 41, 43; standardized data collection in, 25; study of modernity in, 183; and sustainability, 11–12; and tourism, 5; World War II in, 176–81, 183
Pacific Ocean, 2, 3, 40, 41
Pacific Rim, 68
Palmer, OR, *134*, 151
Palus people, 113
Parks Canada, 29
Parsley, Colleen, 170

Passport-in-Time (PIT) projects, 185
Peace River, *2*, 40, 44, 46
Peace River region, 195
Pearl Harbor, 178
Pearl River delta, 122
Pend d'Oreille people, 83
Pend Oreille River, 143
Penelakut Island, 129
Penelakut people, 129
Perez, Juan, 40
Pickett, George E., 100
Pierce, ID, *134*, 146, 148
Pig War, 99, 101, 102, 103
Pioneer Square cemetery, 119
Pioneer woman's grave, 115–16, 117
Pittsburgh, PA, 59
Plateau, *2*, 3, 52, 113
Poet, Rebecca McClelland, 77
Point Defiance Park, 67
Poole, James, 140
Porcelain: African Americans and, 174; American, 126; Asian, 168; bowls, 39, 79, 124, 125, 147, 154; British, 126; children's tea sets, 167; Chinese, 18, 37, *38*, 48, 50, 57, 79, 125, 126, 147, 163, 167, 172; cups, 39, 125, 154; dating of, 37, 106; and dating of other artifacts, 49; decoration on, 38, 79, 124, 125, 126, 147, 163, 172; dishes, 154; doll parts and dishes, 126, 167, 172; false teeth, 74; figurines, 39, 168; German, 167; globular box-shapes, 39; Indigenous peoples and, 18, 37, *38*, 39; Japanese, 154, 163, 172; Japanese-style, 172; plates, 39, 154; quality of, 174; saucers, 147; sherds, 39, 126; spoons, 172; and status, 106; tableware, 126; teapots, 154; teaware, 134; tobacco pipes, 106; vase or bottle, 39; vessels, 125, 168
Port Blakely, WA, *134*, 154
Porter, John E. P., 65
Portland, OR: burials and cemeteries in, 121–22, 125–26; Chinese and Chinese descendants in, 125–26, 169, 170, 196; incarceration of Japanese and Japanese descendants near, 178; and logging and lumbering, 148; map of, *2*; original name of, 148; as population center, 5; and proximity to Oregon Trail, 115; and railroads, 162; and urbanization, 196
Portland Basin, 55
Portland State University, 43, 55, 93, 187, 188
Portland West Hills/Willamette Stone, 132
Port Townsend, WA, 103
Portuguese, 140
Pow Wow grounds, 106, 107
Prentiss, Anna Marie, 82
Prentiss, Clarissa, 75
Prentiss, Stephen, 75
Presbyterians, 73
Prince, Paul, 128
Progressive movement, 33
Prohibition, 162, 184
Prostitution, 162–63, 169
Protestants, 74, 118
Puget Sound, 1, 51, 66, 85, 128
Puget Sound Agricultural Company (PSAC), 66, 67
Puget Sound Indian War, 92, 94
Pullman, WA, 183
Puyallup, WA, 67, 178
Puyallup Valley, 135

Quackenbush, William George, 62
Qua-to-mah people, 98
Quebec, Canada, 121
Queen Charlotte Islands/Haida Gwaii, 40, 52
Queen Mary (Takelma woman), 96
Quimby, George I., 17

Race and ethnicity: and American exceptionalism, 19; American settlers and, 83; and burials and cemeteries, 118, 121; Chinese and Chinese descendants and, 6, 122, 124, 146, 148; and citizenship, 141; and community archaeology, 186; and depiction of mining towns, 140–41; diversity of, 5; historical archaeology and, 10, 17–18, 19, 24, 25, 96, 107, 160, 165, 173, 191, 193, 195, 197; increased study of, 191; and interpretation of past events, 95–96; and land and property rights, 132, 141; and legal testimony against Whites, 141; legislation enforcing, 132; and mining, 140–41, 146; and mixed-race households, 140; perseverance against, 197; and prohibitions on interracial marriage, 141; railroads and, 168; and Rogue River War, 94, 96; settlers and, 10, 65, 74, 83, 96, 108–10, 132, 135, 141, 167, 195; and status, 173; and structural/institutionalized racism, 160, 168; and taxes, 141; terms for, 5n1; U.S. Army

and, 92, 173–74, 179; and Victorianism, 159; and violence, 141, 143
Raft River Crossing, 85
Railroads: and access to goods and markets, 31, 136, 150, 158, 162; Chinese and Chinese descendants and, 161, 162; communities and towns along, 161, 162; construction and operations camps for, 157, 161; and construction technology, 162; and gender, 161; homesteaders and, 160; impact of, on general stores, 158; intercontinental, 168, 173; at Japanese internment camps, 179; and logging and lumbering, 150, 152, 153; maps of, *153, 159*; and population growth, 150, 166; and race and ethnicity, 168; and settlement patterns, 140, 150, 152, 153, 161, 162; and status, 165; transcontinental, 150, 162; and urbanization, 164; U.S. Army and, 152, 173
Ramsay, Barnett, 17
Rathje, William, 197
Reconstruction. *See* Historic reconstruction
Regiment of Mounted Riflemen, 84, 91
Repatriation, 47, 114, 126, 191
Richardson Ranch, 23, *36*, 55
Ridgefield, WA, 39, 55
Riordan, Timothy Benedict, III, 192
River Basin Surveys, 29
River Street project, 168–69, 186–87
Riverview cemetery, 122
Rock Island Creek, 143
Rocky Mountain Fort, *36*, 44, 45, 46
Rocky Mountain House, 54
Rocky Mountain Portage House, 44
Rocky Mountains, 2, 41, 85
Roenke, Karl, 30
Rogue River, 96, 97, 139, 140
Rogue River Canyon, 97
Rogue River people, 90, 140
Rogue River War, 92, 94–99, 103, 104, 185
Rogue Valley, 94
Roosevelt, Franklin D., 174
Rose, Chelsea, 141, 170
Ross, Alexander, 49, 63
Ross, Douglas Edward, 30, 138, 139, 169
Ross, Lester A., 30, 187
Ross Bay Cemetery, 119–20, 124
Roulette, Bill R., 165, 176
Royal Engineers, 92
Royal Marines, 100, 101, 102, 144

Ruiz, Chris, 141
Russians, 24, 40

Saanich peninsula, 119
Saanich people, 103
Sainte Marie de Willamette, 76
Salem, OR, 73, 88, 121, 122, 126–27, 130
Salem Landmarks Commission, 126
Salmon River, 115
Sanborn Fire Insurance maps, 28, 141, 165
Sandpoint, ID, *159*, 162–64, 185
Sand Point Lumber Company/Humbird Lumber, 162
San Francisco, CA, 97, 143
San Juan Islands, 20, 23, *86*, 99–103, 113
San Juan Town, 101
San Lorenzo de Nutka, 40
San Miguel Island, 40
Sanpoil/Nespelem people, 83
Santiam people, 135
Santiam River, 131
Santo Christo de Burgos (ship), 38, 39
Sauer, Sandra R., 136
Sauvies Island, 113
Scandinavians, 137
Scappoose, OR, 55
Schaepe, David M., 7
Scheans, Daniel J., 30
Schumacher, Paul J. F., 42, 43
Schwantes, Carlos Arnaldo, 3
Sciousin (Nisqually dairyman), 67
Scots, 68
Scott, Winfield, 100
Seattle, WA, *2*, 5, 148–49, 181
Secwepemc Kamloops Village /Thompson's River Post/Fort Kamloops site, 54
Sekani people, 62
Sequalitchew Creek, 67
Serbians, 168
Settler colonialism: in Canada, 63; definition of, 9; Indigenous peoples and, 9, 10, 13, 156, 196; marginalized groups and, 13, 192; and resistance, 10, 13; and Rogue River War, 95, 98; scholarship on, 10, 24, 185. *See also* Colonialism
Settlers: activities of, 43, 135; American, 59, 83, 84–85, 102, 103, 104, 108–10, 115–17, 120–21, 122, 132, 133, 140, 141, 164, 195; and burials and cemeteries, 13, 16, 108–9,

115–18, 119–22; Canadian, 59, 119–20; and Chinese and Chinese descendants, 141; and consumerism, 133, 195; descendants of, 185; dwellings of, 42, 43, 156; environmental impact of, 197; and health, 116–17, 118, 120, 135; and identity, 13; impact of, on Pacific Northwest, 4; impact of fur trade on, 195; interest of, in their heritage, 16; and land rights, 132, 133, 164; and manifest destiny, 83, 92, 97; and missionaries, 74; motives of, 84, 103; narratives of, 6, 38, 63, 76, 92, 95, 97, 117, 130, 185; and nationality, 83; need for future research on, 192, 193; and Oregon Trail, 13, 84, 115–16, 120, 195; and perspectives on Pacific Northwest, 84; and political and economic power, 4; and race and ethnicity, 10, 65, 74, 83, 96, 108–10, 132, 135, 141, 167, 195; and religion, 83, 85, 121; and resistance, 10; scholarship on, 23, 42, 115; and social status, 83, 96, 167–68; sources of goods for, 133, 140; and technological change, 194; and U.S. government, 97; and U.S. military, 92, 94, 97, 100, 104; veneration of, 115–16, 117, 121; and violence, 84–85, 92, 95, 96, 99, 100, 103, 117, 120–21, 132. *See also* Indigenous peoples, and settlers

Sexyel (Captain Charlie; Stó:lō man), 81
Seymour Valley, *134*, 154
Shasta people, 95, 97, 140
Sheep Creek, 143
Shepard, Cyrus, 121
Shevlin-Hixon camp, 152
Shield Site, *36*, 51
Shipwrecks, 27, 35, 37–38, 39, 55
Short, Esther, 164
Shoshone-Bannock people, 16, 51
Shoshone people, 51, 86
Shwayip/sxoie'łpᵘ people, 64
Shxwowhamel cemetery, 128
Silcott, WA, 22–23, 158, 165
Similkameen River, 143
Simon Fraser site, *36*
Simon Fraser University, 144
Simons, Eric, 129–30
Simpson, George, 60, 64
Smith, Harlan Ingersoll, 113
Smith, Lisa Michelle, 82
Smithsonian Institution, 29, 185
Snake River, 61, 63, 117, 148, 158

Snake River plain, 2, 178
Snohomish, WA, 67
Snxwemi'ne/Upper Spokane people, 47
Society for American Archaeology, 191
Society for Historical Archaeology, 20
Soda Springs, ID, 85
Soldiers: activities of, 104, 105; artifacts of, 93, 97, 98, 101, 104–5, 173–74; and Battle of Hungry Hill, 96; and Bear River Massacre, 86; as consumers, 94, 106; diet of, 105, 106; distribution of, 173; documentary research on, 101, 104; enlisted, 104, 105, 106; housing for, 92, 97, *98*, 152, 173; and logging, 152; and occupation of San Juan Island, 100; and race and ethnicity, 92, 173–74, 180, 193; and reoccupation of Whitman mission buildings, 74; scholarly focus on, 106; and settlers, 92; and socioeconomic status, 106; volunteer, 74, 86, 96. *See also* Officers, military
Sonoma State functional classification system, 21
South, Stanley, 21–22, 23, 89, 102, 104
Southern Oregon University: and collaboration with Indigenous peoples, 107; and excavation of Jacksonville Chinese Quarter, 141; and excavations at Fort Lane, 98; online collections of, 30, 194; and research on Battle of Hungry Hill, 96; and research on Rogue River War, 95
Southern Pacific Railroad, 162
Southern Plateau people, 51
South Thompson River, 54
Southwest Oregon Research Project, 24
Spain and Spanish, 40, 41, 43, 127
Spanish American War, 174
Spoehr, Alexander, 17
Spokane, Portland & Seattle (SP&S) Railroad, 164, 165
Spokane, WA, *2*, 5
Spokane International Railway, 162
Spokane people, 48, 83, 114
Spokan House/Fort Spokane. *See* Fort Spokane/Spokan House
Sprague, Roderick: on archaeology of Indigenous peoples, 102–3; and artifact typology, 21, 29, 64, 89, 104; on collaborating with Indigenous peoples, 191; on historical archaeology, 15, 16; and Palus burial site, 113; and Society for Historical Archaeology, 20

Springfield, OR, 116
Spruce Mill, 152, 174
Spruce Production Division, 152. *See also* U.S. Army
Sqilxw people, 136–37
Staffordshire, England, 167
Stanstead, Quebec, Canada, 121
Stark, Vicki Hall, 191
State Asylum cemetery, 121
State Historic Preservation Offices, 20
State of Jefferson movement, 3
St'át'imc ancestral site/Bridge River site, *60,* 82
St'át'imc people, 82, 145, 195
Steele, Harvey W., 24
Stein River Valley, 196
St. Francis Xavier Mission, 76
Stilson, Leland M., 31
St. James Catholic Mission, 69
St. Joseph's College, 76, 77
St. Louis, MO, 78
Stó:lō people, 81, 128, 135
St. Paul, OR, 121
St. Paul Mission, 60, 76–78
Straus, Kirsten, 111
Strong, W. Duncan, 112
Stuart Lake, 43, 62
Sullivan, Daniel D., 24, 30
Sung Lee/Cum Sing Laundry, 170
Survivance (term), 35. *See also* Indigenous peoples, persistence and survivance of
Sussman, Lynne, 30
Swanson, Earl, 49
Sweet ruling (1889), 141
Sxoie'łpᵘ/Shwayip people, 64

Taber, Emily Celene, 166
Table Rock Reservation, 94
Table Rock Treaty, 94
Tacoma, WA, 67, 94
Tahiti, 123
Takelma people, 94, 95, 96
Tamura, Anna Hosticka, 179
Taylor, Zachary, 98
Thompson, David, 46
Thompson's River Post/Fort Kamloops/*Secwepemc* Kamloops Village, 54
Tiede, Kristen, 180
Tillamook, OR, 37
Tillamook peoples, 18, 37

Tl-ell region, 52
Tlingit peoples, 18
Transportation: along Indigenous trails, 44; by boat, 44, 59; by canoe, 44; and ferries, 161; of goods to market, 194; by horse or mule, 44, 51, 59, 149; and logging, 149, 150; mining-related system of, 144; by oxen, 149; by river, 161; and roads and highways, 158, 161, 164, 184, 192; routes for, 170; by ship, 31, 91, 102, 195; by stage, 117, 136; and steamboats, 59, 161; and technological change, 194; by tractor, 150; and urbanization, 158, 159; by wagon, 44, 59, 75, 88, 136, 168; wagons, 84; water routes for, 44, 161. *See also* Railroads
Trestle City (Jose Trestle) Construction Camp, *159,* 161
Troy, ID, *134*
Tsek'ehne Village, 24, 62, 195
Tseriadun site, 98
Tsilhquot'in people, 145
Tsimshian people, 81
Ts'qó:ls village, 81
Tualatin Plains, 113, 131
Tuck, Janna Beth, 175
Tuckkwiowhum, British Columbia, *134,* 143, 144
Tveskov, Mark Axel, 95, 97, 98, 185
Twin Falls, ID, 178
Tyee Joe (Chief Joseph Lane), 96
Tyee John (Shasta man), 97
Tyler, Thomas R., 103

Umpqua encampment, 106, 107
Umpqua people, 106, 140
United States: bicentennial of, 20, 78; cemeteries in, 119; Civil War in, 94, 97, 166; and colonization, 72, 92; cultural resources management in, 193; and Great Britain, 99–100, 103; and Great Depression, 174; historic preservation in, 27; and Indigenous peoples, 24, 103, 132; and Japanese and Japanese descendants, 160, 176, 178–81; northern boundary of, 32, 99, 132; numbering of archaeological sites in, 29; racism in, 155; and San Juan Islands, 99–100; and World War II, 160, 176, 177, 178
University of British Columbia Okanagan, 184
University of Idaho: and archaeology of Kooskia Work Camp, 180; and Bolvile Run project, 184; and Campus Trash Project, 183, 184;

and classification of artifacts, 21; and collaboration with Indigenous peoples, 191; and Fort Colvile excavations, 21, 64; and Indigenous site excavations, 64; and repatriation of Indigenous remains, 191; and research on Boise, ID, 166, 167; and San Juan Island excavations, 100–101
University of Montana, 82
University of Oregon, 24, 141
University of Washington, 43, 101, 106, 107
Unruh, John D., Jr., 131
Upper Chinook, 55
Upper Columbia River, 113
Upper Fraser Hops Farms, *134*
Upper Peace River, 61
Upper Salmon Falls, *86*, 88
Upper Spokane people (Snxwemi'ne), 47
U.S. Army: African Americans and, 173; and alienation, 92; and American settlers, 104; and Civilian Conservation Corps, 175; diet in, 105, 106; and environment, 92; 1st Cavalry of, 173; First Artillery of, 91; First Regiment of Dragoons of, 97; forts and posts of, 63, *86*, 91–94, 104, 172–73; 442nd Regimental Combat Team of, 179; 4th Infantry of, 97; and hierarchy, 97; immigrants in, 92; and Indigenous peoples, 92, 95, 103; Japanese and Japanese descendants and, 179; and logging industry, 151–52; 9th Cavalry of, 173–74; officers of, 92; and race and ethnicity, 92, 173–74, 179; Regiment of Mounted Riflemen of, 84, 91; and Rogue River War, 95, 96; and social inequality, 92; and spaces vacated by Hudson's Bay Company, 71; Spruce Production Division of, 152, 174; standards of, 175; and training, 172–73; and transportation, 173; and Victorianism, 93; and World War I, 151
U.S. Bureau of Indian Affairs Agency School, 190
U.S. Bureau of Land Management, 28
U.S. Coast Survey map, 42
U.S. Congress, 20, 133
U.S. Department of Agriculture, 175
U.S. Department of Labor, 175
U.S. Department of the Interior, 174–75
U.S. Forest Service, 175, 185
U.S. Fort Vancouver. *See* Fort Vancouver/Camp Vancouver/Vancouver Barracks
U.S. General Land Office, 28, 132
U.S. Indian Agency and agents, 156, 157
U.S. Military Fort Spokane. *See* Fort Spokane/Spokan House
U.S. Military Fort Walla Walla. *See* Fort Nez Percé/Fort Walla Walla
U.S. National Park Service: and Barclay House, 108; and community collaboration, 188; and establishment of sites, 33; and Fort Clatsop, 42, 43; and Fort Vancouver, *18*, 69, 74; John Latschar and, 85; Kids Dig! program of, 188, *189*; Louis Caywood and, *18*, 42, 69; and Middle Village, 58; and Oregon Trail sites, 85; and public archaeology, 188–89; and San Juan Island, 100; Stan Young and, 85; university partners of, 188; and Waiilatpu Mission, 74–75
U.S. National Register of Historic Places, 192
U.S. Public Land Survey System, 132
U.S. War Department, 174
U.S. War Relocation Authority (WRA), 178, 180
U.S. Wartime Civilian Control Agency (WCCA), 178
Utah State University, 87

Vancouver, British Columbia, 2, 5, 124, *159*, 169, 196
Vancouver, WA, 50, *159*, 164–65, 166, 176
Vancouver Barracks. *See* Fort Vancouver/Camp Vancouver/Vancouver Barracks
Vancouver Island, 61, 99, 113
Vancouver Island University, 170
Vancouver Waterfront, 165
Vanport shipyard, 177
Veit, Richard F., 110
Vernon, British Columbia, 136
Victoria, British Columbia: artifacts from, 36; brewery in, 102; burials and cemeteries in, 119, 124; Chinese and Chinese descendants in, 123, 124; Hudson's Bay Company headquarters in, 71; manufacture of grave stones in, 127; as population center, 5
Victoria, Queen, 9, 99
Victoria Harbor, 79
Victorianism: and burials and cemeteries, 117, 118, 119, 120; and consumerism, 133, 167; and cultural space, 93, 197; definition of, 9; and gender, 9, 93, 133, 141, 151, 168, 193; and hunting and shooting, 167–68; ideals

of, 93, 141; Irish American immigrants and, 121; and race and ethnicity, 159; U.S. Army and, 93
Vogel, George, *18*

Waiilatpu Mission: and Cayuse War, 74, 79, 88, 92; historical archaeology at, 29, 74–76; history of, 73–74; location of, *60, 86;* and veneration of colonial past, 59
Waiilatpu village, 73
Wallace House, 88
Walla Walla, WA, 161
Walla Walla Community College, 173
Walla Walla River, 50
Walters Ferry, 117
Walula City, WA, 63
Walula people, 63
Warner, Mark S., 186
Warren, ID, 123, *134,* 139, 146
Warrendale Cannery, *134,* 139
Washington Archaeological Research Center, 20
Washington County, OR, 175
Washington State: African Americans in, 173–74; Alien Land legislation in, 178; archaeological sites in, *4, 18,* 19, 22–23, 39, *44,* 47–48, 49–50, 55–59, 60, 61, 63–65, 66–71, 73–76, 82, 90–91, 92–94, 99, 100–103, 151, 152, *153,* 154, 158, 165–66, 173–74, 175, 176–77; Basques in, 127; British military in, 100, 101–2; canneries in, 137; Cascade Range in, 3; Chinese and Chinese descendants in, 165; Civilian Conservation Corps camps in, 175; climate in, 160; Forest Service Passport-in-Time projects in, 185; fur trade in, 17, 19, 36, *44, 47*–48, 49, 50, 51, 60, 61, 63, 64, 66, 67, 68, 69, 71; gold mining in, 143, 170; and Great Depression, 158, 160, 165, 166; historic preservation in, 20–21, 49, 66–67, 191; Indian reservations in, 50, 71, 103; Indigenous peoples in, 9, 47, 48, 49, 50, 51, 55–58, 61, 63, 64, 65, 67, 68, 69, 71–72, 73, 74, 75, 76, 82–83, 92, 101, 102–3; industrialization in, 160; Japanese and Japanese descendants in, 154, 181; Japanese incarceration camps in, 178; Kids Dig! program in, 188, *189;* lumbering in, 151, 152, 154; maps of, *2, 36, 60, 86, 134, 159;* as part of Inland Empire, 19; as part of Pacific Northwest, 1, 5; population and settlement patterns in, 1, 5, 165; present-day research in, 188; Pullman study in, 183; railroads in, 165; roads in, 161; and San Juan Islands, 99; social status in, 165–66; technological changes in, 158; urbanization in, 160; U.S. military in, 91–94, 99, 100, 101, 102, 103, 173–74; as U.S. territory, 99; volunteer troops from, 104; and World War I, 152, 160, 173; and World War II, 176–77
Washington State University, 48, 93, 173, 183, 188
Washington Territory, 99
Watson, Bruce M., 83
Weapons and ammunition: buckshot, 61; cannons, 69; cartridges, 156, 173; conical rifle bullets, 98; flintlock musket parts, 47; gun flints, 75; gun hammers, 76; gun parts, 156; gunsmithing materials, 75; hunting knife and sheath, 114; lead bullets, 87; lead shot, 66, 96, 98; musket ball extractor, 98; musket balls, 46, 96; nipple pick fragments, 98; percussion caps, 61, 98; ramrods, 98; shot, 61; and technological change, 194; unspecified weapons, 30, 48, 106, 157, 167
Wegars, Priscilla, 30, 122
Wells Reservoir, 49, 50
Welsh, 68, 121
Wenatchee, WA, 143
West Borneo, 145
Western Oregon University/Oregon College of Education, 89
Western Washington State Fairgrounds, 178
Weston, David, 89
Weyerhaeuser Camp 2, *134,* 152, *153*
Weyerhaeuser Company, 66–67
Whale Cove, OR, 35, *36*
Whatcom County, WA, 99
Whidbey Island, 113
Whitman, Marcus, 59, 73–75, 76
Whitman, Narcissa, 59, 73–74, 75, 76
Wild Horse Creek Provincial Historic Site, 78, 123–24
Wilhelm I, Kaiser, 100
Willamette Meridian, 132
Willamette Mission cemetery, 121
Willamette Mission site, 16, *60,* 72–73, 76
Willamette Post, 88
Willamette River, 72, 84, 88, 89, 127
Willamette Stone/Portland West Hills, 132
Willamette Valley: agriculture in, 85; archaeol-

ogy in, 90, 113, 116, 133; Aurora colony in, 133; bricks from, 30; burials and cemeteries in, 20, 116, 118–19, 121; and California gold rush, 76; ceramics production in, 16–17, 132; French Canadians in, 88; fur traders in, 61, 85; horses in, 51; Indigenous peoples in, 88, 128, 135; migration to, 118; missions and missionaries in, 72, 78, 88; sawmills in, 131; settlement in, 85, 88, 89, 90, 118, 121, 133; townships in, 132; Tualatin area of, 113; William Earl in, 131
William Earl Homestead, 131, 133–35
Williams, Scott S., 38
Williamson, Henry, 164
Wilson, Douglas C., 1
Wind River Lumber Company, 151
Wing Hong Hai Company, *159*, 170–72
Wisconsin, 118
Wolf, Eric, 23
Work camps, 25, 160, 161, 168, 180, 182
World War I: as demarcation point, 9, 150, 151, 152, 159; impact of, 160; and prisoners of war, 174; reactivation of Army forts during, 173

World War I Spruce Mill, *134*
World War II: artifacts from, 13; changes after, 192, 197; Chinese burial customs during, 124; Civilian Conservation Camp participants and, 175; as demarcation point, 11, 15, 17, 158; and gender, 176, 193; incarceration of Japanese and Japanese descendants during, 160, 175; industrial production during, 197; in Pacific Northwest, 176–81, 183; recycling and salvage during, 177; Vancouver, WA, population during, 164, 176
Wyeth, Nathaniel, 61, 72, 85, 90, 112, 137

Yakama Indian Reservation, 103
Yakama people, 51–52
Yakima War, 1, 63, 92, 99
Yamhill River, 105, 106
Yellowhorn, Eldon Carlyle, 62
York Factory, 64
Young, Ewing, 90, 94
Young, Stan, 85
Yreka, CA, 131
Yukon Territory, 6
Yuquot site, *36*, 40, 41, *60*, 79, 80

Douglas C. Wilson is an archeologist with the National Park Service and an Adjunct Associate Professor at Portland State University. He has written extensively on colonial and historical archaeology of the Pacific Northwest, including "The Fort and the Village: Landscape and Identity in the Colonial Period of Fort Vancouver" in *British Forts and Their Communities: Archaeological and Historical Perspectives* and "Decolonizing Fort Vancouver through Archaeological Interpretation" (with Amy Clearman and Kaitlyn Hosken) in *Creating Participatory Dialogue in Archaeological and Cultural Heritage Interpretation*.

The American Experience in Archaeological Perspective

Michael S. Nassaney, Founding Editor

Krysta Ryzewski, Coeditor

The American Experience in Archaeological Perspective series was established by the University Press of Florida and founding editor Michael S. Nassaney in 2004. This prestigious historical archaeology series focuses attention on a range of significant themes in the development of the modern world from an Americanist perspective. Each volume explores an event, process, setting, institution, or geographic region that played a formative role in the making of the United States of America as a political, social, and cultural entity. These comprehensive overviews underscore the theoretical, methodological, and substantive contributions that archaeology has made to the study of American history and culture. Rather than subscribing to American exceptionalism, the authors aim to illuminate the distinctive character of the American experience in time and space. While these studies focus on historical archaeology in the United States, they are also broadly applicable to historical and anthropological inquiries in other parts of the world. To date the series has produced more than two dozen titles. Prospective authors are encouraged to contact the series editors to learn more.

The Archaeology of Collective Action, by Dean J. Saitta (2007)
The Archaeology of Institutional Confinement, by Eleanor Conlin Casella (2007)
The Archaeology of Race and Racialization in Historic America, by Charles E. Orser Jr. (2007)
The Archaeology of North American Farmsteads, by Mark D. Groover (2008)
The Archaeology of Alcohol and Drinking, by Frederick H. Smith (2008)
The Archaeology of American Labor and Working-Class Life, by Paul A. Shackel (2009; first paperback edition, 2011)
The Archaeology of Clothing and Bodily Adornment in Colonial America, by Diana DiPaolo Loren (2010; first paperback edition, 2011)
The Archaeology of American Capitalism, by Christopher N. Matthews (2010; first paperback edition, 2012)
The Archaeology of Forts and Battlefields, by David R. Starbuck (2011; first paperback edition, 2012)
The Archaeology of Consumer Culture, by Paul R. Mullins (2011; first paperback edition, 2012)
The Archaeology of Antislavery Resistance, by Terrance M. Weik (2012; first paperback edition, 2013)
The Archaeology of Citizenship, by Stacey Lynn Camp (2013; first paperback edition, 2019)
The Archaeology of American Cities, by Nan A. Rothschild and Diana diZerega Wall (2014; first paperback edition, 2015)
The Archaeology of American Cemeteries and Gravemarkers, by Sherene Baugher and Richard F. Veit (2014; first paperback edition, 2015)
The Archaeology of Smoking and Tobacco, by Georgia L. Fox (2015; first paperback edition, 2016)
The Archaeology of Gender in Historic America, by Deborah L. Rotman (2015; first paperback edition, 2018)
The Archaeology of the North American Fur Trade, by Michael S. Nassaney (2015; first paperback edition, 2017)
The Archaeology of the Cold War, by Todd A. Hanson (2016; first paperback edition, 2019)
The Archaeology of American Mining, by Paul J. White (2017; first paperback edition, 2020)
The Archaeology of Utopian and Intentional Communities, by Stacy C. Kozakavich (2017; first paperback edition, 2023)
The Archaeology of American Childhood and Adolescence, by Jane Eva Baxter (2019)

The Archaeology of Northern Slavery and Freedom, by James A. Delle (2019)
The Archaeology of Prostitution and Clandestine Pursuits, by Rebecca Yamin and Donna J. Seifert (2019; first paperback edition, 2023)
The Archaeology of Southeastern Native American Landscapes of the Colonial Era, by Charles R. Cobb (2019)
The Archaeology of the Logging Industry, by John G. Franzen (2020)
The Archaeology of Craft and Industry, by Christopher C. Fennell (2021)
The Archaeology of the Homed and the Unhomed, by Daniel O. Sayers (2023)
The Archaeology of Contemporary America, by William R. Caraher (2024)
The Historical Archaeology of the Pacific Northwest, by Douglas C. Wilson (2024)